Emotion and
Social Behavior

Emotion and Social Behavior

Editor
MARGARET S. CLARK

14
REVIEW of PERSONALITY and SOCIAL PSYCHOLOGY

Published in cooperation with the Society for Personality and Social Psychology, Inc.

SAGE Publications
International Educational and Professional Publisher
Newbury Park   London   New Delhi

For information address:

SAGE Publications, Inc.
2455 Teller Road
Newbury Park, California 91320

SAGE Publications Ltd.
6 Bonhill Street
London EC2A 4PU
United Kingdom

SAGE Publications India Pvt. Ltd.
M-32 Market
Greater Kailash I
New Delhi 110 048 India

Printed in the United States of America

International Standard Book Number: 0-8039-4745-3 (p)
0-8039-4744-5 (c)

International Standard Series Number: 0270-1987

Library of Congress Card Number: 80-649712

92 93 94 95   10 9 8 7 6 5 4 3 2 1

Sage Production Editor: Tara S. Mead

Contents

Editor's Introduction

MARGARET S. CLARK

Margaret S. Clark is Professor of Psychology at Carnegie Mellon University, where she has been since receiving her Ph.D. from the University of Maryland, College Park, in 1977. Her research interests are in the areas of interpersonal relationships and emotions. Following publication of the current volume, her duties as editor of the *Review* end, and she assumes the role of series editor.

This volume is the fourteenth in the *Review* series. It includes chapters on emotion and social behavior and is intended to be a companion book to the thirteenth volume of the *Review*, which also deals with emotion.

Proposals for both volumes were solicited by sending out flyers to all members of the International Society for Research on Emotion (ISRE)—an interdisciplinary group—as well as to many additional researchers who had published in the area of emotion. We also placed a call for proposals in the newsletter of the Society for Personality and Social Psychology—the sponsoring group for this *Review* series. Fifty-seven proposals were received. Each was read and rated by a number of reviewers. Ultimately, 22 proposals were selected for the thirteenth and fourteenth volumes of the *Review*. There was not a separate call for chapters for one volume versus the other. Rather, once the 22 accepted proposals were in hand, I tried to divide them between the two volumes in a sensible way. The result is a first volume, the thirteenth in our series, which focuses primarily on basic theoretical issues having to do with emotion, and the present volume which, although still dealing with theoretical issues of emotion, focuses on the links between emotion and social behavior to a greater extent than does the prior volume. I would emphasize, however, that given no clear dividing line between 11 proposals that could clearly by categorized one way and 11 others that could clearly be categorized another, and given the preferences of a few authors to be represented in a particular volume due to personal schedules, the division is a rough one.

Tim Wilson begins this volume with a chapter focusing on how our affective expectations can influence our affective responses to stimuli in our environment. As he notes, his chapter differs from much other work on emotion in taking a "top down" rather than a "bottom up" approach to understanding emotional reactions. He persuasively argues that our a priori expectations of how we will feel about things influence how we actually do feel about them as well as how quickly we can assess those feelings. The general idea that "top down" processes can influence emotional experience is echoed as well in Chapter 3 by John Cacioppo, Gary Berntson, and David Klein. These authors discuss how the emotional schemata that we possess and that may be activated at any given time can influence how we interpret and experience undifferentiated or ambiguous somatovisceral afference. More generally, these authors present a new theoretical approach to understanding emotions that are accompanied by peripheral physiological changes. Their approach falls somewhere between prior models—which hold that discrete emotional experiences stem from distinct somatovisceral patterns, and prior models, which hold that discrete emotional experiences stem from cognitive appraisals initiated by the perception of undifferentiated physiological arousal. As the authors note, their approach may be viewed as complementary to rather than competing with the earlier approaches. An updated view of the latter approach is presented in Chapter 3. This chapter, by Craig Smith and Lois Pope, reviews an appraisal approach and elaborates on it by developing hypotheses concerning the dispositional and situational antecedents of some specific appraisals.

Two of the chapters in this volume (Chapter 4 by Jerome Kagan and Chapter 5 by Nancy Eisenberg and Richard Fabes) have a developmental flavor. At the same time they both include a focus on individual differences in emotional expression and behavior. In Chapter 4, Kagan reviews his theoretical ideas regarding temperamental contributions to children's emotional and social behavior. In Chapter 5, Eisenberg and Fabes review a great deal of literature dealing with individual differences in experiencing emotion and with individual differences in self-regulation of emotion. Then they present their own new view of how social behavior is likely to be influenced by the *interaction* of emotional arousability (including reactivity and intensity) and regulatory/coping skills.

Chapter 7, by Marianne LaFrance and Mahzarin Banajii, also includes a focus on the general question of individual differences in emotionality. More specifically, it focuses on the question of whether men and women differ in emotionality. Although the popular view seems to be that women are more emotional, this chapter demonstrates that the answer to whether men and women differ in emotionality is not at all clear nor even an easy question to address. LaFrance and Banajii review a tremendous amount of literature dealing variously with phenomenal experiences of emotion (mostly reported verbally), nonverbal behavior, and physiological activity. They break down the evidence from each of these categories into subcategories in efforts to make sense of the available findings. They demonstrate that what conclusions you reach about whether and, if so, how men and women differ in emotionality depend on how, methodologically, you ask the questions. In doing so they call into question glib assumptions that women are more emotional than men.

The remaining chapters deal with some more specific issues regarding emotion and social behavior. In Chapter 6, Elaine Hatfield, John Cacioppo, and Richard Rapson review evidence demonstrating that a phenomenon they call *emotional contagion* exists. That is, they provide evidence that we often come to feel as our social companions feel. They also discuss possible mechanisms behind this phenomenon. In Chapter 8, Rowland Miller and Mark Leary discuss the social sources of embarrassment, as well as the interactive functions embarrassment serves and its possible evolutionary significance. They also use the case of embarrassment to make a more general point that at least some emotions are not just cognitive responses to physiological, cultural, or structural factors (as one might think on the basis of the majority of the existing literature on emotion). Rather they often are social actions that have developed because they facilitate ongoing social interactions. In Chapter 9, William McIntosh and Leonard Martin point out that research indicates that people's objective life situations are not very good predictors of their happiness. They then propose a new model of what makes us happy or unhappy that can account for this surprising fact. Whether we believe that we must attain goals we have *in order* to be happy appears to have a great deal to do with tendencies to experience positive or negative affect day-to-day, which in turn influence our general sense of happiness. In Chapter 10, Diane Mackie, Arlene Asuncion, and Francine

Rosselli discuss the impact of positive affect on persuasion processes. First they present a processing model of persuasion, then they systematically discuss ways in which positive affect might influence processing at each stage of this model. They present available empirical evidence for their model as they work through it. Their chapter represents a far more complete discussion of how affect might influence persuasion than has been available to date. Finally, Constantine Sedikides closes the volume with a chapter on how mood can influence judgments about the self. He reviews the now very large literature on the impact of mood on self-judgments and discusses various theoretical perspectives from which one might understand these effects.

As in the case of its companion volume, I have found editing this volume to be enjoyable and interesting. I have learned a good deal about emotion in the process.

Once again I thank the entire editorial board for their assistance. They have all worked hard and have supplied both me and the individual authors with much valuable feedback. I extend special thanks to Rebecca Deuser for her help as an editorial assistant. I also extend special thanks (and an apology) to John Levine who has served on the editorial board of all the volumes of the *Review* I have edited but whose name was inadvertently left off the list of editorial board members for Volume 13. I would also like to thank the authors themselves for not only preparing their own chapters and for being so responsive to reviewers' comments but for also, in almost all cases, commenting on one or more of the other chapters in the present volume or the prior one.

At this point I am at the end of my term as editor of the *Review*. I have enjoyed the experience and thank the publications board of the Society for Personality and Social Psychology for having given me the opportunity to serve in this role.

The end of my term marks a change in the editorial policy of the *Review*. Since the inception of this series, a single editor has edited multiple volumes. The earliest volumes in this series, edited by Ladd Wheeler, each included chapters on a wide range of topics. The policy has changed over time in that regard. Under the direction of the various subsequent editors—Phil Shaver, Clyde Hendrick, and myself—and the publications board and at the urging of the publisher, the policy has changed such that each volume now focuses on a specific theme. Yet, as this change took place the tradition of appointing a single editor for multiple volumes remained the same. Given the change to a thematic structure it now makes sense to move to having a different editor for each volume—one who is an expert in the area represented by that volume. Thus beginning with Volume 15 a series editor, along with the publications board, will select an individual editor for each volume. In the short run, I will serve as the series editor. I welcome inquiries from potential editors interested in working on an individual volume. Soon a new series editor will be selected. When that occurs, an announcement will appear in the newsletter for the Society, *Dialogue*, along with instructions regarding how to submit proposals for individual volumes.

"Expectation Whirls Me Round"

THE ROLE OF AFFECTIVE EXPECTATIONS IN AFFECTIVE EXPERIENCE

TIMOTHY D. WILSON
KRISTEN J. KLAAREN

Timothy D. Wilson is Associate Professor of Psychology at the University of Virginia. His research interests are in the general area of cognitive social psychology, including the effects of introspection on attitudes and decision making, the interplay of affect and expectations, and "mental contamination," that is, when a judgment, impression, or emotion is influenced by any unwanted piece of information.

Kristen J. Klaaren is a graduate student in social psychology at the University of Virginia. Her research interests include affective expectations, confronting everyday forms of racism, the effects of introspection on attitudes and decision making, and the role of self-reference in impression formation.

> I am giddy, expectation whirls me round.
> The imaginary relish is so sweet
> That it enchants my sense.
> Shakespeare, *Troilus and Cressida*, III.ii.17

The study of emotion is both one of the oldest and one of the freshest topics in psychology. Some of the earliest work in the field concerned such issues as the functions and origins of the emotions (e.g., Darwin, 1872; James, 1884; Lange, 1885). A perusal of the contents of this volume, and the previous one in the series (Clark, 1992), illustrates that research on these and related issues is still thriving. Considerable progress has been made, though there are certain questions that seem to defy resolution. In this chapter, we will focus on one of these questions:

AUTHORS' NOTE: The writing of this chapter, and the research it describes, were supported by National Institute of Mental Health Grant MH41841. We wish to thank Irving Kirsch, Phil Shaver, Robert Thayer, and an anonymous reviewer for their thoughtful comments on a previous draft. Address correspondence to Timothy D. Wilson, Department of Psychology, Gilmer Hall, University of Virginia, Charlottesville, VA 22903-2477 (E-mail: tdw@virginia).

Exactly what are the determinants of a person's emotions, preferences, and moods? We certainly do not claim to have "the answer" to such a large and complex question. Nor, given our space limitations, will we present a comprehensive review of the many studies that address it. Our goal is to explore a heretofore neglected determinant of emotional experience, namely, people's expectations about their own affect. We will discuss the role of affective expectations, describe some studies we have performed to examine their influence, and then discuss the relation between our approach and other positions.

Historically, there have been major disagreements about the determinants of emotions. Some theorists suggest that we know how we feel by observing our bodily reactions (James, 1884; Laird & Bresler, 1992; Lange, 1885), whereas others argue that emotion results from generalized arousal and the cognitive appraisal of the source of that arousal (Clark, 1982; Schachter & Singer, 1962; Zillmann, 1978). Others question the necessity of cognition in affective experience (Zajonc, 1980; Zajonc, Murphy, & Inglehart, 1989).

These positions disagree so drastically about the origin of affect that an important similarity between them has been obscured. All share the view that affect is primarily data driven, caused by something that happens in the current situation (e.g., one's bodily reactions, one's cognitive appraisals of current events). The assumption that emotions are bottom-up, data-driven phenomena is in striking contrast to the dominance of theory-driven models in most other areas of psychology. Most current theories of perception, memory, judgment, person perception, and self-perception are top-down models, in the sense that these responses are said to be influenced by preexisting knowledge structures (in their various incarnations of schemata, theories, categories, models, expectancies, hypotheses, prototypes, scripts, frames, and personaes). People's theories and expectations, for example, have been shown to guide the way information about themselves and others is gathered and processed and to persevere in the face of contradictory information (Nisbett & Ross, 1980; Rosenthal & Jacobson, 1968; Snyder, 1984; Swann, 1984).

In recent years, theories of emotion have begun to incorporate top-down features as well. This is most apparent in the cognitive appraisal approach to emotion, which argues that emotion results from the appraisal of events in relation to people's needs, wishes, and expectations (Frijda, 1986; Ortony, Clore, & Collins, 1988; Roseman, 1984; Scherer,

1984; Shaver, Schwartz, Kirson, & O'Connor, 1987; Smith & Ellsworth, 1985; Smith & Pope, this volume; Weiner, 1985). Consider, for example, two people who watch the Minnesota Twins win the last game of baseball's World Series. To the extent that the two people have different needs and expectations about baseball, they will construe this event very differently, resulting in quite different emotional reactions. The one who is a lifelong Twins fan, and had a large wager on the outcome of the series, will obviously have a different reaction than someone who cares little about baseball. Though both have access to the same "data," their needs and expectations cause quite different appraisals of the events, resulting in different emotions. Another example of a top-down approach to emotion is the hypothesized role of affective memories, whereby previous affective reactions are triggered when that stimulus is encountered again (Fiske, 1982; Fiske & Pavelchak, 1986; Hoffman, 1986; Leventhal, 1980, 1984; Zajonc, Pietromonaco, & Bargh, 1982). In addition, clinical researchers have demonstrated that people's expectations about the effectiveness of therapeutic techniques influence the extent to which these techniques alter their affective states (e.g., their fear of snakes; see Kirsch, 1985; Kirsch, Tennen, Wickless, Saccone, & Cody, 1983).

Like these recent approaches, our concern is with top-down determinants of affective experience. We have investigated a type of top-down processing that has not received much attention: The effects of people's expectations about how they will feel on their actual reactions. We suggest that affective reactions are often formed with reference to prior expectations about how people thought they would feel. In this sense, affect can result from a top-down process, determined as much by affective expectations as by information in the situation at hand.

SOURCES OF AFFECTIVE EXPECTATIONS

We define *affective expectations* as people's predictions about how they will feel in a particular situation or toward a specific stimulus. Affective expectations are distinct from people's expectations about the occurrence of an event, which have been discussed by several emotion theorists. For example, a student who expects to do well on a test but gets a failing grade is likely to have a different emotional reaction than a student who expected to fail (see, e.g., Abelson, 1983;

Kahneman & Miller, 1986; Mandler, 1982; Ortony et al., 1988). Our concern is with people's expectations about their own *feelings,* such as how anxious they think they will feel while taking an exam, how much they think they will like another person, how funny they think a movie will be, or how they expect to feel on their wedding day. These expectations are one class of what Kirsch (1985) has called *response expectancies.*

There seems to be little doubt that people possess such affective expectations. Some are similar to what Jones and McGillis (1976) termed *target-based expectancies,* which are expectations based on one's own previous reactions to a stimulus. Thus a person might expect to like a meal at the Peking Palace because he or she has always had good meals there. Other expectations are similar to what Jones and McGillis (1976) termed *category-based expectancies,* which are based on other people's reactions to a stimulus. Thus a person might never have been to the Peking Palace but expect to have a good meal there because all of his or her friends rave about it. Finally, expectations can be based on what Hochschild (1979) termed *cultural feeling rules.* These are cultural norms dictating how we expect to feel in different social situations, such as happy at weddings and sad at funerals. A person could never have been to a funeral or known anyone who has but still expect to be sad, due to cultural feeling rules about funerals.

It is interesting to consider the accuracy of affective expectations. Consider, for example, three people who go to the same movie. One has no expectation about how enjoyable it will be, the second expects to like it, and the third expects to dislike it. Suppose the movie turns out to be very enjoyable (i.e., in the absence of any expectation, all three would like it). Will the affective reactions of the three moviegoers differ, due to their varying expectations? In what way? How easily will they decide how much they like the movie? We suggest that the relation between people's expectations and the actual value of a stimulus can be divided into four categories. These categories are not meant to be exhaustive, nor are the boundaries between them meant to be rigid. They are a means of conceptualizing the relationship between affective expectations and stimulus values and will clarify the hypotheses we have tested in our research.

Case 1: No Affective Expectation

The first case is one in which people evaluate a stimulus devoid of any expectation about how much they will like it, as with our moviegoer who has no expectation about how much he or she will like the movie. In everyday life, there are probably few such pure cases of no expectations, because people almost always know enough about a stimulus to form at least a rudimentary expectation about their reaction to it (e.g., knowing one's "baseline" level of enjoyment at the movies). People constantly categorize their environments (e.g., "This movie is a romantic comedy"), and these categorizations produce expectations about liking. Nonetheless, it seems best to include the case in which evaluations are primarily data driven, with little reference to expectations or norms. It may be a matter of degree only, but this situation is distinguishable from the second case, in which people have a firm expectation that is consistent with the value of the stimulus.

Case 2: Stimulus Value Confirms an Affective Expectation

Sometimes our affective expectations are on the mark. We expect to like a movie that is, in fact, first rate. We expect a faculty meeting to be interminably dull and, sure enough, it is. These situations differ from Case 1 in that people need not spend as much time examining the stimulus to determine their liking. When expectations are weak or nonexistent, the stimulus must be examined with some care in order to form an evaluation of it. If people have an expectation about their reaction that is confirmed, less processing is necessary to determine how they feel. The assumption is that expectations lead to confirmation checks of the sort discussed by advocates of the "New Look" theory of perception (Bruner, 1957; Postman, 1951). Once the stimulus has been quickly examined to see whether its value is consistent with what was expected, it is not necessary to examine it further to see how much one likes it. In this way, affective expectations may operate similarly to highly accessible attitudes, which have been shown to facilitate the processing of attitude-relevant information (Fazio, Sanbonmatsu, Powell, &

Kardes, 1986). Accessible attitudes, argue Fazio et al. (1986), "free the individual from the processing required for reflective thought about his or her evaluation of the object" (p. 237). We suggest that affective expectations—which may or may not be based on a prior attitude toward the object—operate in the same manner.

Case 3: The Stimulus Value Is Discrepant From an Affective Expectation, but the Discrepancy Is Not Noticed

The next two cases, in which the value of the stimulus conflicts with an expectation, are perhaps the most interesting. Case 3 occurs when people do not realize that such a discrepancy exists. For example, people might expect to like a movie so much that they do indeed like it, not realizing that in the absence of an expectation they would have found it to be rather tedious. When this occurs, the processing of the stimulus is hypothesized to occur relatively quickly, just as in Case 2. Case 3 differs from Case 2 in that the stimulus is objectively *in*consistent with the expectation; that is, without the expectation, people would evaluate it quite differently. When they have the affective expectation, however, people do not recognize the discrepancy, with the following consequences: They (a) examine the stimulus relatively quickly; (b) rate the stimulus consistently with their expectation—that is, assimilation occurs—and (c) engage in less conscious thought about the stimulus while evaluating it.

Case 4: The Stimulus Value Is Discrepant From an Affective Expectation, but the Discrepancy Is Noticed

In Case 4, people realize that there is a discrepancy between their expectation and the value of the stimulus. A confirmation check reveals discrepancies that cannot be ignored, and people are likely to stop and try to resolve the discrepancy. This should trigger slower processing, with the following hypothesized consequences: (a) People take the longest amount of time to examine the stimulus; (b) contrast effects are likely to occur, such that people evaluate the stimulus in a direction *away* from their expectations; and (c) people engage in more conscious thought about the stimulus while evaluating it.

We would like to emphasize that these categories are not meant to be exhaustive. They are relatively pure examples of how affective expectations and stimulus values interact to produce affective reactions. There are, of course, other possible relations between expectations and stimulus values. For example, we have deliberately made an extreme argument for Case 3, arguing that at times people have no idea that the stimulus value is inconsistent with their expectation, such that their evaluation is the result of their expectation and not the value of the stimulus. We will present evidence consistent with the existence of this case below. Without doubt, however, there are also less extreme cases, where people have some recognition that the stimulus is inconsistent with their expectations but are still able to assimilate it to the expectation. For example, people might realize that a movie was not as good as they expected it to be, but the discrepancy might be small enough that assimilation occurs. In this case, their evaluation would be the result of an averaging of their expectation and the stimulus value, much as Anderson's (1981) integration theory would suggest. Such an example can be considered to be somewhere between cases 3 and 4, in that people notice that there is a discrepancy but do not notice the *magnitude* of the discrepancy. Despite these instances that do not fit neatly into our four cases, we find our categorization scheme a useful heuristic for formulating the hypotheses we have addressed in our research.

RESEARCH EVIDENCE

There seems to be little doubt that people have affective expectations as well as ideas about how they operate. Curiously, however, there has not been much research exploring their influence (an exception is Kirsch's, 1990, work on expectancies and fear, which will be discussed later). One reason for this may be that the very idea of expectation-driven processing suggests a cold, reasoned, logical inference, while affect is notoriously "hot." In addition, a top-down approach seems to imply that the determination of affect is a lengthy process in which information from a stimulus must first be processed through a knowledge structure before people know how they feel. A model that postulates the dependence of affect on the occurrence of lengthy cognitive processes is open to the criticism that affect is experienced very quickly, before such processes have the opportunity to occur (e.g., see Cannon's, 1927, criticisms of James's, 1884, bodily reaction theory, and Leventhal & Tomarken's, 1986, criticisms of Schachter and Singer's, 1962, two-factor theory of emotion). Our argument that people often compare the positive and negative attributes of a stimulus with their affective expectations, before forming an evaluation, might appear to be open to similar criticisms. A central part of our position, however, is that the comparison between stimulus attributes and affective expectations often occurs quickly and automatically, facilitating rather than impeding the formation of preferences.

The facilitative effect of affective expectations was illustrated in a study reported by Wilson, Lisle, Kraft, and Wetzel (1989, Study 1). The chief purpose of this study was to illustrate the existence of Case 3, which is, perhaps, the most controversial. Are there circumstances in which people's expectations determine their feelings, even when the value of the stimulus is discrepant from these expectations? To demonstrate that there are, Wilson et al. (1989) asked subjects to look at six single-panel cartoons and created relatively strong expectations that the subjects would like them. The experimenter mentioned off-handedly that previous participants thought they were funny, and the first three that subjects saw were, in fact, funny. The last three, however, were ones that most people think are mediocre at best. The question was this: How funny would people think these last cartoons were, given their expectations that they would like them?

To answer this question, Wilson et al. (1989) included a no-expectation group who saw the same six cartoons but were not told that previous participants thought they were funny. The fact that the first three were funny might create a weak expectation about the final three cartoons, but because subjects had no reason to assume that all six were of the same type or from the same source, they should be able to recognize that the last three were not very funny. This is what occurred, as seen in the top panel of Figure 1.1. Subjects with no expectation found the first three cartoons to be funny but rated the last three as significantly less funny. What about people in the expect-to-like condition? They too liked the first three cartoons. When they saw the last three, they seem to have been blinded by their expectations, in that they reported that the final three cartoons were as funny as the first three. It is possible, of course, that they did not really think the last three cartoons were funny but reported that they were so as not to appear deviant from previous participants. To rule out this possibility, we videotaped people, unbeknownst to

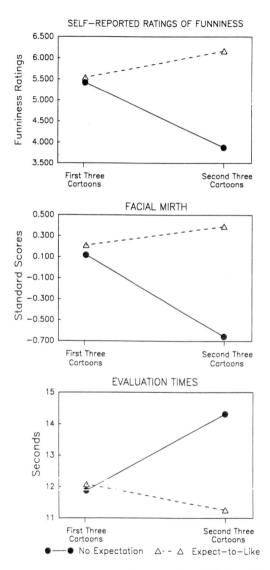

Figure 1.1. Funniness Ratings of the Cartoons, Facial Mirth, and Evaluation Time

SOURCE: From Wilson et al. (1989, Study 1); copyright 1989 by the American Psychological Association.
NOTE: The funniness ratings were made on 9-point scales ranging from *not at all funny* (1) to *extremely funny* (9). The facial mirth scores are the average of the standardized ratings of two independent coders. The higher the number, the greater the facial mirth.

them, and coded how much mirth they expressed while watching the cartoons (all participants subsequently gave us their permission to keep and code the videotapes). As seen in the middle panel of Figure 1.1, people in the expect-to-like condition also laughed and smiled more at the final three cartoons. Because subjects were unaware that they were being observed, the facial mirth results suggest that they genuinely believed the cartoons were funny and did not simply say they were because of self-presentational concerns.

Earlier, we suggested that, when people have affective expectations, they perform rapid confirmation checks to see if the value of the stimulus matches their expectation. If this check results in an affirmative answer, people know how they feel relatively quickly. If people notice that their expectation is wrong, however, they take longer to evaluate the stimulus. To test these hypotheses, we recorded how much time people spent looking at the cartoons before rating them. Subjects in the no-expectation condition probably formed weak expectations on the basis of the first three cartoons that the last three would be funny. They noticed that the last three were not funny, however, causing them to take longer to evaluate them, as seen in the bottom panel of Figure 1.1. By the time subjects in the expect-to-like condition had evaluated the first three cartoons, thereby seeing that the experimenter was correct in saying that they were funny, they should have had a firm expectation about the last three cartoons, leading to quick confirmation checks. Consistent with this view, people in the expect-to-like condition spent significantly less time examining the final three cartoons than did people in the no-expectation condition.

This study provides evidence for Case 3, in which people rapidly assimilate discrepant affective information to an expectation. Apparently, there are times when we do not recognize that our expectations are wrong, and we end up feeling just as we expected. This raises the question, however, of when people will realize that their expectations are incorrect. As hypothesized in Case 4, sometimes we recognize that our affective expectations are incorrect, causing us to stop and reflect about how we feel. When are people likely to note such discrepancies? (That is, when will Case 4 versus Case 3 apply?)

We hypothesize that the ease with which people can assimilate a stimulus to their affective expectations will determine whether Case 3 or Case 4 applies. In short, if a quick confirmation check can succeed in finding attributes of the stimulus that confirm the expectation, then

Case 3 should apply. If the confirmation check fails, people spend time trying to resolve the discrepancy between their expectation and the value of the stimulus, leading to longer evaluation times (Case 4). This hypothesis is a straightforward extension of other models of theory-driven processing to the realm of affect. For example, it is similar to Piaget's (1951) discussion of the determinants of assimilation versus accommodation as well as the determinants of assimilation versus contrast in social judgment theory (C. Sherif, 1979; M. Sherif & Hovland, 1961). Several factors have been identified that influence the ease of assimilation, including the magnitude of the discrepancy between an expectation and the stimulus (Herr, Sherman, & Fazio, 1983), the strength of the expectation, and the ambiguity of the stimulus (C. Sherif, 1979).

We examined factors that might influence the ease with which people can assimilate stimuli to their affective expectations in two studies, which we will briefly summarize. In both studies, people initially evaluated how much they liked 20 stimuli (cartoons in one, reproductions of abstract paintings in the other). After rating their liking for each stimulus, people were given feedback about its source (which magazine it came from in the cartoon study, which style of painting it represented in the art study). In this way, we manipulated people's expectations about how much they liked each style of cartoon or painting. For example, in one condition of the cartoon study, each time people gave a cartoon a high rating, they were told it was from *Punch* magazine, to create the expectation that they liked cartoons from this source. In another condition, people were told that all of the cartoons they disliked were from *Punch,* and in a third condition none of the 20 cartoons was said to be from *Punch.* After evaluating the 20 stimuli, people were asked to evaluate new stimuli, all of which were said to be from the same source (e.g., *Punch* magazine). Thus, in one condition, people expected to like the new cartoons, based on their previous experience with that type. In another condition, people expected to dislike the new cartoons, and in a control condition, people had no affective expectations.

Cross-cutting the expectation manipulation, we also varied the ambiguity of the conditions under which people viewed the new stimuli. In the cartoon study, we accomplished this by asking people to rate the funniness of each of the new cartoons and then to rate how funny they were overall. The others saw the four cartoons without rating them and then rated how funny they were overall. Our reasoning was that a stimulus (in this case, the set of four new cartoons) is more ambiguous when evaluated globally, because people are less likely to perceive that it has both positive and negative attributes (Linville, 1982). For example, consider two people who expect to enjoy a meal at a highly rated restaurant. One person makes separate evaluations of the service, the ambience, the price of the wine, and the quality of each course of the meal. The other, at the conclusion of the meal, makes only one evaluation of the overall experience. Our hypothesis was that the person who rates the different components is more likely to notice a discrepancy between his or her expectations and the experience (i.e., be in Case 4), because of the likelihood that at least one of these components (e.g., the disappointing hors d'oeuvre) conflicts with the expectation. In contrast, people who make one, overall evaluation were hypothesized to be less likely to notice a discrepancy (i.e., be in Case 3). In the art study, we manipulated the ambiguity of the new paintings more directly. We gave half of the subjects color reproductions of the new paintings, whereas we gave the others black-and-white photocopies. (The experimenter told the latter subjects that she only had the black-and-white copies but to try to imagine what they looked like in color.) The black-and-white versions were considerably more ambiguous; that is, it was more difficult to tell what the paintings actually looked like.

Thus, in both studies, people viewed stimuli (new cartoons or paintings) with the expectation that they would like them, dislike them, or with no affective expectations. In the cartoon study, the new cartoons were generally liked by our subject population; thus people in the expect-to-like condition had their expectations confirmed, whereas people in the expect-to-dislike condition had their expectations disconfirmed. In the art study, the new paintings were generally disliked by our subject population, thus people in the expect-to-dislike condition had their expectations confirmed, whereas people in the expect-to-like condition had their expectations disconfirmed. In both studies, half of the people viewed the stimuli under relatively ambiguous conditions (the overall rating condition in the cartoon study, the black-and-white condition in the art study). When people's expectations were confirmed in the ambiguous conditions, we expected people's reactions to be characterized by Case 2: Their liking should be the same as that of people with no expectations, but they should form their evaluation relatively quickly and with relatively little thought about the stimuli (people were asked, at the end of the study, to list the thoughts they remembered having while evaluating the new cartoons). When people's expectations

The emotion itself is hypothesized to include a distinctive subjective feeling state, pattern of physiological activity, and action tendency. Theoretically, one function of this response is to prepare and motivate the person to respond adaptively to the environmental demands (another is to communicate the person's emotional state and likely behaviors to others in the social environment; e.g., Frijda, 1986; Scherer, 1984; Smith & Lazarus, 1990). The subjective feeling state serves as a compelling signal that the person is faced with a particular type of harm or benefit, and it motivates the person to contend with this fact (e.g., Frijda, 1986; Smith & Lazarus, 1990). The associated pattern of physiological activity prepares the individual to cope with the adaptational demands, and the action tendency suggests a particular type of coping response (e.g., to flee in fear or to aggress in anger; Frijda, 1986; Plutchik, 1980; Scherer, 1984; Smith & Lazarus, 1990).

The action tendencies are not the sole determinants of coping, however, and, at all but the most extreme levels of emotional arousal, one can suppress the specific action tendencies and select from a wide array of coping options (Smith, 1991; Smith & Lazarus, 1990). Although the action tendency may not be directly enacted, the emotion nonetheless provides a strong motivational incentive to react to the environmental demands in some way and thereby increases the likelihood that the person will maximize the benefit or minimize the harm that has elicited the emotion. Thus, even though individual emotions may not be reliably associated with specific behaviors, they are likely to result in behaviors that are in some way functionally equivalent.

It is the fact that emotions theoretically link adaptationally similar stimulus conditions with functionally equivalent behavioral responses that makes advances in emotion theory relevant to understanding the relationship between personality and social behavior: The influence of personality on behavior is posited to be most evident in the linkage between functionally equivalent stimuli and functionally equivalent behaviors, and emotion is hypothesized to represent an important mechanism for achieving this linkage. To date, there has been substantially more work examining the elicitation of emotion than the relationship between emotion and behavior (see, however, Frijda et al., 1989). Therefore the current focus is on the elicitation of emotion.

APPRAISAL THEORY AND EMOTION

As noted at the outset, appraisal theorists have attempted to specify the personal meanings associated with a variety of emotions (e.g., Frijda, 1986; Roseman, 1984; Scherer, 1984; Smith & Ellsworth, 1985; Smith & Lazarus, 1990). In their efforts, they have adopted an interactional approach in which the appraisal process is hypothesized to combine consideration of the properties of both the person and the situation (Lazarus & Launier, 1978; Smith & Lazarus, 1990). It is through this approach that appraisal theory achieves the potential to explain individual variation in emotion through the operation of a highly structured and deterministic system. Different emotions are hypothesized to be fixed and universal responses to particular appraised meanings. If a person appraises his or her circumstances in a certain way, then the associated emotional response inevitably follows. If two individuals make the same appraisals, they will experience the same emotions, but if they appraise their circumstances in different ways, they will experience different ones (Smith & Lazarus, 1990). Because the outcome of appraisal is a function of both the person and the situation, however, different individuals will often appraise seemingly identical circumstances differently and react with different emotions. Conversely, the same individuals might appraise seemingly different circumstances similarly and respond with similar emotions. Although on the surface such outcomes might appear disorganized, an adequate consideration of the individuals, their circumstances, and their appraisals would reveal the outcomes to be products of a highly organized system.

Fortunately, the meaning analysis, or appraisal, resulting in emotion appears to be theoretically tractable. In theory, its purpose is to evaluate the person's circumstances in terms of a relatively small number of categories of adaptational significance, corresponding to the harms and benefits associated with various emotions (Smith & Lazarus, 1990). Thus only a limited number of evaluation outcomes result in emotion, and it is possible to derive testable models depicting these appraisals. Several such models have been proposed and have begun to be tested (e.g., Ellsworth & Smith, 1988; Frijda et al., 1989; Roseman, 1991; Roseman et al., 1990; Scherer et al., 1986; Smith & Ellsworth, 1985; Smith & Lazarus, 1991). Although these models differ in certain important respects (see Roseman et al., 1990; Smith, Lazarus, & Pope, 1991), they provide a surprisingly convergent view of appraisal. Below we outline the model proposed by Smith and Lazarus (1990), which is the one with which we have worked most extensively.

This model was derived with several objectives in mind. First, it explicitly attempted to integrate the results of previous work on appraisal and emotion (cited above) with the general theory of stress and coping developed by Lazarus and colleagues (e.g., Lazarus & Folkman, 1984). Second, it sought to isolate and differentiate appraisals—evaluations of significance for personal well-being that directly produce emotions—from other types of cognition, including causal attributions, that are less directly related to emotion (see Smith & Lazarus, 1990; Smith, Lazarus, & Pope, 1991). Finally, the model was derived through rational analysis to illustrate the highly logical structure of the emotion system. This analysis started with the premise that the purpose of appraisal is to evoke functionally appropriate emotions under adaptationally relevant conditions, and then it considered the functions served by individual emotions as proposed by a number of theorists (e.g., Izard, 1977; Plutchik, 1980; Tomkins, 1963). The analytic task was then to identify the information a person would logically require to determine whether one or another adaptational function (served by particular emotions) would be needed under a variety of circumstances. The resulting model is generally consistent with the previous work cited above, and it has received direct support in two studies designed to test it (Smith & Lazarus, 1991; Smith, Lazarus, & Pope, 1991).

For instance, using a vignette methodology, Smith and Lazarus (1991) systematically manipulated the appraisals hypothesized to produce anger, guilt, sadness, and fear/anxiety and found that the appraisal manipulations produced changes in subjects' reported feelings of anger, guilt, and fear/anxiety in a manner highly consistent with the model. Support for the model's predictions concerning sadness was weaker, largely due to the ineffective manipulation of the relevant appraisal variables. Nonetheless, reported levels of sadness were found to covary with the theoretically relevant appraisals within the experimental conditions.

In a subsequent study examining subjects' remembered past experiences, Smith, Lazarus, and Pope (1991) found that theoretically relevant appraisals strongly covaried with reported experiences of anger, guilt, fear/anxiety, sadness, happiness, and hope/challenge. In addition, they found the observed appraisal-emotion relationships to be stronger and more direct than the relationships between a variety of causal attributions and the emotions.

A SPECIFIC APPRAISAL MODEL

The model describes appraisal at two distinct and complementary levels of analysis. The first is a molar, categorical level that summarizes the significant outcomes of appraisal corresponding to the various emotions. These outcomes, referred to as *relational themes,* are the personal meanings hypothesized to produce emotion. Each emotion is produced by its own theme, which represents a distinct type of harm or benefit. For example, the relational theme for fear is appraised *danger* or *threat;* for anger, *other blame*; and so on (see Smith & Lazarus, 1990).

The second level is more molecular and describes the individual *components* of appraisal, which correspond to the appraisal dimensions described in other models (e.g., Roseman, 1984; Scherer, 1984; Smith & Ellsworth, 1985). These components represent the specific *questions* or issues evaluated in appraisal, the answers to which are used to classify one's circumstances in terms of the kinds of harm or benefit represented by the relational themes. Each relational theme can be defined as a particular configuration of evaluation outcomes across several appraisal components, and the appraisal associated with a particular emotion can be described at either level.

Each appraisal component addresses one of the two global issues originally proposed by Lazarus and colleagues in their theory of stress and coping (e.g., Lazarus & Folkman, 1984). The first, *primary appraisal,* concerns whether and how one's circumstances are relevant for personal well-being (e.g., whether anything important is at stake). The second, *secondary appraisal,* concerns the person's resources and options for coping with the situation. The model includes two components of primary appraisal and four of secondary appraisal.

The components of primary appraisal are motivational relevance and motivational congruence (or incongruence). *Motivational relevance* is an evaluation of the extent to which the situation touches upon personal goals or concerns (i.e., the situation's importance). *Motivational congruence* refers to the extent to which the circumstances are consistent or inconsistent with the person's goals (i.e., the situation's desirability). Evaluations along both components are involved in every emotional encounter. An evaluation of high motivational relevance is hypothesized to be necessary for strong emotion, because the degree of relevance determines the person's level of affective involvement. Assessments of motivational congruence combine with relevance to determine whether the encounter is *stressful* or *benign* (Smith, 1991; Smith & Lazarus, 1990). Benign encounters are appraised as motivationally relevant and motivationally congruent (i.e., both important and desired), whereas stressful ones are appraised as motivationally relevant and motivationally incongruent (i.e., important but, in some way, not as desired).

It should be noted that primary appraisal does not include the identity of the stakes involved in the encounter (i.e., which specific goal or concern is implicated). This information is relevant to primary appraisal because the evaluation of one's circumstances in terms of motivational relevance or motivational congruence would be impossible without taking into account what one sees as being at stake in the encounter, one's desires with respect to that stake, and the strength of those desires. This information, however, does not contribute directly to the emotional response. Emotions have considerable flexibility with regard to the range of stimuli that can evoke them (see Smith & Lazarus, 1990), and it is precisely the lack of goal-content specificity in primary appraisal that enables just about any objective stimulus, within the proper context, to elicit just about any emotion.

The components of secondary appraisal are accountability, problem-focused coping potential, emotion-focused coping potential, and future expectancy. The *accountability* evaluation provides direction and focus to the emotional response and the coping it motivates. It determines who or what (oneself or someone or something else) is to receive the credit (if the situation is motivationally congruent) or the blame (if it is motivationally incongruent) for the situation.

The other three components all have to do with the evaluation of the potential for improving an undesirable situation or maintaining a desirable one. The two components of coping potential represent the person's evaluations of his or her abilities to engage in the two global types of coping identified by Lazarus and Folkman (1984). *Problem-focused coping* encompasses one of the major ways of reducing discrepancies between one's circumstances and one's desires—namely, altering the undesirable circumstances—and *emotion-focused coping* encompasses the other—altering one's interpretations, desires, and/or beliefs (see Kimble, 1990; Lazarus & Folkman, 1984; Scherer, 1984; Smith, 1991; Smith & Lazarus, 1990). Thus *problem-focused coping potential* reflects evaluations of the person's ability to act directly to bring (or keep) the situation in line with his or her desires, and *emotion-focused coping potential* refers to the perceived prospects of psychologically adjusting to the encounter should things not work out as desired. *Future expectancy* refers to the perceived possibilities, for *any* reason (i.e., independent of whether the individual plays a role), for changes in the actual or psychological situation that could alter the encounter's motivational congruence.

For illustrative purposes, Table 2.1 depicts the appraisals, described in terms of both components and relational themes, theoretically associated with the four emotions, as well as the emotions' proposed adaptive functions. A more general treatment of the model can be found in Smith and Lazarus (1990) and Smith (1991).

All four emotions are associated with appraisals of high motivational relevance and, in all but one, this appraisal is combined with evaluations of motivational incongruence to define the circumstances as stressful (Smith, 1991). Of the four, only happiness is associated with evaluating the circumstances as motivationally congruent. This evaluation combines with the evaluation of motivational relevance to define the relational theme for happiness—"success." The relational themes for the three remaining stress-related emotions are all differentiated by their associated components of secondary appraisal.

The proposed function of fear/anxiety is to motivate the person to avoid potential harm (see Izard, 1977; Plutchik, 1980; Tomkins, 1963), and the associated relational theme is an appraisal of "danger" or "threat." The secondary appraisal component that defines this theme is uncertain or low coping potential, especially of the emotion-focused variety. The appraisal of emotion-focused coping potential is an evaluation of the person's ability to accept and adjust to a bad situation should things not work out as desired. Holding other factors constant, one's sense of danger, and hence fear/anxiety, should be particularly acute when, beyond seeing potential or actual harm in the situation, the person also believes he or she will be unable to adjust to this harm, should it occur. The motivational consequence of appraising emotion-focused coping potential as low is to push the person to attempt to escape or avoid the harm through problem-focused means, such as by leaving the situation or by altering it to eliminate the harm.

In contrast, the function of sadness/resignation is to motivate the person to get help and support in the face of harm or loss and to disengage from lost commitments (see Izard, 1977; Klinger, 1975;

TABLE 2.1 Appraisals Associated With Four Emotions

Emotion	Proposed Adaptive Function	Relational Theme	Important Appraisal Components
Happiness	Reward success	Success	(a) Motivationally relevant (b) Motivationally congruent
Fear/Anxiety	Avoid potential harm	Danger/Threat	(a) Motivationally relevant (b) Motivationally incongruent (c) Low/uncertain (emotion-focused) coping potential
Sadness/ Resignation	Get help and support in the face of harm/ Disengage from a lost commitment	Irrevocable loss/Hope-lessness about harm or loss	(a) Motivationally relevant (b) Motivationally incongruent (c) Low (problem-focused) coping potential (d) Low future expectancy
Challenge/ Determination	Sustain coping/ Motivate mastery	Effortful optimism/ Potential for success	(a) Motivationally relevant (b) Motivationally incongruent (c) High (problem-focused) coping potential (d) High future expectancy

Plutchik, 1980). The relational theme for this emotion is an appraisal of "irrevocable loss" or "hopelessness about harm or loss." The secondary appraisal components hypothesized to define this theme are a combination of low future expectancy and low coping potential, especially of the problem-focused variety. In a condition of irrevocable loss, the focus is on the inability to do anything to undo the harm, and there is less focus on whether or not the person will ultimately be able to adjust to it. The focus on the inability to repair things through problem-focused means pushes the person to adjust to the circumstances in an emotion-focused manner, such as by seeking emotional support from others or by disengaging from the lost commitment.

Whereas fear/anxiety and sadness/resignation both motivate the person to act in ways that ameliorate harm, challenge/determination reflects a more positive side to stress, akin to the construct of "eustress" discussed by Selye (1974). This emotion motivates sustained striving toward mastery and gain (Smith, 1991), and its relational theme is "effortful optimism"—the belief that, if the person tries hard enough, he or she will be able to improve matters. This theme includes the combined appraisals of motivational relevance and motivational incongruence associated with stress but, in direct contrast to the relational theme for sadness, it includes high levels of problem-focused coping potential and future expectancy. The assessment that positive change is possible motivates the person to persevere and to expend the effort necessary to bring about the desired outcome.

TOWARD AN INTERACTIONAL MODEL: DISPOSITIONAL AND SITUATIONAL ANTECEDENTS OF APPRAISAL

Although appraisal models like the one outlined above clearly are interactional, much of the empirical work examining them has not been interactional. Instead, this work has been directed toward establishing the validity of the proposed nomothetic relationships between appraisals and emotions, and it typically has started with individuals appraising their circumstances in a particular manner and has ended with their emotional reactions. Little attention has been devoted to either the antecedents of the appraisal or the consequences of the emotion. This work has served as an important prerequisite for examining the interactional implications of the appraisal approach by providing a firm foundation for more interactional research. Some of our recent efforts have begun to build on this foundation to examine the situational and dispositional antecedents of appraisal from an interactional perspective, and we describe these efforts below.

A central issue in the more recent work has been to assess the degree to which individual differences in emotion could be understood through the operation of a nomothetic appraisal model. According to appraisal theory, individual differences in emotion are directly caused by individual differences in appraisal. If two individuals appraise the same circumstances differently, they will experience different emotions. Thus the key to understanding individual differences in emotion should lie in identifying the factors that lead some individuals to appraise their circumstances one way and others to appraise the same circumstances another way.

We believe that an examination of the antecedents of the individual appraisal components represents a promising avenue toward such understanding. Each component is hypothesized to represent a specific issue or question evaluated in appraisal. Careful consideration of the nature of this question should provide considerable guidance toward identifying the situational and dispositional factors that systematically contribute to evaluations along the component.

Below we describe our efforts to identify and examine the antecedents of two appraisal components: motivational relevance and problem-focused coping potential. For the two components in turn, we first illustrate how the appraisal model can be used to derive predictions concerning the dispositional and situational antecedents of that component, and then we describe recent research designed to test those predictions. We have focused our discussion on motivational relevance and problem-focused coping potential because these are the components for which we have so far developed clear theoretical predictions. In illustrating the manner in which these predictions were derived, we hope to encourage others to extend an interactional analysis to a broader range of appraisals. As with the basic appraisal model, our predictions were derived through rational analysis. We began with the specific question addressed by the particular appraisal component and, with this question clearly in mind, we attempted to identify the types of information an individual logically would need to answer it.

Hypothesized Antecedents of Appraisals of Motivational Relevance

The evaluation of motivational relevance assesses the degree to which (actual or potential) events in a situation are relevant to issues or concerns to which the person is committed. Colloquially, the question evaluated by this appraisal component is this: "How important to me is what is happening (or might happen) in this situation?" This question is inherently interactional, and it cannot be assessed without reference to both the person's goals and the implications of the situation for those goals. An evaluation of high motivational relevance requires the person to see the circumstances as relevant to an issue to which he or she is committed. A situation could have implications for many things but would be appraised as having little motivational relevance if the person did not care about those things. Conversely, a person could be passionately committed to a particular issue but would appraise little motivational relevance if the circumstances were seen as unrelated to that issue.

This conceptualization of motivational relevance provides considerable guidance in identifying the dispositional and situational factors most likely to contribute to appraisals along this component. On the dispositional side, the most relevant variables include the nature of the person's goals, needs, and values, which we collectively refer to as the person's *commitments*. On the situational side, the most relevant variables include the implications of the *situational content* (i.e., the actual or potential events occurring in the situation) for various commitments. To the extent that the situational content touches upon concerns to which the person is committed, the person's circumstances should be appraised as motivationally relevant. Thus, all else being equal, given that a situation touches upon a particular concern, an individual's appraisals of motivational relevance should be positively correlated with his or her degree of commitment to that concern.

Depending on one's purposes, an individual's commitments can be assessed with any of a number of motivational variables concerned with the individual's values, goals, and needs (reviewed in Cantor & Zirkel, 1990). Such measures vary considerably in their breadth. At one extreme, one can assess the person's degree of commitment to very broad and general domains, such as those captured by the basic needs proposed by Murray (1938; e.g., commitment to affiliation and commitment to achievement). At the other extreme, one can assess the person's degree of commitment to very task-specific goals, such as "proximal goals" as discussed by Bandura (1986) or "current concerns" as discussed by Klinger (1975).

In a similar manner, situational content can be assessed at various levels of generality. At any particular level, however, the main aspect to assess is the degree to which the situation has positive or negative implications for various goals and commitments. This assessment can range from evaluating the implications of a specific set of circumstances for a particular goal to normatively classifying a broad range of situations as to their relevance to broad motivational domains (e.g., classifying general types of situations as to their achievement or affiliation relevance). In any case, it is the situational implications as perceived by the individual that contribute directly to the appraisal of motivational relevance. Thus a situation may be normatively classified as having strong implications for a particular motivational domain, but if these implications are not perceived by the individual, they will not contribute to the appraisal of motivational relevance.

We have begun to examine the antecedents of appraised motivational relevance at a broad level of analysis. We have focused on assessing individuals' levels of commitment to achievement and affiliative concerns, two of Murray's (1938) broad-based needs. In two studies that we describe below, we attempted to examine the ability of measures of commitment within these domains to predict individual differences in appraisals of motivational relevance across situations selected for their relevance to one or the other domain (Pope & Smith, 1991). We have begun at this general level to examine the validity of our theorizing across a broad range of experience. We recognize, however, that it will be important to extend this work to examine explicitly the contributions to appraised motivational relevance of more specific goals and more specific settings.

An Empirical Examination of Commitment, Situational Content, and Appraised Motivational Relevance

In the first study, 137 undergraduates described their appraisals and emotions during past experiences they had recalled in response to probes designed to factorially vary the valence (positive versus negative) and situational content (achievement related versus affiliation related) of the experiences. For example, two of the achievement-related situations involved a time when the subject had performed either particularly well or particularly poorly on an exam. One of the affiliation-related situations involved the subject having an argument with his or her dating partner, and another involved finding out that a person in whom the subject had romantic interests was also interested in him or her. In addition to describing their assigned experience, subjects completed a battery of personality scales that included measures of their levels of commitment to both achievement and affiliation. These latter scales combined items from the achievement and affiliation subscales of the Personality Research Form (Jackson, 1967) with items developed by Novacek and Lazarus (1990).

Consistent with the theoretical rationale outlined above, it was predicted that appraisals of motivational relevance would be correlated with an individual's level of commitment to a particular domain (achievement or affiliation) in situations relevant to that domain but would not be correlated with commitment level in situations not relevant to the domain. These predictions were confirmed for commitment to achievement, but not for commitment to affiliation.

The top panel (a) of Figure 2.1 depicts the results for commitment to achievement. As can be seen, there was a statistically significant interaction of commitment and situational content ($p < .05$; all reported probabilities are two tailed), indicating that one's level of commitment to achievement and appraisals of motivational relevance were essentially uncorrelated in affiliation-related situations (β [standardized slope] = .04) but were positively correlated in achievement-related ones ($\beta = .41$).

Contrary to predictions, the analogous commitment by situational content interaction was not observed for commitment to affiliation ($p > .15$, not depicted). Instead, collapsing on situational content, the person's level of commitment to affiliation interacted with situational valence ($p < .05$), such that appraisals of motivational relevance were positively correlated with commitment to affiliation for positive situations ($\beta = .42$), but not negative ones ($\beta = .06$). A possible interpretation of this interaction is that it reflects a tendency of individuals highly committed to affiliation to emphasize the positive aspects of their circumstances. This interpretation is supported by valence by commitment interactions, similar to the one observed for motivational relevance, that were observed for appraisals of motivational congruence, problem-focused coping potential, and success as well as for feelings of happiness (all $ps < .05$). In every case, commitment to affiliation was positively correlated with the appraisal or emotion for positive situations (all $\beta s > .30$) but was essentially uncorrelated with it for negative ones (all $|\beta|s \leq .10$). Moreover, as indicated by statistically reliable main effects (all $ps < .05$), individuals highly committed to affiliative concerns reported stronger appraisals of future expectancy and effortful optimism and stronger feelings of hope/challenge across all types of situations (both positive and negative) than did their less committed counterparts (all $\beta s > .20$). It is possible that, by emphasizing the positive aspects of their circumstances, individuals highly committed to affiliation were

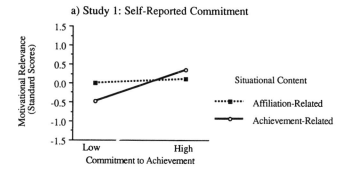

a) Study 1: Self-Reported Commitment

b) Study 2: Self-Reported Commitment

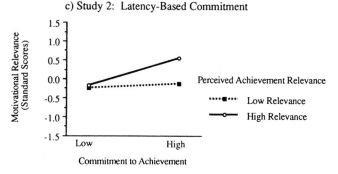

c) Study 2: Latency-Based Commitment

Figure 2.1. Interactive Effects of Situational Content and Commitment to Achievement on Appraisals of Motivational Relevance Using Self-Report and Latency-Based Measures of Commitment

SOURCE: Data from Pope and Smith (1991).

strategically attempting to respond in socially desirable ways that would maximize their chances of being liked.

The second study, involving 43 undergraduates, conceptually replicated the first but with the following changes: First, using a directed imagery task, each subject imagined him- or herself in a series of standardized vignettes designed to manipulate situational valence and situational content (relevance to achievement versus affiliation) factorially. These vignettes were modeled closely after specific experiences subjects had recalled in response to the prompts used in the first study. Second, the subjects' own perceptions of situational content (i.e., the degree of achievement and affiliation relevance perceived by the subjects for each situation) were directly assessed, and these perceptions were used as the primary indicators of situational content in the data analyses. Finally, using a self-description task developed by Markus (1977), the self-report measures of commitment were supplemented with more indirect measures based on the latencies with which subjects endorsed affiliation- and achievement-related adjectives as self-descriptive.

The results of this study largely paralleled those of the first. As depicted in the bottom two panels of Figure 2.1, both the self-report (panel b) and the latency-based (panel c) measures of commitment to achievement demonstrated the predicted commitment by situational content interaction (both $ps < .05$). For both measures, appraisals of motivational relevance were positively correlated with one's level of commitment to achievement when perceived achievement relevance was high (self-report $\beta = .33$, latency $\beta = .34$) but were uncorrelated with commitment levels when perceived achievement relevance was low (self-report $\beta = .01$, latency $\beta = .04$).

Neither measure of commitment to affiliation, however, demonstrated the analogous commitment by situational content interaction (both $ps > .50$). Moreover, commitment to affiliation was once again associated with a tendency to emphasize the positive, although this tendency was more clearly captured by the new schema-based measure than by the original self-report measure. For instance, for the self-report measure, there was a general tendency for an individual's level of commitment to affiliation to be positively correlated with his or her appraisals of problem-focused coping potential ($\beta = .31$) but, for the latency-based measure, a similar tendency was more pervasive and involved appraisals of motivational congruence ($\beta = .37$), emotion-focused coping potential (β = .32), and future expectancy (β = .38; all $ps < .05$).

Further, subjects' perceptions of situational content were found to vary as a function of commitment. Collapsing across situations, commitment to a domain (primarily as assessed by the self-report measures) was positively correlated with the tendency to perceive one's circumstances as relevant to that domain. That is, commitment to achievement was associated with seeing one's circumstances as achievement related (β = .45), and commitment to affiliation was associated with seeing them as affiliation related (β = .34; both $ps < .05$). This result is reminiscent of the work conducted within the New Look approach to perception (e.g., Bruner, 1957) and suggests that, beyond contributing to appraisals of the importance of situational features perceived as being related to one's concerns, one's commitments further influence which situational aspects will be perceived as being related to those concerns in the first place.

In combination, the two studies provide some support for the hypothesized contributions of motivational variables to individual differences in emotional response. The predicted influences on appraisals of motivational relevance were found for commitment to achievement but not for commitment to affiliation. In part, the lack of predicted findings for commitment to affiliation may have been due to a ceiling effect on appraisals of motivational relevance in both studies. Perhaps due to the reliance on remembered (and thus memorable) experiences in Study 1 and on hypothetical vignettes designed to be emotionally evocative in Study 2, appraisals of motivational relevance were consistently high in both studies, with a mean rating of approximately 7.5 (SD = 1.5) on a 9-point (1-9) scale. Moreover, there was a general tendency for affiliation-related situations to be appraised as slightly more motivationally relevant than achievement-related ones. We suspect that future work examining situations associated with a broader range of appraised motivational relevance will find less ambiguous support for the hypotheses.

Nonetheless, the additional findings in both studies—the association between commitment to affiliation and the tendency to emphasize the positive, and the general tendency to see one's commitments as being implicated across a variety of situations—clearly indicate that the systematic influence of the commitment variables on the subjects' responses went considerably beyond their predicted effects on primary appraisal.

Hypothesized Antecedents of Appraisals of Problem-Focused Coping Potential

The evaluation of problem-focused coping potential is an assessment of the degree to which the individual has the ability to act directly upon his or her (social or physical) circumstances to increase or maintain their motivational congruence. Colloquially, the question represented by this appraisal component is this: "Can I successfully do something that will make (or keep) the situation (more) the way I want it to be?" In many respects, the appraisal of problem-focused coping potential is similar to efficacy-related evaluations as discussed by Bandura (1986). However, whereas efficacy judgments are usually restricted to refer to assessments of one's ability to perform specific tasks, the evaluation of coping potential is a broader judgment that reflects the individual's perceived ability to influence his or her circumstances in desired ways through any available courses of action.

The assessment of problem-focused coping potential involves a comparison of the perceived difficulty of successfully performing the tasks required to alter the circumstances with the person's self-perceived abilities to perform such actions. To the extent that one's abilities are evaluated as exceeding the task demands, then appraisals of problem-focused coping potential should be high, but, to the extent that the demands are seen as exceeding one's abilities, then appraisals of problem-focused coping potential should be low.

From this analysis, the dispositional and situational factors most likely to contribute to appraisals of problem-focused coping potential are easily derived. On the dispositional side, it is important to assess the person's *self-perceived ability*. Depending upon one's purposes, these assessments could range in specificity from task-specific self-efficacy judgments (Bandura, 1986) to global competence beliefs (e.g., Smith, Dobbins, & Wallston, 1991). On the situational side, it is important to assess the *difficulty* of the task(s) the person needs to perform to improve or maintain the situation. The factors entering into this assessment could range in specificity from the particular knowledge and skills required to perform the task successfully to more general considerations of the degree to which the person's circumstances are controllable and amenable to change. As with situational content, however, it is task difficulty as perceived by the individual, rather than as normatively defined, that will contribute directly to the appraisal.

In our preliminary work examining the antecedents of appraised problem-focused coping potential, we have adopted an intermediate level of analysis. We have assessed subjects' self-perceived and actual abilities within the domain of mathematical problem solving and then confronted high and low ability subjects with a mathematical problem-solving task in which difficulty was experimentally manipulated. We expected the systematic combination of individuals of known ability with a task of known difficulty to influence appraisals of problem-focused coping potential in highly predictable ways.

An Empirical Examination of Ability, Task Difficulty, and Problem-Focused Coping Potential

The subjects in this study (Smith et al., 1990) were 28 undergraduates selected for either high or low mathematical ability as determined by both math-SAT scores (above 670 versus below 600, respectively) and self-reported mathematical competence. Each subject was randomly assigned to work on one of two sequences of algebra word problems (easy versus difficult). Both sequences were identical, and easy, for the first five problems. Subsequent problems in the easy sequence remained easy, but those in the difficult sequence became virtually unsolvable. Subjects expected to work on 20 problems over the course of an hour, but the experiment was halted after the seventh problem, and appraisals and emotions were retrospectively assessed for the fifth and seventh problems. For each problem, subjects were given up to four attempts to answer the problem correctly and, after each incorrect attempt, they had the option of receiving a hint concerning the problem's solution. Thus the subject could take up to three hints while working on each problem.

In accord with the above theoretical analysis, it was predicted that, in the easy sequence, all subjects would remain relatively confident of their potential to succeed at the task, and appraisals of problem-focused coping potential would be generally high. In the difficult sequence, however, the difficulty of the sixth and seventh problems was expected to lead subjects to question their abilities and to reassess their coping potential. High ability subjects were expected to remain relatively confident of their abilities, to continue to appraise their problem-focused coping potential as high, and thus to report both appraisals of effortful optimism and feelings of challenge/determination. In contrast, low ability subjects were expected to evaluate themselves as lacking the abilities necessary for success and thus to show large reductions in their appraised problem-focused coping potential. Accordingly, these subjects were further expected to demonstrate decreases in effortful optimism and challenge/determination but to demonstrate increases in hopelessness and sadness/resignation (see Table 2.1). The key findings are presented in Figure 2.2.

As can be seen, the results generally corresponded to predictions. Although, for unknown reasons, the low ability subjects facing the difficult task demonstrated lower levels of appraised coping potential (panel a; all scales ranged from 1 to 9) in response to problem 5 (which was before the task became difficult) than did the other subjects, they also demonstrated greater reductions in appraised coping potential between the fifth and seventh problems: After controlling for levels of appraised coping potential associated with problem 5, appraised coping potential was significantly lower during problem 7 for these subjects than for the others ($p < .05$). In accord with predictions, the reduction in coping potential was accompanied by decreases in effortful optimism (panel b) and challenge/determination (panel c) and increases in hopelessness (panel d) and resignation (panel e; all $ps < .01$). Thus appraisals of problem-focused coping potential were successfully manipulated by combining theoretically relevant dispositional traits with equally relevant situational properties, and these manipulated appraisals had predicted effects on emotional state.

Moreover, within the difficult sequence, subjects' self-reported appraisals and emotional reactions during problem 7 received convergent validation from an examination of the subjects' hint-taking behavior during problem 6, the first of the difficult problems. Within our experimental setting, subjects were conservative about hint taking, and it seemed to be limited to cases in which the subject was preparing to give up on the task. Hint taking thus appeared to represent a form of help seeking that theoretically might be expected to be associated with sadness/resignation. Consistent with this interpretation, virtually no hints were taken in the easy sequence, and, in the difficult sequence, the number of hints taken while working on problem 6 was negatively correlated with self-perceived math competence ($r = -.70, p < .01$). On average, high ability subjects took only one of the three hints available to them ($M = 1.11$), whereas the low ability subjects almost always took all three of them ($M = 2.89$). Notably, despite the small sample within

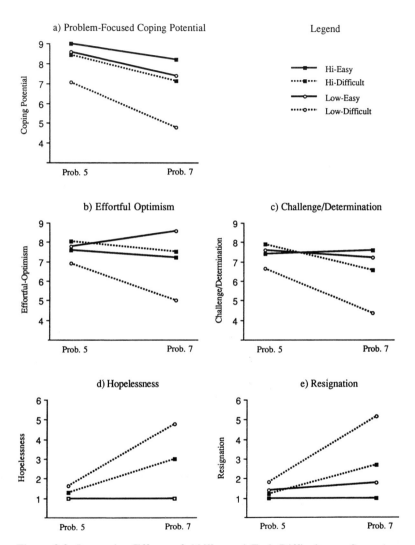

Figure 2.2. Interactive Effects of Ability and Task Difficulty on Secondary Appraisals of Problem-Focused Coping Potential, Associated Relational Themes (effortful optimism and hopelessness), and Associated Emotions (challenge/determination and resignation)

SOURCE: Data from Smith, Ellsworth, and Pope (1990).

the difficult sequence ($N = 18$), the number of hints taken on problem 6 was negatively correlated with subjects' appraisals of problem-focused coping potential ($r = -.49$, $p < .05$) and positively correlated with their feelings of resignation ($r = .48$, $p < .05$) while working on problem 7.

CONCLUSIONS AND FUTURE DIRECTIONS

The above examples, combined with the review of the theory from which they were derived, are meant to illustrate the promise of an explicitly interactional approach to the study of emotion. It should be evident that the adoption of an interactional perspective has contributed both theoretically and empirically to a rich and still developing understanding of emotional phenomena. As illustrated above, this perspective is helping students of emotion understand how emotion simultaneously can be variable across individuals and the product of a deterministic system.

In addition, this review was meant to illustrate the potential contributions of emotion theory to the development of a more general interactional psychology of social behavior. If, as currently believed, personality yields its most consistent effects at the level of personal meanings, then the appraisal approach can offer considerable guidance for understanding those meanings and how they operate. The language of appraisal is important for understanding the subjective functional equivalence of stimuli. The relational themes associated with various emotions provide a rich, yet constrained set of variables for describing subjective functional equivalences that are important in organizing subjective experience and behavior. Further, the theory describing the generation of these relational themes provides considerable guidance as to how dispositional and situational factors combine to produce these functional equivalences (appraisals). Nevertheless, the potential contributions of an interactional approach to the study of both emotion and social behavior are largely that—potential contributions. Therefore we conclude by briefly considering some of the limitations of the work reviewed above as well as what we see as some of the most important issues to be addressed in future work.

First, it should be noted that virtually all of existing work within the appraisal framework has been limited to the study of emotional reactions associated with remembered past experiences or hypothetical vignettes, and has relied almost exclusively on verbal self-report measures. We believe that the reliance on these relatively weak methodologies was a necessary step in the development of specific models of appraisal-emotion relationships because the use of these techniques permitted investigators to examine appraisals and emotions across a broad range of experience that would have been otherwise impossible to capture within the context of any single study.

Nonetheless, the exclusive reliance on such techniques has had its costs. First, the reliance on remembered and hypothetical experiences necessarily entails some interpretive ambiguity concerning whether subjects are describing actual emotional reactions or whether they are describing their intuitive theories of emotion. Such problems become particularly acute when one wishes to examine either the antecedents of appraisal or the behavioral consequences of emotion. For instance, in our examination of the antecedents of appraised motivational relevance, it is difficult to know whether the highly affiliative subjects' apparent tendency to emphasize the positive aspects of their situations reflected what they actually did (or would have done) within the remembered (or hypothetical) circumstances or whether these reports reflected idealized responses that the subjects most likely would not have enacted during an ongoing encounter.

We believe that such ambiguities can only be resolved by moving away from the study of remembered and hypothetical experiences and moving toward an examination of individuals' appraisals and emotional reactions during ongoing meaningful experiences. Such studies are necessarily complicated and difficult to perform. We feel, however, that the specific models produced as a result of the earlier work provide the theoretical guidance necessary to support this more difficult research. In addition, the study of ongoing experiences provides the opportunity for supplementing subjects' self-reports with a variety of more behavioral measures that can be used to provide convergent validation of the self-reports.

The examination of the antecedents of appraised problem-focused coping potential that we reported above (Smith et al., 1990) represents our preliminary attempt to advance our research in these directions. In this study, we were able to observe subjects' appraisals and emotional reactions while they were engaged in a meaningful task. In addition, we were able to "manipulate" subjects' appraisals systematically in an interactional fashion by exposing individuals selected for theoretically relevant dispositional traits to situations in which key situational properties were experimentally manipulated. Moreover, by observing the subjects' performances in the ongoing task, we were able to collect behavioral data that helped validate the subjects' self-reports.

We are currently attempting to develop this interactional methodology further. In doing so, we have identified a number of issues we believe are especially important to address. First, there is an obvious need to replicate and extend the research we have described. The examination of the antecedents of motivational relevance should be replicated in a context involving an ongoing experience. Such a context not only should be likely to increase the variance of appraisals of motivational relevance (and thereby give our hypotheses concerning the antecedents of these appraisals a fairer test) but also would allow one to observe subjects' actual (as opposed to idealized) reactions. Similarly, the examination of the antecedents of problem-focused coping potential consisted of a preliminary feasibility study using a small sample, and it needs to be replicated using a larger one. In addition, it is important to extend the theory and research to examine the antecedents of additional appraisal components such as motivational congruence, accountability, and emotion-focused coping potential. The theoretical and empirical illustrations we have provided are intended to guide such attempts.

Moreover, the models specifying the cognitive antecedents of emotion need to be complemented by equally specific models outlining the relationships between emotions and behavior. Much of the current interest in emotion theory is derived from an assumption that emotion plays a significant role in shaping social behavior. This assumption has received surprisingly little direct theoretical or empirical attention, however. One promising step toward addressing this omission would be to integrate the study of emotion more extensively with that of stress and coping. As discussed elsewhere (e.g., Lazarus, 1991; Smith, 1991), research on stress and emotion has largely developed along independent lines. Stress and emotion, however, represent two sides of the same coin, and there is much to be gained by integrating their study (see Smith, 1991).

Finally, the emerging *interactional* approach to the study of emotion could be profitably developed into a more *transactional* one. Virtually all proponents of an interactional psychology distinguish between two types of "interaction" (e.g., Bowers, 1973; Magnusson, 1990). The first is largely static and cross-sectional and depicts how at a given point in time properties of the person and situation combine (or interact) to produce some outcome. The appraisal model and associated research presented above largely correspond to this type of interaction. The second is more dynamic and depicts the person and situation as continual mutual influences on one another. For instance, as discussed by Buss (1987) and others, individuals do not merely react passively to the situations in which they happen to find themselves, but they are often active agents in determining the very nature of those circumstances. They can *select* which situations to enter and which to avoid; they can unintentionally *evoke* certain properties of the situation that might otherwise remain latent; and they can strategically *manipulate* the situation to further their goals. In a similar manner, the social environment is not inert but often responds to the person's behaviors in ways that actively hinder or facilitate his or her goals. This latter type of interaction has been labeled "transaction" by some (e.g., Lazarus & Launier, 1978; Pervin, 1968) to emphasize the dynamic and reciprocal influences of the person and situation.

Even though the research presented above was conducted within a largely static interactional framework of the first type, hints of transactional influences of the second type were observable in the data, particularly in the studies examining motivational relevance. For instance, the seeming attempts of individuals highly committed to affiliative concerns to emphasize the positive aspects of their circumstances could be interpreted as manipulative attempts to evoke desired outcomes from their social environment (i.e., to encourage others to like them). Similarly, the tendency of commitment to heighten the salience of the potential commitment-related implications of one's circumstances could be an example of individuals selectively perceiving and thus evoking properties of their circumstances that might otherwise remain latent. That these hints of transactional processes were observed in a context that was not particularly designed to detect them suggests their importance for understanding social behavior. It is only through the development of approaches that explicitly take these more dynamic transactional processes into account that the true potential of an "interactional" psychology will be fully actualized.

REFERENCES

Allport, G. W. (1937). *Personality: A psychological interpretation.* New York: Holt.

Averill, J. R. (1983). Studies on anger and aggression: Implications for theories of emotion. *American Psychologist, 38,* 1145-1160.

Bandura, A. (1986). *Social foundations of thought and action: A social-cognitive theory.* Englewood Cliffs, NJ: Prentice-Hall.

Bem, D. J., & Funder, D. C. (1978). Predicting more of the people more of the time: Assessing the personality of situations. *Psychological Review, 85,* 485-501.

Ben-Porath, Y. S., & Tellegen, A. (1990). A place for traits in stress research. *Psychological Inquiry, 1,* 14-16.

Bowers, K. S. (1973). Situationism in psychology: An analysis and a critique. *Psychological Review, 80,* 307-336.

Bruner, J. S. (1957). On perceptual readiness. *Psychological Review, 64,* 123-152.

Buss, D. M. (1987). Selection, evocation, and manipulation. *Journal of Personality and Social Psychology, 53,* 1214-1221.

Cantor, N., & Zirkel, S. (1990). Personality, cognition, and purposive behavior. In L. A. Pervin (Ed.), *Handbook of personality: Theory and research* (pp. 135-164). New York: Guilford.

Ekman, P. (1984). Expression and the nature of emotion. In K. R. Scherer & P. Ekman (Eds.), *Approaches to emotion* (pp. 329-343). Hillsdale, NJ: Lawrence Erlbaum.

Ellsworth, P. C., & Smith, C. A. (1988). From appraisal to emotion: Differences among unpleasant feelings. *Motivation and Emotion, 12,* 271-302.

Endler, N. S., & Magnusson, D. (1976). Personality and person by situation interactions. In N. S. Endler & D. Magnusson (Eds.), *Interactional psychology and personality* (pp. 1-25). New York: John Wiley.

Epstein, S. (1979). The stability of behavior: I. On predicting most of the people much of the time. *Journal of Personality and Social Psychology, 37,* 1097-1126.

Frijda, N. H. (1986). *The emotions.* New York: Cambridge University Press.

Frijda, N. H., Kuipers, P., & ter Schure, E. (1989). Relations among emotion, appraisal, and emotional action readiness. *Journal of Personality and Social Psychology, 57,* 212-228.

Funder, D. C. (1991). Global traits: A neo-Allportian approach to personality. *Psychological Science, 2,* 31-39.

Funder, D. C., & Colvin, C. R. (1991). Explorations in behavioral consistency: Properties of persons, situations, and behaviors. *Journal of Personality and Social Psychology, 60,* 773-794.

Izard, C. E. (1977). *Human emotions.* New York: Plenum.

Jackson, D. N. (1967). *Personality Research Form manual.* Goshen, NY: Research Psychologists Press.

Kimble, G. A. (1990). Mother nature's bag of tricks is small. *Psychological Science, 1,* 36-41.

Klinger, E. (1975). Consequences of commitment to and disengagement from incentives. *Psychological Review, 82,* 1-25.

Lazarus, R. S. (1968). Emotions and adaptation: Conceptual and empirical relations. In W. J. Arnold (Ed.), *Nebraska Symposium on Motivation* (Vol. 16, pp. 175-266). Lincoln: University of Nebraska Press.

Lazarus, R. S. (1991). *Emotion and adaptation.* New York: Oxford University Press.

Lazarus, R. S., & Folkman, S. (1984). *Stress, appraisal, and coping.* New York: Springer.

Lazarus, R. S., & Launier, R. (1978). Stress-related transactions between person and environment. In L. A. Pervin (Ed.), *Perspectives in interactional psychology* (pp. 287-327). New York: Plenum.

Magnusson, D. (1990). Personality development from an interactional perspective. In L. A. Pervin (Ed.), *Handbook of personality: Theory and research* (pp. 193-222). New York: Guilford.

Markus, H. (1977). Self-schemata and processing information about the self. *Journal of Personality and Social Psychology, 35,* 63-78.

Mischel, W. (1968). *Personality and assessment.* New York: John Wiley.

Mischel, W. (1973). Toward a cognitive social learning reconceptualization of personality. *Psychological Review, 80,* 252-283.

Murray, H. A. (1938). *Explorations in personality.* New York: Oxford University Press.

Novacek, J., & Lazarus, R. S. (1990). The structure of personal commitments. *Journal of Personality, 58,* 693-715.

Pervin, L. A. (1968). Performance and satisfaction as a function of individual-environment fit. *Psychological Bulletin, 69,* 56-68.

Plutchik, R. (1980). *Emotion: A psychoevolutionary synthesis.* New York: Harper & Row.

Pope, L. K., & Smith, C. A. (1991). *Contributions of commitment to primary appraisal and emotional response.* Manuscript in preparation, Vanderbilt University.

Roseman, I. J. (1984). Cognitive determinants of emotion: A structural theory. In P. Shaver (Ed.), *Review of personality and social psychology: Vol. 5. Emotions, relationships, and health* (pp. 11-36). Beverly Hills, CA: Sage.

Roseman, I. J. (1991). Appraisal determinants of discrete emotions. *Cognition and Emotion, 5,* 161-200.

Roseman, I. J., Spindel, M. S., & Jose, P. E. (1990). Appraisals of emotion-eliciting events: Testing a theory of discrete emotions. *Journal of Personality and Social Psychology, 59,* 899-915.

Scherer, K. R. (1984). Emotion as a multicomponent process: A model with some cross-cultural data. In P. Shaver (Ed.), *Review of personality and social psychology: Vol. 5. Emotions, relationships, and health* (pp. 37-63). Beverly Hills, CA: Sage.

Scherer, K. R., Wallbott, H. G., & Summerfield, A. B. (Eds.). (1986). *Experiencing emotion: A cross-cultural study.* New York: Cambridge University Press.

Selye, H. (1974). *Stress without distress.* Philadelphia: J. B. Lippincott.

Smith, C. A. (1991). The self, appraisal, and coping. In C. R. Snyder & D. R. Forsyth (Eds.), *Handbook of social and clinical psychology: The health perspective* (pp. 116-137). Elmsford, NY: Pergamon.

Smith, C. A., Dobbins, C. J., & Wallston, K. A. (1991). The mediational role of perceived competence in psychological adjustment to rheumatoid arthritis. *Journal of Applied Social Psychology, 21,* 1218-1247.

Smith, C. A., & Ellsworth, P. C. (1985). Patterns of cognitive appraisal in emotion. *Journal of Personality and Social Psychology, 48,* 813-838.

Smith, C. A., Ellsworth, P. C., & Pope, L. K. (1990). Contributions of ability and task difficulty to appraisal, emotion, and autonomic activity [Abstract]. *Psychophysiology, 27,* S64.

Smith, C. A., & Lazarus, R. S. (1990). Emotion and adaptation. In L. A. Pervin (Ed.), *Handbook of personality: Theory and research* (pp. 609-637). New York: Guilford.

Smith, C. A., & Lazarus, R. S. (1991). *Appraisal components, relational themes, and emotion.* Manuscript submitted for publication, Vanderbilt University.

Smith, C. A., Lazarus, R. S., & Pope, L. K. (1991). *In search of the "hot" cognitions: Attributions, appraisals, and their relationship to emotion.* Manuscript submitted for publication, Vanderbilt University.

Tomkins, S. S. (1963). *Affect, imagery, consciousness: Vol. 2. The negative affects.* New York: Springer.

3

What Is an Emotion?

THE ROLE OF SOMATOVISCERAL AFFERENCE, WITH SPECIAL EMPHASIS ON SOMATOVISCERAL "ILLUSIONS"

JOHN T. CACIOPPO
GARY G. BERNTSON
DAVID J. KLEIN

John T. Cacioppo is Professor of Psychology at The Ohio State University. His research reflects a psychophysiological perspective on social processes and individual differences. His current research interests include the physiological contributions to individual differences and personality processes, emotion, and health; rudimentary determinants of attitude formation and change; electrocortical, somatic, and autonomic markers of evaluative and emotional processes; and reciprocal effects of social (e.g., contextual, social support, cultural) factors on attitudes, emotions, and health. He is currently Associate and Methodology Editor of *Psychophysiology* and the Associate Editor of the *Psychological Review*.

Gary G. Berntson is Professor of Psychology, Psychiatry, and Pediatrics at The Ohio State University. His research interests range from the biological mechanisms underlying cognition and affect to social processes in primates. Among his recent research interests are the organization and control of autonomic nervous system activity, electrocortical markers of evaluative activation, and the control and interpretation of respiratory sinus arrhythmia. He has served as the Associate Editor and Editor of *Physiological Psychology*.

David J. Klein is a graduate student in social psychology at The Ohio State University. Currently, his research concerns individual differences in autonomic reactivity and expressivity in emotion. He is also interested in the role affect plays in attitude development and change.

More than a century has passed since William James (1884) published his influential article titled "What Is an Emotion?" James's provocative answer to this question was that emotional feelings were consequences rather than antecedents of peripheral physiological changes brought about by some stimulus:

AUTHORS' NOTE: Preparation of this manuscript was supported by National Science Foundation Grant No. BNS-8940915 to JTC, National Science Foundation Grant No. BNS-8820027 to GGB, and a National Science Foundation Fellowship to DJK. Address correspondence concerning this manuscript to John T. Cacioppo, Department of Psychology, The Ohio State University, 1885 Neil Avenue, Columbus, OH 43210-1222 (E-mail: Cacioppo.1@osu.edu).

Our natural way of thinking about these standard emotions is that the mental perception of some fact excites the mental affection called the emotion, and that this latter state of mind gives rise to the bodily expression. My thesis on the contrary is that *the bodily changes follow directly the* PERCEPTION *of the exciting fact, and that our feeling of the same changes as they occur* IS *the emotion.* (James, 1884, p. 190)

James's theory has stimulated debate (e.g., Baldwin, 1894; James, 1894; Levenson, 1992; Zajonc & McIntosh, 1992) and research (e.g., Ax, 1953; Cannon, 1927; Ekman, Levenson, & Friesen, 1983; Marañon, 1924; Schachter & Singer, 1962; Stemmler, 1989) for more than a century. Research on the influence of cognitive appraisals in emotion (e.g., Smith & Ellsworth, 1987; Valins, 1966; see, also, Smith & Pope, this volume) and on emotions in the spinal cord injured (e.g., Chwalisz, Diener, & Gallagher, 1988) suggests that afferent information from peripheral activity is not a *necessary* condition for emotional experience. James (1884), however, viewed emotions as being multiply determined. For instance, individuals might recall earlier emotional episodes, including their feelings, and, in so doing, they might reexperience the emotion. If the remembered emotion was weak originally (e.g., it involved little or no somatovisceral activation), reexperiencing the emotion might occur in the absence of significant peripheral bodily disturbances. James (1884) therefore stated at the outset that "the only emotions I propose expressly to consider here are those that have a distinct bodily expression" (p. 189), a limiting condition of which James reminded his critics a decade later (James, 1894). James maintained that, within this broad class of emotional phenomena, discrete emotional experiences could be identified with unique patterns of bodily changes, and that the perception of one of these specific patterns of peripheral physiological changes *was* the emotional experience.

Numerous theories of emotion have been proposed since James (1884), but those dealing with the same class of phenomena (i.e., emotions accompanied by significant peripheral physiological changes) are bracketed by (a) models that hold that discrete emotional experiences stem from distinct somatovisceral patterns (e.g., Ekman, in press; Ekman et al., 1983; Levenson, Ekman, & Friesen, 1990) and (b) models that hold that discrete emotional experiences derive from cognitive appraisals that were initiated by the perception of undifferentiated physiological arousal (e.g., Mandler, 1975; Schachter & Singer, 1962).[1]

Our goal in this chapter is to begin to sketch an alternative answer to James's (1884) classic question—what is an emotion?—that falls between these brackets.[2] We do not maintain that the mechanism we describe in this chapter is the only, or even the predominant, determinant of specific emotional percepts; that is for future research to determine. We end by outlining a broad framework within which to view the role of reafference in emotions accompanied by significant somatovisceral changes.

THE PERCEPTION AND INTERPRETATION OF PERIPHERAL BODILY ACTIONS

James (1884) identified three sources of somatovisceral afference that he thought contributed to discrete emotions: the muscles, the skin, and the viscus. Subsequent theorists have differed in the emphasis they have placed on proprioceptive and visceral cues (e.g., Kleck et al., 1976; Laird, 1984; Strack, Martin, & Stepper, 1988; Tomkins, 1962), but Ekman et al. (1983) have recently returned to James's (1884) emphasis on somatovisceral patterning in specific emotional states. Ekman et al. (1983) suggested that previous investigators had failed to isolate specific emotions for a sufficient period of time to allow accurate autonomic assessments, and they used prototypical facial expressions to create or identify epochs during which subjects were experiencing specific emotions (see, also, Levenson et al., 1990). Results indicated that several specific facial configurations of emotions (e.g., happiness, fear, anger) were associated with distinct emotional reports and patterns of visceral responses. These data are compatible with James's (1884) suggestion that there are emotion-specific autonomic patterns of activation. Ekman, Levenson, and their colleagues (Ekman et al., 1983; Levenson, 1992; Levenson, Carstensen, Friesen, & Ekman, 1991; Levenson et al., 1990), like James (1884), have suggested that the distinctive proprioceptive and interoceptive cues associated with basic emotions constitute sensory information, the perception of which can determine emotional experience. Thus this line of theorizing specifies that distinct emotional feelings arise from the perception of discrete and unambiguous sensory information transmitted through the somatovisceral system just as assuredly as distinct visual percepts, such as the image of the old woman depicted in the left panel of Figure 3.1, arise from physically discrete sensory information transmitted through the visual system.

Although the research on the autonomic differentiation of emotions by Levenson, Ekman, and their colleagues is interesting, the cumulative evidence for emotion-specific autonomic patterns remains inconsistent (e.g., see Lang, Bradley, & Cuthbert, 1990; Stemmler, 1989; Wagner, 1989). Zajonc and McIntosh (1992) further note that the evidence for the autonomic differentiation of happiness, sadness, anger, fear, disgust, and surprise is inconsistent even when one focuses exclusively on the research reported by Ekman, Levenson, and their colleagues over the past decade using what they suggested were methodologically superior procedures. Heart rate appears to be the best discriminator of these emotions, with anger, fear, and sadness sharing comparable elevations in heart rate with respect to the other emotions. Zajonc and McIntosh note, however, that even heart rate is far from discriminating consistently or fully among the emotions in these studies. For instance, Ekman et al. (1983) found heart rate did not discriminate between the emotions in emotional imagery conditions, and it differentiated only anger, fear, and sadness from happiness, disgust, and surprise in a conceptual replication using facial-muscle manipulation to induce discrete emotions. Furthermore, contrary to the findings of Levenson, Ekman, and their colleagues, heart rate was one of the four physiological measures that differentiated anger from fear in Ax's (1953) classic study in which he used realistic and intense manipulations of anger and fear.

Of course, all of the potential elements and patterns of autonomic activity have yet to be studied. Moreover, potential patterns may not be describable by gross measures of end-organ response (e.g., heart rate; see Berntson, Cacioppo, & Quigley, 1991). Thus emotion-specific autonomic changes may indeed exist and may yet be identified. Nevertheless, whether or not the conditions for and the elements of emotion-specific autonomic patterns of activity can be identified, it appears that discrete emotional percepts can occur even when the autonomic changes do not discriminate fully the emotions that are experienced. Is it possible for discrete emotional percepts to be sculpted from an ambiguous or undifferentiated pattern of afference?[3] If so, how is this transformation from ambiguous visceral input to unequivocal emotional percept accomplished? Cannon's (1927) answer to the first question was no; autonomic events were too slow, too insensitive, and too undifferentiated to contribute to emotions. Schachter and Singer (1962) revolution-

Figure 3.1. An Old Woman
SOURCE: Adapted from Boring (1930).

ized thinking about emotions when they suggested that undifferentiated autonomic activity *could* subserve discrete emotions. The mechanism by which this was accomplished, according to Schachter and Singer (1962; Schachter, 1964; see, also, Mandler, 1975; Reisenzein, 1983), was as follows: Given a state of physiological arousal for which an individual has no immediate explanation, an "evaluative need" is created that motivates the individual to understand and label cognitively his or her bodily feelings. The consequent attributional process was thought to produce specific emotional states and influence emotional behavior.[4]

In sum, emotion theorists such as James (1884) and Ekman et al. (1983) have suggested that the sensory information is unambiguous, and the consequent perception of this sensory input yields a spontaneous and discrete emotional experience. Emotion theorists such as Schachter and Singer (1962) and Mandler (1975), on the other hand, have emphasized the ambiguity in the interoceptive information associated with discrete emotional percepts. The primary roles this interoceptive information plays in emotion, according to their perspective, are to motivate the individual to search for a label for the perceived but unexplained physiological state and to establish the intensity of the labeled emotional state. We propose in this chapter that there is yet a third distinct way in which peripheral bodily reactions may contribute to emotional experience, an active perceptual process by which an ambiguous pattern of somatovisceral afference is disambiguated to produce an immediate, spontaneous, and indubitable emotional percept. We turn next to the mechanism by which transformations of this form occur.

AMBIGUOUS FIGURES AND SOMATOVISCERAL "ILLUSIONS"

James's (1884) theory of emotion can be viewed as a perceptual theory about the mental consequence of a particular kind or pattern of somatovisceral afference. Theory and research on other sensory systems (e.g., vision) may therefore provide useful insights into the psychological mechanism underlying emotional percepts that are derived from somatovisceral information. For instance, in addition to the class of perceptual phenomena illustrated by unambiguous images (e.g., see the old woman in the left panel of Figure 3.1 and the young woman in the left panel of Figure 3.2), there is a second, interesting class of perceptual phenomena illustrated in the right panels of figures 3.1 and 3.2. These pictures are adaptations of a classic example of an ambiguous visual figure originally published in *Puck* by W. E. Hill (1915) as "My Wife and My Mother-in-Law" and introduced to psychology by Boring (1930). Naive subjects who look at Figure 3.1 *or* Figure 3.2 report seeing strikingly different images (e.g., Leeper, 1935). Subjects who are exposed to Figure 3.1 report seeing two pictures of the same old woman, whereas subjects who are exposed to Figure 3.2 report seeing two pictures of the same young woman. Moreover, the perceptual experience created by viewing the pair of pictures within Figure 3.1 or within Figure 3.2 is that the pictures are virtually identical, and the picture depicted in the right panel of Figure 3.1 is perceived to be quite different from the picture depicted in the right panel of Figure 3.2. These strikingly different perceptions are immediate, effortless, self-evident, and discrete. Naive subjects do not perceive any of the pictures to be ambiguous. This, of course, is something of an "illusion," because the pictures depicted in the right panels of figures 3.1 and 3.2 are identical. Ambiguous visual figures therefore illustrate how the visual system can be presented with physically invariant stimulus (e.g., contour) information that can be perceived in strikingly different ways.

Figure 3.2. A Young Woman
SOURCE: Adapted from Boring (1930).

Although what one sees when looking at an ambiguous visual figure appears to be the work of neural events in the brain beyond the visual cortex (i.e., top-down processes; Sekuler & Blake, 1985), the sensory information provided by the ambiguous figure clearly contributes to this perception. For instance, Leeper (1935) compared the effects of verbal and perceptual preparation on the perception of Boring's ambiguous figure. Verbal preparation involved giving a detailed description of one of the possible organizations—the old or young woman—including the direction the person would be facing, how the person was dressed, and prominent features of the person. Perceptual preparation involved showing the subjects one of the two figures depicted in the left panels of figures 3.1 and 3.2. Leeper found that subjects who had been given verbal preparation did not differ significantly from a control group who received no preparation: Approximately 65% of the subjects reported seeing only the young woman and approximately 35% reported seeing only the old woman. As noted above, however, perceptual preparation had dramatic effects on what subjects perceived when they looked at the ambiguous figure: All of the subjects who first looked at the unambiguous figure of the young women saw only the young woman when they looked at Boring's ambiguous figure, whereas 97% (i.e., all but one) of the subjects who first looked at the unambiguous figure of the old woman saw only the old woman when they looked at the ambiguous figure. Thus prior exposure to the young or old woman primed the form of the discrete and unambiguous image such that the perception of the subsequently presented ambiguous figure was perceived to be a discrete and unambiguous image.

Subsequent research suggests that verbal instructions regarding what viewers should look at in ambiguous figures are sufficient to influence what they see, but the nature of the instructions are important. For instance, global instructions such as those used by Leeper (1935) are less effective than specific instructions about what focal area contains features that are significant for the perception of one image but not the other (Tsal & Kolbert, 1985). Moreover, once both unambiguous pictures have been identified or primed, it is possible to switch back and forth between the two images in the ambiguous figure by attending to a focal area that contains features significant for one percept but not for the other (Tsal & Kolbert, 1985). It is important that only one unambiguous picture can be perceived at any given moment. You can confirm this for yourself by focusing on the image of the old woman in the right panel of Figure 3.1: The perceptual experience is that the "ambiguous figure" is not ambiguous at all. Looking at the same figure can yield a strikingly different perceptual experience a moment later, as you "switch" between the two images. Note that, when this switch is made, the perceptual experience again is coherent and unambiguous (even though one recognizes the figure must be ambiguous to be capable of producing such strikingly different perceptual experiences). The belief that the picture depicts a young woman and an old woman is derived through direct experience; the belief that the picture is ambiguous is derived through inference.

Ambiguous visual figures are constructed using elements from two (or more) unambiguous images in such a way that the figure created by overlapping or slightly modifying the elements of the unambiguous images can be interpreted in multiple discrete ways (Sekuler & Blake, 1985). Ambiguous figures therefore have sometimes been referred to as figure-figure reversals (Boring, 1930), which differ from other reversible figures in which the figure and ground reverse (e.g., the chalice/profiles image). Despite our reference to ambiguous figures as "illusions," they are not illusions in the strict sense because there is no distortion of the stimulus features that contradicts reality (Soltis, 1966). The fact that the same sensory information in an ambiguous figure can produce such strikingly different, immediately obvious, and unambiguous perceptions, however, led Leeper (1935) to refer to ambiguous figures as reversible illusions. It is in this sense that we use the term *illusion* in this chapter.

It is important that, although the invariant information in the ambiguous visual figure can produce very different perceptions through the influences of activated cognitive schemata or categories, the phenomenon of reversible illusions depends fundamentally on the afferent information produced by viewing the figure. Chambers and Reisberg (1985), for instance, reported that subjects could not reverse an ambiguous figure in mental imagery even though these subjects were able to draw an ambiguous figure from their mental image and then reverse the figure in their drawing. Thus the afferent information appears not only to be contributory but to be essential for the class of perceptual phenomena illustrated by reversible visual illusions. The ambiguous sensory information, which can give rise to two or more discrete percepts, is transformed by the active process of perception to yield an immediate and unambiguous perceptual experience. In sum, both the activated schema and the sensory data are important in the production of the percept.

Consider the implications if the active perceptual processes underlying reversible visual illusions are not limited to visual information processing but can also operate on interoceptive (e.g., visceral) and proprioceptive (e.g., postural, facial, vocal) input.[5] The architecture of the somatovisceral apparatus is more likely to yield ambiguous afference than is the visual system (Reed, Harver, & Katkin, 1990), and it seems likely that events as important and commonplace as the emotions have cognitive representations that include somatovisceral attributes. Thus two important features required for the production of somatovisceral illusions are plausibly in place. A unique prediction that follows from the notion of somatovisceral illusions is that discrete emotions can result from the perception of the same somatovisceral input when this input contains somatovisceral attributes of two or more discrete emotions. A second important prediction is that these discrete emotional percepts are "reversible" as different emotional schema are activated. Thus, just as top-down processes make it possible for people looking at Figure 3.3 to alternate quickly between seeing the face of an Egyptian woman who is located behind a candlestick and the right and left profiles of identical twins looking at one another, they also make it possible for the person on a ride at an amusement park to alternate rapidly between the states of happy excitement and near-panic fear. With practice, the discrete emotional percepts stemming from ambiguous somatovisceral input should be controllable, much like the visual percepts stemming from ambiguous visual figures. Such practice should produce little or no control over emotional percepts, however, when (a) the somatovisceral input is unambiguous rather than ambiguous or (b) there is a dominant emotion category whose activation in the context has been automated by virtue of prior experience.

We know a great deal about the nature of the unambiguous visual arrays that produce visual perceptions, and this makes it possible to construct ambiguous visual figures and to identify the focal areas in which unambiguous visual information is located in ambiguous figures. Unfortunately, we still know very little about the unambiguous visceral afference that underlies specific emotions or whether emotion-specific autonomic profiles even exist. Indeed, empirical research showing that the *same* pattern (at least superficially) of somatovisceral afference can be associated with discrete emotional experiences, and quite different patterns of somatovisceral afference can be associated with the *same* emotional experience, has been taken as evidence that somatovisceral afference has little or no instrumental role in the production of discrete emotions. Thus another important implication of the notion of somatovisceral illusions is that these empirical results are not *necessarily* incompatible with somatovisceral afference playing an instrumental role in the production of discrete emotions. This is because, although the visual information underlies the images seen in ambiguous figures such as those shown in figures 3.1, 3.2, and 3.3, the same visual information can produce discrete visual percepts, and different patterns of visual information can produce the same visual percepts.

In the next section, we outline in more detail two models of emotional percepts as somatovisceral "illusions" based on the work in perception on reversible visual illusions. Both models assume that emotion-specific somatic (e.g., facial) patterning exists. In the first, we also assume that emotion-specific autonomic patterns exist; in the second, we assume that they do not exist. Because the details of the proposed model differ somewhat given these different assumptions, research designed to clarify the presence and nature of emotion-specific autonomic afference is

Figure 3.3. An Ambiguous Figure Constructed From Overlapping Unambiguous Elements

SOURCE: From *Mind Sights*, by Roger N. Shepard. Copyright © (1990) by Roger N. Shepard. Reprinted by permission of W. H. Freeman and Company.
NOTE: The picture depicts (a) the face of a woman who is located behind a candlestick and (b) the right and left profiles, respectively, of identical twins looking at one another. These discrete images are derived from the same sensory information and, although one can switch rapidly between these images, one cannot perceive both images simultaneously.

particularly important. We should also note, however, that these two models are not mutually exclusive but can be viewed as complementary. We will return to this point below.

Model 1: Emotional percepts derived from overlapping sets of specific autonomic patterns. To begin, let us assume that at least some discrete emotions can be differentiated autonomically. Ekman et al.

(1983), for instance, reported that the skin temperature of the middle finger of the right hand differentiated anger from fear and sadness, and this result was replicated by Levenson et al. (1990). Skin temperature is not homogeneous, however. Skin temperature can vary across the surface of the body at a given point in time and it can vary at the same site across time. This is precisely the kind of ambiguous sensory input—ambiguous interoceptive information formed by the coincidence of two or more unambiguous patterns of inputs—that enables an activated schema to transform the ambiguous sensory information into one of several possible immediate, discrete, and compelling percepts.

Emotional percepts no doubt involve more than sensations of skin temperature. Studies of people's perception of skin temperature, however, provide evidence that the kind of perceptual transformation that underlies reversible visual illusions also operates on interoceptive input. For instance, Pennebaker and Skelton (1981) asked subjects to track their skin temperature and were told they would be exposed to an "ultrasonic sound." Some subjects were told the ultrasonic sound could cause their skin temperature to increase, others were told it could cause their skin temperature to decrease, and yet others were told that it could cause their skin temperature to remain constant. Finger temperature was monitored while subjects "listened" to the noise. No noise was actually presented. As expected, measures of finger temperature indicated skin temperature was comparable across conditions and varied across time within conditions. Despite the similarities in the dynamic visceral activity found to occur across conditions, the perceptions of skin temperature varied in a manner consistent with the primed effects of the ultrasonic noise; moreover, just as the discrete visual images that can be seen in the right panels of figures 3.1 and 3.2 correspond to a focusing of attention on particular configurations of stimulus features, the reports of changes in finger temperature by subjects in Pennebaker and Skelton's (1981) experiment corresponded to actual changes in finger temperature. Thus subjects who expected their finger temperature to increase noticed actual increases more than actual decreases in skin temperature, and subjects who expected their finger temperature to decrease noticed actual decreases more than actual increases in skin temperature.

This leaves us with several important but unresolved issues: (a) How are overlapping patterns of emotion-specific afference initiated unless there is some central determination of what emotion-specific patterns are to be activated in the first place? (b) What governs which emotion schema is activated? These are important and general issues to which we return after discussing the second model of emotion as a special instantiation of reversible illusions.

Model 2: Emotional percepts derived from "undifferentiated" autonomic activation in emotion. How can emotional percepts be somatovisceral "illusions" if there are no emotion-specific autonomic patterns, if, instead, all emotions are characterized by myriad catabolic reactions, the intensity and profile of which depend on individual and stimulus response stereotypies, the intensity of the emotion, and the anticipated metabolic requirements of the behavioral response? Schachter (1964) conceded that the particulars of peripheral physiological activation in emotion might differ, but he maintained that the most salient perceptual cue derived from the dynamic interoceptive inputs was arousal. Consistent with this reasoning, research on the accuracy of detecting specific peripheral changes such as heart rate (e.g., Blascovich & Katkin, 1983; Brener & Jones, 1974; Pennebaker, 1982), gastric activity (e.g., Adam, 1978; Whitehead & Drescher, 1980), and finger pulse volume (Pennebaker, Gonder-Frederick, Stewart, Elfman, & Skelton, 1982) has revealed that naive subjects perform at or near chance levels (but see Pennebaker & Skelton, 1981; Skelton & Pennebaker, 1990). Zillmann (1984) has suggested that circulating catecholamines are increased during activity or emotion and that the amount of circulating catecholamines varies with the intensity of the activity or emotion. Zillmann (1983, 1984) reviews evidence that emotional feelings as different as lust and anger can be reversed by allowing the previously activated schema to decay and by activating the alternative emotion schema.

Of course, the fact that people perform poorly when trying to identify a specific peripheral change that occurs in isolation does not mean that the perception of a complex of visceral changes cannot be sculpted by an activated schema for a particular emotion. For instance, intense physiological variations, as might occur in intense emotions, are much better perceived than are moderate physiological changes (Jones & Hollandsworth, 1981; see Reed et al., 1990). Moreover, we do not mean to suggest that the deliberate, accurate perception of specific variations in somatovisceral activity constitutes the emotion any more than the accurate perception of the contours in an ambiguous figure constitutes the perception of the visual pictures. Top-down processes transform these sensory components to produce an immediate, holistic perception.

It is interesting that recent studies of the peripheral changes people *report* to have experienced during emotional states have revealed consistent, emotion-specific, and cross-culturally shared patterns of somatovisceral cues (e.g., Nieuwenhuyse, Offenberg, & Frijda, 1987; Pennebaker, 1982; Rime, Philippot, & Cisamolo, 1990; Scherer, Wallbott, & Summerfield, 1986; Shaver, Schwartz, Kirson, & O'Connor, 1987; Shields, 1984; Wallbott & Scherer, 1986). Although these studies have focused on belief systems of emotions, these belief systems may be based in part on somatovisceral components of emotion. Rime et al. (1990), for instance, reported that (a) joy was associated with warm temperature, changes in cardiac activity, muscle relaxation, and breathing changes; (b) anger was characterized by feeling hot, changes in cardiac activity, muscle tension, and breathing changes; (c) fear was associated with perspiration, changes in cardiac activity, muscle tension, and breathing changes; and (d) sadness was associated with changes in cardiac activity, muscle tension, and a lump in the throat. Rime et al. (1990) considered it "paradoxical that although evidence for actual physiological patterns in emotions is lacking, a very consistent set of data supports the existence of differentiated and reliable patterns based on subjects' self-reports" (p. 39).

A potential resolution to this paradox is that emotional experience, at least under specifiable sensory conditions, is a special instantiation of reversible illusions. Analogous to the distinct images that can arise from looking at the right panels of figures 3.1 and 3.2 or at Figure 3.3, discrete emotions may arise from somatovisceral afference even if there are few or no objective differences in the somatovisceral information traveling to the brain. For this reasoning to be plausible when autonomic activity is not emotion specific, we should again be able to identify parallels between the important visual cues in ambiguous visual figures and the somatovisceral cues in emotion. There are at least two lines of empirical research that support this reasoning.

Recall that reversible visual illusions are formed by overlapping (or modifying slightly) the elements from two or more unambiguous visual figures (e.g., compare the left and right panels of figures 3.1 and 3.2). Research on peripheral *somatic* responses has long demonstrated that skeletomuscular actions are faster and more sensitive than are visceral actions (Cacioppo, Petty, & Tassinary, 1989; Leventhal & Mosbach, 1983), and there is now compelling evidence for specific somatic configurations for at least a subset of human emotions (Duclos et al., 1989; Ekman, 1989; Izard, 1990). Moreover, Ekman (1985, in press) has suggested that the facial actions and expressions identified with a specific emotion are transient, usually lasting no longer than a few seconds, and can be preceded and followed by facial actions and expressions that are identified with other emotions. Given the mercurial nature of proprioceptive cues in emotion, the variability in the proprioceptive cues that can emanate from various points on the body, and the relatively sluggish nature of visceral afferents, proprioception may be an important component of the ambiguous somatovisceral input to the brain.

In addition, recent research in psychobiology indicates that central (brain) states can modulate ascending afferent transmission, which can affect an individual's sensitivity to specific features of a homogeneous reafference pattern. One example is hunger-induced priming of gustatory transmission, which can be seen at the level of the primary central neurons (*nucleus tractus solitarius*) of the gustatory pathway (Scott & Yaxley, 1989). Another example derives from the marked reduction in pain sensitivity and reactivity that can be observed following uncontrollable aversive stimuli (Maier, 1986, 1989). This hypoalgesia appears to be mediated, at least in part, by descending opiate and nonopiate pathways to the spinal cord (Basbaum & Fields, 1984). Both the degree of hypoalgesia, and the relative contributions of opiate and nonopiate systems, have been shown to be dependent on psychological factors, including the predictability and controllability of the aversive event (Maier, 1986, 1989). The effects of these psychological variables appear to be mediated by both associative and nonassociative factors and depend in part on the inherent response dispositions of the subjects to the aversive stimuli (Minor, Dess, & Overmeir, 1991; see review by Berntson, Boysen, & Cacioppo, in press). Finally, Montoya, Schandry, and Muller (1991) recently found that attentional factors can influence event-related brain potentials to visceral responses. Subjects were identified as being "good" and "poor" at cardiac perception, and event-related brain potentials were time-locked to the R-spike of the cardiac cycle (i.e., the cardioelectrical event corresponding to left ventricular contraction). Analyses revealed that focusing attention on the heartbeat signal had similar effects to focusing attention on external stimuli, and these effects were larger for "good" rather than "poor" heartbeat perceivers.

Returning to the bodily changes people associate with distinct emotions, one finds evidence for considerable overlap in bodily symptoms across emotions.[6] All four of the emotions examined by Rime et al. (1990), for instance, were believed to be associated with changes in heart rate, and three of the four were believed to be associated with breathing changes and muscle tension. Moreover, most of the symptoms of emotions identified by Rime et al. (1990) are characteristic of sympathetic-adrenal discharge, and bodily responses such as skin temperature and muscle tension show both increases and decreases across the body during sympathetic-adrenal discharge (Johnson & Anderson, 1990). Even when autonomic activity does not differentiate emotions, the details of this activity can be quite complex. General increases in heart rate, for instance, tend to be characterized by beat-by-beat increases and decreases in rate. Such a pattern of autonomic activation is reminiscent of Pennebaker and Skelton's (1981) observations of skin temperature, which was comparable across groups who believed an ultrasonic noise would increase or decrease skin temperature but was variable across time within groups. As we noted above, the groups of subjects in Pennebaker and Skelton's study produced a reliable and differentiated pattern of symptom reports, and these symptom reports were related to actual physiological changes, even though there was no overall difference in the physiological changes among these groups. Activation of a schema for the physiological changes led to very different perceptions of the same sensory input. Thus the visceral afference, even when "undifferentiated" across emotions (see Note 3), may contribute to the construction of an ambiguous somatovisceral figure.

In sum, research on the peripheral bodily changes people associate with discrete emotions has revealed specific syndromes of symptoms across cultures. Several of the elements that constitute these syndromes are common across the discrete emotions and are common to the peripheral physiological changes found during sympathetic-adrenal discharge. Other symptoms, such as thermal sensations, muscle tension, and perspiration, tend to vary across the surface of the body and across time, providing overlapping unambiguous elements that together constitute an ambiguous sensory input. Further specificity can be provided by the proprioceptive cues arising from facial, postural, and vocal actions, which also can change from moment to moment. Thus, in Model 1 and Model 2, the sensory cues available through the somatovisceral afferents share important features with the visual cues in reversible illusions (see Figure 3.3). In theory, all that needs to be added to the somatovisceral afference outlined in Model 1 or 2 to create an immediate, discrete, and vivid emotional percept is an activated emotion schema whose fundamental components are included in the incoming afference. Thus the current conceptualization shares features with both James's (1884) and Schachter and Singer's (1962) formulations but differs from each one in subtle ways, including the constitution of the somatovisceral input, the role ascribed to the activation of emotional schemata prior to the registration of somatovisceral afference, the immediacy and automaticity of the discrete emotional percept that accompanies the registration of the somatovisceral afference, and the reversibility of emotional percepts.

Unresolved Questions

In the preceding sections, we found parallels between the sensory features of a visual reversible illusion and the sensory information available through the somatovisceral afferents in emotion whether we assumed differentiated (Model 1) or undifferentiated (Model 2) autonomic activation in emotion. In this section, we address two important but unresolved issues: (a) How are overlapping patterns of emotion-specific afference initiated unless there is some central determination of what emotion-specific patterns are to be activated in the first place? (b) What governs which emotion schema is activated?

First, if discrete emotional experiences stem in part from active perceptual processes acting on overlapping patterns of emotion-specific information, then a rapid appraisal of the activating event must occur to initiate these overlapping patterns of emotion-specific response. One possible answer to this question holds that activating events (e.g., a gunshot) are evaluated quickly at a rudimentary level to determine their likely appetitive or aversive importance, and that somatovisceral changes capable of supporting a host of appetitive or aversive actions are initiated as a result of this preliminary appraisal. In parallel with this multipurpose somatovisceral activation, more detailed cognitive appraisals of the evocative event can produce somatic actions (e.g., a driver swerving to avoid a head-on collision) and prime-specific emotion categories (see below) prior to or during the central processing of sensations arising from visceral activation. Consistent with this reasoning, parallel circuits appear to be involved in the evaluation of the potential significance of stimuli. Through classical thalamo-cortical pathways, sensory information may be perceived, and complex (e.g., relational) cognitive appraisals of its emotional significance can be performed. Additional routes, comprising subcortical circuits, appear to be involved in faster, more rudimentary analyses of the emotional significance of stimuli. LeDoux and his colleagues, for instance, have identified a neural pathway from the thalamus to the amygdala, which may support aversive classical conditioning along simple stimulus dimensions even when the primary sensory area in the cortex has been destroyed (e.g., LeDoux, Iwata, Cicchetti, & Reis, 1988; LeDoux, Romanski, & Xagoraris, 1989; see reviews by LeDoux, 1986, 1987). Thus a rapid but crude evaluation of the emotional significance of stimuli may be accomplished within these subcortical circuits. The potential somatovisceral variations stemming from these rapid and crude evaluations may result in precisely the kind of ambiguous sensory input that enables primed cognitive categories to sculpt immediate, compelling, and strikingly distinct percepts.

Another possibility is that ongoing events are evaluated initially at a rudimentary level to determine the likely metabolic demands on the organism, that visceral changes capable of supporting the anticipated metabolic demands are put into motion, and that certain classes of emotions are sculpted from the resulting afference. What distinguishes this from the preceding account is that the autonomic outflow is governed by metabolic rather than emotional demands. Such a mechanism implies either that certain subsets of emotions are tied to distinct levels or types of metabolic demands or that all of the emotions shaped by bodily inputs involve catabolic reactions that are not emotion specific. This mechanism, of course, is much more compatible with the somatovisceral-illusion model based on the assumption of undifferentiated autonomic activity across emotions (see Model 2, above).

If the ambiguous sensory input is to lead to a distinct emotional percept, it is also important for a distinct emotional category to be perceptually primed. Of particular interest is research showing that discrete emotions can be characterized by unique patterns of stimulus appraisal along emotionally relevant dimensions (e.g., Roseman, 1984; Weiner & Graham, 1984). Smith and Ellsworth (1985, 1987; see, also, Smith & Pope, this volume), for instance, found that more than a dozen distinct emotions (e.g., happiness, fear, anger, disgust, contempt, pride, shame) could be differentiated by appraisals of the situation along six dimensions (i.e., pleasantness, anticipated effort, attentional activity, certainty, human agency, and situational control). Moreover, the activation of discrete emotions did not appear to require appraisals of the situation along all six dimensions. Typical instances of anger were found to be associated with appraisals of uncertainty and high anticipated effort, but the essential dimensions of appraisal for anger appeared to involve only the dimensions of unfairness and other agency. Smith and Ellsworth (1987) make an interesting speculation that emotional blends may result from appraisals along subsets of dimensions:

> Thus, if a person appraises a situation to be unfair and caused by someone else, to now be beyond one's control, and to have unpleasant implications for the future, we might expect that person to experience a blend of anger, sadness, and fear. (Smith & Ellsworth, 1987, p. 486)

The blending of emotions has been questioned by Ortony and Turner (1990; Turner & Ortony, in press), but the questions that have been raised leave unresolved how individuals could vacillate among several discrete emotions in close temporal proximity. The current analysis provides such a mechanism. For instance, the images of the old woman and the young woman are not "blended" when a perceiver switches quickly and repeatedly between the two images in Boring's (1930) figure but the person nevertheless experiences these discrete perceptual images nearly simultaneously. An analogous mechanism controlled by an individual's varying cognitive appraisals of the situation may also underlie the complex emotional experiences that Smith and Ellsworth (1987) attributed instead to the workings of an emotional blender.

To illustrate how some emotions may be somatovisceral illusions, imagine that you are driving an automobile along a two-lane highway. An oncoming truck is about to go by when you suddenly see a car that has been following the truck move into your lane in a vain attempt to pass the truck. You swerve reflexively toward the shoulder of the highway to avoid the head-on collision and, as the car and truck pass, you swerve back to avoid hitting an upcoming bridge abutment. Only moments have passed, the road ahead is now clear, and you have not yet had time to think about anything other than steering out of trouble. At a somewhat slower pace, the somatovisceral feedback aroused by the preceding events is making its way into consciousness. These bodily

sensations create such an immediate, intense, and indubitable feeling
of fear that you pull off the highway to reflect on what just happened
and to gain your composure. Although the fear that flooded over you as
the effect of the initial wave of somatovisceral afference made its way
to consciousness certainly *seemed* unambiguous, you may have just
experienced a somatovisceral "illusion."

How is the somatovisceral "illusion" model of emotion related to
other theories of emotion? William James (1884) spoke about emotions
as a perceptual consequence of somatovisceral afference in which the
somatovisceral activity was unambiguous and unique across emotions—
much like the visual information one detects in an unambiguous picture.
This latter proposition represents a major distinction between our
somatovisceral illusion model of emotion and existing peripheral theories of emotions. James's theory therefore can be viewed as a special
case within a broader model of the role of somatovisceral afference in
emotion (see below).

In addition, Schachter and Singer's (1962) theory represents a comple-
menting rather than competing perspective on the role of somatovisceral
afference in emotion. In the illustration described above on the arousal
of fear by a near-head-on collision, there is no evaluative need or
misattribution. Moreover, the notion of somatovisceral illusions posit
that (a) the somatovisceral input constrains the emotional percepts that
are possible (just as the visual arrays in figures 3.1, 3.2, and 3.3 constrain
the visual experiences that result from viewing these pictures), and (b)
different configurations of the somatovisceral afference are salient in
different emotions (just as different visual contours in the right panel
of Figure 3.1 are salient if you see an old woman or a young woman).
Finally, Schachter and Singer (1962, 1979) neither included somatic
(e.g., facial, postural) feedback in their analysis nor emphasized the
activation of an emotional schema *prior* to the perception of autonomic
activation because one or both of these processes could undermine the
arousal of an evaluative need. Thus the current model owes an obvious
debt to Schachter and Singer's (1962) seminal theory for pointing to the
importance of top-down processes in emotion, but the processes highlighted in the current formulation are not isomorphic with Schachter
and Singer's cognitive labeling theory.

Cognitive appraisal theorists have posited that feedback from the
periphery is neither necessary nor sufficient for discrete emotions. We
agree. But then one can "look" at a mental image of an old woman or a

young woman too. This remarkable feat by the brain does not imply that visual information plays no role in visual images or in reversible visual illusions. Nor do data demonstrating that discrete emotions can be experienced in the absence of somatovisceral afference imply that somatovisceral afference plays no role in emotion (see Chwalisz et al., 1988). For instance, Levenson et al. (1990) reported that, when subjects produced facial configurations that most closely resembled the associated emotional expression, autonomic differences among emotions were most pronounced and self-reports of the associated emotion were most prevalent. We do not maintain that the model we have outlined in this chapter represents the only, or even the predominant, determinant of specific emotional percepts, but that somatovisceral afference can contribute to emotion in ways heretofore not highlighted (e.g., through somatovisceral illusions).

It might also be worthwhile to consider briefly whether the somatovisceral "illusion" model outlined thus far can withstand Cannon's (1927) critique of peripheral theories of emotion. Specifically, Cannon raised five objections to William James's emphasis on interoceptive patterns in emotion.

(1) *"Total separation of the viscera from the central nervous system (CNS) does not alter emotional behavior"* (Cannon, 1927, p. 108, italics in original). Emotional behavior and emotional perception are not equivalent. Demonstration of CNS control over emotional behavior does not preclude the possibility that peripheral events can contribute to emotional perception. Indeed, there is now considerable evidence that suggests peripheral somatic (e.g., Adelman & Zajonc, 1989; Duclos et al., 1989) and autonomic (e.g., Zillmann, 1983) activity contributes to emotional perception and judgment (see, also, Hatfield, Cacioppo, & Rapson, this volume). Thus research on spinal cord-injured humans suggests that, although interoception may not be necessary for emotional experience, it is contributory (Chwalisz et al., 1988).

(2) *"The same visceral changes occur in very different emotional states and in non-emotional states"* (Cannon, 1927, p. 109). We have dealt in some detail with this proposition. Two models were outlined, one based on the presence of emotion-specific visceral patterning and a second based on the absence of emotion-specific autonomic patterning. In either model, somatic activity in emotion adds emotion-specific elements, with the resulting pattern of afference constituting the somatovisceral counterpart to an ambiguous (visual) figure. In addition,

the somatovisceral "illusion" model makes explicit the importance of perceptually primed emotion schema in the experience created by the somatovisceral afference. Although we have emphasized the priming of discrete emotion schema, the perceptual priming of relevant nonemotional schema (e.g., physical exertion) should be capable of sculpting the somatovisceral afference into a discrete nonemotional percept as well.

(3) *"The viscera are relatively insensitive structures"* (Cannon, 1927, p. 111). A key term here is *relatively,* as in relative to somatosensory structures (and the consequent tactile and proprioceptive afference). The somatovisceral afference in the near-crash example described above, however, would not be expected to be subtle. Although in some instances the afference may be subtle, the feature of insensitivity or nonspecificity inherent in the architecture of the viscera is a virtue in the somatovisceral "illusion" model, for it implies that there can be common interoceptive cues that support multiple discrete emotional percepts.

(4) *"Visceral changes are too slow to be a source of emotional feeling"* (Cannon, 1927, p. 112). This feature, too, is a virtue in the somatovisceral "illusion" model for two reasons. First, the faster, more emotionspecific proprioceptive cues can unfold across two or more emotions (thereby contributing multiple overlapping emotion-specific elements to the afference) while the more sluggish visceral reactions contribute ambiguous (and possibly some unambiguous) elements to and a longer temporal integration of the somatovisceral afference. Second, we have implied in this model that the full force of proprioceptive inputs in emotion is felt when the inputs are accompanied by strong autonomic afference and an emotion schema has been perceptually primed. We further suggested that the peripheral events (from which the afference derives) come from a fast but crude evaluation of the emotional significance of the evocative event, whereas the priming of the emotion schema is achieved by a slower but more flexible and relational appraisal of the event. Because the emotion schema must be primed prior to the ambiguous somatovisceral afference reaching the brain for a somatovisceral "illusion" to occur, the sluggishness of the viscera increases the plausibility that somatovisceral "illusions" occur.

(5) *"Artificial induction of the visceral changes typical of strong emotions does not produce them"* (Cannon, 1927, p. 113). As we noted in the preceding points, the priming of an emotion schema is a prerequisite for a somatovisceral "illusion." Thus Cannon's objections to the

role of peripheral physiological responses as determinants of emotion are not problematic for the somatovisceral "illusion" model.

A GENERAL FRAMEWORK FOR THINKING ABOUT THE ROLE OF SOMATOVISCERAL ACTIVITY IN EMOTION

If discrete emotional experiences can stem from mechanisms as different as classical conditioning (e.g., conditioned emotional responses; Miller, 1951; Mower, 1947; Pavlov, 1927), perceptions of specific and unambiguous afference (e.g., facial feedback; emotion-specific ANS feedback; James, 1884), somatovisceral "illusions" (outlined above), cognitive appraisals (e.g., Smith & Ellsworth, 1985, 1987; Smith & Pope, this volume), and attributional labeling (e.g., Schachter & Singer, 1962; see Valins, 1966), what might the moderator variable(s) be? We can only speculate, but at least two variables or dimensions appear important. The first dimension concerns the nature of the somatovisceral afference (i.e., input). Afference is less relevant to cognitive appraisal theories (e.g., Smith & Ellsworth, 1985) and perhaps to theories of conditioned emotional response (see Miller, 1951).[7] Undifferentiated afference (see Note 3) is most compatible with the attributional labeling theories of Schachter and Singer (1962) and Mandler (1975); ambiguous afference (as in Boring's "ambiguous" figure) predicates our somatovisceral "illusion" model; and unambiguous emotion-specific afference underlies James's theory of emotions. The second dimension concerns the extent of informational analysis or cognitive elaboration to which the stimulus is subjected prior to the emergence of emotional experience. Conditioned emotional responding, for instance, can occur with minimal informational analysis; the cognitive appraisal (and visceral "illusion") models require more cognitive processing; and cognitive labeling theories tend to require the most. Neither dimension alone completely distinguishes among these various theories, but the two dimensions together do.

These considerations yield a general framework within which to view the various mechanisms by which somatovisceral afference influences emotional experience (see Figure 3.4). This Somatovisceral Afference Model of Emotion, or SAME, specifies possible mechanisms by which and conditions under which (a) the *same* pattern of somatovisceral afference leads to discrete emotional experiences and (b) quite different patterns of somatovisceral afference lead to the *same* emotional experience.

The SAME is designed to explain emotional states that stem from somatovisceral feedback. A stimulus undergoes at least a rudimentary evaluation, which leads to significant changes in somatovisceral activity. These variations can range from emotion-specific patterns of activation to undifferentiated activation, with ambiguous somatovisceral activation (i.e., partially differentiated activation patterns specific to multiple emotions) falling between these two end points along a continuum of somatovisceral patterning (see Figure 3.4, left column). The nodes along this continuum therefore represent important transitions in the constitution of the autonomic response, but the openings between these nodes underscore the continuous nature of this dimension. The pattern of somatovisceral activation produces a parallel continuum of somatovisceral sensory input to the brain. The arrows between nodes denote the major pathways for information flow.

In addition to these peripheral events, the emotional significance of the stimulus and the somatovisceral afference undergo more extensive cognitive evaluation. Thus Figure 3.4 also depicts the cognitive operations performed on the somatovisceral afference required to produce discrete emotional states. The extent of the cognitive elaboration of the somatovisceral afference required to produce an emotional experience ranges from simple informational analyses such as pattern recognition (e.g., James's theory of emotion as the perception of discrete patterns of somatovisceral afference) to much more complex attributional analyses and hypothesis testing (e.g., Schachter and Singer's two-factor theory of emotion), with simple cognitive appraisals of the stimulus and perceptual priming of an emotion schema falling between these two end points (e.g., emotional percepts as somatovisceral "illusions"). The more extensive these cognitive operations, the longer it requires for them to be completed and, consequently, the longer it takes for the somatovisceral afference to affect emotional experience. Thus simple pattern recognition can produce an emotional experience relatively quickly, whereas detailed cognitive appraisals, attributional analyses, and systematic hypothesis testing can take longer.[8] Note that quite different patterns of somatovisceral afference (see Figure 3.4, left column) can lead to the same emotional experience via three very different psychophysiological mechanisms (see Figure 3.4, right column), whereas the same pattern of somatovisceral afference can lead to discrete emo-

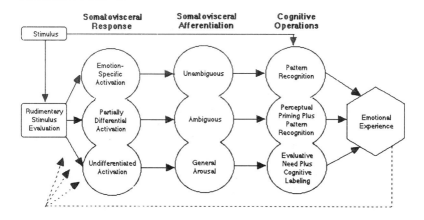

Figure 3.4. The Somatovisceral Afference Model of Emotion (SAME)

NOTE: The same pattern of somatovisceral activity has been associated with surprisingly different emotions, and the same emotion has been associated with quite different patterns of somatovisceral activity. These results have been viewed as evidence against the importance of somatovisceral afference in emotion. The SAME, depicted above and described in the text, encompasses both of these findings while emphasizing the instrumental role of somatovisceral afference and cognitive/perceptual processes in producing each.

tional experiences by two distinct psychophysiological mechanisms: (a) somatovisceral "illusions" when the afference is ambiguous and an emotion schema has been primed and (b) cognitive labeling when the perception of the afference is undifferentiated with respect to an emotion and there is an evaluative need.

Inspection of Figure 3.4 also indicates some of the boundary conditions of these theories. For instance, James's (1884) theory focused on the mechanism outlined in the nodes at the top of the continua, and he did not consider the direct effects of the evaluation of the evocative stimulus on the emotional state. Cannon's (1927) theory of emotion was limited to the direct effects of the evaluation of the evocative stimulus on the rudimentary evaluative processing circuit and on the resulting (but emotionally inconsequential) activation of the viscera. Cognitive labeling theories such as Schachter and Singer's two-factor theory of emotion have focused more on the mechanism represented in the nodes at the bottom of the continua in Figure 3.4, although their emphasis on top-down processes in the interpretation of visceral reactions in emotion predates the current model. Finally, the somatovisceral "illusion" models discussed above are represented by the middle nodes in these continua.

Of course, the arousal of an emotional state often marks an interruption of an ongoing action and the redirection of biological and cognitive resources toward some stimulus or goal. The resulting efferent volleys can have dramatic effects on somatovisceral variations and patterns (see Figure 3.4, dotted line). An interesting implication of this efferent circuit is that an emotional experience need not begin with an external stimulus. If a frightening external stimulus were presented, the general formulation depicted in Figure 3.4 specifies three separate mechanisms by which somatovisceral activity could contribute to the emotion of fear. In addition, (a) if fear has been perceptually primed (e.g., by having viewed a truly frightening movie; by having observed a frightening medical procedure), this central state can affect perception and emotion in an otherwise innocuous context; (b) vivid mental imagery or remembering an emotional period in one's life can produce somatovisceral changes, afference, and escalations or changes in emotional experience; (c) autonomic variations can be triggered chemically (e.g., Schachter & Singer, 1962) or by exertion, and these autonomic responses feed forward to produce an emotion if and only if the requisite cognitive operations are in place; and (d) central states may be manipulated directly by stimulation or pathology (e.g., "amygdalar rage," psychomotor epilepsy, Dyscontrol Syndrome). Thus the SAME is a closed loop with varying weights assigned to specific paths to emotional experience dependent on factors such as the sensory figure stemming from the somatovisceral activation and the timing and nature of the cognitive/perceptual operations performed on the somatovisceral input.

How might one go about testing the SAME? Creating an ambiguous visceral afferent array from unambiguous visceral components of discrete emotions is precluded given the current state of knowledge about the visceral components of discrete emotion. Research spearheaded by Tomkins (1962), Ekman (1971), and Izard (1971, 1977), however, has provided a clearer set of findings regarding the prototypical facial configurations associated with discrete emotions. Hence it should be possible to construct an ambiguous array of facial feedback by combining catabolic activity with unambiguous portions of the expressions of two different emotions. The successful construction of an ambiguous facial configuration should result in an ambiguous *visual* figure from the perspective of an observer, and an ambiguous array of *facial affer-*

ence from the perspective of the actor. According to the SAME, the emotional consequence of evoking such a somatovisceral configuration is not a blending of the two emotions, rather it specifies a mechanism by which one of the discrete emotions is perceived or both "co-occur" in the sense that the perceptual experience vacillates between the two discrete emotional percepts. Thus, if unambiguous components of the facial expressions associated with disgust and anger were combined to form an ambiguous visual figure, the priming of one or the other emotion schema should foster the arousal of the emotion of disgust or anger.

The SAME also suggests that the immediate emotional percept arising from an evocative event (e.g., the narrow avoidance of a fatal automobile accident; the feelings aroused when one believes one has been treated unjustly) differs quantitatively if not qualitatively when somatovisceral afference is present versus absent. Chwalisz et al. (1988) found that the spinal cord injured experience emotions much like the noninjured, and they interpreted this to mean that somatovisceral afference does not play a major role in emotion. The language people use to describe their feelings, however, can be influenced dramatically by changes in judgmental perspectives (Cacioppo, Andersen, Turnquist, & Tassinary, 1989; Ostrom & Upshaw, 1968), such as in terms of what constitutes an "intense" emotional experience. Thus it may be noteworthy that Chwalisz et al. (1988) interviewed handicapped individuals who were active, nonhospitalized, and had had a long time to adapt to their disabilities. Hohmann (1966), in contrast, asked a sample of outpatients at a Veterans Administration hospital to compare their emotional life at the time of the interview with their experiences prior to their injury. Hohmann (1966) found that the intensity of emotional experiences was reduced proportionally with higher lesions. Although the study by Chwalisz et al. (1988) was methodologically superior to Hohmann's along several dimensions (e.g., psychometric properties of the assessments), Hohmann's procedures were less likely to confound the extent of spinal cord injury with changes in the judgmental perspective. Thus somatovisceral afference may play a more important role in emotion than is implied by the Chwalisz et al. (1988) study.

CONCLUSION

A fundamental assumption of the framework outlined in this chapter is that there are direct parallels between the perception of sensory information carried through the visual system in reversible illusions and the perception of sensory information carried through the somatovisceral system in emotion. We further propose that these parallels stem from their adaptive significance. The model outlined in Figure 3.4 affords tremendous flexibility and adjustment in the pattern of somatovisceral activation rallied to deal with an environmental challenge while also allowing the operation of powerful and largely automatic inferential principles to transform the somatovisceral afference into a generally adaptive (e.g., organizing) emotional percept. Illustrative of the flexibility highlighted by the SAME are the predictions that the same pattern of somatovisceral activation can lead to discrete emotional experiences, and the same emotion can result from different patterns of somatovisceral activation. The constraints on this flexibility derive from two sources: the priming of an emotion schema and the specificity of the somatovisceral activity that is aroused by the evocative event. These constraints are an important source of adjustment for individuals in a complex world because they are generally adaptive. Thus Shepard's (1990) discussion of the behavioral significance of visual illusions, ambiguities, and anomalies applies equally well to somatovisceral afference:

> The illusions, ambiguities, and other visual anomalies that have been explored by artists and by perceptual psychologists are not manifestations of arbitrary quirks, glitches, or design faults of the human visual system. Rather, these perceptual aberrations arise from the operation of powerful and automatic inferential principles that are well tuned to the general properties of the natural world. We owe our very existence to the effectiveness with which these principles have served our ancestors. (p. 212)

It is important that these constraints can also be modified based on the unique contingencies encountered by individuals, thereby contributing further to the adjustment afforded by emotions guided by a mechanism such as that depicted in Figure 3.4. To illustrate, viewing a frightening sequence of events should prime a fear schema and enhance the likelihood that undifferentiated or ambiguous somatovisceral afference would be perceived as fear. Thus a spatiotemporal context in which fearful events are common is likely to be dangerous, and wariness in the face of an ambiguous evocative event in that context is likely to be adaptive. Of course, certain contexts featuring fearful events (e.g., movies) are not dangerous, and an individual's learning history can attenuate the emotional priming that would otherwise result from exposures to the fearful events.

Regardless of the ultimate usefulness of the details of the models we have outlined in this chapter, theory and research on perception may have more to contribute to the study of emotion than typically has been recognized. First, many perceptual processes are invariant across sensory modality. Indeed, this fact forms the theoretical foundation for methodologies involving cross-modal matching. The identification and application of these invariant processes to the study of somatovisceral afference and emotion may illuminate mechanisms underlying some aspects of emotional experience.

Second, a number of theories of emotion are in part perceptual theories about the mental consequence of a particular kind or pattern of somatovisceral afference. The precise nature of these patterns of somatovisceral afference is still in dispute, however (e.g., see Turner & Ortony, in press). Therefore it may be informative to use external stimuli acting upon a telereceptive sensory (e.g., visual, auditory) system to model the perceptual implications of the sensory information posited by these theories.

Third, demonstrations that one can "see" strikingly different images even though the sensory input is identical (e.g., see the right panels of figures 3.1 and 3.2 or see Figure 3.3) underscore how invariant sensory information can be sculpted by powerful and automatic inferential principles to produce discrete mental phenomena. Thus we examined the stimulus features and cognitive components underlying a class of perceptual phenomena termed reversible *illusions* to examine how analogous patterns of somatovisceral activity might be sculpted during the active process of perception to form discrete emotional experiences. Related to this, demonstrations that one can "see" the same image even though the sensory input differs (e.g., see the left and right panels of Figure 3.2; see Figure 3.3) underscore how there are multiple means of achieving the same percept—a possibility we have suggested holds for emotional percepts as well. Thus the general framework proposed in Figure 3.4 to organize and stimulate theory and research on the role of somatovisceral afference in emotion takes as a given the very pair of observations that have been interpreted heretofore as evidence against the importance of somatovisceral activity in emotion.

NOTES

1. We do not mean by this that physiological arousal per se is depicted as being undifferentiated in these theories but only that the *perception* of the peripheral physiological activation is general and diffuse. Although not the focus of this chapter, differentiated reafference that does not reach the level of awareness that permits verbal description or cognitive elaboration may nevertheless exert a notable impact on central substrates for emotion. An example is baroreceptor activity, which can modulate afferent transmission and central reactivity. Here we focus on perceptual features.

2. James's (1884) theory focused on the role of the feedback from facial and peripheral bodily responses in what people felt during what were consensually regarded as "emotions" (e.g., fear, anger, sadness, happiness). Interesting theoretical work has addressed the definitional question of what an emotion is (e.g., Bindra, 1969; Ortony & Turner, 1990; Pribram, 1970; Zajonc, Murphy, & Inglehart, 1989), but our focus in this chapter is more limited (e.g., see James, 1884; Schachter & Singer, 1962).

3. There is now considerable evidence that is inconsistent with the notion that autonomic activity increases in a general and diffuse manner during emotion. For instance, reliable individual and situational stereotypies have been documented (e.g., see reviews by Cacioppo et al., 1992; Lang et al., 1990). Moreover, neural changes within the sympathetic nervous system can be highly fractionated (see Johnson & Anderson, 1990), and different patterns of sympathetic and parasympathetic activity can underlie similar-appearing autonomic responses (Berntson Cacioppo & Quigley, 1991). Hence, by "undifferentiated" pattern of autonomic response, we mean only that the autonomic responses (from which interoceptive feedback is derived) do not differentiate specific emotions such as fear and anger.

4. This poses an interesting question on the potential role of reafference in animals, because they are not likely to have been subject to social reinforcement or survival advantage in explicitly defining, describing, or characterizing reafference patterns. On the other hand, the ability to perceive emotional states in others (e.g., by piloerection, pupillodilation, facial configurations) may have been extremely important in survival and may be the evolutionary origin of the disposition to attribute emotional states to others and ultimately to oneself.

5. There are also limitations to the usefulness of the analogy to visual processes. For instance, in the perception of ambiguous visual figures, the stimulus is a visual array outside the body. The central nervous system, however, serves to create and interpret both the stimulus and the response to somatovisceral information. In this regard, visual processes are somewhat more like somatic instrumental processes than visceral processes. Both differ from visceral perception, for instance, in the distinctiveness of the reafference. In the somatic case, the accuracy of response is readily ascertainable, and correctable, by somatosensory and visual feedback. In the visceral domain, there is no "intended" outcome in the conscious sense (although there are target outcomes in an automatic or homeostatic sense). Hence visceral perception differs from somatic and visual perception in that there is no discrete criterion (or "correct" perception) for which an individual is

consciously looking. For this reason, visceral afference may be particularly prone to misperceptions and "illusions."

6. If the emotion schemata are characterized by some distinctive visceral cues, the question arises about the origin of these features in emotion schemata. Several possibilities have been suggested. Rime et al. (1990), for instance, suggested that strongly differentiated patterns of autonomic activity may characterize intense emotions and that people's identification of these peripheral changes as occurring during these emotional states results in these symptoms becoming salient features in the emotion schema. This view is consistent with the cross-cultural stability in emotion schemata found by Rime et al. (1990; see, also, Rime & Giovannini, 1986; Wallbott & Scherer, 1986). Rime et al. (1990), however, favored a social constructivist explanation for the distinctive symptoms in emotion schemata. In this view, people learn what bodily symptoms are supposed to occur in each emotion by descriptive expressions in daily interactions, literary productions, tales, legends, poems, and so forth. A third possibility is that the central organization of emotion includes circuits that, when activated, prime emotion schemata. These schemata would be complete with somatovisceral features and would require only the feedback from the somatovisceral events unleashed to deal with the evocative event to yield a discrete emotional experience of an intensity proportional to the intensity of the somatovisceral feedback. Although future research can be conducted to distinguish among these hypotheses, there is now considerable evidence to suggest that "individuals are endowed with a set of expectations about the peripheral changes to be experienced in various emotional states" (Rime et al., 1990, p. 48). This is the important point here, because the existence of emotion schemata, regardless of their origin, is a prerequisite for the sculpting of discrete emotional perceptions from ambiguous somatovisceral afference.

7. The simultaneous or short forward temporal coupling of discrete conditioned (CS) and unconditioned stimuli (UCS) fosters the development of conditioned responses (CR) that are linked explicitly to the conditioned stimulus. Conditioned emotional responses developed under contingent associations of this type may result in but not rely on somatovisceral input. It is interesting that CS-UCS contingencies characterized by long (e.g., 2 s) temporal lags result in CRs that are more generally associable (Klein & Mowrer, 1989). Conditioned emotional responses therefore are not all alike. Somatovisceral afference is likely to play a more important role in the latter than in the former conditioned emotional responses. Cacioppo, Petty, Losch, and Kim (1986) similarly reasoned that facial feedback may become empowered to influence emotions by virtue of its loose temporal coupling with affective experiences. Thus the proprioception from expressing sadness sporadically when feeling sad could, over time, alter the emotional significance of this proprioceptive feedback. Nevertheless, the close temporal pairing of discrete conditioned and unconditioned stimuli should rely much less on somatovisceral afference in the production of conditioned emotional responses.

8. Feature detection and discriminative processing, of course, also occur during complex cognitive appraisals, but the proximal cognitive operations that combine with the somatovisceral afference to produce the discrete emotional states are what are of interest here.

REFERENCES

Adam, G. (1978). Visceroception, awareness, and behavior. In G. E. Schwartz & D. Shapiro (Eds.), *Consciousness and self-regulation: Advances in research and theory* (Vol. 2, pp. 199-213). New York: Plenum.

Adelman, P. K., & Zajonc, R. B. (1989). Facial efference and the experience of emotion. *Annual Review of Psychology, 40*, 249-280.

Ax, A. F. (1953). The physiological differentiation between fear and anger in humans. *Psychosomatic Medicine, 15*, 433-442.

Baldwin, J. M. (1894). The origin of emotional expression. *Psychological Review, 1*, 610-623.

Basbaum, A. L., & Fields, H. L. (1984). Endogenous pain control systems: Brainstem spinal pathways and endorphin circuitry. *Annual Review of Neuroscience, 7*, 309-338.

Berntson, G. G., Boysen, S. T., & Cacioppo, J. T. (in press). Neurobehavioral organization and the cardinal principle of evaluative bivalence. In F. M. Crinella & J. Yu (Eds.), *Brain mechanisms, 1990: Papers in memory of Bob Thompson.* New York: New York Academy of Sciences.

Berntson, G. G., Cacioppo, J. T., & Quigley, K. S. (1991). Autonomic determinism: The modes of autonomic control, the doctrine of autonomic space, and the laws of autonomic constraint. *Psychological Review, 98*, 459-487.

Bindra, D. (1969). A unified interpretation of emotion and motivation. *Annals of the New York Academy of Sciences, 159*, 1071-1083.

Blascovich, J., & Katkin, E. S. (1983). Visceral perception and social behavior. In J. T. Cacioppo & R. E. Petty (Eds.), *Social psychophysiology: A sourcebook* (pp. 493-509). New York: Guilford.

Boring, E. G. (1930). A new ambiguous figure. *American Journal of Psychology, 42*, 444.

Brener, J., & Jones, J. M. (1974). Interoceptive discrimination in intact humans: Detection of cardiac activity. *Physiology and Behavior, 13*, 763-767.

Cacioppo, J. T., Andersen, B. L., Turnquist, D. C., & Tassinary, L. G. (1989). Psychophysiological comparison theory: On the experience, description, and assessment of signs and symptoms. *Patient Education and Counseling, 13*, 257-270.

Cacioppo, J. T., Petty, R. E., Losch, M. E., & Kim, H. S. (1986). Electromyographic activity over facial muscle regions can differentiate the valence and intensity of affective reactions. *Journal of Personality and Social Psychology, 50*, 260-268.

Cacioppo, J. T., Petty, R. E., & Tassinary, L. G. (1989). Social psychophysiology: A new look. *Advances in Experimental Social Psychology, 22*, 39-91.

Cacioppo, J. T., Uchino, B. N., Crites, S. L., Snydersmith, M. A., Smith, G., Berntson, G. G., & Lang, P. J. (1992). The relationship between facial expressiveness and sympathetic activation in emotion: A critical review, with emphasis on modeling underlying mechanisms and individual differences. *Journal of Personality and Social Psychology, 62*, 110-128.

Cannon, W. B. (1927). The James-Lange theory of emotions: A critical examination and an alternative theory. *American Journal of Psychology, 39*, 106-124.

Chambers, D., & Reisberg, D. (1985). Can mental images be ambiguous? *Journal of Experimental Psychology: Human Perception and Performance, 11*, 317-328.

Chwalisz, K., Diener, E., & Gallagher, D. (1988). Autonomic arousal feedback and emotional experience: Evidence from the spinal cord injured. *Journal of Personality and Social Psychology, 54,* 820-828.

Duclos, S. E., Laird, J. D., Schneider, E., Sexter, M., Stern, L., & Van Lighten, O. (1989). Emotion-specific effects of facial expressions and postures on emotional experiences. *Journal of Personality and Social Psychology, 57,* 100-108.

Ekman, P. (1971). Universals and cultural differences in facial expressions of emotion. In J. Cole (Ed.), *Nebraska Symposium on Motivation* (Vol. 19, pp. 207-283). Lincoln: University of Nebraska Press.

Ekman, P. (1985). *Telling lies: Clues to deceit in the marketplace, politics, and marriage.* New York: Norton.

Ekman, P. (1989). The argument and evidence about universals in facial expressions of emotion. In J. Wagner & A. Manstead (Eds.), *Handbook of social psychophysiology* (pp. 143-164). New York: John Wiley.

Ekman, P. (in press). A set of basic emotions. *Psychological Review.*

Ekman, P., Levenson, R. W., & Friesen, W. V. (1983). Autonomic nervous system activity distinguishes among emotions. *Science, 221,* 1208-1210.

Hohmann, G. W. (1966). Some effects of spinal cord lesions on experienced emotional feelings. *Psychophysiology, 3,* 526-534.

Izard, C. E. (1971). *The face of emotion.* New York: Appleton-Century-Crofts.

Izard, C. E. (1977). *Human emotions.* New York: Academic Press.

Izard, C. E. (1990). Facial expressions and the regulation of emotions. *Journal of Personality and Social Psychology, 58,* 487-498.

James, W. (1884). What is an emotion? *Mind, 9,* 188-205.

James, W. (1894). The physical basis of emotion. *Psychological Review, 1,* 516-529.

Johnson, A. K., & Anderson, E. (1990). Stress and arousal. In J. T. Cacioppo & L. G. Tassinary (Eds.), *Principles of psychophysiology: Physical, social, and inferential elements* (pp. 216-252). New York: Cambridge University Press.

Jones, G. E., & Hollandsworth, J. G. (1981). Heart rate discrimination before and after exercise-induced augmented cardiac activity. *Psychophysiology, 18,* 252-257.

Kleck, R. E., Vaughan, R. C., Cartwright-Smith, J., Vaughan, K. B., Colby, C. Z., & Lanzetta, J. T. (1976). Effects of being observed on expressive, subjective, and physiological responses to painful stimuli. *Journal of Personality and Social Psychology, 34,* 1211-1218.

Klein, S. B., & Mowrer, R. (1989). *Contemporary learning theories: Pavlovian conditioning and the status of traditional learning theory.* Hillsdale, NJ: Lawrence Erlbaum.

Laird, J. D. (1984). The real role of facial response in the experience of emotion: A reply to Tourangeau and Ellsworth, and others. *Journal of Personality and Social Psychology, 47,* 909-917.

Lang, P. J., Bradley, M. M., & Cuthbert, B. N. (1990). Emotion, attention, and the startle reflex. *Psychological Review, 97,* 377-395.

LeDoux, J. E. (1986). Sensory systems and emotion. *Integrative Psychiatry, 4,* 237-248.

LeDoux, J. E. (1987). Emotion. In F. Plum (Ed.), *Handbook of physiology. 1: The nervous system: Vol. 5. Higher functions of the brain* (pp. 419-460). Bethesda, MD: American Physiological Society.

LeDoux, J. E., Iwata, J., Cicchetti, P., & Reis, D. J. (1988). Different projections of the central amygdaloid nucleus mediate autonomic and behavioral correlates of conditioned fear. *Journal of Neuroscience, 8,* 2517-2529.

LeDoux, J. E., Romanski, L., & Xagoraris, A. (1989). Indelibility of subcortical emotional memories. *Journal of Cognitive Neuroscience, 1,* 238-243.

Leeper, R. (1935). A study of a neglected portion of the field of learning: The development of sensory organization. *Journal of Genetic Psychology, 46,* 41-75.

Levenson, R. W. (1992). Autonomic nervous system patterning in emotion. *Psychological Science, 3,* 23-27.

Levenson, R. W., Carstensen, L. L., Friesen, W. V., & Ekman, P. (1991). Emotion, physiology, and expression in old age. *Psychology and Aging, 6,* 28-35.

Levenson, R. W., Ekman, P., & Friesen, W. V. (1990). Voluntary facial action generates emotion-specific autonomic nervous system activity. *Psychophysiology, 27,* 363-384.

Leventhal, J., & Mosbach, P. A. (1983). The perceptual-motor theory of emotion. In J. T. Cacioppo & R. E. Petty (Eds.), *Social psychophysiology: A sourcebook* (pp. 353-390). New York: Guilford.

Maier, S. F. (1986). Stressor controllability and stress-induced analgesia. *Annals of the New York Academy of Sciences, 467,* 55-72.

Maier, S. F. (1989). Determinants of the nature of environmentally induced hypalgesia. *Behavioral Neuroscience, 103,* 131-145.

Mandler, G. (1975). *Mind and emotion.* New York: John Wiley.

Marañon, G. (1924). Contribution à l'étude de l'action émotive de l'adrénaline. *Revue Française d'Endocrinologie, 2,* 301-325.

Miller, N. E. (1951). Learning drives and rewards. In S. S. Stevens (Ed.), *Handbook of experimental psychology* (pp. 435-472). New York: John Wiley.

Minor, T. R., Dess, N. K., & Overmeir, J. B. (1991). Inverting the traditional view of "learned helplessness": A reinterpretation in terms of anxiety and modulator operations. In M. R. Denny (Ed.), *Aversive events and behavior.* Hillsdale, NJ: Lawrence Erlbaum.

Montoya, P., Schandry, R., & Muller, A. (1991). The influence of cardiac awareness and focus of attention on the heartbeat evoked potential [Abstract]. *Psychophysiology, 28,* S40.

Mower, O. H. (1947). On the dual nature of learning: A reinterpretation of "conditioning" and "problem solving." *Harvard Educational Review, 17,* 102-148.

Nieuwenhuyse, B., Offenberg, L., & Frijda, N. H. (1987). Subjective emotion and reported body experience. *Motivation and Emotion, 11,* 169-182.

Ortony, A., & Turner, T. J. (1990). What's basic about basic emotions? *Psychological Review, 97,* 315-331.

Ostrom, T. M., & Upshaw, H. S. (1968). Psychological perspectives and attitude change. In A. G. Greenwald, T. C. Brock, & T. M. Ostrom (Eds.), *Psychological foundations of attitudes.* New York: Academic Press.

Pavlov, I. (1927). *Conditioned reflexes* (G. V. Anrep, Trans.). London: Oxford University Press.

Pennebaker, J. W. (1982). *The psychology of physical symptoms.* New York: Springer-Verlag.

Pennebaker, J. W., Gonder-Frederick, L. A., Stewart, H., Elfman, L., & Skelton, J. A. (1982). Physical symptoms associated with blood pressure. *Psychophysiology, 19,* 201-210.

Pennebaker, J. W., & Skelton, J. A. (1981). Selective monitoring of physical sensations. *Journal of Personality and Social Psychology, 41,* 213-223.

Pribram, K. H. (1970). Feelings as monitors. In M. B. Arnold (Ed.), *Feelings and emotions: The Loyola Symposium* (pp. 41-53). New York: Academic Press.

Reed, S. D., Harver, A., & Katkin, E. S. (1990). Interoception. In J. T. Cacioppo & L. G. Tassinary (Eds.), *Principles of psychophysiology: Physical, social, and inferential elements* (pp. 253-294). New York: Cambridge University Press.

Reisenzein, R. (1983). The Schachter theory of emotion: Two decades later. *Psychological Bulletin, 94,* 239-264.

Rime, B., & Giovannini, D. (1986). The physiological patterning of emotional states. In K. R. Scherer, H. G. Wallbott, & A. B. Summerfield (Eds.), *Experiencing emotion: A cross-cultural study* (pp. 84-97). Cambridge: Cambridge University Press.

Rime, B., Philippot, P., & Cisamolo, D. (1990). Social schemata of peripheral changes in emotion. *Journal of Personality and Social Psychology, 59,* 38-49.

Roseman, I. J. (1984). Cognitive determinants of emotion: A structural theory. In P. Shaver (Ed.), *Review of personality and social psychology* (Vol. 5, pp. 11-36). Beverly Hills, CA: Sage.

Schachter, S. (1964). The interaction of cognitive and psychological determinants of emotional state. *Advances in Experimental Social Psychology, 1,* 49-80.

Schachter, S., & Singer, J. E. (1962). Cognitive, social, and physiological determinants of emotional state. *Psychological Review, 69,* 379-399.

Schachter, S., & Singer, J. E. (1979). Comments on the Maslach and Marshall-Zimbardo experiments. *Journal of Personality and Social Psychology, 37,* 989-995.

Scherer, K. R., Wallbott, J. G., & Summerfield, A. B. (Eds.). (1986). *Experiencing emotion: A cross-cultural study.* New York: Cambridge University Press.

Scott, T. R., & Yaxley, S. (1989). Interaction of taste and ingestion. In R. H. Cagan (Ed.), *Neural mechanisms of taste* (pp. 148-177). Boca Raton, FL: CRC Press.

Sekuler, R., & Blake, R. (1985). *Perception.* New York: Knopf.

Shaver, P., Schwartz, J., Kirson, D., & O'Connor, C. (1987). Emotion knowledge: Further exploration of a prototype approach. *Journal of Personality and Social Psychology, 52,* 1061-1086.

Shepard, R. N. (1990). *Mind sights.* San Francisco: Freeman.

Shields, S. A. (1984). Distinguishing between emotion and nonemotion: Judgments about experience. *Motivation and Emotion, 8,* 355-369.

Skelton, J. A., & Pennebaker, J. W. (1990). The verbal system. In J. T. Cacioppo & L. G. Tassinary (Eds.), *Principles of psychophysiology: Physical, social, and inferential elements* (pp. 631-657). New York: Cambridge University Press.

Smith, C. A., & Ellsworth, P. C. (1985). Patterns of cognitive appraisal in emotion. *Journal of Personality and Social Psychology, 48,* 813-838.

Smith, C. A., & Ellsworth, P. C. (1987). Patterns of appraisal and emotion related to taking an exam. *Journal of Personality and Social Psychology, 52,* 475-488.

Soltis, J. F. (1966). *Seeing, knowing, and believing: A study of the language of visual perception.* London: Allen & Unwin.

Stemmler, G. (1989). The autonomic differentiation of emotions revisited: Convergent and discriminant validation. *Psychophysiology, 26,* 617-632.

Strack, F., Martin, L. L., & Stepper, S. (1988). Inhibiting and facilitating conditions of the human smile: A nonobtrusive test of the facial feedback hypothesis. *Journal of Personality and Social Psychology, 54,* 768-777.

Tomkins, S. S. (1962). *Affect, imagery, and consciousness: Vol. 1. The positive affects.* New York: Springer.

Tsal, Y., & Kolbert, L. (1985). Disambiguating ambiguous figures by selective attention. *Quarterly Journal of Experimental Psychology, 37,* 25-37.

Turner, T. J., & Ortony, A. (in press). Basic emotions: Can conflicting criteria converge? *Psychological Review.*

Valins, S. (1966). Cognitive effects of false heart-rate feedback. *Journal of Personality and Social Psychology, 4,* 400-408.

Wagner, H. (1989). The physiological differentiation of emotions. In H. Wagner & A. Manstead (Eds.), *Handbook of social psychophysiology* (pp. 77-89). New York: John Wiley.

Wallbott, H. G., & Scherer, K. R. (1986). How universal and specific is emotional experience? Evidence from 27 countries on 5 continents. *Social Science Information, 25,* 763-795.

Weiner, B., & Graham, S. (1984). An attributional approach to emotional development. In C. E. Izard, J. Kagan, & R. B. Zajonc (Eds.), *Emotions, cognition, and behavior* (pp. 167-191). New York: Cambridge University Press.

Whitehead, W. E., & Drescher, V. M. (1980). Perception of gastric contractions and self-control of gastric motility. *Psychophysiology, 17,* 552-558.

Zajonc, R. B., & McIntosh, D. N. (1992). Emotions research: Some promising questions and some questionable promises. *Psychological Science, 3,* 70-74.

Zajonc, R. B., Murphy, S. T., & Inglehart, M. (1989). Feeling and facial efference: Implications of the vascular theory of emotions. *Psychological Review, 96,* 395-416.

Zillmann, D. (1983). Transfer of excitation in emotional behavior. In J. T. Cacioppo & R. E. Petty (Eds.), *Social psychophysiology: A sourcebook* (pp. 215-242). New York: Guilford.

Zillmann, D. (1984). *Connections between sex and aggression.* Hillsdale, NJ: Lawrence Erlbaum.

4

Temperamental Contributions to Emotion and Social Behavior

JEROME KAGAN

Jerome Kagan is Professor of Psychology at Harvard University. His research interests focus on continuity and discontinuity in personality development with a special emphasis on the influence of temperament. His most recent books include *The Nature of the Child* and *Unstable Ideas.*

Although the ideas of temperament, emotion, and behavior share some features, each concept has a distinct meaning. An *acute emotion* is a profile of physiological, cognitive, and motor reactions to a class of incentives but need not involve social behavior. *Social behavior* refers to interactive response profiles that need not involve any acute emotional state. The concept of *temperament* refers to an inherited physiological bias that predisposes a child to particular emotional and behavioral reactions in specific contexts. An illustration of the differences among the three terms is contained in the following example. Most young children react with an acute emotion of mild fear or anxiety and behavioral restraint for several minutes upon encountering a large group of unfamiliar children. This is an almost universal phenomenon. But there is a small group of about 15% of children who react with an extreme degree of fear to a group of unfamiliar children, as well as other unfamiliar events, and will avoid interacting with them for a half hour or more because of an inherited temperamental characteristic.

Until recently, psychologists have been reluctant to award much power to the temperamental factors that contribute to the ease with which certain emotional states are provoked, the intensity of those states, and their associated social behaviors.

This lacuna is due to two relatively independent factors. One is attributable to the Western egalitarian ethic that dislikes the idea that people vary endogenously in their susceptibility to certain emotions. A

AUTHOR'S NOTE: The research reported in this chapter was supported by grants from the John D. and Catherine T. MacArthur Foundation and the Leon Lowenstein Foundation.

second reason for the past indifference to temperament was the absence of powerful theoretical ideas to guide empirical work. Research during the last 10-15 years, however, has begun to remedy this state of affairs. Neurobiologists have discovered individual variation in chemical and physiological processes that can serve as the basis for variation in emotional experience and expression (Adamec & Stark-Adamec, 1989; Applegate, Kapp, Underwood, & McNall, 1983; Aston-Jones, 1985; Davis, 1986; Dunnette & Weinshilboum, 1982) and developmental scientists have begun to carve out coherent profiles of behavior that are moderately stable over time and associated with theoretically relevant physiological characteristics (Kagan, 1989; Porges, 1986). This chapter, which addresses the contribution of two temperamental factors to specific emotional and behavioral profiles, describes the behavioral and physiological characteristics of these two types of children and the early signs of their temperaments in infancy. Finally, the text speculates on the implications of these temperamental categories for larger issues in social psychology and personality.

THE MEANING OF TEMPERAMENT

The meaning of a theoretical term is based on a synthesis of sense and referential meanings (Frege, 1979). The former refers to the abstract ideas that define an object or event; the latter to the actual phenomena implied by the sense meaning. The referential meaning is central to validity in empirical science and gives operational reality to sentences about temperament and behavior. The sense meaning of *anxiety* is an unpleasant psychological state. The referential meaning could be the report of a person who is experiencing distress or an increase in heart rate and blood pressure in a stressful situation. These two referential meanings are different. The sense meaning of *temperament* held by most contemporary scientists is defined by stable, biologically based affect/behavior profiles that appear early in life. Some believe temperamental profiles are inherited (Plomin, 1986); those who are less insistent on the contribution of genes are either agnostic regarding heredity or award power to prenatal, perinatal, and early postnatal events not under genetic control that affect the central nervous system to create stable psychological profiles. Because prenatal events might have such potency, it is reasonable to assume that there are at least two different categories of temperament—one influenced by heredity and the other by a variety of other biological factors, including drug addiction or alcoholism in a pregnant mother.

This sense definition of *temperament* fails, however, to specify either particular psychological phenomena or their sources of evidence. At the moment, there are two popular but different referential meanings of *temperament*. One involves questionnaires given to parents about their children or to adults who provide self-descriptions. The other involves direct observations of children or adults. The two referential meanings are not the same. Some people who report they are extroverts on a questionnaire do not appear to be sociable when they are observed in a situation with strangers.

Two contrasting scientific styles can be detected in those who probe a new domain like temperament. One group, resembling Plato, begins with an a priori idealized conception of the phenomena of interest based on deep ideological premises. The second group, akin to Aristotle, prefers to infer powerful constructs from a corpus of evidence and awards less power to a priori conceptions. Both styles are necessary in science and I suspect that different personality types are attracted to these complementary strategies. I side with the second group and, at the moment, prefer an inductive, Baconian strategy. The work to be summarized reflects that prejudice. Thus, instead of assuming a priori that emotion, activity, and sociability are the three most basic temperamental types, I avoided decisions about the most fundamental temperamental traits and began by observing children. These observations suggested that some children were consistently shy and restrained in unfamiliar contexts while others were sociable and bold; as a result, our laboratory decided to study these two types of children.

INHIBITED AND UNINHIBITED TEMPERAMENTS

There are two qualitatively different types of children, each characterized by a consistent behavioral style to unfamiliarity and, by inference, different thresholds for the provocation of the emotions we normally call *anxiety, fear,* and *guilt.* One group is usually shy, restrained, and timid in unfamiliar contexts; the other is social, affectively spontaneous, and bold in the same unfamiliar situations. We call the former children *inhibited* and the latter *uninhibited* (Kagan, Reznick, & Snidman, 1988).

The contrast between inhibited and uninhibited children would be assimilated easily by Galen, a perceptive second-century physician, who posited four fundamental personality types: melancholic, sanguine, choleric, and phlegmatic. Galen believed that each person could be characterized by his or her position on the opposed qualities of warm versus cold and dry versus moist, which were based on the balance in the body between blood and phlegm. The melancholic, anxious person was cold and dry; the outgoing, sanguine person was warm and moist. Kant accepted Galen's four types and Eysenck (1953) elaborated them almost two millennia later in his descriptions of extroverts and introverts.

Although Galen's speculations may initially appear bizarre to modern readers, they are not fundamentally different in form than the contemporary speculations that schizophrenics have an excess of dopamine and depressives too little norepinephrine. The basic premise is that bodily substances can influence mind, mood, and behavior.

Our current research had its origin in a longitudinal study conducted at the Fels Research Institute in which a large corpus of normative information on 89 Caucasian adults, born between 1929 and 1939 and studied from infancy through adolescence, was related to their adult status in the third decade (Kagan & Moss, 1962). The most provocative result was that children characterized by extreme fear and avoidant behavior to novelty and challenge during the first three years retained that quality through adolescence and adulthood. The fearful children were, as adults, psychologically more dependent on their spouse or love object and more introverted than the majority of subjects. They sought jobs with structure that did not require continuous interaction with unfamiliar people or a great deal of uncertainty.

This finding lay dormant for 15 years until Richard Kearsley, Philip Zelazo, and I reflected on data we had gathered on Chinese American and Caucasian infants enrolled in a longitudinal project designed to assess the effects of day-care attendance on young infants (Kagan, Kearsley, & Zelazo, 1978). We observed these children from 3 to 29 months of age with extensive laboratory assessments at 7 ½, 9 ½, 11 ½, 13 ½, 20, and 29 months. The Chinese American children, whether reared at home or at our experimental day-care center, were consistently more fearful than the Caucasians and the Chinese American mothers were more likely than the Caucasians to describe their children as wary and fearful.

These results implied a temperamental characteristic and were the incentive for Cynthia Garcia-Coll's dissertation. Garcia-Coll selected children 21 months old who were either extremely inhibited or extremely uninhibited in their behavior in a variety of laboratory settings consisting of unfamiliar rooms, people, and objects (Garcia-Coll, Kagan, & Reznick, 1984). In one situation, an unfamiliar woman entered a playroom in which the mother and child had been playing, sat down, and remained quiet for 30 seconds and then called the child by name and asked him or her to approach. The child's behaviors across six different unfamiliar situations were coded for the occurrences of fretting or crying, withdrawal from the unfamiliar event, latency to approach and/or contact the unfamiliar toys or adults, and cessation of play. An aggregate index of inhibition was constructed by summarizing the separate, correlated signs of inhibited behavior across the six situations and, based on that score, children were classified as extremely inhibited or uninhibited. Even though the situations the children encountered were identical, the aggregate index of inhibition was stable across the two sessions ($r = .63$).

A second longitudinal cohort, which Nancy Snidman (1984) studied for her dissertation, was composed of Caucasian children 31 months old who were classified as inhibited or uninhibited based on a slightly different set of laboratory procedures. These children first played with an unfamiliar peer of the same sex and age with both mothers present in the room. At the end of the play session, a woman dressed in an unusual costume entered the room and sat on the floor. Behaviors indexing inhibition were similar to those used with Garcia-Coll's cohort; namely, long latencies to initiate contact with the toys, the unfamiliar child, or the unfamiliar woman; inhibition of speech; and long periods of time spent close to the mother. Groups of extremely inhibited and uninhibited children were selected and the inhibited and uninhibited children from Garcia-Coll's and Snidman's cohorts were combined to yield 54 inhibited and 53 uninhibited children selected from an initial screening group of more than 400 children.

These two groups of children were observed several times, at 18-24 month intervals, with the last major assessment occurring at 7 ½ years of age. The evaluations at 7 ½ years included, first, a peer play session in which a group of 7 to 10 unfamiliar children of the same sex and age played in a large room. In the second setting on a different day, a female examiner administered a series of cognitive tests over a one-hour period. Behavior in both situations differentiated the two groups.

In the peer play context, about two thirds of the original group of inhibited children were very quiet and spent more than 40% of their time, especially during the unstructured intervals, spatially distant from any other child. By contrast, two thirds of the original group of uninhibited children spoke a great deal and were in close contact with one or more peers during the 90-minute session. During the session with the female examiner, 90% of inhibited children either spoke less than 30 times or took longer than five minutes to utter their sixth spontaneous comment. By contrast, two thirds of the uninhibited children spoke more than 30 times and their first six spontaneous comments were uttered in the first five minutes. When we combined standard scores for each child's behaviors across the two different procedures to create a standard score for inhibited behavior at 7 ½ years, 81% (35 of 43) of the inhibited children had scores above the median, while 76% of the uninhibited children had scores below the median. Less than a quarter of the children changed their behavioral category from the time of the original classification to 7 ½ years. Thus the different styles of social behavior of the two groups were preserved through late childhood for about three quarters of the children. The children who had been classified as inhibited in their second year are reserved and show less spontaneous affect than those who were classified as uninhibited. But the two groups are not different in school achievement. Thus it appears that more inhibited than uninhibited children will grow up to fit Jung's (1924) description of an introvert while uninhibited children will be closer to his description of the extravert. An educated mother described her inhibited son when he was 11 years old, "If something is new and different, his inclination is to be quiet and watch. He is aware of this and has compensating and coping strategies. So, his friends don't see him as shy. It is unfamiliarity that is the cause of his behavior, not only unfamiliar people—it has to do with newness."

Physiological Differences

The argument for a genetic contribution to these two temperamental categories would be strengthened if a distinct physiological profile were associated with each of the two types. There is evidence to support that assumption, for the temperamental groups differ in the reactivity of the sympathetic nervous system. Two sites in the brain that exert a major influence on sympathetic reactions and influence each other are the amygdala and the hypothalamus. The amygdala is an almond-shaped organ tucked up against the temporal lobe; the hypothalamus is a collection of neurons located under the thalamus and above the pituitary gland. We are not suggesting that the origins of the psychological differences to be described lie in these particular places; rather, these anatomical sites participate in neural circuits that contribute to peripheral physiological and behavioral characteristics. The origin of the daily tides is in neither the moon nor the earth but in the gravitational attraction between each of these objects.

We have measured several different variables that reflect the activity of the sympathetic nervous system and found that inhibited, compared with uninhibited, children showed greater sympathetic reactivity. For example, inhibited children showed larger increases in heart rate over a battery of different cognitive procedures as well as during particular cognitive tests. For example, at 5 ½ years of age, each child heard a narrated story while watching 20 slides that were chromatic drawings of two child characters in the story, one child depicted as fearful and the other as fearless. Inhibited children displayed large cardiac accelerations to a larger number of the 20 slides than did the uninhibited children (Kagan, Reznick, & Snidman, 1987).

A second index of sympathetic activity is a large rise in diastolic blood pressure when a child changes his or her position from sitting to standing. A rise to the standing position produces an automatic, sympathetically mediated vasoconstriction in the vessels of the arterial tree to prevent blood from leaving the head. The older inhibited children had a larger rise in diastolic blood pressure than did the uninhibited children, implying greater sympathetic reactivity. Magnitude of dilation of the pupil is a third sympathetically mediated response, and inhibited children had significantly larger pupils during a brief 15-minute cognitive battery at 5 ½ years of age.

A fourth index of sympathetic reactivity is vasoconstriction of the arteriovenous anastomoses lying under the surface of the skin. A primary function of these small muscular structures, which are sympathetically innervated, is to prevent heat from escaping through the skin surface by constricting the flow of blood to surface capillaries. One additional fact is important in interpreting the results. The sympathetic nervous system is a bit more reactive on the right than on the left side of the body (Rogers, Battit, McPeek, & Todd, 1978; Saper, Loewy, Swanson, & Cowan, 1976). If inhibited children have a more reactive sympathetic system, they should show an asymmetry in the constriction of the anastomoses and therefore greater cooling on the right compared with the left side. Groups of inhibited children showed a greater increase in cooling on the right, compared with the left, side of the face when their initial facial temperatures were compared with the coolest temperature attained during a succeeding set of mildly stressful procedures. By contrast, uninhibited children showed greater cooling on the left side of the face.

Thus four different indexes of sympathetic activity to mildly stressful incentives—rise in heart rate, increase in diastolic blood pressure, pupillary dilation, and asymmetry in facial cooling favoring a cooler right side—suggest that inhibited children possess a sympathetic system more reactive to imposed challenge. We do not yet know the deeper reasons for this variation in the activity of the sympathetic nervous system. Future research will have to resolve that issue. The two temperamental groups also differ in other biological characteristics. Even casual observation reveals that inhibited children have greater muscle tension than uninhibited youngsters, especially in the face and trunk. To quantify this difference, we took advantage of the fact that increased tension of the muscles of the vocal cords and larynges, which are skeletal, is accompanied by a decrease in the variability of vocal utterances. This increased tension has two sources: one is derivative of activity of the *nucleus ambiguus* serving the larynx; the other is sympathetic in origin and is the result of vasoconstriction of the arterioles serving these muscles. Computer programs written by Philip Lieberman of Brown University permitted us to quantify changes in the variability of the pitch periods—the actual index is the standard deviation of the normalized distribution of twice the difference between two successive pitch periods divided by the sum of the periods. Variability of the pitch periods was measured first during a minimally stressful context in which the child simply had to speak single words like *dog, tub,* and *cake.* After repeating these words in a recall memory task, the child was asked a series of six questions for which these words were the correct answer. Inhibited children showed significantly lower variability, suggesting greater tension in the muscles of the larynx and vocal cords as a result of the cognitive stress of trying to remember the correct answer from the set of six words (Coster, 1986).

Finally, we assessed levels of cortisol in the saliva of the longitudinal sample of inhibited and uninhibited children when they were 5 ½ and 7 ½ years of age during the early morning on three days before the stress of the day had begun. Cortisol, a hormone produced by the adrenal cortex and monitored by the hypothalamus and pituitary, typically increases to a variety of psychological or physical stressors. The inhibited children were more likely than the uninhibited ones to have high cortisol values at both ages. Nine inhibited children with very high cortisol values at both 5 ½ and 7 ½ years differed from the inhibited children with low cortisol values in important ways. In a play session with an unfamiliar peer of the same sex and age, three of these nine children remained proximal to their mother for the first 5-10 minutes of the play session. The fourth child sat passively in the middle of the room doing nothing and a fifth glanced at her mother frequently during the 30-minute play session. Interviews with the mothers revealed that six of the nine showed signs of physiological arousal as well as intense fears. One child was constipated during infancy, retained urine during the first three years of life, and showed many contemporary fears. A second had been extremely irritable as an infant and at 4 years of age had a fear of blood, bugs, and defecation. The third had allergies, chronic constipation, and colic during infancy and was afraid of playing alone. A fourth had a spastic colon as an infant, was plagued with nightmares, and was afraid of being alone and apart from the parents. A fifth displayed extreme separation fear during infancy and was asthmatic. A sixth was constipated as an infant, showed chronic fear of nursery school, and was afraid of leaving her backyard. None of the uninhibited children, even those with high cortisol levels, showed these symptoms. Thus the high cortisol levels in inhibited children may be reflecting a temperamental vulnerability to anxiety.

Although the inhibited children differed from the uninhibited on each of the physiological measures described above, the correlations among the varied measures were low. This is not uncommon. Many investigators report low intercorrelations among a diverse set of physiological variables, each of which is presumed to index a state of uncertainty or anxiety (Nesse et al., 1985). But we assumed that children who were high on two or three of these variables were under greater limbic arousal than those who were high only on one. We standardized each physiological variable gathered at 5 ½ years of age on the cohort that was selected at 21 months: cortisol level in the laboratory, heart rate during the cognitive tasks, heart rate variability during the cognitive tasks (reversed so that a low heart rate variability indexed limbic arousal), pupillary dilation, variability of pitch periods during cognitive stress (reversed), the standard deviation of all the fundamental frequency values (reversed), and total norepinephrine level estimated from a urine sample. The aggregate index was related to the index of inhibited behavior at every age of assessment. The multiple correlation predicting inhibited behavior at 5 ½ years from (a) behavior at 21 months and (b) the physiological index was 0.62, compared with only 0.52 when only the behavior at 21 months was used as a predictor.

Very low values on the physiological variables described above, however, were more characteristic of uninhibited children than were high values characteristic of inhibited children. That is, there were no fearful children with very low and variable heart rates, small pupils, and very low cortisol levels; but there were a few fearless children with high heart rates, large pupils, and high cortisol levels. This asymmetry in the relation between physiology and behavior implies that the biological conditions that mediate low reactivity of limbic sites are different from those that mediate high reactivity in the same circuits. An analogy may help. Fatigue, fever, and a depressed mood can be a result of a flu virus but high levels of energy, fearlessness, and happy mood do not occur just because the person is free of a flu virus.

Heritability. The most important source of evidence for the idea that inhibited and uninhibited children are physiologically different is the finding from studies of twins that the two types are heritable. Matheny (1989) computed indexes of behavioral inhibition on monozygotic and dizygotic twins and found that the former were significantly more similar than the latter, suggesting heritability of inhibited behavior. Analyses of the behaviors of monozygotic and dizygotic twins who are members of the MacArthur Longitudinal Twin Study administered at the Institute of Behavioral Genetics at the University of Colorado provided additional support for the heritability of inhibited behavior (Plomin et al., 1990). These twins were observed, at 14 and 20 months of age, at home and in the laboratory where they encountered unfamiliar objects and people. The child's tendency to remain close to the mother and to show long latencies before approaching unfamiliar people or objects— indexes of inhibition—were recorded. Inhibited behavior showed evidence of heritability at 14 and 20 months.

These children were observed again at 24 months in a laboratory situation in which pairs of unfamiliar twins played together with the mothers present. An index of inhibited behavior based on time proximal to the mother, total time staring at an unfamiliar child, and reluctance to approach an unfamiliar child also indicated the heritability of inhibited behavior. There were 18 very inhibited children in this evaluation; 14 of the 18 were made up of seven pairs of monozygotic twins. It is unlikely that a single gene is responsible for each of these temperamental types and more likely that each of the profiles is due to the actions of many genes.

Faith in the heritability of the inhibited and uninhibited profiles is enhanced by the presence of a small number of physical differences between the two groups. Significantly more inhibited children are blue eyed, and come from families where at least one half of the first-degree relatives are blue eyed, while significantly more uninhibited children have brown eyes and come from families where more than half of the adults have brown eyes (Rosenberg & Kagan, 1987, 1989). Further, inhibited children are more likely to suffer from allergic rhinitis and eczema, and significantly more first- and second-degree adult relatives of inhibited, compared with uninhibited, children report the same two symptoms (Kagan, Snidman, Sellars, & Johnson, 1991). Because both eye color and these atopic allergies are under partial genetic control, it appears that the genes that create the conditions for the development of inhibited and uninhibited behavior also participate in the production of melanin in the iris and susceptibility to selected atopic allergies.

THE PREDICTION FROM INFANCY

Although the physiological profiles and heritability data add credibility to the hypothesis of genotypic differences between inhibited and uninhibited children, the children in the longitudinal studies described above were not seen for the first time until the second year of life. Hence some scientists might argue that environmental forces could have shaped both the behavior and the physiological profiles. Thus the argument for a genetic contribution would be strengthened if we could predict inhibited and uninhibited behavior in the second year from behavior during early infancy. The final part of this chapter summarizes the evidence for this claim.

The rationale for the procedures to be described is based on the hypothesis, stated earlier, that inhibited children have a low threshold of reactivity in the amygdala and its separate projections to the hypothalamus, sympathetic chain, and skeletal motor system. The lower threshold could be the result of a special neurochemistry in these areas. Because the amygdala receives all classes of sensory information, reactivity to unfamiliar stimulus events might reflect variation in thresholds of excitability. That is, infants born with an excitable amygdala should become more aroused to stimulation than infants with a less excitable amygdala. One source of support for this idea comes from the work of LaGasse, Gruber, and Lipsitt (1989), who found that newborn infants who showed a major increase in sucking rate when the water they were ingesting through a nipple suddenly changed to a sweet sucrose solution were more likely to be inhibited two years later than were newborns who showed a minimal increase in sucking rate following the change in taste. The difference in motor activity to the change in taste could be due to differences in the excitability of sites in the amygdala that project to the motor centers serving the sucking response.

A second possible predictor of inhibited behavior is crying to unfamiliar stimulation. A site in the amygdala called the central nucleus projects to parts of the cortex and midbrain that mediate distress calls in cats and monkeys and, by extrapolation, crying in infants (de Lanerolle & Lang, 1988; Jurgens, 1982). There is evidence to suggest that infants who fret or cry readily to unfamiliar stimulation are more likely to become fearful children than are minimally irritable infants (Crockenberg, 1981; Crockenberg & Smith, 1982; van den Boom, 1989).

Because both motor activity and crying to unfamiliar ecologically valid events could reflect an excitable amygdala, we presented various sources of such stimulation to 4-month-old infants. The infants belonged to one of two longitudinal samples. Infants in the first sample were presented with visual and auditory stimulation (colored mobiles and human speech); infants in the second sample were presented with the same visual, auditory stimulation and, in addition, olfactory stimulation. Degree of motor activity and fretting/crying to the varied stimulus episodes were quantified. The first sample contained 102 healthy, 4-month-old Caucasian infants seen in the laboratory and the second sample contained 250 healthy Caucasian infants visited at home at the same age.

Levels of motor activity and irritability to the varied stimulus episodes revealed four different groups of infants. About 20% showed both high motor activity and frequent crying. About 40% showed the complementary profile of low motor activity and low crying; 25% showed low motor activity and high crying; and 15% showed high motor activity and low irritability. Each infant was reliably assigned to one of these four groups. We observed these children again when they were 9, 14, and 21 months of age in the laboratory to see whether they differed in inhibited or uninhibited behavior, expecting that the infants who were high motor-high cry at 4 months would be inhibited while those who were low motor and low cry would be uninhibited.

The degree of inhibited and uninhibited behavior was assessed in a variety of laboratory settings with the mother present continually. The indexes of each of the two temperamental types were based on the frequency of display of fear to unfamiliar people, objects, or situations. The specific unfamiliar stimuli presented to the child varied with age so that the battery was age appropriate. A *fear response* was defined as the occurrence of fretting or crying following encounter with an unfamiliar context, object, person, or procedure or failure to approach an unfamiliar person or object following an invitation to do so. The stimulus events that elicited a fear response most often included crying and resistance to the placement of heart rate electrodes on the child's chest, placement of a blood pressure cuff, facial disapproval from the examiner or the mother, a noisy rotating wheel, a request from the examiner to taste liquid from a dropper, and failure to approach a metal robot or an unfamiliar adult despite an invitation to do so. No child failed to become subdued or show some degree of wariness to one or two of the unfamiliar incentives. Thus a low fear score means that the infant rarely cried to unfamiliar events or, after initial restraint to the appearance of a stranger or robot, subsequently approached them.

The results reveal stability of fear behavior from 9-14 and 14-21 months, with stability correlations of 0.4. Moreover, less than 15% of the children changed from high fear at one age to low fear at another or from low fear at one age to high fear at another. More important, approximately 20% of the infants in both samples who had been classified at 4 months as high motor-high cry had the highest levels of fear at all ages, while the 40% of all infants who were classified as low motor-low cry showed the lowest levels of fear. The other two groups showed inter-mediate fear. For example, at 14 months of age, the high motor-high cry children in sample 1 had a mean of 5.0 fears while the low motor-low cry children had a mean of 1.8 fears ($p < .001$). The other two groups had intermediate fear scores (3.1 and 3.5) (Kagan & Snidman, 1991).

This relation between early reactivity at 4 months and level of fear in the second year was replicated in the second, larger sample: 60% of the high motor-high cry infants showed four or more fears; 25%, two or three fears; and 15% showed zero or one fear at 14 months. By contrast, among the low motor-low cry infants, only 10% showed four or more fears; 32%, two or three fears; and 56%, zero or one fear ($p < .001$). Of the 158 children in this second cohort who were observed at both 14 and 21 months, 32 showed four or more fears at both ages; 16 of these 32 had been high motor-high cry infants at 4 months of age and only 3 had been low motor-low cry. By contrast, 29 of these children showed zero or one fear at both ages, and 21 of these 29 had been low motor-low cry at 4 months and only 3 had been high motor-high cry infants when they were seen at 4 months of age ($p < .001$).

These data support the hypothesis that inhibited and uninhibited behavior, as reflected in avoidance of and fear to unfamiliarity in the second year, is due in part to differential thresholds of excitability in the amygdala and its projections to the hypothalamus and sympathetic and motor systems. It is important to add that the high motor-high cry infants who become inhibited 2-year-olds also show greater sympathetic reactivity than the low motor-low cry uninhibited children. For example, the former have higher heart rates during sleep at 2 weeks of age, larger heart rate accelerations to challenge at 14 and 21 months, and greater cooling on the right compared with the left side of the face at 21 months of age. The reader will recall that these sympathetic reactions also differentiated the older inhibited and uninhibited children. The physiological profile that predisposes an infant to become inhibited or uninhibited in the second year is not deterministic, how-ever. The family environment during the first year can affect the probability that a high motor-high cry infant will develop extremely inhibited behavior.

Doreen Arcus (1991) studied 12 infants who were high motor and high cry and 12 who were low motor and low cry at 4 months of age. She visited the homes of these 24 infants and filmed the mother and infant in a naturalistic context when the infants were 5, 7, 9, 11, and 13 months old. The high motor-high cry infants, who became highly fearful in the second year, experienced a maternal environment different from the smaller number of high motor-high cry infants who did not become highly fearful. The mothers of the former group were more likely to hold the infant for longer periods of time when the infant was only mildly distressed and were less likely to set limits in situations in which the infant might have learned to cope with uncertainty or fear. A combination of the two variables explained 40% of the variance in fear behavior for the high motor-high cry infants. Because low motor-low cry infants were not very fearful, however, these two maternal variables were not related to the child's fear score.

Support for this relation between maternal behavior and fearfulness is found in another source of data. Mothers of the 158 infants in sample 2 were asked, at the end of the 21-month battery, to rank, from most to least desirable, 14 child qualities the mother would like to see in her 5-year-old child. Some of the items were (a) "I would like my child to be able to play alone," (b) "I want my child not to worry about school grades," (c) "I want my child to be emotionally close to me." Another item read, "I want my child to obey me most of the time." The mothers who ranked this last item in ranks 1-7 (that is, as relatively desirable) had less fearful children than the mothers who ranked this item as less important (ranks 8-14). Specifically, among the mothers of children who were minimally fearful at 14 and 21 months, 65% ranked the obedience item as desirable, while among the mothers of highly fearful children, only 35% ranked this item as desirable (chi square = 6.2; $p < .01$).

One possible interpretation of these results rests on the idea that mothers of high motor-high cry infants are reluctant to set limits, perhaps because they do not want to make their child anxious. This practice may make it more, rather than less, difficult for this category of infant to learn to cope with stress. Put more plainly than the data warrant, an infant born with a high motor-high cry profile may need a family environment that provides opportunities to cope with stress and uncertainty rather than an environment that protects the child from these experiences.

DISCUSSION

The evidence summarized suggests that some extremely shy, timid children show very high reactivity of limbic sites while some extremely extroverted, social children show the complementary profile. The evidence supports the idea that temperamental variables make a contribution to the child's susceptibility to the emotions of fear or anxiety to unfamiliarity as well as to shy behavior in situations with unfamiliar people or timidity in unfamiliar contexts. Thus scientists interested in the social behavior of children or adolescents should be acutely aware of the role of temperament. It is likely that a proportion of the shy adults who are the focus of concern of social psychologists were inhibited children. The remaining shy adults probably acquired their external demeanor as a product of experience, probably after school entrance. Both types, however, are at risk for chronic loneliness (Jones, Hobbs, & Hockenbury, 1982).

Because inhibited children are more likely to be shy with others and more likely to show signs of internalization, rather than externalization, the work on temperament engages a major concern of social psychologists.

The developmental course of an inhibited or an uninhibited temperamental style will depend on the specific family and peer experiences encountered. An inhibited child born to middle-class parents who value academic achievement is likely to devote a great deal of time to schoolwork because of his or her desire to avoid social groups. As a result, the child will encounter success and therefore is likely to choose a vocation that permits him or her to avoid unexpected interactions with unfamiliar people. In this sense, the child's temperament influences his or her choice of environments. The inhibited child in a lower-class home that does not value academic achievement is likely to have a more difficult time of adjustment, at least in contemporary, democratic societies. By contrast, the uninhibited child raised in a neighborhood or home that is permissive of asocial behavior may be at risk for conduct disorder. The same child raised in a neighborhood that punishes asocial behavior is likely to become popular and a leader with his or her peers.

Thus it appears that Galen was correct when he suggested that there was a temperamental contribution to melancholic versus sanguine personalities. Acceptance of this conclusion has implications for research on emotion. Most laboratory studies of emotion, especially those that try to induce an affect and quantify behavioral indexes of that state, assume implicitly that all subjects in the sample are equally susceptible to induction of the emotion. This assumption may be incorrect.

A nice example of this claim is seen in the work of Manuck, Cohen, Rabin, Muldoon, and Bachen (1991), who found that the response of the immune system to an antigen differed for subjects who were low versus high on an index of sympathetic reactivity of the cardiac system. Those adults who showed high sympathetic reactivity prior to the experimental intervention—as indicated by higher heart rates and higher blood pressure—showed a reduced immune response, while those with low sympathetic reactivity showed no compromise of the immune response to stress. This finding matches our intuition. Some people become very anxious in times of stress while others remain calm. There are very few laboratory or life situations in which all individuals react similarly to a particular, emotionally arousing event. It appears that temperamental characteristics influence this variation.

One of the premises of Western society, derivative of the Christian assumption that will (or mind) controls body, is that each of us should be able to monitor our moods. Some chronically tense or dysphoric adults believe they are immature or insufficiently intelligent if they cannot control their feelings. Monk's (1990) biography of Wittgenstein reveals that his temperament kept him in a state of tension and anxiety for most of his life. The suicides of several of his brothers implies a genetic component to his depressed mood. But in none of his published letters or diary entries did Wittgenstein acknowledge that possibility. Instead, he came to the opposite conclusion, for he wrote in despair in his early fifties that he was still prone to moods of anxiety and attributed these feelings to his lack of wisdom. In the diary entry for April 1, 1942, he wrote, "I have suffered much but I am apparently incapable of learning from my life. I suffer still just as I did many years ago. I have not become any stronger or wiser" (Monk, 1990, p. 443).

How much conscious control of his mood did Wittgenstein have? This question is not amenable to a crisp answer. At one extreme are well-functioning adults who, in a matter of weeks, become deeply depressed for the first time and cannot, without professional help, regain their former good mood. These unfortunate individuals could not control the acute onset of their depression. By contrast, we assume that a person who is sad because of a job failure or afraid to ask for a raise in salary is able to cope with those affects. Further, we believe that an individual who has insulted his neighbor also could have controlled that action and we hold him responsible for the uncivil act. But the middle ground, where Wittgenstein lived, is ambiguous. Do adults who are chronically suspicious, angry, depressed, or worried have the capability of muting their emotions? I recall an extremely inhibited child from the

Fels study who, as an adult, told me that when he was an adolescent he decided he must conquer his extreme fear. He began by asking the most attractive girl in the senior class to the spring dance. She accepted his invitation. Thus inhibited children do have some power to cope with their vulnerability to anxiety and avoidant behavioral style.

The issue of developing coping mechanisms has pragmatic consequences, for, unconsciously, our reactions toward others depend upon our interpretations of their psychological surface. If I believe a colleague can control his angry outbursts, I experience moral outrage and become irritated with him because he has violated a community standard of acceptable behavior. I become more forgiving, however, if I believe his biology makes it difficult for him to suppress angry outbursts. That is why we do not hold young children or adults with Tourette's Syndrome responsible for actions that in normal adults would invite severe sanctions.

The increasing public awareness of temperamental dispositions will render this conflict more acute. One of the consequences is that some of us may, on occasion, become too tolerant of extreme emotional reactions in others if we believe that psychological characteristics originating in biology are less subject to personal control than those that originate only in past experience. That assumption is probably invalid most of the time for it is extremely difficult to change the chronically anxious mood of a child who has been in seven foster homes during the first 10 years of life. Nonetheless, the concept of will, which is a psychological rather than a biological construct, is so central to Western conceptions of human nature, it is easier for most of us to be persuaded that we can monitor our moods and behaviors more effectively if they were learned than if they were influenced, in part, by our biology. Although this belief is neither logical nor empirically valid, it represents a danger to which we should remain alert as temperamental constructs gain favor in the years ahead.

REFERENCES

Adamec, R. E., & Stark-Adamec, C. (1989). Behavioral inhibition and anxiety. In J. S. Reznick (Ed.), *Perspectives in behavioral inhibition* (pp. 93-124). Chicago: University of Chicago Press.

Applegate, C. D., Kapp, B. S., Underwood, M. D., & McNall, C. L. (1983). Autonomic and somatomotor effects of amygdala central nucleus stimulation in awake rabbits. *Physiology and Behavior, 31,* 353-360.

Arcus, D. M. (1991). *The experiential modification of temperamental bias in inhibited and uninhibited children.* Unpublished doctoral dissertation, Harvard University.

Aston-Jones, G. (1985). Behavioral functions of the locus ceruleus derived from cellular attributes. *Physiological Psychology, 13,* 118-126.

Coster, W. (1986). *Aspects of voice and conversation in behaviorally inhibited children.* Unpublished doctoral dissertation, Harvard University.

Crockenberg, S. (1981). Infant irritability, mother responsiveness, and social support influences on the security of infant attachment. *Child Development, 52,* 857-865.

Crockenberg, S., & Smith, P. (1982). Antecedents of mother-infant interaction and infant irritability in the first three years of life. *Infant Behavior and Development, 5,* 105-119.

Davis, M. (1986). Pharmacological and anatomical analysis of fear conditioning using the fear potentiated startle paradigm. *Behavioral Neuroscience, 100,* 814-824.

de Lanerolle, N. C., & Lang, F. F. (1988). Functional neural pathways for vocalization in the domestic cat. In J. D. Newman (Ed.), *Physiological control of mammalian vocalization* (pp. 21-42). New York: Plenum.

Dunnette, J., & Weinshilboum, R. (1982). Family studies of plasma-dopamine beta hydroxylase. *American Journal of Human Genetics, 34,* 84-99.

Eysenck, H. J. (1953). *The structure of human personality.* London: Methuen.

Frege, G. (1979). *Posthumous writings.* Chicago: University of Chicago Press.

Garcia-Coll, C., Kagan, J., & Reznick, J. S. (1984). Behavioral inhibition in young children. *Child Development, 55,* 1005-1019.

Jones, W. H., Hobbs, S. A., & Hockenbury, D. (1982). Loneliness and social skill deficits. *Journal of Personality and Social Psychology, 42,* 682-689.

Jung, C. G. (1924). *Psychological types.* New York: Harcourt Brace.

Jurgens, U. (1982). Amygdalar vocalization pathways in the squirrel monkey. *Brain Research, 241,* 189-196.

Kagan, J. (1989). Temperamental contributions to social behavior. *American Psychologist, 44,* 668-674.

Kagan, J., Kearsley, R., & Zelazo, P. (1978). *Infancy and its place in human development.* Cambridge, MA: Harvard University Press.

Kagan, J., & Moss, H. A. (1962). *Birth to maturity.* New York: John Wiley.

Kagan, J., Reznick, J. S., & Snidman, N. (1987). The physiology and psychology of behavioral inhibition. *Child Development, 58,* 1459-1473.

Kagan, J., Reznick, J. S., & Snidman, N. (1988). Biological bases of childhood shyness. *Science, 240,* 167-171.

Kagan, J., & Snidman, N. (1991). Infant predictors of inhibited and uninhibited behavioral profiles. *Psychological Science, 2,* 40-44.

Kagan, J., Snidman, N., Sellars, M. J., & Johnson, M. O. (1991). Temperament and allergic symptoms. *Psychosomatic Medicine, 53,* 332-340.

LaGasse, L. L., Gruber, C. P., & Lipsitt, L. P. (1989). The infantile expression of avidity in relation to later assessments of inhibition and attachment. In J. S. Reznick (Ed.), *Perspectives of behavioral inhibition* (pp. 159-176). Chicago: University of Chicago Press.

Manuck, S. B., Cohen, S., Rabin, B. S., Muldoon, M. F., & Bachen, E. A. (1991). Individual differences in cellular immune response to stress. *Psychological Science, 2*, 111-115.

Matheny, A. P. (1989). Children's behavioral inhibition over age and across situations. *Journal of Personality, 57*, 215-231.

Monk, R. (1990). *Ludwig Wittgenstein*. New York: Free Press.

Nesse, R. M., Curtis, G. C., Thyer, B. A., McCann, D. S., Huber-Smith, M., & Knopf, R. F. (1985). Endocrine and cardiovascular responses during phobic anxiety. *Psychosomatic Medicine, 47*, 320-332.

Plomin, R. (1986). *Development, genetics, and psychology*. Hillsdale, NJ: Lawrence Erlbaum.

Plomin, R., Campos, J., Corley, R., Emde, R. N., Fulker, D. W., Kagan, J., Reznick, J. S., Robinson, J., Zahn-Waxler, C., & De Freis, J. C. (1990). Individual differences during the second year of life: The MacArthur Longitudinal Twin Study. In J. Colombo & J. Fegan (Eds.), *Individual differences in infancy* (pp. 431-455). Hillsdale, NJ: Lawrence Erlbaum.

Porges, S. W. (1986). Respiratory sinus arrhythmya. In P. Grossman, R. H. Janssen, & D. Vaitl (Eds.), *Cardiorespiratory and cardiosomatic psychophysiology* (pp. 101-106). New York: Plenum.

Rogers, M. C., Battit, G., McPeek, P., & Todd, D. (1978). Lateralization of sympathetic control of the human sinus node. *Anesthesiology, 48*, 139-141.

Rosenberg, A., & Kagan, J. (1987). Iris pigmentation and behavioral inhibition. *Developmental Psychobiology, 20*, 377-392.

Rosenberg, A., & Kagan, J. (1989). Physical and psychological correlates of behavioral inhibition. *Developmental Psychobiology, 22*, 753-770.

Saper, C. B., Loewy, A. D., Swanson, L. W., & Cowan, W. M. (1976). Direct hypothalamo-autonomic connections. *Brain Research, 117*, 305-312.

Snidman, N. (1984). *Behavioral restraint and the central nervous system*. Unpublished doctoral dissertation, University of California, Los Angeles.

van den Boom, D. C. (1989). Neonatal irritability and the development of attachment. In J. A. Kohnstamm, J. E. Bates, & M. K. Rothbart (Eds.), *Temperament in childhood*. New York: John Wiley.

5

Emotion, Regulation, and the Development of Social Competence

NANCY EISENBERG
RICHARD A. FABES

Nancy Eisenberg is Regents' Professor of Psychology at Arizona State University. Her research interests are in social and emotional development, including the development of altruism, moral reasoning, social competence, and empathy and related emotional responses. She is the author of *Altruistic Emotion, Cognition, and Behavior* and *The Roots of Prosocial Behavior in Children* (coauthored with Paul Mussen). She is editor (with Janet Strayer) of *Empathy and Its Development*.

Richard A. Fabes is Associate Professor of Child Development in the Department of Family Resources and Human Development at Arizona State University. Currently, his research examines the relation between children's emotionality and their social interactions. He has written numerous articles on social and emotional development and has edited a volume (with Nancy Eisenberg) titled *Emotion and Self-Regulation in Childhood*.

After decades of neglect, there has been a flurry of recent work on the development and regulation of emotion in normal populations. As a consequence of this work, it has become clear that the emotions children express, and the ways they deal with their emotions, are related to a variety of social behaviors and to others' perceptions of the child. For example, variations in children's style of attachment to caregivers have been described as reflecting different styles of emotional regulation (Cicchetti, Ganiban, & Barnett, 1991; Pipp & Harmon, 1987)—styles believed to persist into adolescence and adulthood (Main, Kaplan, & Cassidy, 1985). Infants with anxious/avoidant attachments seem to overregulate to prevent becoming overwhelmed by negative emotion. In contrast, babies with anxious/ambivalent attachments seem to be underregulated and become overwhelmed by, and preoccupied with, negative emotion (Cicchetti et al., 1991).

AUTHORS' NOTE: The writing of this chapter was supported by a grant from the National Science Foundation (BNS8807784) to both authors and a Research Scientist Development Award from the National Institute of Mental Health (K02 MH00903-01) to Nancy Eisenberg.

The ways children manage and express their emotions also appear to be correlates of preschool and elementary school children's social competence and social status (Cummings & Cummings, 1988; Denham, 1986; Fabes & Eisenberg, 1992). For example, children tend to avoid those who express anger (Denham, 1986). Indeed, anger frequently seems to cause aggression (e.g., Camras, 1977; Cummings & Cummings, 1988), and hostile aggression seems to be associated with peer rejection (Coie, Dodge, & Kupersmidt, 1990). Children who cope with anger by means of behaviors such as revenge, venting of emotion, or tattling to adults tend to be less popular and are viewed as less socially competent by adults than children who deal more constructively with their anger (e.g., by asserting themselves; Fabes & Eisenberg, 1992).

Children experience negative emotions not only as a consequence of their own direct experience but also from vicariously induced negative emotions. Moreover, there are individual differences in how children deal with exposure to others' emotional arousal. For example, the observation of others' anger can result in dysregulated behavior, behavioral constriction, or concern for the person or persons expressing the anger, depending on the child's style of coping with the emotion (Cummings & Cummings, 1988).

In our own work, we have been particularly interested in individuals' emotional reactions to others' negative emotions or need. People exposed to others' sadness, distress, or need frequently experience empathy (i.e., experience the same, or nearly the same, emotion as the other person), and this empathic response sometimes is expressed as sympathy (i.e., other-oriented concern and sorrow based on the apprehension of the other's emotion or condition) and sometimes as predominantly personal distress (a self-focused, aversive reaction such as anxiety or discomfort in response to apprehending another's emotional state or condition). Those who experience sympathy frequently try to assist others in distress even if they can escape from dealing with the distressed person (Batson, 1987; Eisenberg & Fabes, 1990); in contrast, children who are anxious or distressed in reaction to others' negative emotions often avoid dealing with the distressing situation (Eisenberg & Fabes, 1990) or may even respond aggressively (Radke-Yarrow & Zahn-Waxler, 1984).

We view these individual differences as partially due to differences among people in level of vicarious emotional responding. Hoffman (1982) suggested that overarousal due to empathy results in a self-focus;

consistent with this view, negative emotional arousal in general seems to engender a focus on the self (e.g., Wood, Saltzberg, & Goldsamt, 1990; Wood, Saltzberg, Neale, Stone, & Rachmiel, 1990). We believe empathic overarousal is experienced as self-focused personal distress (Eisenberg, Bernzweig, & Fabes, 1992). If this is the case, individuals who are unable to maintain their emotional reactions within a tolerable range (and therefore tend to become overaroused) would be expected to focus on their own needs and to behave in ways that do not necessarily facilitate positive interactions in social situations involving negative emotion.

Our findings in regard to vicarious emotional responding and children's social behaviors also have led us to believe that children's abilities to regulate their vicarious emotional responding are linked to their general social competence. For example, we have found that children prone to sympathetic responding are relatively likely to spontaneously assist others in their social interactions (Eisenberg, McCreath, & Ahn, 1988). Moreover, in prior work, we found that children who tend to assist others spontaneously are emotionally expressive in response to peers' behaviors (Eisenberg, Cameron, Tryon, & Dodez, 1981), are relatively social and assertive (Eisenberg, Pasternack, Cameron, & Tryon, 1984; Eisenberg et al., 1981), and tend to express relatively low levels of egoistic moral reasoning and high levels of other-oriented, primitive empathic reasoning (Eisenberg-Berg & Hand, 1979; Eisenberg et al., 1984).

In contrast, children prone to express personal distress appear to be relatively nonassertive with their peers and perform relatively high levels of compliant prosocial behaviors (Eisenberg et al., 1988, 1990). Children (particularly boys) who perform high levels of compliant behaviors seem to be seen as easy victims by peers and do not receive positive reactions from peers when they assist (Eisenberg et al., 1981, 1988; also see Rubin & Borwick, 1984). Moreover, children who frequently perform compliant prosocial behaviors are less sociable than are children who are high in spontaneous prosocial behavior (although they are not extremely low in social interactions; Eisenberg et al., 1981), and compliant prosocial behavior does not seem to be related to children's prosocial moral reasoning (Eisenberg et al., 1984).

In general, then, it appears that children who are prone to sympathetic reactions are well regulated in regard to both their emotional responding and their behavior in social interactions. This conclusion is consistent with the argument that sympathetic/empathic involvement in others' emotional states, as well as the capacity to cope with aversive or distressing emotions, are components of social and emotional competence (Saarni, 1990; Salovey & Mayer, 1990). In contrast, children who experience high levels of personal distress, particularly boys, seem to be nonassertive and relatively low in social competence. We hypothesize that these children have difficulty dealing with their own and others' emotions and therefore frequently comply with others' demands and requests as a way of curtailing unpleasant social interactions and the resultant negative emotion. People who are easily overaroused by negative emotion typically may have difficulty dealing constructively with emotionally evocative situations.

Research such as that just described has led to questions about the factors that influence whether individuals become emotionally overaroused in social interactions and the implications of style of emotion management for social behavior. We now turn to these larger issues.

DETERMINANTS OF LEVEL OF EMOTIONAL AROUSAL

We recently have begun to focus on two person variables that probably influence whether individuals become emotionally overaroused in social contexts: (a) the individual's dispositional level of emotional responsivity, particularly the intensity and threshold of responding (which may be aspects of temperament; Rothbart & Derryberry, 1981; Thomas, Chess, & Birch, 1968), and (b) individuals' abilities to regulate (modulate) their emotional reactions and cope with the evocative situation (Derryberry & Rothbart, 1988; Lazarus & Folkman, 1984). Of course, we believe many other factors contribute to the development of sympathy, including the nature of one's ties to others and socialization experiences (e.g., Eisenberg, Fabes, Carlo, & Karbon, 1992; Eisenberg, Fabes, Schaller, Carlo, & Miller, 1991).

Emotional Intensity

By *emotional intensity* (EI), we mean stable individual differences in the typical intensity with which individuals experience their emotions (affective intensity, as defined by Larsen & Diener, 1987) and in threshold to relatively intense levels of emotional responding (which should be highly correlated with frequency of responding). Although emotional intensity and threshold to emotional responding are not identical, they are moderately highly correlated (Mary Rothbart, personal communication, 1991). Both the intensity of emotional experiences and the ease with which individuals respond intensely would be expected to contribute to the degree to which individuals become emotionally aroused in a given situation. Similar to others, we view EI as an aspect of temperament, one with considerable intraindividual consistency (Larsen & Diener, 1987; Rothbart & Derryberry, 1981; also see Plomin & Stocker, 1989).

In line with Larsen's definition of affective intensity, we believe that EI can reflect intensity and threshold of both positive and negative emotional responding, particularly for adults (Larsen & Diener, 1987). This definition contrasts with those of emotionality (Buss & Plomin, 1984), neuroticism (Eysenck, 1967), and negative affectivity (Watson & Clark, 1984)—all of which refer only to negative emotionality. Consistent with this argument, Larsen's measure of affective intensity is positively correlated with negative affectivity (Larsen & Diener, 1987) as well as with subjective ratings of positive events (Larsen, Diener, & Emmons, 1986; although it is unrelated to global indexes of well-being; Larsen & Diener, 1987). However, given that the amount of variance accounted for by the correlation between negative and positive affective intensity is approximately 50%, it is possible that some people who score high in affective intensity experience particularly intense negative emotions (and not intense positive emotions) whereas others experience particularly intense positive emotions. Only a portion of individuals high in emotional intensity may be prone to high-intensity positive and negative emotions.

As might be expected, individual differences in emotional intensity appear to be associated with emotional reactions in specific distressing or stressful situations. For example, Eisenberg et al. (1991) found that adults' scores on a scale of dispositional affective intensity (the AIM; Larsen & Diener, 1987) were modestly positively associated with skin conductance in response to a sympathy-evoking film ($r = .26, p < .05$) and reported vicarious emotional responding to a distressing film ($r = .28, p < .01$). In another study with adults, Derryberry and Rothbart (1988) obtained positive correlations between measures of dispositional autonomic reactivity and sadness, fear, frustration, and discomfort. In addition, people who tend to react empathically or sympathetically to others in distress seem to be relatively high in emotional intensity and low in the tendency to screen or block less essential sensory stimulation (Larsen, Diener, & Cropanzano, 1987; Mehrabian, 1980).

In thinking about emotional intensity, it is useful to differentiate it not only from negative emotionality (e.g., Watson & Clark, 1984) but also from baseline physiological reactivity. Larsen (Larsen & Diener, 1987) has proposed that people high in affective intensity use emotion for stimulation, that is, they "develop strong emotional responsiveness to compensate for an otherwise chronically low level of baseline arousal" (p. 30). In his view, people high in EI apparently do not go out and seek emotionally charged situations (i.e., sensation seek; Zuckerman, 1979); rather, they seem more reactive to the stimuli they do encounter (Larsen et al., 1986). The data support this argument (Larsen et al., 1986); they suggest that sensation seeking, stimuli augmentation (i.e., augmenting sensory stimuli), and intensifying emotional responses are alternative (but not mutually exclusive) ways of regulating baseline reactivity. It is possible, however, that some individuals low in baseline arousal are low in part because they have high thresholds to stimulation. If this is true, emotional intensity and low baseline physiological arousal may not be positively related.

Regulatory Processes

The second individual difference of interest, relevant regulation processes, can be viewed in at least two different but interrelated ways. First, regulation as viewed by persons studying temperament involves regulation of impinging stimuli and internal states, using mechanisms such as shifting attention away from an arousing or unpleasant stimulus to modulate distress (attentional shifting), the ability to sustain attention (attentional focusing), activational control (voluntary initiation or continuance of action, i.e., approach mechanisms), and inhibitory control (inhibition of action; Rothbart & Derryberry, 1981). People who can regulate their emotional reactivity through allocating attention appear to react more positively to stressful events. For example, the abilities to shift or focus attention have been negatively associated with reported susceptibility to negative emotion, particularly frustration and fear (Derryberry & Rothbart, 1988). Moreover, among adults, inhibitory control has been negatively related to autonomic reactivity and frustration and has been positively related to falling reactivity as well as attentional shifting and focusing (Derryberry & Rothbart, 1988). In addition, children, especially infants, may regulate their emotional arousal with self-stimulatory or self-soothing behaviors (Rothbart, Ziaie, & O'Boyle, 1992), and people of all ages may regulate emotional inputs from others by means of their social communications (e.g., facial, gestural, and vocal expressions; Rothbart & Derryberry, 1981).

Second, regulation can be viewed as changing cognitive and behavioral efforts to manage specific external or internal demands that are appraised as taxing or exceeding the resources of the individual (i.e., coping; Lazarus & Folkman, 1984). Two general modes of coping have been differentiated: problem focused (efforts to modify the source of the problem) and emotion focused (efforts to reduce emotional distress). Thus coping behaviors include ways of modulating the degree of emotional arousal by altering the experience of emotion (e.g., with reality-distorting processes, by switching one's attention to some different aspect of the situation, or by involving oneself in a distracting or soothing activity in a given situation) as well as mechanisms for changing aspects of the emotion-laden situation (e.g., by orienting to the situation, by displaying postural and facial cues indicative of one's inner state, and by enacting behaviors that alter the situation; also see Case, Hayward, Lewis, & Hurst, 1988). Although regulatory and coping skills tend to be implemented somewhat differently (e.g., temperament researchers tend not to study problem-focused coping but are more likely than coping researchers to assess behaviors directly such as allocation of attention), emotional regulation is an inherent aspect of emotion-focused coping. Moreover, individuals who can regulate their emotional arousal are likely to cope in relatively constructive and controlled ways; indeed, Lazarus and Folkman (1984) argued that in many situations people first need to regulate negative emotions to facilitate problem-solving coping.

Models of the Role of Self/Emotion Regulation and Emotional Arousability in Social Behavior

We believe that social behavior varies as a function of the interaction between emotional arousability (including reactivity and intensity) and regulatory/coping skills. Prior to presenting our own model, we briefly review some of the ways that psychologists have discussed this interaction.

Fox's model and the research on heart rate variability. Fox (1989a) explicitly predicted the behavioral outcomes that result from the interaction between reactivity and self-regulation. He based his predictions on the results of research on the relation of vagal tone to infants' behaviors and expressivity.

Vagal tone is a measure of heart rate (HR) variability that is believed to reflect the individual's level of parasympathetic nervous system regulation (Porges, 1991). Researchers have argued that the vagal tone may provide a physiological metaphor for the regulation of emotional states (Porges, 1991), the interaction of reactivity and self-regulation (Fox, 1989a; Stifter & Fox, 1990), and coping with stress (Jemerin & Boyce, 1990).

Research findings on the relation of vagal tone to infants' behavior are not straightforward. In general, infants with high vagal tone (high HR variability) appear to display negative reactions when frustrated but are active, expressive, and unafraid of novelty (Fox, 1989a, 1989b). High vagal tone infants seem to have good attentional regulation (Porges, 1991) but appear to be somewhat difficult. For example, they may be difficult to soothe (Stifter & Fox, 1990) and often appear to be insecurely attached (Izard et al., 1991). Porges (1991) argued that vagal tone is correlated with self-regulation, but some infants with high vagal tone are fussy because they have difficulty self-soothing and maintaining a calm state.

After infancy, however, high vagal tone and other measures of HR variability (all of which tend to be significantly associated, although some measures may reflect sympathetic as well as parasympathetic nervous system responding; Fox, 1989b; Izard et al., 1991) generally have been associated with behaviors that appear to reflect optimal self-regulation and expressivity. For example, by the time children enter nursery school, those with high vagal tone were rated by their mothers as having an easy temperament and showed a greater increase in play and in group entry behavior during the first six weeks of nursery school than did children with lower vagal tone (Fox, 1989b). Moreover, children with high HR variability appear to be sociable, expressive, and uninhibited whereas those with high, stable HRs tend to be shy, inhibited, and more fearful (Fox, 1989a; Reznick et al., 1986; see Reznick, 1989).

Based on findings such as those just described, Fox (1989a) proposed a model of how levels of reactivity and regulation interact to produce different modes of infant behavior (see Table 5.1). For example, those high in regulation and reactivity are expected to be expressive, social, and uninhibited whereas those high in reactivity and low on regulation are uncontrollable and hyperactive.

Although Fox's model may be useful for summarizing the findings concerning infants' and young children's vagal tone, we had difficulty adapting it for the prediction of children's social behaviors and social competence. One difficulty concerns the definition of *regulation* in the various cells. In the high reactivity-*high* regulation cell, the infant is described as expressive, social, and uninhibited; thus infants in this cell appear to be somewhat *low* in inhibitory control and relatively high in activational control (the ability to initiate and maintain behavior). Low reactivity-*high* regulation infants (described as nonexpressive, inhibited, and highly controlled), however, would seem to be *high* in inhibitory control, low in activational control, and low to moderate in attentional control (because, if attentional self-regulation were being used effectively, high inhibition probably would not be necessary).

Thus the definition of *high regulation* changes in the high versus low reactivity cells. Moreover, in the high reactivity-low regulation cell, the children are described as low in inhibitory regulation (i.e., as uncontrollable and hyperactive), whereas, in the low-low cell, they are described in ways that suggest moderate to high inhibitory control, low activation control, and perhaps low attentional regulation (i.e., as depressed and socially withdrawn). Again, the definition of *regulation* is varied. Moreover, one wonders if children low in both reactivity and regulation would be depressed and socially withdrawn; it seems reasonable to hypothesize that they might be erratic in their behavior and perhaps even sensation seeking and manipulative if low reactivity reflects low baseline arousal level (see Eysenck, 1967; Zuckerman, 1979).

The Blocks' dimensions of ego control and ego resiliency. An analysis of Fox's model led us to the conclusion that it was necessary to consider both inhibitory and activational regulation, as well as attentional processes and other modes of coping, in a model of the interaction between emotional intensity and self-regulation in children. The work of Block and Block (1980) on ego control and ego resiliency is useful for conceptualizing the role of inhibitory regulation in social behavior.

TABLE 5.1 Interaction of Reactivity and Regulation

Reactivity	Regulation	
	High	*Low*
High	Expressive Sociable Uninhibited	Uncontrollable Hyperactive
Low	Nonexpressive Inhibited Highly controlled	Depressed Socially withdrawn

SOURCE: From Fox (1989b, in *Developmental Psychology*); used by permission of the American Psychological Association.

According to the Blocks, *ego control* refers to the threshold or operating characteristic of an individual with regard to the expression or containment of impulses, feelings, and desires. *Overcontrol* is characterized by "the containment of impulse, delay of gratification, inhibition of action, and insulation from environmental distractors" (p. 43). The opposite end of the continuum, *undercontrol,* is described as "insufficient modulation of impulse, the inability to delay gratification, immediate and direct expression of motivations and affects, and vulnerability to environmental distractors" (p. 43). Presuming equivalence in motivation and the environmental context,

> the ego overcontroller is expected to have a high modal threshold for response, to be constrained and inhibited, to manifest needs and impulses relatively indirectly, to delay gratification unduly, to show minimal expression of emotion, to tend to be categorical and overly exclusive in processing information, to be perseverative, nondistractible, less exploratory, relatively conforming, with narrow and unchanging interests, to be relatively planful and organized, and to be made uneasy by and therefore avoidant of ambiguous or inconsistent situations. In contrast, the ego undercontroller can be expected to have a low modal threshold for response, to be expressive, spontaneous, to manifest needs and impulses relatively directly into behavior, to tend toward the immediate gratification of desires, to readily manifest feelings and emotional fluctuations, to be overly inclusive in processing information, to have many but relatively short-lived enthusiasms and interests, to be distractible, more ready to explore, less conforming, relatively comfortable with or undiscerning of ambiguity and incon-

sistency, to manifest actions that cut across conventional categories of response in ways that are (for better or for worse) original, and to live life on an ad hoc, impromptu basis. (p. 44)

The Blocks' second dimension, *ego resiliency,* refers to the dynamic capacity of individuals to modify their modal level of ego control as a function of the demands of the environment. At one extreme of the dimension, *ego resiliency* is defined as resourceful adaptation to changing circumstances and contingencies, analysis of the fit between situational demands and behavioral possibilities, and the flexible use of the available repertoire of problem-solving strategies (broadly defined to include social and personal as well as cognitive strategies). The other end of the continuum, called *ego brittleness,* implies little adaptive flexibility, an inability to respond to changing demands, a tendency to perseverate or become disorganized when confronted with changes in circumstances or when stressed, and difficulty in recovering from traumatic experiences.

The Blocks differentiated the construct of ego resiliency from that of coping because coping often is defined in ways that are not independent of the outcome, that is, of whether the behavior "works." Their notion of ego resiliency, however, is quite similar to Lazarus and Folkman's (1984) definition of coping.

In an impressive longitudinal study, the Blocks obtained considerable support for their constructs. For example, undercontrolled preschool children (as assessed outside the classroom) were classified by their teachers as more active, assertive, aggressive, competitive, outgoing, attention seeking, unable to delay gratification, overreactive to frustration, jealous, and exploitive and less compliant, orderly, yielding, shy, reflective, private, helpful, or considerate than overcontrolled children. Ego resilient children, in comparison with ego brittle children, were able to cope with stress and were empathic, self-accepting, bright, appropriate in their expression of emotion, novelty seeking, fluent, self-reliant, creative, and competent. They also were less in need of assurance, conflicted and anxious, suspicious, and sulky. At age 7, the findings were similar, albeit fewer in number (perhaps due to the method of measurement).

The Blocks repeatedly noted that they found no statistical relation between measures of ego resiliency and ego control and argued that the two constructs were independent. They also noted, however, that "extreme placement at either end of the ego-control continuum implies a constancy in mode of behavior that, given a varying world, can be expected to be adaptively dysfunctional" (p. 44). This statement seems to reflect the belief that moderate ego control is adaptive and entails flexibility. Indeed, children who are not overly or undercontrolled would probably be good copers and possess many of the positive qualities associated with ego resiliency. Thus we would predict that there is a relation between ego control and ego resiliency, but this relation is nonlinear. Specifically, we would expect ego resiliency to be negatively related to both ego overcontrol and undercontrol but to be positively related to moderate control.

We are not claiming that the constructs of ego control and ego resiliency are synonymous; moderate ego control may not always be associated with the flexibility and ability to adapt that is the hallmark of the construct of ego resiliency. Nonetheless, ego resiliency, by definition, would seem to be very different from, and negatively related to, under- or overcontrol (which are not characterized by flexibility), and ego resiliency generally would be expected to be evidenced in individuals who are not over- or undercontrolled. Consistent with this argument is Arend, Gove, and Sroufe's (1979) finding that securely attached children were high on resiliency and between the avoidant babies (who were overly controlled) and the anxious/resistant babies (who were low on ego control) on ego control.

Pulkkinen's model. Pulkkinen (1982, 1986), like the Blocks, has conducted longitudinal research concerning self-control; however, the primary focus of her work has been on aggression. Nonetheless, her work is relevant to this chapter.

Pulkkinen presents a model of impulse control in which the two major dimensions are "neutralization of the intrinsic or emotional aspect of aggression" and the "suppression of the extrinsic or behavioral aspects of aggression" (1982, p. 68). Thus Pulkkinen differentiates between control of emotion and suppression of the outward expression of emotionally driven behavior. For example, children who do not neutralize emotional experience and have weak self-control are hypothesized to exhibit uncontrolled expression of impulses (i.e., aggression); those who do not neutralize the emotion but suppress the overt behavior are described as exhibiting uncontrolled inhibition of impulses (e.g., anxiety). High neutralization of emotion and high suppression of behavior are seen as producing controlled inhibition of impulses (i.e., submission), and neutralization of emotional impulses with high levels of behavioral expression is seen as resulting in the controlled expression of impulses (i.e., constructive behavioral responses).

Pulkkinen (1982, 1986) suggested that cognitive appraisals and cognitive coping strategies frequently are used to neutralize the emotional aspect of aggression, and that the cognitive capacities used to control emotion develop with age. One also might hypothesize, however, that the likelihood of neutralizing emotion depends, in part, on the intensity of the individual's emotional response. In contrast, Pulkkinen argues that the suppression of the behavioral aspect of aggression is dependent on external controllers such as the superior power of an attacker or parental negative sanctions. As a result of suppression, an individual's responses are avoidant, and he or she uses behaviors such as crying or withdrawal.

In a circumplex model, Pulkkinen (1982) mapped her theoretical model onto the characteristics of adolescents (20-year-olds). Based on a factor analysis, she obtained two bipolar factors for the adolescents' behaviors: Reveller versus Loner and Striver versus Loser. The Strivers were well adjusted, successful, made friends easily, had strong self-control, and were constructive. Pulkkinen viewed them as relatively high on inhibition of impulses and as not suppressing behavior (e.g., as being relatively active and exhibiting controlled expression of impulses). The Losers had problems of adjustment and lacked self-confidence; had difficulties concentrating; were afraid of the future and dissatisfied with choices; did poorly in school, were unemployed, and had few plans for themselves; watched TV excessively; smoked excessively; had no obligations toward society or opinions about politics; and had difficulty making friends. These people were characterized as exhibiting weak emotional control and high inhibition of behavior. The Revellers were sociable and made friends easily; were not dependent on parents; had conflicts with them, and often were angry and quarreled; smoked, drank, and had sex at a young age; were active and energetic; and spent free time in discos and restaurants. They were viewed as neither neutralizing emotions nor suppressing behavior. Finally, the Loners, who were viewed as controlling impulses and inhibiting behavior, were socially passive, shy, tense, quiet, dependent on parents, had few friends, and did not use drugs, alcohol, or date.

Thus, in Pulkkinen's model and research, the most positive outcomes seem to be associated with strong emotional control and low levels of suppression of behavior (i.e., with being socially active). As defined in her research, behavioral suppression is not advantageous for people who can control their emotions. Pulkkinen's definition of behavioral suppression, however, is general passivity versus activity, and suppression is viewed as externally driven; thus she does not seem to be talking about internalized behavioral control based on mature self-control or coping skills. We would argue that mature coping and self-regulation skills can be the basis for both the neutralization of emotion and the suppression of behavior. In addition, like the Blocks, we suggest that flexible and moderate levels of control probably are optimal. We agree with Pulkkinen, however, that inhibition of behavior frequently results in anxiety or submissiveness, and the lack of emotional or behavioral controls is associated with aggressive and erratic behavior. Also, we believe that her distinction between the regulation of emotional arousal (henceforth called emotion regulation) and of behavior (henceforth called self-regulation) is important.

A Model of the Role of Regulation in Emotional and Behavioral Responding

Figure 5.1 is a model of our current thoughts about the role of emotion regulation and self-regulation in emotional responding. This model is adapted from Rothbart and Derryberry's (1981) model of a framework for studying temperament.

In this model, features of a stimulus or social situation are evaluated in terms of their potential for reward and punishment (Gray, 1971), and this evaluative process usually elicits the use of various forms of emotion regulation. These regulatory processes, in turn, may influence what characteristics of stimuli are processed and the nature of evaluative processes. Internal response systems such as the autonomic nervous system and endocrine system may be directly activated by aspects of the stimulus situation (such as the intensity of the stimulus); moreover, emotion regulation processes influence the reactions of internal response systems.

Once internal responses are activated, they result in the internal experience of emotion. Resultant internal emotional responses may elicit further use of emotional regulation mechanisms in an attempt to modulate the intensity or duration of emotional responding. In addition, the experience of emotion results in behavioral and cognitive responses (including self-regulatory processes) such as the overt expression or

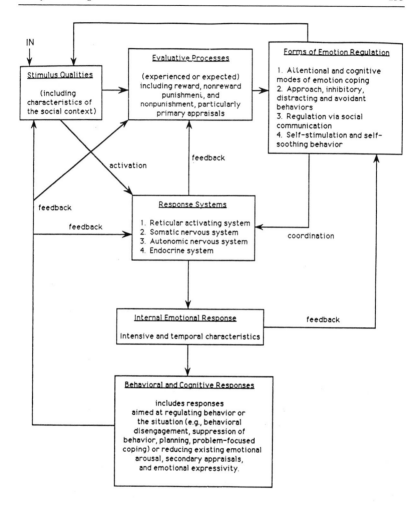

Figure 5.1. Model of the Role of Self-Regulation in Emotion and Emotion-Based Behavior

SOURCE: Adapted from Rothbart and Derryberry (1981).

inhibition of emotion (e.g., gestural and facial reactions), further cognitive appraisals regarding the possible implications of the situation and experiencing the given emotion, suppression of behavior, planning, problem-focused coping, and/or behavioral responses such as aggression. The resultant behavioral responses generally are attempts to deal with the situation or regulate one's own behavior. Finally, some reactions such as the facial expression of emotion may feed back and influence the internal experience of emotion (e.g., Izard, 1990); moreover, behaviors and cognitions that result from the experience of emotion may alter the context (e.g., may alter others' responses to the individual) and how the person assesses the potential for reward or punishment in the given context.

Although not represented clearly in Figure 5.1, it is also important to note that the environment shapes, in part, children's coping strategies and the development of regulatory processes and socially relevant cognitions (Kopp, 1982; Rizzo & Corsaro, 1988; Vygotsky, 1978). Self-regulation in social interaction appears to have at least some of its origins in the cognitive structures that are constructed in the social context. Moreover, as noted above, the individual's reactions to emotional arousal help to shape his or her social environment.

For the purpose of this chapter, perhaps the most important feature of the model is that there are forms of regulation that more directly control the experience of emotion (emotion regulation) and those that are involved in the expression, suppression, and shaping of behaviors that result from the experience of emotion (self-regulation). Which behaviors people use to regulate their own emotion, behavior, or the emotion-laden situation likely vary due to an interaction between the individual's cognitive appraisals and strategies, abilities (including the ability to inhibit behavior and to use mental strategies), and values, needs, and goals.

Correlates of the Interaction Between Regulatory Style and Emotional Intensity

In Table 5.2, we present a model of the hypothesized correlates associated with different levels of EI and style of regulation (especially emotion regulation). Our predictions generally are based on both theory and existing empirical research, but in some cases they are based more on logic than available data. We view this model as a heuristic for thinking about the roles of emotionality and regulation in social behavior.

In this model, the construct of *emotional intensity* is defined as stable differences in the strength with which individuals typically experience emotions (see our earlier discussion). These differences are due to individual differences in both the magnitude with which emotions are experienced (when they are experienced) as well as in the ease with which people experience intense emotions. We believe that this dimension is in part the consequence of how people regulate emotion (so one can never totally separate emotional intensity and regulation). In the model, we discuss *moderately* high and low levels of emotional intensity; it is likely that people who are extremely high or low in emotional intensity differ in important ways from other people and that extremes in intensity are associated with psychopathology.

It was difficult to decide how to conceptualize levels of regulation in the model because there are so many types of emotion regulation and self-regulation (e.g., attentional mechanisms, inhibitory control, positive cognitive restructuring), and regulation can occur in terms of modulating the experience of the emotion or the associated behavior or situation (see Table 5.2). Moreover, it sometimes is difficult to separate regulation of emotion and regulation of emotionally based behavior because similar overt behaviors can be used for both (e.g., inhibition of behavior to limit exposure to stimulation or to control unwanted behaviors). Given this caveat, we tried to select dimensions that capture some of the interesting patterns in the literature, and we did not try to clearly differentiate between mechanisms used to alter one's own emotional experience, the situation, or one's own behavior.

The levels of regulation chosen were (a) highly controlled, which involves high use of inhibition and underuse of adaptive strategies such as attentional strategies and activation control, (b) optimal regulation, which is defined by flexibility and the ability to respond effectively to changing environmental conditions and demands (and probably involves quite a few attentional processes), and (c) underregulation, which reflects low use of inhibitory control and other adaptive strategies such as attentional mechanisms and planning. In this model, we assume that the relatively high use of attentional mechanisms generally is adaptive because individuals can shift and focus attention as needed and thereby regulate both their level of emotion (Derryberry & Rothbart, 1988; Gianino & Tronick, 1988; Rothbart, Ziaie, & O'Boyle, 1992) and their ability to delay and regulate behavior (Block & Block, 1980; Mischel & Mischel, 1976; Silverman & Ragusa, 1990). As with nearly any mechanism, however, the extreme use of attentional mechanisms may be maladaptive (e.g., may result in very high levels of avoiding input).

TABLE 5.2 The Interaction of Self-Regulation and Emotional Reactivity: Hypothesized Correlates

Emotional Intensity (disregarding valence)	Style of Regulation		
	Highly Controlled (high inhibitory control; low activational control; underuse of adaptive attentional, social communicative, and other mechanisms)	*Optimal Regulation* (moderate use of inhibitory control; relatively high use of activational control, attentional and social communicative mechanisms, planning and problem-focused coping; flexible use of self-regulatory mechanisms)	*Underregulation* (low in inhibition; underuse of adaptive attentional, activational control, problem-focused or emotion-focused mechanisms)
Moderately high	Inhibited Expressive at a young age but learns to inhibit overt expressions of emotion Shy Low to average social skills Prone to reactive (emotion-induced) withdrawal Lack of flexibility in coping Prone to anxiety and personal distress	Expressive Interpersonally engaging Sociable Socially competent and popular Constructive coping behaviors Resilient Prone to sympathy and spontaneous prosocial behavior Prone to high levels of positive emotion	Uncontrolled, active behavior Sociable or extroverted Frequently controversial or rejected children (particularly boys) Nonconstructive ways of coping with emotion Prone to reactive aggression Low in prosocial behavior Prone to personal distress, frustration, and negative affectivity

Moderately low		
Inhibited and passive	Placid	Erratic behavior
Highly controlled	Average expressiveness	Extroverted and sensation seeking
Nonexpressive	Sociable	Low to average popularity
Unsociable or introverted	Socially competent and popular	Often nonconstructive coping
Prone to proactive withdrawal	Constructive coping behaviors	Prone to proactive aggression and manipulative behavior
Low to average social skills and popularity	Resilient	Low in prosocial behavior and vicarious emotional responding
Lack of flexibility in coping	Moderately high in prosocial behavior and sympathy	
Somewhat flat effect	Prone to positive emotion	

In the model, we also try to differentiate among shyness, sociability, introversion, and extroversion. Shyness is viewed as inhibited and awkward behavior with strangers or acquaintances, accompanied by feelings of tension and distress and a tendency to want to escape from the social situation (Buss & Plomin, 1984). Thus it involves behavioral inhibition and avoidance tendencies (see Bruch, Gorsky, Collins, & Berger, 1989; Gersten, 1989), although these may be combined with anxiety due to some desire to approach others (Asendorpf, 1990; Buss & Plomin, 1975; Cheek & Buss, 1981). In contrast, unsociable or introverted people display a nonfearful preference for not affiliating with others (i.e., they prefer solitude but have the ability to interact when necessary; Asendorpf, 1990; Bruch et al., 1989), whereas sociability implies the preference for affiliation or a need to be with people and perhaps interest in people (Asendorpf, 1990; Buss & Plomin, 1975; Cheek & Buss, 1981). Finally, extroverted people approach others and like to affiliate, but extroversion (as viewed by Eysenck, 1967) involves using people as a source of stimulation rather than true social interest in others (Buss & Plomin, 1975; Eysenck, 1967). Among these various constructs, it is shyness that appears to be most associated with negative affect and dysfunctional behaviors (Bruch et al., 1989; Reznick, 1989).

In our model, optimal regulation, like ego resiliency (Block & Block, 1980), is associated with the most positive, adaptive behavior, although social behavior is seen as varying somewhat as a function of individual differences in emotional intensity. Children and adults who can use inhibitory and activational control and attentional and other modes of regulation flexibly and appropriately are seen as sociable, relatively popular, socially competent, and prone to experience positive emotion. Those high in emotional intensity also are viewed as expressive, interpersonally engaging, and prone to experience sympathy and to assist others spontaneously . These predictions are consistent with Block and Block's (1980) findings and with research indicating an association of emotional intensity with sociability and reactivity (Larsen & Diener, 1987); associations among sympathy, spontaneous prosocial behavior, and expressiveness (e.g., Eisenberg et al., 1981, 1988, 1990); correlations between social competence or social status, adaptive coping behaviors, and sociocognitive development (Coie et al., 1990; Dodge & Feldman, 1990; Fabes & Eisenberg, 1992); and correlations among positive affect, prosocial behaviors, and social competence or popularity (e.g., Coie & Dodge, 1988; Coie et al., 1990; Denham, 1986).

Because people high in emotional intensity are likely to be prone to vicarious emotional arousal (Eisenberg et al., 1991; Larsen et al., 1987) and also have the emotion-regulation skills necessary to modulate vicarious emotional arousal (and thereby prevent feelings of personal distress), they are expected to be relatively sympathetic (Eisenberg, Bernzweig, et al., in press). In fact, effective regulatory skills have been associated with infants' low levels of personal distress (Ungerer et al., 1990).

Because they generally experience less intense levels of emotion, optimally regulated, less emotionally intense people are hypothesized to be somewhat placid, only average in expressiveness, and moderately high in sympathy and prosocial behavior. To our knowledge, however, there is relatively little research concerning the differences between resilient, well-adapted people who are more and less emotionally reactive.

Individuals in the moderately high emotional intensity, underregulated cell are assumed to be uncontrolled and active, to exhibit low levels of delay and high levels of frustration, to be low in social skills and prosocial behavior and prone to personal distress and reactive aggression (i.e., aggression based upon emotional arousal; Hartup, 1974). Although they may be sociable or extroverted, they are expected to be frequently rejected by peers because of their aggression and lack of social skills or to be liked by some peers and disliked by others (i.e., controversial; see Coie & Dodge, 1988; Coie et al., 1990). Underregulated persons who are moderately low in emotional intensity also are assumed to be low in prosocial behavior and sympathy and to engage in nonconstructive modes of coping; however, they are hypothesized to be extroverted and sensation seeking, low to average in popularity, and prone to proactive or instrumental aggression (referring to a relatively nonemotional display of aggression characterized by a focus on goals) and manipulation of others.

These predictions are consistent with a number of findings. First, ego undercontrol is associated with a rapid personal tempo and restlessness; self-assertion, aggression, and teasing of others; low delay of gratification and overreactivity to frustration; sociability and low levels of shyness; low levels of prosocial and cooperative behavior; jealousy and crying easily; lack of obedience, compliance, and planfulness; regression under stress; and inattentiveness and inability to concentrate (Block & Block, 1980). In addition, lack of impulse control and low self-regulation have been associated with aggression and inability to delay behavior (e.g.,

Olson, 1989; Olweus, 1980; Pulkkinen, 1986; Silverman & Ragusa, 1990), although the association between undercontrol and undesirable behaviors may be somewhat weaker in adolescents than in younger children (particularly for girls; see Block & Block, 1980; Block & Gjerde, 1986). Thus one would expect individuals low in self-regulation to have difficulties coping in constructive ways and behaving prosocially.

The research also is consistent with the view that underregulated persons who are high in emotional intensity may be particularly prone to reactive aggression and uncontrolled behavior. People high in EI are active and arousable (Larsen & Diener, 1987), and temperamental intensity has been associated with proneness to angry outbursts, emotional upset, and aggressions (although negative emotionality and activity level account for more variance in aggression than does intensity; Teglasi & MacMahon, 1990). Hotheaded, active boys are particularly likely to aggress (Olweus, 1980), and Thomas et al. (1968) found that young children who were high on intensity, and had low thresholds for response, were active, irregular, low on adaptability, high on distractibility, and prone to behavior problems, including aggression, during childhood. In our own research, we have found that preschoolers high in both intensity of anger experiences and general emotional intensity were particularly likely to become angry, to engage in reactive aggression or avoidance when angered, and to score low on measures of social competence (Fabes & Eisenberg, in press).

In addition, because of their limited ability to regulate emotion, people who are relatively high in emotional intensity and underregulation are unlikely to experience sympathy for others; rather, they are likely to experience personal distress (Eisenberg, Bernzweig, et al., 1992; Ungerer et al., 1990). Further, individuals who are prone to high levels of emotion may process social information differently than other people and therefore may be prone to react inappropriately or aggressively (see Dodge, 1991). Because of their high approach tendencies and their emotional intensity, however, they would be expected to be relatively interested in other people (Larsen & Diener, 1987), albeit not very sensitive to others' needs.

Because many socially rejected children tend to display hyperactivity, disruptiveness, and aggression (particularly boys), aggressive socially rejected children (Coie et al., 1990), especially boys, are expected to cluster in this cell. It is important to note, however, that aggression is not always associated with peer rejection (e.g., Coie & Dodge, 1988), and some rejected children often are socially interactive (Coie & Kupersmidt, 1983). Moreover, aggressive/withdrawn children also may fall into this grouping. Rubin, LeMare, and Lollis (1990) discussed one group of children who are hostile, aggressive, and rejected by their peers and, in middle to late childhood, may become isolated from their peer group. Such children are hypothesized to be fussy, overactive, and difficult to soothe as neonates and are seen as becoming hostile and aggressive as a consequence of the interaction between their temperament and maternal characteristics (e.g., aggressive, anxious, low in nurturance) and attitudes (e.g., authoritarian, hostile, with limited concern for socializing and social competence), with the latter maternal variables being influenced by socioecological conditions (e.g., the financial situation, cultural norms) and the personal-social setting of the parent (e.g., mental health status, availability of emotional and social support). These children are not viewed initially as being shy or behaviorally inhibited; rather, they become socially withdrawn as a consequence of peer rejection. Nonetheless, because of their isolation from peers, they, as well as aggressive, nonwithdrawn children, are deprived of the developmental benefits of peer negotiation, discourse, and play and are likely to develop a variety of deficits in sociocognitive and social skills (Rubin, Hymel, & Chen, in press; Rubin et al., 1990).

It is quite possible that people who are underregulated and relatively high in EI are prone to negative emotions. In general, high EI is related to negative emotionality (Larsen & Diener, 1987), and proneness to several negative emotions (i.e., discomfort, fear, frustration, and sadness) has been correlated with autonomic reactivity, rate of rising reactivity (for fear only), and falling reactivity (for all but sadness; Derryberry & Rothbart, 1988). Moreover, negative emotionality tends to be associated with lack of inhibitory control or emotional control (e.g., Zuckerman, Kuhlman, & Camac, 1988) and has been linked with nonspecific general arousal (Wallace, Newman, & Bachorowski, 1991). In addition, recent findings indicate that rejected, aggressive junior high students are prone to depression (Hodgens & McCoy, 1989), and depression among 18-year-old men (but not women) is associated with undercontrolled, self-aggrandizing, aggressive behavior from age 7 years onward (Block, Gjerde, & Block, 1991).

Because people low in EI tend to experience less intense emotions, underregulated, low emotional intensity individuals would be expected to be somewhat less prone to frustration and anger than high EI, underregulated people. Therefore they are expected to be less prone to explosive behavior and reactive aggression than high EI, underregulated people. These individuals, however, may account for the relation between underregulation and manipulativeness in some studies (e.g., Block & Block, 1980; also see Strelau, 1983), and their aggressive behaviors may be less due to emotional reactivity than to the desire for certain ends combined with relatively low levels of behavioral control. Individuals in this cell who are extroverted may be those who seek to modulate low baseline levels of responding with extroverted behavior and sensation seeking rather than heightened emotional responding (see Eysenck, 1967; Larsen & Diener, 1987).

Because children in this group are less likely to "fly off the handle" than are high EI, underregulated children, they may be somewhat less likely to be rejected. Most likely they are low to average in popularity, depending on the degree to which they exhibit behaviors such as manipulativeness and proactive aggression. Certainly, their lack of inhibitory control is expected to be linked to a pattern of nonconstructive coping, which probably affects sociometric status. In addition, their low level of emotional reactivity, combined with underregulation, is hypothesized to result in relatively low levels of either sympathy or personal distress in response to others' emotional responding.

The high EI, highly controlled cell is a particularly interesting one. People in this cell are characterized by an inhibited style, that is, behavioral inhibition (e.g., Kagan, 1989; Rothbart, 1989). Hypothesized correlates include shyness and what we have labeled reactive withdrawal (withdrawal based on emotional factors), proneness to negative emotion and distress as well as personal distress, low to average social skills, and inflexible coping (see Table 5.2). Because these people are relatively emotional, they also are expected to be emotionally expressive in childhood; however, with age and due to their inhibited social style, they may learn to inhibit external signs of emotion.

There is considerable empirical support for these predictions. Behaviorally inhibited children tend to be shy with unfamiliar peers and adults, cautious in situations involving mild risk, socially withdrawn, and rejected (Kagan, 1989; Reznick, Gibbons, Johnson, & McDonough, 1989; Reznick et al., 1986; see Reznick, 1989; Rubin et al., 1990). Moreover, there are theoretical and empirical reasons to believe that shyness and behavioral inhibition are associated with negative emotionality and fears (Bruch et al., 1989; Cheek & Buss, 1981; Jones, Briggs,

& Smith, 1986; Plomin & Stocker, 1989; Radke-Yarrow, Richters, & Wilson, 1988). For example, among girls, depression in adolescence appears to be associated with overcontrol (Block et al., 1991). Further, inhibition in childhood is correlated with low vagal tone and low heart rate variability, and low vagal tone children seem to have difficulty adapting to a new social situation (Fox & Field, 1989). Although some behaviorally inhibited children seem to have adequate social skills and friends (Gersten, 1989), in general, social withdrawal is linked to relatively low levels of popularity (Coie & Dodge, 1988; Rubin et al., 1990), particularly for girls (Coie et al., 1990).

It is likely that the emotionality of inhibited people is not due to seeking stimulation to compensate for low baseline physiological responding (Larsen & Diener, 1987). Rather, Kagan (Kagan, Reznick, & Snidman, 1987) has argued that the threshold of responsivity in limbic and hypothalamic structures to unfamiliarity and challenge is tonically lower for inhibited than uninhibited children. In fact, inhibited children exhibit more evidence of limbic system arousal than do uninhibited children (Kagan, 1989).

Similarly, Rubin et al. (1990) hypothesized that inhibited, withdrawn children have a low threshold to stimulation and are difficult to comfort. He further suggests that these characteristics interact with maternal attitudes and behaviors (e.g., insensitivity, nonresponsivity, neglect, lack of affection; authoritarian or permissive parenting) to cause insecurity, anxiety, and socially unsuccessful behavior. These social failures and negative feelings, enhanced by the child's awareness of his or her social inadequacy as he or she ages, are seen as resulting in social anxiety, further withdrawal, and peer rejection.

There is reason to believe that there are sex differences in the frequency and perhaps in quality and correlates of behavioral inhibition and shyness. Although the findings are not always consistent (Stevenson-Hinde, 1989), more girls than boys appear to be inhibited (Kagan, 1989; Reznick et al., 1989; see Rothbart, 1989) and susceptible to problems involving inhibition of action (rather than aggression and acting out; Achenbach, 1982). As noted previously, there is also evidence that overcontrol is related to depression among adolescent girls whereas undercontrol is related for adolescent boys (Block et al., 1991). Moreover, shyness in girls has been associated with positive maternal perceptions of daughters (maternal sensitivity and enjoyment of child, joint activities with mother and with father, and a positive relationship with the older sibling) and negatively related to negative perceptions (e.g., actively hostile to mother, child not engaged with mother, child hostile to peers). The opposite pattern seems to hold for boys (Stevenson-Hinde, 1989; also see Radke-Yarrow et al., 1988). Thus any biologically based sex difference in behavioral inhibition is likely to be reinforced by the fact that socializers seem to respond more positively to inhibition and shyness in girls than boys.

The overcontrolled, low EI cell is perhaps the most speculative. Individuals in this cell are hypothesized to be behaviorally inhibited but less prone to negative emotions than people in the analogous high EI cell. Because they are relatively low in emotionality as well as inhibited, they may appear to be rather flat in affective tone. Such people are hypothesized to be unsociable rather than shy; that is, they are not expected to desire high levels of social contact or to experience anxiety about social interactions (i.e., they are low on both approach and avoidance social tendencies). Thus these people are characterized by proactive withdrawal (nonfearful preference for not affiliating with others). Moreover, as hypothesized by Buss and Plomin (1984), because children low in sociability are relatively unmotivated to acquire social skills and are less likely than other children to endure the negatives of social interaction, unsociable people would be expected to have poorer social skills and receive fewer rewards in social contexts than would more sociable people.

CONCLUSIONS

In this chapter, we have argued that examination of the interaction between individual differences in emotional intensity and style of regulation can be a fruitful approach to understanding differences among people in personality and social behavior. In our review of the relevant research, we have drawn heavily from research and theory on personality and temperament as well as on the larger developmental literature on social development. Consistent with research on the stability of personality characteristics during the life span and the behavioral genetics literature (e.g., Buss & Plomin, 1975, 1984; Kagan, 1989; Pedersen, Plomin, McClearn, & Friberg, 1988), we believe that there are genetic underpinnings to individual differences in emotional intensity, behavioral inhibition, and impulsivity as well as sociability. Thus, in our view, it is important to examine individual differences in person-

ality and temperament when studying the development and maintenance of social behaviors.

We also believe, however, that social and situational factors, including the socialization of emotional responding (Eisenberg, Fabes, Carlo,
& Karbon, 1992; Lewis & Saarni, 1985) and self-regulation (Kopp,
1982), influence style and degree of regulation, the expression of
emotion, and related social responses such as aggression (see Parke &
Slaby, 1983; Rubin et al., 1990; Vygotsky, 1978). An important question, then, concerns how socialization variables and other contextual
factors interact with temperamental predispositions in affecting socially relevant competencies and behaviors. Emotional intensity as
experienced by the individual is probably less susceptible to modification by the environment than are regulatory style, emotional expressivity, social skills, and social behaviors, although sensitive parenting may
counteract or moderate children's tendencies to experience anxiety and
distress (Cicchetti et al., 1991; Rubin et al., 1990). Thus, in future research,
it may be productive to focus on the role of socialization in children's and
adults' expression of felt emotion, style of coping with negative emotion,
and regulation of emotionally based behavior. In doing so, we may learn
more about the development of a variety of processes and behaviors central
to coping, social competence, and socioemotional functioning.

REFERENCES

Achenbach, T. M. (1982). *Developmental psychopathology* (2nd ed.). New York: John
Wiley.

Arend, R., Gove, F. L., & Sroufe, L. A. (1979). Continuity of individual adaptation from
infancy to kindergarten: A predictive study of ego-resiliency and curiosity in preschoolers. *Child Development, 50,* 950-959.

Asendorpf, J. B. (1990). Beyond social withdrawal: Shyness, unsociability, and peer
avoidance. *Human Development, 33,* 250-259.

Batson, C. D. (1987). Prosocial motivation: Is it ever truly altruistic? In L. Berkowitz
(Ed.), *Advances in experimental social psychology* (Vol. 20, pp. 65-122). New York:
Academic Press.

Block, J. H., & Block, J. (1980). The role of ego-control and ego-resiliency in the
organization of behavior. In W. Andrew Collins (Ed.), *Development of cognition,
affect, and social relations: The Minnesota Symposia on Child Psychology* (Vol. 13,
pp. 39-101). Hillsdale, NJ: Lawrence Erlbaum.

Block, J., & Gjerde, P. F. (1986). Distinguishing between antisocial behavior and
undercontrol. In D. Olweus, J. Block, & M. Radke-Yarrow (Eds.), *Development of*

antisocial and prosocial behavior: Research, theories, and issues (pp. 177-206). Orlando, FL: Academic Press.

Block, J., Gjerde, P. F., & Block, J. H. (1991). Personality antecedents of depressive tendencies in 18-year-olds: A prospective study. *Journal of Personality and Social Psychology, 60,* 726-738.

Bruch, M. A., Gorsky, J. M., Collins, T. M., & Berger, P. A. (1989). Shyness and sociability reexamined: A multicomponent analysis. *Journal of Personality of Social Psychology, 57,* 904-915.

Buss, A. H., & Plomin, R. (1975). *A temperament theory of personality development.* New York: John Wiley.

Buss, A. H., & Plomin, R. (1984). *Temperament: Early developing personality traits.* Hillsdale, NJ: Lawrence Erlbaum.

Camras, L. A. (1977). Facial expressions used by children in a conflict situation. *Child Development, 48,* 1431-1435.

Case, R., Hayward, S., Lewis, M., & Hurst, P. (1988). Toward a neo-Piagetian theory of cognitive and emotional development. *Developmental Review, 8,* 1-51.

Cheek, J. M., & Buss, A. H. (1981). Shyness and sociability. *Journal of Personality and Social Psychology, 41,* 330-339.

Cicchetti, D., Ganiban, J., & Barnett, D. (1991). Contributions from the study of high-risk populations to understanding the development of emotion regulation. In J. Garber & K. A. Dodge (Eds.), *The development of emotion regulation and dysregulation* (pp. 15-48). Cambridge: Cambridge University Press.

Coie, J. D., & Dodge, K. A. (1988). Multiple sources of data on social behavior and social status in the school: A cross-age comparison. *Child Development, 59,* 815-829.

Coie, J. D., Dodge, K. A., & Kupersmidt, J. B. (1990). Peer group behavior and social status. In S. R. Asher & J. D. Coie (Eds.), *Peer rejection in childhood* (pp. 17-59). Cambridge: Cambridge University Press.

Coie, J. D., & Kupersmidt, J. B. (1983). A behavioral analysis of emerging social status in boys' groups. *Child Development, 54,* 1400-1416.

Cummings, E. M., & Cummings, J. L. (1988). A process-oriented approach to children's coping with adults' angry behavior. *Developmental Review, 8,* 296-321.

Denham, S. A. (1986). Social cognition, prosocial behavior, and emotion in preschoolers: Contextual validation. *Child Development, 57,* 194-201.

Derryberry, D., & Rothbart, M. K. (1988). Arousal, affect, and attention as components of temperament. *Journal of Personality and Social Psychology, 55,* 958-966.

Dodge, K. A. (1991). Emotion and social processing. In J. Garber & K. A. Dodge (Eds.), *The development of emotion regulation and dysregulation* (pp. 159-181). Cambridge: Cambridge University Press.

Dodge, K. A., & Feldman, E. (1990). Issues in social cognition and sociometric status. In S. R. Asher & J. D. Coie (Eds.), *Peer rejection in childhood* (pp. 119-155). Cambridge: University of Cambridge Press.

Eisenberg, N., Bernzweig, J., & Fabes, R. A. (1992). Coping and vicarious emotional responding. In T. Field, P. McCabe, & N. Schneiderman (Eds.), *Stress and coping in infancy and childhood* (pp. 101-117). Hillsdale, NJ: Lawrence Erlbaum.

Eisenberg, N., Cameron, E., Tryon, K., & Dodez, R. (1981). Socialization of prosocial behavior in the preschool classroom. *Developmental Psychology, 17,* 773-782.

Eisenberg, N., & Fabes, R. A. (1990). Empathy: Conceptualization, assessment, and relation to prosocial behavior. *Motivation and Emotion, 14,* 131-149.

Eisenberg, N., Fabes, R. A., Carlo, G., & Karbon, M. (1992). Emotional responsivity to others: Behavioral correlates and socialization antecedents. In N. Eisenberg & R. A. Fabes (Eds.), *Emotion and its regulation in early development: New directions in child development.* San Francisco: Jossey-Bass.

Eisenberg, N., Fabes, R. A., Miller, P. A., Shell, C., Shea, R., & May-Plumee, T. (1990). Preschoolers' vicarious emotional responding and their situational and dispositional prosocial behavior. *Merrill-Palmer Quarterly, 36,* 507-529.

Eisenberg, N., Fabes, R. A., Schaller, M., Carlo, G., & Miller, P. A. (1991). The relations of parental characteristics and practices to children's vicarious emotional responding. *Child Development, 62,* 1393-1408.

Eisenberg, N., Fabes, R. A., Schaller, M., Miller, P. A., Carlo, G., Poulin, R., Shea, C., & Shell, R. (1991). Personality and socialization correlates of vicarious emotional responding. *Journal of Personality and Social Psychology, 61,* 459-470.

Eisenberg, N., McCreath, H., & Ahn, R. (1988). Vicarious emotional responsiveness and prosocial behavior: Their interrelations in young children. *Personality and Social Psychology Bulletin, 14,* 298-311.

Eisenberg, N., Pasternack, J. F., Cameron, E., & Tryon, K. (1984). The relation of quantity and mode of prosocial to moral cognitions and social style. *Child Development, 55,* 1479-1485.

Eisenberg-Berg, N., & Hand, M. (1979). The relationship of preschoolers' reasoning about prosocial moral conflicts to prosocial behavior. *Child Development, 50,* 356-363.

Eysenck, H. J. (1967). *The biological basis of personality.* Springfield, IL: Charles C Thomas.

Fabes, R. A., & Eisenberg, N. (1992). Young children's coping with interpersonal anger. *Child Development, 63,* 116-128.

Fabes, R. A., & Eisenberg, N. (in press). Young children's emotional arousal and anger/aggressive behaviors. In A. Fraczek & H. Zumkley (Eds.), *Socialization and aggression.* New York: Springer-Verlag.

Fox, N. A. (1989a). Heart-rate variability and behavioral reactivity: Individual differences in autonomic patterning and their relation to infant and child temperament. In J. S. Reznick (Ed.), *Perspectives on behavioral inhibition* (pp. 177-195). Chicago: University of Chicago Press.

Fox, N. A. (1989b). Psychophysiological correlates of emotional reactivity during the first year of life. *Developmental Psychology, 25,* 364-372.

Fox, N. A., & Field, T. M. (1989). Individual differences in young children's adjustment to preschool. *Journal of Applied Developmental Psychology, 10,* 527-540.

Gersten, M. (1989). Behavioral inhibition in the classroom. In J. S. Reznick (Ed.), *Perspectives on behavioral inhibition* (pp. 71-91). Chicago: University of Chicago Press.

Gianino, A., & Tronick, E. (1988). The mutual regulation model: The infant's self and interactive regulation and coping and defensive capacities. In T. M. Field, P. M. McCabe, & N. Schneiderman (Eds.), *Stress and coping across development* (pp. 47-68). Hillsdale, NJ: Lawrence Erlbaum.

Gray, J. A. (1971). *The psychology of fear and stress.* New York: McGraw-Hill.

Hartup, W. W. (1974). Aggression in childhood: Developmental perspectives. *American Psychologist, 27,* 336-341.

Hodgens, J. B., & McCoy, J. F. (1989). Distinctions among rejected children on the basis of peer-nominated aggression. *Journal of Clinical Child Psychology, 18,* 121-128.

Hoffman, M. L. (1982). Development of prosocial motivation: Empathy and guilt. In N. Eisenberg (Ed.), *The development of prosocial behavior* (pp. 281-313). New York: Academic Press.

Izard, C. E. (1990). Facial expressions and the regulation of emotions. *Journal of Personality and Social Psychology, 58,* 487-498.

Izard, C. E., Porges, S. W., Simons, R. F., Haynes, O. M., Hyde, C., Parisi, M., & Cohen, B. (1991). Infant cardiac activity: Developmental changes and relations with attachment. *Developmental Psychology, 27,* 432-439.

Jemerin, J. M., & Boyce, W. T. (1990). Psychobiological differences in childhood stress response. ii. Cardiovascular markers of vulnerability. *Developmental and Behavioral Pediatrics, 11,* 140-150.

Jones, W., Briggs, S. R., & Smith, T. G. (1986). Shyness: Conceptualization and measurement. *Journal of Personality and Social Psychology, 51,* 629-639.

Kagan, J. (1989). The concept of behavioral inhibition to the unfamiliar. In J. S. Reznick (Ed.), *Perspectives on behavioral inhibition* (pp. 1-23). Chicago: Chicago University Press.

Kagan, J., Reznick, J. S., & Snidman, N. (1987). The physiology and psychology of behavioral inhibition in child. *Child Development, 58,* 1459-1473.

Kopp, C. B. (1982). Antecedents of self-regulation: A developmental perspective. *Development Psychology, 18,* 199-214.

Larsen, R. J., & Diener, E. (1987). Affect intensity as an individual difference characteristic: A review. *Journal of Research in Personality, 21,* 1-39.

Larsen, R. J., Diener, E., & Cropanzano, R. A. (1987). Cognitive operations associated with individual differences in affect intensity. *Journal of Personality and Social Psychology, 53,* 767-774.

Larsen, R. J., Diener, E., & Emmons, R. A. (1986). Affect intensity and reactions to daily life events. *Journal of Personality and Social Psychology, 51,* 803-814.

Lazarus, R. S., & Folkman, S. (1984). *Stress, appraisal, and coping.* New York: Springer.

Lewis, M., & Saarni, C. (Eds.). (1985). *The socialization of emotions.* New York: Plenum.

Main, M., Kaplan, N., & Cassidy, J. (1985). Security in infancy, childhood, and adulthood: A move to the level of representation. *Monographs of the Society for Research in Child Development, 50* (102, Serial No. 209), pp. 66-104.

Mehrabian, A. (1980). *Basic dimensions for a general psychological theory.* Cambridge, MA: Oelgeschlager, Gunn, & Hain.

Mischel, W., & Mischel, H. N. (1976). A cognitive social-learning approach to morality and self-regulation. In T. Lickona (Ed.), *Moral development and behavior: Theory, research, and social issues* (pp. 84-107). New York: Holt, Rinehart & Winston.

Olson, S. L. (1989). Assessment of impulsivity in preschoolers: Cross-measure convergences, longitudinal stability, and relevance to social competence. *Journal of Clinical Child Psychology, 18,* 176-183.

Olweus, D. (1980). Familial and temperamental determinants of aggressive behavior in adolescent boys: A causal analysis. *Developmental Psychology, 16,* 644-660.

Parke, R. D., & Slaby, R. G. (1983). The development of aggression. In P. H. Mussen (Ed.), *Handbook of child psychology: Vol. 4. Socialization, personality, and social development* (pp. 547-641; E. M. Hetherington, Series Ed.). New York: John Wiley.

Pedersen, N. L., Plomin, R., McClearn, G. E., & Friberg, L. (1988). Neuroticism, extraversion, and related traits in adult twins reared apart and reared together. *Journal of Personality and Social Psychology, 55,* 950-957.

Pipp, S., & Harmon, R. J. (1987). Attachment as regulation: A commentary. *Child Development, 58,* 648-652.

Plomin, R., & Stocker, C. (1989). Behavioral genetics and emotionality. In J. S. Reznick (Ed.), *Perspectives on behavioral inhibition* (pp. 219-240). Chicago: Chicago University Press.

Porges, S. W. (1991). Vagal one: An autonomic mediator of affect. In J. Garber & K. A. Dodge (Eds.), *The development of emotion regulation and dysregulation* (pp. 111-128). Cambridge: Cambridge University Press.

Pulkkinen, L. (1982). Self-control and continuity from childhood to late adolescence. In P. B. Baltes & O. G. Brim, Jr. (Eds.), *Life-span development and behavior* (Vol. 4.) New York: Academic Press.

Pulkkinen, L. (1986). The role of impulse control in the development of antisocial and prosocial behavior. In D. Olweus, J. Block, & M. Radke-Yarrow (Eds.), *Development of antisocial and prosocial behavior: Research, theories, and issues* (pp. 149-206). Orlando, FL: Academic Press.

Radke-Yarrow, M., Richters, J., & Wilson, W. E. (1988). Child development in a network of relationships. In R. A. Hinde & J. Stevenson-Hinde (Eds.), *Relationships within families: Mutual influences* (pp. 48-67). Oxford: Clarendon.

Radke-Yarrow, M., & Zahn-Waxler, C. (1984). Roots, motives, and patterns in children's prosocial behavior. In E. Staub, D. Bar-Tal, J. Karylowski, & J. Reykowski (Eds.), *Development and maintenance of prosocial behavior: International perspectives on positive behavior* (pp. 81-99). New York: Plenum.

Reznick, J. S. (1989). *Perspectives on behavioral inhibition.* Chicago: Chicago University Press.

Reznick, J. S., Gibbons, J. L., Johnson, M. O., & McDonough, P. M. (1989). Behavioral inhibition in a normative sample. In J. S. Reznick (Ed.), *Perspectives on behavioral inhibition* (pp. 25-49). Chicago: University of Chicago Press.

Reznick, J. S., Kagan, J., Snidman, N., Gersten, M., Baak, K., & Rosenberg, A. (1986). Inhibited and uninhibited children: A follow-up study. *Child Development, 57,* 660-680.

Rizzo, T. A., & Corsaro, W. A. (1988). Toward a better understanding of Vygotsky's process of internalization: Its role in the development of the concept of friendship. *Developmental Review, 8,* 219-237.

Rothbart, M. K. (1989). Behavioral approach and inhibition. In J. S. Reznick (Ed.), *Perspectives on behavioral inhibition* (pp. 139-157). Chicago: Chicago University Press.

Rothbart, M. K., & Derryberry, D. (1981). Development of individual differences in temperament. In M. E. Lamb & A. L. Brown (Eds.), *Advances in developmental psychology* (Vol. 1, pp. 37-86). Hillsdale, NJ: Lawrence Erlbaum.

Rothbart, M. K., Ziaie, H., & O'Boyle, C. G. (1992). Self-regulation and emotion in infancy. In N. Eisenberg & R. A. Fabes (Eds.), *Emotion and its regulation in early development: New directions in child development* (pp. 7-23). San Francisco: Jossey-Bass.

Rubin, K. H., & Borwick, D. (1984). Communicative skills and sociability. In H. E. Sypher & J. L. Applegate (Eds.), *Communication by children and adults* (pp. 152-170). Beverly Hills, CA: Sage.

Rubin, K. H., Hymel, S., & Chen, X. (in press). The socio-emotional characteristics of extremely aggressive and extremely withdrawn children. *Journal of Abnormal Child Psychology.*

Rubin, K. H., LeMare, L. J., & Lollis, S. (1990). Social withdrawal in children: Developmental pathways to peer rejection. In S. R. Asher & J. D. Coie (Eds.), *Peer rejection in childhood* (pp. 217-249). Cambridge: Cambridge University Press.

Saarni, C. (1990). Emotional competence: How emotions and relationships become integrated. In R. A. Thompson (Ed.), *Socioemotional development* (pp. 115-182). Lincoln: University of Nebraska Press.

Salovey, P., & Mayer, J. D. (1990). Emotional intelligence. *Imagination, Cognition and Personality, 9,* 185-211.

Silverman, I. W., & Ragusa, D. M. (1990). Child and maternal correlates of impulse control in 24-month-old children. *Genetic, Social, and General Psychology Monographs, 116,* 435-473.

Stevenson-Hinde, J. (1989). Behavioral inhibition: Issues of context. In J. S. Reznick (Ed.), *Perspectives on behavioral inhibition* (pp. 125-138). Chicago: University of Chicago Press.

Stifter, C. A., & Fox, N. A. (1990). Infant reactivity: Physiological correlates of newborn and 5-month temperament. *Developmental Psychology, 26,* 582-588.

Strelau, J. (1983). *Temperament-personality-activity.* New York: Academic Press.

Teglasi, H., & MacMahon, B. H. (1990). Temperament and common problem behaviors of children. *Applied Developmental Psychology, 11,* 331-349.

Thomas, A., Chess, S., & Birch, H. G. (1968). *Temperament and behavior disorders in children.* New York: New York University Press.

Ungerer, J. A., Dolby, R., Waters, B., Barnett, B., Kelk, N., & Lewin, V. (1990). The early development of empathy: Self-regulation and individual differences in the first year. *Motivation and Emotion, 14,* 93-106.

Vygotsky, L. (1978). *Mind in society.* Cambridge, MA: Harvard University Press.

Wallace, J. F., Newman, J. P., & Bachorowski, J. (1991). Failures of response modulation: Impulsive behavior in anxious and impulsive individuals. *Journal of Research on Personality, 25,* 23-44.

Watson, D., & Clark, L. A. (1984). Negative affectivity: The disposition to experience aversive emotional states. *Psychological Bulletin, 96,* 465-490.

Wood, J. V., Saltzberg, J. A., & Goldsamt, L. A. (1990). Does affect induce self-focused attention? *Journal of Personality and Social Psychology, 58,* 899-908.

Wood, J. V., Saltzberg, J. A., Neale, J. N., Stone, A. A., & Rachmiel, T. B. (1990). Self-focused attention, coping responses, and distressed mood in everyday life. *Journal of Personality and Social Psychology, 58,* 1027-1036.

Zuckerman, M. (1979). *Sensation seeking: Beyond the optimal level of arousal.* Hillsdale, NJ: Lawrence Erlbaum.

Zuckerman, M., Kuhlman, D. M., & Camac, C. (1988). What lies beyond E and N? Factor analyses of scales believed to measure basic dimensions of personality. *Journal of Personality and Social Psychology, 54,* 96-107.

6

Primitive Emotional Contagion

ELAINE HATFIELD
JOHN T. CACIOPPO
RICHARD L. RAPSON

Elaine Hatfield is Professor of Psychology at the University of Hawaii. Her research interests are in passionate love, physical attractiveness, emotional contagion, and emotion. She is both an experimental social psychologist and a clinician. Her books include (with Richard Rapson) *Love, Sex, and Intimacy: Their Psychology, Biology, and History*; (with Susan Sprecher) *Mirror, Mirror: The Importance of Looks in Everyday Life*; and (with John Carlson) *The Psychology of Emotion*.

John T. Cacioppo is Professor of Psychology at The Ohio State University. His research reflects a psychophysiological perspective on social processes and individual differences. His current research interests include the physiological contributions to individual differences and personality processes, emotion, and health; rudimentary determinants of attitude formation and change; electrocortical, somatic, and autonomic markers of attitudinal and emotional processes; and reciprocal effects of social (e.g., contextual, social support, cultural) factors on attitudes, emotions, and health. He is currently Associate and Methodology Editor of *Psychophysiology* and the Associate Editor of the *Psychological Review*.

Richard L. Rapson is Professor of History at the University of Hawaii, having also taught previously at Amherst College and Stanford University. He has written nine books, many of which explore the territories where history and psychology intersect. His most recent book was *American Yearnings: Love, Money, and Endless Possibility*.

A woman talks casually with a friend. Suddenly she notices that she is beginning to feel awkward, uncomfortable, and ill at ease. She worries that she must be boring her friend and begins to try harder to be entertaining. The intensity of the discomfort intensifies, so she apologetically bids her friend farewell. As she walks away feeling somewhat anxious, she recalls that she was feeling fine prior to speaking with her friend. She wonders whether she possibly could have picked up her *friend's* emotion? She realizes that her chum is always ill at ease in company—brief expressions of anxiety cross his face, his voice rises, and he gets "twitchy." The next time they meet, the woman worries less about being witty and charming and more about reassuring her anxious friend. That succeeds in putting them both at ease.

Recently, we have begun to explore this process of emotional contagion. Of course, people's conscious analyses give them a great deal of information about their social encounters. People, however, can also focus their attention on their moment-to-moment emotional reactions to others, during their social encounters. This stream of reactions comes to them via their fleeting observations of others' faces, voices, postures, and instrumental behaviors. Further, as they nonconsciously and automatically mimic their companions' fleeting expressions of emotion, people also may come to *feel* as their partners feel. By attending to the stream of tiny moment-to-moment reactions, people can gain a great deal of information on their own and their partners' emotional landscapes. We begin by defining *emotion* and *emotional contagion* and discussing several mechanisms that we believe might account for this phenomenon. Next, we review the evidence from a variety of disciplines that "primitive emotional contagion" exists. Then we examine the role of individual differences in emotional contagion. Finally, we outline some of the broad research questions researchers might profitably investigate over the next decade.

OVERVIEW

Definitions

Fischer, Shaver, and Carnochan (1990) argue that emotions are

> organized, meaningful, generally adaptive action systems. . . . they are complex functional wholes including appraisals or appreciations, patterned physiological processes, action tendencies, subjective feelings, expressions, and instrumental behaviors. . . . none of these features is necessary for a particular instance of emotion. Emotions fit into families, within which all members share a family resemblance but no universal set of features. (pp. 84-85)

There is still disagreement about what precisely constitutes an emotion family (Ekman, in press; Izard, in press; Ortony & Turner, 1990; Panksepp, in press), but theorists have long argued that emotional "packages" comprise many components. These include conscious awareness; facial, vocal, and postural expression; neurophysiological and autonomic nervous system activity; and gross emotional behaviors. Different portions of the brain process the various aspects of emotion (Gazzaniga, 1985; Lewicki, 1986; MacLean, 1975; Panksepp, 1986; Papez, 1937). Early theorists focused on the "sequence" question—which comes first, the cognitive, somatovisceral, or behavioral aspects of emotion? Recent theorists contend that "it depends." Emotional stimuli may well trigger the conscious, somatovisceral, and behavioral aspects of emotion almost simultaneously. Which appears first depends on the person and the situation. In any case, the brain integrates the emotional information it receives; thus each of the emotional components acts on and is acted upon by the others (Candland, 1977; Carlson & Hatfield, 1992). Our definition of emotion, then, stresses the importance of all the elements of the emotional "package" in shaping emotional experience/behavior.

How should *emotional contagion* be defined? A broad working definition might read something like this: "the tendency to 'catch' (experience/express) another person's emotions (his or her emotional appraisals, subjective feelings, expressions, patterned physiological processes, action tendencies, and instrumental behaviors)." Such emotional contagion, we believe, is best conceptualized as a multiply determined family of psychophysiological, behavioral, and social phenomena. Emotional contagion is *multiply determined,* because innate stimulus features (e.g., a mother's nurturing expressions and actions toward an infant), acquired stimulus significance, and mental simulations or emotional imagery are each capable of producing it. Emotional contagion represents a *family* of phenomena, because it can manifest as similar responses (e.g., as when smiles elicit smiles) or complementary responses (e.g., as when the sight of a stroke aimed leads to a drawing back of the site of the blow). Emotional contagion is a *multilevel phenomenon* because the precipitating stimuli arise from one individual, act upon (i.e., are perceived and interpreted by) one or more other individuals, and yield corresponding or complementary conscious awareness; facial, vocal, and postural expression; neurophysiological and autonomic nervous system activity; and gross emotional behavioral responses in these individuals. Thus an important consequence of emotional contagion is an attentional, emotional, and behavioral synchrony that has the same adaptive utility (and drawbacks) for social entities (dyads, groups) as has emotion for the individual. The focus in this chapter is on primitive emotional contagion—contagion that is relatively automatic, unintentional, uncontrollable, and largely unconscious. This form of *primitive emotional contagion* is defined as "the tendency to automatically mimic and synchronize movements, expressions, postures, and vocalizations with those of another person and, consequently, to converge emotionally."

In this section, we will discuss the mechanisms that might account for emotional contagion (in general) and primitive emotional contagion (in particular). We will review evidence for the mechanisms said to underlie primitive emotional contagion, providing evidence that people do tend to (a) mimic the facial expressions, vocal expressions, and postures of those around them and (b) "catch" others' emotions as a consequence of such facial, vocal, and postural feedback. We will end by observing that primitive emotional contagion may well be critically important in personal relationships because it allows people to track others' feelings moment to moment.

Possible Mechanisms of Emotional Contagion

In characterizing emotional contagion as multiply determined, we suggested that individuals "catch" another's emotions in several ways. Early researchers focused on complex cognitive processes by which people might come to know and feel what those around them felt. Some theorists proposed that conscious reasoning and analysis accounted for the phenomenon. For example, as subjects listen to a target describe his or her emotional experiences, they might remember times they felt much the same way and shared much the same experiences. Such conscious reveries could spark a similar emotional response (Humphrey, 1922; Lang, 1985).

Other researchers argued that contagion had to be learned. Aronfreed (1970), for example, noted that, if an observer's and participant's pain or pleasure are habitually linked, soon the observer will come to share the participant's affective state. That is, emotional contagion can be a conditioned emotional response. Thus if, when a father is upset, he lashes out at his son, soon the sight of a distressed father will come to elicit distress in the son. Through stimulus generalization, emotional contagion could result from the sight of distress in anyone, not just the father.

A few researchers have suggested that some forms of emotional contagion are the result of even more primitive associative processes; specifically, that on occasion people may catch others' emotions be-cause the others' responses generate an *unconditioned* emotional re-sponse. For example, Klinnert, Campos, Sorce, Emde, and Svelda (1983) observe that "abrupt, angular movements, shrill, high-pitched voices, loud or otherwise intense voculations and movements . . . probably elicit emotional reactions" (p. 79). Although individuals might be aware of the unconditioned emotional response, they can also be utterly ignorant of the eliciting stimulus and powerless against the emotional forces unleashed automatically following the perception of the stimulus.

Finally, and most important, considering our interest in primitive emotional contagion, we would add that, in conversation, people continuously mimic and synchronize their movements with the facial expressions, voices, postures, and instrumental behaviors of others (Bavelas, Black, Lemery, & Mullett, 1987; Bernieri, Reznick, & Rosenthal, 1988; Warner, 1988). Most of this mimicry occurs without deliberate or conscious processing (O'Toole & Dubin, 1968). People's emotional experience may be influenced by one of the following: (a) the central nervous system commands that direct such mimicry/synchrony in the first place; (b) the afferent feedback from such facial, postural, or verbal mimicry/synchrony; or (c) self-perception processes wherein individuals draw inferences about their own emotional state based on the emotional expressions and behaviors evoked in them by the emotional state of another (Adelmann & Zajonc, 1989; Izard, 1971; Laird, 1984; Tomkins, 1963).

In sum, various mechanisms for emotional contagion have been proposed, several of which are also capable of producing the automatic transmission of emotions between individuals. These latter mechanisms range from unconditioned and conditioned emotional responses to interactional mimicry and synchrony. The case for unconditioned and conditioned emotional responses subserving emotional contagion is relatively straightforward. Therefore we focus in the remainder of this chapter on the evidence consistent with the notion that primitive emotional contagion can derive from interactional mimicry and synchrony.

If we piece together several facts about the nature of emotion, we can gain some understanding of how and when each of these mechanisms might operate.

Emotional information may be processed consciously or nonconsciously. People often have powerful emotional reactions to others yet are at a loss to explain just why they responded as they did. Neuroscientists have found that people are consciously aware of only a small bit of the information that their brains process moment to moment (Wilson, 1985). Normally, people consciously attend only to the most important, unusual, or difficult information. As Lachman, Lachman, and Butterfield (1979) observe:

Most of what we do goes on unconsciously. It is the exception, not the rule, when thinking is conscious; but by its very nature, conscious thought seems the only sort. It is not the only sort; it is the minority. (p. 207)

Similarly, probably most of the processing of emotional information goes on out of conscious awareness (Ohman, 1988; Posner & Snyder, 1975; Shiffrin & Schneider, 1977). We would argue that primitive contagion is produced by information that is processed outside of conscious awareness.

Despite the subjective experience that information is processed sequentially, the human brain clearly is capable of processing information in parallel (Gazzaniga, 1985). For example, while we are carrying on a rational conversation, we may also be continuously monitoring our partner's emotional reactions to what we have to say. We may unconsciously and automatically scan our partners' faces for second-by-second information as to their feelings. Are they feeling happiness, love, anger, sadness, or fear? We can use a variety of subtle indicators (such clues as facial muscle movements, "micro expressions," "crooked" expressions, or the timing of reactions to decide whether the other person is telling the truth or lying; Ekman, 1985). People may even be able to detect their partner's mood by observing facial muscle movements so minute that they *seem* detectable only in electromyographic (EMG) recordings (Cacioppo & Petty, 1983). People may also respond to other types of emotional information. They can listen to other people's words—to the volume, rhythm, pitch, and speed of their speech or to the length of their pauses. They can observe the way people gesture, move their hands, legs, and feet, and stand. They can observe others' instrumental behaviors.

Given this view of emotion, there is really not much mystery about the observations of therapists and others that—although they are not consciously aware that their clients and others are experiencing joy, sadness, fear, or anger—"somehow" they sense what others are feeling and react to it. Today, emotion researchers assume that the information of which we are consciously aware is only a small portion of the information we possess about ourselves and others.

Emotional packages comprise several components. As Fischer et al. (1990) noted, an emotional package typically includes conscious appraisals, subjective feelings, action tendencies, expressions, patterned physiological processes, and instrumental behaviors. No single feature, not even conscious awareness, is a necessary feature of an emotional episode. Laird and Bresler (1992), for example, suggested that

> all components of the emotional episode are ordinarily generated, more or less independently, by some central mechanism, but activation of any one may increase activity of any other. Their interactive effects might arise because of the way the organism is built (Buck, 1985) or because of classical conditioning, produced by the long history of paired occurrence of emotional responses. (Kleck et al., 1976). (p. 49)

On occasion, of course, the various components may be desynchronized, because the various components may be controlled by very different perceptual and reinforcement contingencies and are processed in different portions of the brain. Such desynchrony may be quite disruptive to responsive social exchanges, however, and thereby foster miscommunication and conflict. One of the benefits of rudimentary emotional contagion therefore is the synchronizing of social exchanges. Let us examine more closely this "synchronization function" of emotional contagion.

People Mimic/Synchronize the Movements of People Around Them

There is no particular need for people to be consciously aware that they are synchronizing their actions with those of others. Any action that is performed continuously is likely to become automatic. Nonetheless, the ability to be "in tune" with those around us is critically important. It allows us to coordinate emotionally and physically with them. The evidence that people synchronize their facial muscle movements, voices, and postural movements with one another, and thus they tend to be in emotional synchrony with one another, comes from several sources, including facial mimicry, vocal synchrony, and movement coordination. We will review this evidence in some detail, because we believe that this is a mechanism that underlies primitive emotional contagion.

Historical background. As early as 1759, Adam Smith observed: "When we see a stroke aimed, and just ready to fall upon, the leg or arm of another person, we naturally shrink and draw back on our leg or our own arm" (1759/1966, p. 4). Smith felt that such imitation was "almost a reflex." Lipps (1906) suggested that empathy is due to an unlearned "motor mimicry" response to another person's expression of affect.

According to Lipps, the observer automatically imitates the other person, with slight movements in posture and facial expression, thus creating in himself inner cues that contribute, through afferent feedback, to his understanding and experiencing of the other person's affect. Bavelas and her colleagues (Bavelas et al., 1987) translate Smith's and Lipps's observations to modern terms: "This is elementary motor mimicry, overt action by an observer that is appropriate to or mimetic of the situation of the other person, rather than one's own. The observer acts as if in the other's place to the point of wincing at his pain, smiling at her delight, or (as Smith described) trying to avoid that person's danger" (p. 317). Since the 1700s, researchers have collected considerable evidence that people do tend to imitate the facial expressions, postures, voices, and behaviors that they see and hear.

Facial mimicry. It has been observed that, when babies open their mouths, mothers tend to open theirs too. This is a nondeliberate reaction on their part, and one of which the mothers can be completely unaware (O'Toole & Dubin, 1968). As we observed earlier, Ekman (cited in Schmeck, 1983), Dimberg (1982), and Vaughan and Lanzetta (1980) have documented that people tend to mimic the expressions of those around them. Bavelas and her colleagues (1987) surveyed the research documenting the existence of motor mimicry. They found that people imitate others' expressions of pain, laughter, smiling, affection, embarrassment, discomfort, disgust, stuttering, reaching with effort, and the like, in a broad range of situations.[1] Ekman (cited in Schmeck, 1983) observes that people's emotions may be shaped by such mimicry. He points out that this may be one reason why smiling faces at parties or grief at a time of mourning are infectious. "The perception of another face is not just an information transfer," contends Ekman, "but a very literal means by which we *feel* the sensations that the other feels" (p. 1). Some researchers contend that we are especially likely to mimic the posture of those we care for (Scheflen, 1964).

Vocal synchrony. Chapple (1982) speculated that people's speech rhythms are related to their biological rhythms. Thus different people prefer different interaction tempos at different periods. When partners interact, if things are to go well, their speech cycles must become mutually entrained. Consistent with this reasoning, there is a good deal of evidence from controlled interview settings supporting interspeaker influence on utterance durations (Matarazzo, Weitman, Saslow, & Wiens, 1963), speech rate (Webb, 1972), and latencies of response (Matarazzo

& Wiens, 1972). Evidence is also available in more freewheeling settings. Capella and Planalp (1981), for example, studied twelve 20-minute dyadic conversations. They found clear evidence that, over time, partners came to match one another's conversational rhythms, even when they examined moment-to-moment reactions. In most dyads, couples talked the same amount. Partners also came to match one another's rhythms, as measured by length of vocalizations, mean pause duration, times between turns, length of talkovers, and the probability of breaking silences. Similar results were secured by Warner, Waggener, and Kronauer (1983) and Warner (1990).

Movement coordination. Finally, communication researchers have noted that people often synchronize their rhythms and movements with those of another person with whom they are interacting (Bernieri, 1988; Kendon, 1970). Condon and Ogston (1966) contend that a speaker's speech and movements are mirrored in the listeners' flow of movements: "Human expression appears to be a function of both speech and body motion inextricably locked together within the flow of behavior, reinforcing and counterpointing one another" (p. 345). To test some of these notions, Kendon (1970) videotaped the conversations of people in a London pub and carefully analyzed the tapes, word by word and frame by frame. He found that speakers' and listeners' streams of behavior were tightly coordinated. When the speaker was speaking and moving, the listener was moving as well. The speaker's movement waves coincide with those of the listener. A typical analysis is as follows:

> When B is moving, his movements are coordinated with T's movements and speech, and that in their form these movements amount in part to a "mirror image" of T's movements: As T leans back in his chair, B leans back and lifts his head; then B moves his right arm to the right, just as T moves his left arm to the left, and he follows this with a headcock to the right, just as T cocks his head to the left. We might say that here B dances T's dance. (Kendon, 1970, p. 110)

Davis (1985) points out that people are probably not able to consciously mimic others very effectively: The process is simply too complex and too fast. For example, it took even the lightening fast Muhammad Ali a minimum of 190 milliseconds to spot a light and 40 milliseconds more to throw a punch in response. Condon and Ogston (1966), however, found that college students could synchronize their movements within

21 milliseconds (the time of one picture frame). Davis (1985) argues that micro synchrony is mediated by basal brain structures and is either "something you got or something you don't; that there is no way that one can deliberately 'do' it" (p. 69). People who consciously try to mirror others, he speculates, are doomed to look phoney.

This is not to suggest that higher-order psychological processes are unimportant in rudimentary forms of emotional contagion. Researchers have speculated that people are most likely to coordinate their movements tightly with those they like and love. Tickle-Degnen and Rosenthal (1987) argue that rapport and coordinated movement are linked. Kendon (1970) argues that synchrony communicates interest and approval. Bernieri (1988) observes that

> high states of rapport are often associated with descriptive terms such as harmonious, smooth, "in tune with," or "on the same wavelength." Likewise states of low rapport are often associated with terms such as awkward, "out of sync," or "not getting it together." (p. 121)

Tronick, Als, and Brazelton (1977) speculate that synchrony may be a way for a child to signal "continue"; dissynchrony may communicate "stop" interaction.

If love and attention facilitate the synchronization of the movements of two people, then it seems reasonable that mothers would show evidence of greater synchrony when interacting with their own children than with the children of others. Bernieri et al. (1988) measured three kinds of synchrony in parent-child interactions: (a) simultaneous movement (does, for example, a mother begin to turn her head at the precise moment her child lifts an arm off the table?); (b) tempo similarity; and (c) coordination and smoothness (does the interactants' flow of behavior mesh evenly and smoothly?). They found that mothers showed more synchrony when they were interacting with their own children than when they were interacting with strangers. Presumably, mothers were more loving and attentive to their own children than to the children of strangers.

Emotional Experience and Facial, Vocal, and Postural Feedback

Researchers have also found evidence that people's emotional experience and somatic expression are tightly linked. In this section, we consider briefly some of the evidence indicating that emotional experience is affected by changes in the skeletal musculature.

The facial feedback hypothesis. Darwin (1872/1965), Izard (1977), and Tomkins (1982) predicted that emotional experience is profoundly affected by feedback from the facial muscles. Several emotions (e.g., fear, anger, sadness, disgust, joy) are associated with different patterns of facial muscle activity. Joy feels different from sadness in part, suggested these theorists, because smiling feels different from frowning. The sight of a face that is happy, loving, angry, sad, or fearful, we suggest, can cause the viewer to mimic elements of that face and, consequently, to catch the other's emotions. We considered evidence for the first part of this mechanism in the preceding section. Let us now consider the evidence for the second part of this mechanism.

Although contemporary theorists do not agree on exactly how facial feedback affects emotional experience, most agree that the two are somehow coupled (Adelmann & Zajonc, 1989; Lanzetta & McHugo, 1986). Two types of experiments have led to this conclusion. In one type, subjects are asked to exaggerate or play down their naturally occurring emotional facial expressions. For example, in some experiments, subjects are told to try to deceive an observer about what they are really feeling. Then they are shown an amusing movie or given painful electric shocks. Later, subjects are asked what they really felt during the funny movie or the electric shock. Subjects report that the movie was funnier or the shocks more painful when they exaggerated their amusement or pain than when they muted their facial reactions (see Kleck et al., 1976; Kopel & Arkowitz, 1974; Kraut, 1982; Lanzetta, Biernat, & Kleck, 1982; McCaul, Holmes, & Solomon, 1982; Zuckerman, Klorman, Larrance, & Speigel, 1981).

In the second type of experiment, careful steps are taken to avoid alerting subjects to the fact that the experimenters are studying emotions or manipulating subjects' emotional expressions. Typically, subjects are told that the experimenters are interested in studying the action of the subjects' facial muscles. Then the experimenters unobtrusively arrange the subjects' faces into happy or angry expressions. For example, subjects might be asked to "contract the muscles between your eyebrows by drawing them down and together, and clench your teeth" thus producing a scowl. With such procedures, researchers find that subjects' emotional feelings and/or behaviors are affected by feedback from their facial expressions. Subjects feel emotions consistent with those poses and have trouble experiencing emotions inconsistent with those poses (Duclos et al., 1989; Kellerman, Lewis, & Laird, 1989; Larsen, Kasimatis, & Frey, 1990; Rutledge & Hupka, 1985; Strack, Martin, & Stepper, 1988). Exceptions to this principle can be found when the facial efference is very weak (Cacioppo, Bush, & Tassinary, 1991) and when the emotional stimulus evokes extensive cognitive appraisals of strong affect (e.g., conditioned emotional responses) independent of the posed emotion (Matsumoto, 1987; Tourangeau & Ellsworth, 1979).

We were able to find only one article that investigated the link between love and feedback from expressions of love. In two experiments, Kellerman et al. (1989) asked opposite-sex pairs of subjects to gaze into one another's eyes continuously for two minutes. Compared with control subjects, who gazed at each other's hands, the mutual gaze subjects reported greater feelings of romantic love for each other.

Finally, researchers find that a happy face (Bush, Barr, McHugo, & Lanzetta, 1989; Hsee, Hatfield, Carlson, & Chemtob, 1991a, 1991b; Hsee, Hatfield, & Chemtob, 1992; Uchino, Hatfield, Carlson, & Chemtob, 1991), sad face (Hsee, Hatfield, & Chemtob, 1992; Hsee et al., 1991a, 1991b; Uchino et al., 1991), loving face, angry face (Lanzetta & Orr, 1986), or fearful face (Lanzetta & Orr, 1981) can provoke the corresponding emotion and facial display in viewers.

In a variety of studies, then, we find that people tend to feel the emotions consistent with the facial expressions they adopt and have trouble feeling emotions inconsistent with those poses. Further, the link between emotion and facial expression appears to be quite specific. When people produced facial expressions of fear, anger, sadness, or disgust, they were more likely to feel the emotion associated with those specific expressions rather than just any unpleasant emotion (i.e., people who make a sad expression feel sad, not angry; Duclos et al., 1989). Of course, emotions are not solely or perhaps even primarily shaped by facial feedback. Nevertheless, to the extent that emotions are influenced by facial feedback, spontaneous facial mimicry should contribute to emotional contagion.

The postural feedback hypothesis. Bull (1951) reports that, when hypnotized subjects are told to experience certain emotions, they consistently adopt appropriate postures. Conversely, when subjects are told only to adopt certain postures, they consistently experience the appropriate emotion as well. They also have unusual difficulty experiencing emotion opposite to that of the locked-in posture. Duclos et al.

(1989) manipulated subjects into sad, angry, and fearful postures and found that subjects' feelings came to match their postures precisely. For example, when subjects were placed in sad postures, they felt sad but not angry or fearful.

In a variation on the facial feedback and postural studies, Cacioppo et al. (in press) hypothesized that a static flexion of the arms and torso that implies approach, in contrast to a static extension that implies withdrawal, results in positive attitudes toward unrelated, novel stimuli in focal attention. In their first experiment, subjects categorized Chinese ideographs as liked or disliked while pressing upward (flexion) or downward (extension) on a table. Afterward, subjects distributed the ideographs equally across six bins, whose labels ranged from "extremely unpleasant" to "extremely pleasant." Results revealed that the ideographs that had been shown during flexor contraction were subsequently rated as being more pleasant than the ideographs that had been shown during extensor contraction. Experiment 2 replicated the results of Experiment 1. Experiment 3 provided evidence that flexion led to more positive attitudes, and extension led to more negative attitudes, when compared with a no-contraction control condition. Thus affective reactions toward neutral, nonassociative stimuli can be influenced by somatic factors as rudimentary as arm flexor or extensor contraction.

The vocal feedback hypothesis. There is also evidence that feedback from the facial muscles and/or the production of emotional sounds can influence emotional experience. For example, Hatfield, Costello, Schalenkamp, Hsee, and Denney (1991) asked subjects to read, as realistically as possible, short tape scripts of joyous, loving, sad, or angry telephone conversations. The authors assessed subjects' emotions in two ways: (a) subjects described their own emotional states (via a series of self-report measures) and (b) judges' rated the subjects' faces as they read the emotional tape scripts. Subjects' self-reports of emotion and facial expressions of emotion were affected by feedback from the emotional messages they delivered. In a second experiment, the scientists made every effort to hide the fact that they were interested in the subjects' emotions. They asked subjects to reproduce a series of supposedly random *sounds*. These sounds had been carefully designed to mimic sounds associated with joy, love, anger, fear, and sadness. As before, subjects were asked to rate their own emotions after reproducing one of the sounds. Again, the authors found evidence that people's emotions were affected by feedback from their vocal productions.

Finally, in a series of studies, Zajonc, Murphy, and Inglehart (1989) asked subjects to make sounds like the long "e" sound in "cheese" (which required them to make a smilelike expression) and the "ü" sound in German (which required subjects to pucker their lips, as if mimicking a negative emotional expression). Here, too, the subjects' experiences matched their vocal expressions. People tended to feel the emotions their voices and faces were induced to express.

Thus far, we have focused on primitive emotional contagion. Researchers from a range of disciplines have been interested in the process of emotional contagion, *broadly defined*. It will be evident to readers that many factors, including primitive contagion, may account for these data. They are, however, included in the interest of completeness.

ADDITIONAL EVIDENCE THAT EMOTIONAL CONTAGION EXISTS

Developmental Research

Child psychologists have long been interested in emotional contagion and the related concepts of empathy and sympathy. Titchener (1909) argued that people could never *know* what another felt by reasoning. They could only know by *feeling themselves into* the other's feelings: "Not only do I see gravity and modesty and pride and courtesy and stateliness, but I feel or act them in the mind's muscle" (p. 21). Later researchers speculated about how this process might work. Allport (1961) thought that it involved "the imaginative transposing of oneself into the thinking, feeling, and acting of another" (p. 536). This involved "the imitative assumption of the postures and facial expressions of other people" (p. 530). Murphy (1947) speculated that people came to feel as others felt because of *motor mimicry*—"his muscles tighten as he watches the tug of war; his larynx tires and his heels rise as the soprano strains upward" (p. 414). Today, theorists make clear distinctions between the process in which we are interested, primitive emotional contagion, and "empathy" or "sympathy" (Eisenberg & Miller, 1987).

Child psychologists have collected some evidence that, from the start, both parents and children are powerfully "enmeshed"; both parents and children show evidence of emotional contagion (Thompson, 1987). In one experiment, for example, Simner (1971) found that 2- to 4-day-old newborns began crying when they heard the cry of another newborn. These newborns seemed to be responding specifically to the other infant's emotional distress rather than to noise per se because the newborns did not cry when they heard a synthetic cry.

Hoffman (1973) has also suggested that caretakers teach their infants to feel what they feel via physical handling. For example, if, when a mother is distressed, her body stiffens, the infant will also experience distress. Subsequently, he speculates, the facial and verbal expressions that initially accompanied the mother's distress will serve as conditioned stimuli that evoke distress in the child. Stimulus generalization ensures that other distressed people also become able to evoke distress in the child. In summarizing such research, Hoffman (1987) observes:

> Infants may experience empathetic distress through the simplest arousal models . . . long before they acquire a sense of others as distinct from the self. Distress cues from the dimly perceived other are confounded with unpleasant feelings empathetically aroused in the self. Consequently, infants may at times act as though what happened to the other happened to themselves. Infants also seem to catch their parents' fears and anxiety. (p. 51)

Hoffman cites as examples the case of a child who buries its face in its mother's lap upon seeing another child fall and cry, or who strikes his doctor in anger when another child is seen receiving an injection. Researchers have found that infants begin to mimic the experimenter's facial gestures shortly after birth. Infants stick out their tongues, purse their lips, open their mouths, and the like shortly after the model does (Meltzoff, 1988; Reissland, 1988). In an interesting extension of this line of research, Haviland and Lelwica (1987) found that 10-week-old infants could and would imitate their mother's facial expressions of happiness, sadness, and anger.

Parents seem to "catch" the emotions of newborns as well. Frodi and her colleagues (1978) found that parents who were asked to observe a sad-angry newborn reported feeling more "annoyed, irritated, distressed, disturbed, indifferent and less attentive and less happy" than those who viewed a smiling infant. When parents viewed a sad-angry child, their diastolic blood pressure rose and their skin conductance increased as well. Although mothers were most likely to "catch" and mimic their infants' positive emotions (interest, enjoyment, and surprise), they also mimicked the infants' negative emotions (pain, sadness, and anger) to some extent (Malatesta & Haviland, 1982).

Although these interesting lines of research do not speak definitively to the hypothesis that parents and children are genetically predisposed to take on one another's emotional reactions, the potential adaptive significance for a species of synchronizing the attention, emotions, and behaviors of caretaker and newborn is undeniable. Of course, this line of reasoning also predicts that newborns or children characterized by sickly or unpleasant (e.g., colicky) temperaments are placed at risk for abuse or neglect. The limited data that do exist are, unfortunately, consistent with this hypothesis (Bugental, Blue, & Lewis, 1990).

Clinical Research

Therapists have long observed that clinicians tend to catch their clients' feelings. Clinicians point out that it is difficult to work with depressed clients; one keeps nodding off. Something about the clients' slow voices, sad facial expressions, or the endless, hopeless details they recite keep putting one to sleep. It is hard to concentrate and attend long enough to be helpful. For example, Jung (1968) observed:

> Emotions are contagious. . . . In psychotherapy, even if the doctor is entirely detached from the emotional contents of the patient, the very fact that the patient has emotions has an effect upon him. And it is a great mistake if the doctor thinks he can lift himself out of it. He cannot do more than become conscious of the fact that he is affected. If he does not see that, he is too aloof and then he talks beside the point. It is even his duty to accept the emotions of the patient and to mirror them. (p. 155)

Reik (1948) described the process by which clinicians move in close enough to glimpse their clients' emotions and then move back far enough to deal with them. Clinicians have speculated about how the process of "countertransference" may operate and how such emotional information might be used therapeutically. Tansey and Burke (1989), for instance, suggest that therapists may respond to clients' emotions in two different ways. They may feel exactly what the client feels (*concordant identification*) or they may feel emotions that are *complementary* to the clients' own emotions (for example, feeling hurt at a client's angry attack). The authors assume that therapists are generally provoked to feel what clients *wish* them to feel.[2]

Clinical researchers have also collected considerable evidence as to the impact manic, depressed, anxious, and angry people make on those around them. In some of these research reports, we find clear evidence of contagion (Coyne, 1976; Howes, Hokanson, & Lowenstein, 1985).

Social-Psychological Research

Early sociologists such as Le Bon (1896) were interested in the "group mind" and the "madness" of crowds. Since then, researchers have explored the process of "mass hysteria" in a variety of societies.[3] In the Middle Ages, in the wake of the Black Plague, dancing manias swept through Europe (Hecker, 1970). In Malaysia, entire communities have fallen prey to contagious depression (Teoh, Soewondo, & Sidhartha, 1975); in East Africa, to hysterical laughter and crying (Ebrahim, 1968); in the New Guinea Highlands, to anger, giddiness, and sexual acting out (Reay, 1960); and, in Singapore, to hysterical fear (Chew, Phoon, & Mae-Lim, 1976).

Wheeler (1966) and other social psychologists have found that Western group members seem particularly susceptible to catching the laughter (Leventhal & Mace, 1970), fear, and panicky behavior of other group members (Kerckhoff & Back, 1968; Schachter & Singer, 1962). Wheeler attempted to distinguish "true" contagion (the rapid transfer of emotion from one person to others in the group) from other types of social influence, such as conformity, conscious imitation, responsiveness to social pressure, and social facilitation.

Psychophysiological Research

Haggard and Issacs (1966) observed that people's emotional experiences and accompanying facial expressions may change with incredible speed. They found that unique facial expressions could appear and disappear within a span of 125 to 200 milliseconds: "Occasionally the expression on the patient's face would change dramatically within three to five frames of film (as from smile to grimace to smile), which is equivalent to a period of from one-eighth to one-fifth of a second."

Psychophysiological investigations have further found that people's emotional experiences and facial expressions, as measured by electromyographic (EMG) procedures, tend to mimic the changes in emotional expression of those they observe, and that this motor mimicry can occur at levels so subtle that people produce no observable facial expressions (Cacioppo, Tassinary, & Fridlund, 1990). For example, Dimberg (1982) measured subjects' facial EMG activity as they looked at pictures of happy and angry facial expressions. He found that happy and angry faces evoked different facial EMG response patterns. Specifically, minute muscular actions were found to increase over the *zygomaticus major* (cheek) muscle region when subjects observed happy facial expressions, whereas minute muscular actions decreased over the *corrugator supercilli* (brow) muscle region (the muscle that pulls the forehead into a frown) when they observed angry facial stimuli. Similar results were secured by Vaughan and Lanzetta (1980) and Voglmaier and Hakeren (1989).

How powerful are these contagion effects? Some research suggests that the process of contagion is relatively fragile (Cacioppo et al., 1991). For instance, if people are caught up in emotions of their own that are very different from those others are feeling, the contagion process can be totally disrupted. In an illustrative study, subjects competed with an experimental confederate in a stock market game (Englis, Vaughan, & Lanzetta, 1982). Subjects quickly learned that, when their partner winced in pain, it was a telltale sign that their own guess was correct and they had won money. When the confederate smiled, they figured they had guessed wrong and that they would soon be receiving an electric shock. Under those conditions, subjects' faces (and facial muscle activity) reflected *their own* pleasure or pain (which was directly opposite to that expressed by the confederate) rather than mimicking the confederate's facial displays of emotion. Thus the usual process of contagion completely disappeared when the context of the social interaction led subjects to focus on and think about the personal consequences implied by another's emotional expressions.

We see then that developmental, clinical, and social psychologists are among the scientists who have observed phenomena that appear to meet the criteria of "emotional contagion." In the next section, we consider the role of individual differences in emotional contagion—individual differences in people's potency as "carriers" of emotional contagion and in people's vulnerability to emotional contagion.

INDIVIDUAL DIFFERENCES

Are there individual differences in susceptibility to emotional contagion? Does everyone experience and display other people's joy, sadness, love, anger, and fear or do people differ markedly in their ability to mirror others' emotions? We assume that people's genetic heritage, gender, personality, and early experiences should make them more or less likely to "catch" versus resist experiencing others' emotions. Orimoto and Hatfield (1992) developed a measure of people's vulnerability to contagion. The Emotional Contagion Scale consists of 15 items designed to assess people's susceptibility to catching fear/anxiety, anger, sadness/depression, joy/happiness, love, and emotions in general. With the development of the Emotional Contagion Scale, investigators can begin to examine individual differences in emotional contagion. Some of the possibilities in which emotional contagion may be more likely are these:

- Mothers may be especially prone to display and experience their infant's emotions. (In fact, the mother-infant relationship may be a prototype of the "loss of boundaries" between emotional displays of two individuals.)
- Women may have been taught to be more "sensitive" to other people's feelings and thus are more likely to experience and display other people's emotions than are men.
- Couples who are passionately in love (and other intimates) may be especially likely to display and experience their mates' emotions.
- Certain social roles may promote emotional contagion. For instance, social roles that require one to make a psychological investment in another may promotion contagion. Thus psychotherapists may be prone to emotional contagion with their clients; teachers, with their students; and caretakers, with their dependents.
- People who are particularly good at decoding emotions should be more susceptible to emotional contagion.
- Individuals who are sympathetically reactive by disposition may be more likely to "catch" the emotions of those around them.
- Some people are generally unaware of their own feelings. Such people may be less likely to display and experience the feelings of others.

Logically, it would seem that several characteristics should make individuals especially susceptible to (or resistant to) emotional contagion: (a) People should be more likely to catch others' emotions if their attention is riveted on the others than if they are oblivious to others' emotions. (b) People should be more likely to catch others' emotions if they construe themselves in terms of their interrelatedness to the others than if they construe themselves in terms of their independence and uniqueness. (c) Those able to read others' emotional expressions, voices, gestures, and postures should be especially vulnerable to contagion. (d)

Those who tend to mimic facial, vocal, and postural expressions should be especially vulnerable to contagion. (e) Those who are aware of their own emotional responses (people whose subjective emotional experience is tempered by facial, vocal, postural, and movement feedback) should be more vulnerable to contagion. (f) Emotionally reactive people should be more vulnerable to contagion.

Recently, Hatfield and her colleagues (Hsee, Hatfield, & Chemtob, 1992; Hsee et al., 1991a, 1991b; Uchino et al., 1991) proposed that it is when people are paying careful attention to, loving, identifying with, or taking responsibility for others that they are most likely to catch others' emotions. Illustrative situations in which people are especially attuned to others include when they love or like others (as opposed to being disinterested in them), when they identify with or feel responsible for others, and when they believe the others have power over them.

Are some people especially likely to shape others' emotions? Some people may be especially able to shape emotional encounters. Some individuals, for instance, have such contagious laughs that no one can resist; other people get lost in the crowd. Friedman and Riggio (1981) argue that "expressive" people (as measured by the Affective Communication Test) are more likely to provoke contagion than are their "inexpressive" peers. Sullins (1991) provides evidence that "strongly expressive" people are more likely to be carriers of emotional contagion than are "weakly expressive" people.

We would argue that powerful senders should probably possess at least three characteristics. (a) They must feel, or at least appear to feel, strong emotion. (b) They must be able to express these emotions (c) They should be relatively insensitive to the feelings of those who are experiencing emotions incompatible with their own.

CONCLUSIONS

In this chapter, we have reviewed evidence that people often catch the emotions of those around them. They sense, moment to moment, what others are feeling. First, we reviewed some of the processes that may underlie such primitive emotional contagion. We found that people are capable of processing a great deal of information outside of conscious awareness. We found that people tend to mimic/synchronize their movements with the movements of those around them. They mimic the facial, vocal, and postural expressions of others. Emotional experience is often shaped by feedback from the facial musculature as well as by vocal and postural feedback. We ended by reviewing evidence from a variety of disciplines that both primitive emotional contagion and broader ranging emotional contagion exist.

What are the implications of such findings? Of course, people's conscious analytic skills can help them figure out what makes other people "tick." But, if people pay careful attention to the emotions they experience in the company of others, they may well gain some extra information as to others' emotional states. In fact, researchers (Hsee, Hatfield, & Chemtob, 1992) provide some evidence that what people think may be very different from what they feel emotionally. Both provide invaluable information as to others' emotional states.

Of course, emotional contagion research is still in its infancy. Much more research is needed to tease apart the factors that shape the tangled skein of primitive emotional contagion. We believe that the importance of emotional contagion for synchronizing and maintaining adaptive social interactions and the potential richness of this area of research will make a program of research into the antecedents and consequences of primitive emotional contagion worthwhile.

NOTES

1. Bavelas et al. (1987) argue, of course, that such mimicry is a communicative act, conveying a rapid and precise nonverbal message to another person.

2. Presumably, in concordance, the client wishes the therapist to share his or her experiences; in complementarity, to fill a very different, but facilitative, role—playing, say, stern disciplinarian to the client's child.

3. Tseng and Hsu (1980) define mass hysteria as a "sociocultural psychological phenomenon in which a group of people, through social contagion, collectively manifest disturbances for a brief period of time" (p. 77). We wish to thank Lois Yamuchi for sharing her research on this topic with us.

REFERENCES

Adelmann, P. K., & Zajonc, R. (1989). Facial efference and the experience of emotion. *Annual Review of Psychology, 40*, 249-280.

Allport, G. W. (1961). *Pattern and growth in personality.* New York: Holt, Rinehart & Winston.

Aronfreed, J. (1970). The socialization of altruistic and sympathetic behavior: Some theoretical and experimental analyses. In J. Macaulay & L. Berkowitz (Eds.), *Altruism and helping behavior* (pp. 103-126). New York: Academic Press.

Bavelas, J. B., Black, A., Lemery, C. R., & Mullett, J. (1987). Motor mimicry as primitive empathy. In N. Eisenberg & J. Strayer (Eds.), *Empathy and its development* (pp. 317-338). New York: Cambridge University Press.

Bernieri, F. J. (1988). Coordinated movement and rapport in teacher-student interactions. *Journal of Nonverbal Behavior, 12,* 120-138.

Bernieri, F. J., Reznick, J. S., & Rosenthal, R. (1988). Synchrony, pseudosynchrony, and dissynchrony: Measuring the entrainment process in mother-infant interactions. *Journal of Personality and Social Psychology, 54,* 243-253.

Buck, R. (1985). Prime theory: An integrated view of motivation and emotion. *Psychological Review, 92,* 389-413.

Bugental, D. B., Blue, J., & Lewis, J, (1990). Caregiver beliefs and dysphoric affect directed to difficult children. *Developmental Psychology, 26,* 631-638.

Bull, N. (1951). The attitude theory of emotion. *Nervous and Mental Disease Monographs, 81,* 1-18.

Bush, L. K., Barr, C., L., McHugo, G. J., & Lanzetta, J. T. (1989). The effects of facial control and facial mimicry on subjective reactions to comedy routines. *Motivation and Emotion, 13,* 31-52.

Cacioppo, J. T., Bush, L. K., & Tassinary, L. G. (1991). Microexpressive facial actions as a function of affective stimuli: Replication and extension. *Personality and Social Psychology Bulletin.*

Cacioppo, J. T., & Petty, R. E. (1983). *Social psychophysiology: A sourcebook.* New York: Guilford.

Cacioppo, J. T., Tassinary, L. G., & Fridlund, A. J. (1990). Skeletomotor system. In J. T. Cacioppo & L. G. Tassinary (Eds.), *Principles of psychophysiology: Physical, social, and inferential elements* (pp. 325-384). New York: Cambridge University Press.

Cacioppo, J. T., Uchino, B. N., Crites, S. L., Snyder, M. A., Smith, G., Berntson, G. G., & Lang, P. (in press). The relationship between facial expressiveness and sympathetic activation in emotion: A critical review with emphasis on modeling underlying mechanisms and individual differences. *Journal of Personality and Social Psychology.*

Candland, D. K. (1977). The persistent problems of emotion. In D. K. Candland, J. P. Fell, E. Keen, A. I. Leshner, R. Plutchik, & R. M. Tarpy (Eds.), *Emotion.* Monterey, CA: Brooks/Cole.

Cappella, J. N., & Planalp, S. (1981). Talk and silence sequences in informal conversations III: Interspeaker influence. *Human Communication Research, 7,* 117-132.

Carlson, J. G., & Hatfield, E. (1992). *Psychology of emotion.* Fort Worth, TX: Harcourt Brace Jovanovich.

Chapple, E. D. (1982). Movement and sound: The musical language of body rhythms in interaction. In M. Davis (Ed.), *Interaction rhythms: Periodicity in communicative behavior* (pp. 31-52). New York: Human Sciences Press.

Chew, P. K., Phoon, W. H., & Mae-Lim, H. A. (1976). Epidemic hysteria among some factory workers in Singapore. *Singapore Medical Journal, 17,* 10-15.

Condon, W. S., & Ogston, W. D. (1966). Sound film analysis of normal and pathological behavior patterns. *Journal of Nervous Mental Disorders, 143,* 338-347.

Coyne, J. C. (1976). Depression and the response of others. *Journal of Abnormal Psychology, 85*, 186-193.

Darwin, C. (1965). *The expression of the emotions in man and animals.* Chicago: University of Chicago Press. (Original work published 1872)

Davis, M. R. (1985). Perceptual and affective reverberation components. In A. B. Goldstein & G. Y. Michaels (Eds.), *Empathy: Development, training, and consequences* (pp. 62-108). Hillsdale, NJ: Lawrence Erlbaum.

Dimberg, U. (1982). Facial reactions to facial expressions. *Psychophysiology, 19*, 643-647.

Duclos, S. E., Laird, J. D., Schneider, E., Sexter, M., Stern, L., & Van Lighten, O. (1989). Emotion-specific effects of facial expressions and postures on emotional experience. *Journal of Personality and Social Psychology, 57*, 100-108.

Ebrahim, G. J. (1968). Mass hysteria in school children: Notes on three out-breaks in East Africa. *Clinical Pediatrics, 7*, 437-438.

Eisenberg, N., & Miller, P. (1987). Empathy, sympathy, and altruism: Empirical and conceptual links. In N. Eisenberg & J. Strayer (Eds.), *Empathy and its development* (pp. 292-316). New York: Cambridge University Press.

Ekman, P. (1985). *Telling lies.* New York: Berkeley Books.

Ekman, P. (in press). Are there basic emotions? A reply to Ortony and Turner. *Psychological Review.*

Englis, B. G., Vaughan, K. B., & Lanzetta, J. T. (1982). Conditioning of counterempathic emotional responses. *Journal of Experimental Social Psychology, 18*, 375-391.

Fischer, K. W., Shaver, P. R., & Carnochan, P. (1990). How emotions develop and how they organize development. *Cognition and Emotion, 4*, 81-127.

Friedman, H. S., & Riggio, R. E. (1981). Effect of individual differences in nonverbal expressiveness on transmission of emotion. *Journal of Nonverbal Behavior, 6*, 96-101.

Frodi, A. M., Lamb, N. E., Leavitt, L. A., Donovan, W. L., Neff, C., & Sherry, D. (1978). Fathers' and mothers' responses to the faces and cries of normal and premature infants. *Developmental Psychology, 14*, 490-498.

Gazzaniga, M. S. (1985). *The social brain: Discovering the networks of the mind.* New York: Basic Books.

Haggard, E. A., & Issacs, F. S. (1966). Micromomentary facial expressions as indicators of ego mechanisms in psychotherapy. In C. A. Gottschalk & A. Averback (Eds.), *Methods of research in psychotherapy* (pp. 154-165). New York: Appleton-Century-Crofts.

Hatfield, E., Costello, J., Schalenkamp, M., Hsee, C., & Denney, C. (1991). *The impact of vocal feedback on emotional experience.* Unpublished manuscript, University of Hawaii, Honolulu.

Haviland, J. M., & Lelwica, M. (1987). The induced affect response: 10-week-old infants' responses to three emotion expressions. *Developmental Psychology, 23*, 97-104.

Hecker, J. F. (1970). *The dancing mania of the Middle Ages* (B. Babington, Trans.). New York: Burt Franklin.

Hoffman, M. L. (1973). *Empathy, role-taking, guilt, and the development of altruistic motives* (Developmental Psychology Report No. 30). Ann Arbor: University of Michigan.

Hoffman, M. L. (1987). The contribution of empathy to justice and moral judgement. In N. Eisenberg & J. Strayer (Eds.), *Empathy and its development* (pp. 47-80). New York: Cambridge University Press.

Howes, M. J., Hokanson, J. E., & Lowenstein, D. A. (1985). Induction of depressive affect after prolonged exposure to a mildly depressed individual. *Journal of Personality and Social Psychology, 49,* 1110-1113.

Hsee, C., Hatfield, E., Carlson, J. G., & Chemtob, C. (1991a). The effect of power on susceptibility to emotional contagion. *Cognition and Emotion, 4,* 327-340.

Hsee, C., Hatfield, E., Carlson, J. G., & Chemtob, C. (1991b). *Emotional contagion and its relationship to mood.* Unpublished manuscript, University of Hawaii, Honolulu.

Hsee, C., Hatfield, E., & Chemtob, C. (1992). The effect of targets' emotional appraisals/expressions on observer's appraisals/expressions. *Journal of Clinical and Social Psychology, 11,* 119-128..

Humphrey, G. (1922). The conditioned reflex and the elementary social reaction. *Journal of Abnormal and Social Psychology, 17,* 113-119.

Izard, C. E. (1971). *The face of emotion.* New York: Appleton-Century-Crofts.

Izard, C. E. (1977). *Human emotions.* New York: Plenum.

Izard, C. E. (in press). Basic emotions, relations among emotions, and emotion-cognition relations. *Psychological Review.*

Jung, C. G. (1968). Lecture five. In *Analytical psychology: Its theory and practice* (pp. 151-160). New York: Random House.

Kellerman, J., Lewis, J., & Laird, J. D. (1989). Looking and loving: The effects of mutual gaze on feelings of romantic love. *Journal of Research in Personality, 23,* 145-161.

Kendon, A. (1970). Movement coordination in social interaction: Some examples described. *Acta Psychologica, 32,* 1-25.

Kerckhoff, A. C., & Back, K. W. (1968). *The June bug: A study of hysterical contagion.* New York: Appleton-Century-Crofts.

Kleck, R. E., Vaughan, R. C., Cartwright-Smith, J., Vaughan, K. B., Colby, C. Z., & Lanzetta, J. T. (1976). Effects of being observed on expressive, subjective, and physiological responses to painful stimuli. *Journal of Personality and Social Psychology, 34,* 1211-1218.

Klinnert, M. D., Campos, J. J., Sorce, J. F., Emde, R. N., & Sveida, M. (1983). Emotions as behavior regulators: Social referencing in infants. In R. Plutchik & H. Kellerman (Eds.), *Emotion: Theory, research, and experience* (Vol. 2, pp. 57-86). New York: Academic Press.

Kopel, S., & Arkowitz, H. S. (1974). Role playing as a source of self-observation and behavior change. *Journal of Personality and Social Psychology, 29,* 677-686.

Kraut, R. E. (1982). Social pressure, facial feedback, and emotion. *Journal of Personality and Social Psychology, 42,* 853-863.

Lachman, R., Lachman, J. L., & Butterfield, E. C. (1979). *Cognitive psychology and information processing: An introduction.* Hillsdale, NJ: Lawrence Erlbaum.

Laird, J. D. (1984). The real role of facial response in the experience of emotion: A reply to Tourangeau and Ellsworth and others. *Journal of Personality and Social Psychology, 47,* 909-917.

Laird, J. D., & Bresler, C. (1991). The process of emotional feeling: A self-perception theory. In M. Clark (Ed.), *Review of personality and social psychology: Vol. 13. Emotion.* Newbury Park, CA: Sage.

Lang, P. J. (1985). The cognitive psychophysiology of emotion: Fear and anxiety. In A. H. Tuma & J. D. Maser (Eds.), *Anxiety and the anxiety disorders* (pp. 131-170). Hillsdale, NJ: Lawrence Erlbaum.

Lanzetta, J. T., Biernat, J. J., & Kleck, R. E. (1982). Self-focused attention, facial behavior, autonomic arousal and the experience of emotion. *Motivation and Emotion, 6,* 49-63.

Lanzetta, J. T., & McHugo, G. J. (1986, October). *The history and current status of the facial feedback hypothesis.* Paper presented at the 26th Annual Meeting of the Society for Psychophysiological Research Montreal, Quebec, Canada.

Lanzetta, J. T., & Orr, S. P. (1981). Stimulus properties of facial expressions and their influence on the classical conditioning of fear. *Motivation and Emotion, 5,* 225-234.

Lanzetta, J. T., & Orr, S. P. (1986). Excitatory strength of expressive faces: Effects of happy and fear expressions and context on the extinction of a conditioned fear response. *Journal of Personality and Social Psychology, 50,* 190-194.

Larsen, R. J., Kasimatis, M., & Frey, K. (1990). *Facilitating the furrowed brow: An unobtrusive test of the facial feedback hypothesis applied to negative affect.* Unpublished manuscript, University of Michigan, Ann Arbor.

Le Bon, G. (1896). *The crowd: A study of the popular mind.* London: Ernest Benn.

Leventhal, H., & Mace, W. (1970). The effect of laughter on evaluation of a slapstick movie. *Journal of Personality, 38,* 16-30.

Lewicki, P. (1986). *Nonconscious social information processing.* New York: Academic Press.

Lipps, T. (1906). Das Wissen von fremden Ichen. *Psychologische Untersuchnung, 1,* 694-722.

MacLean, P. D. (1975). Sensory and perceptive factors in emotional function of the triune brain. In R. G. Grenell & S. Gabay (Eds.), *Biological foundations of psychiatry* (Vol. 1, pp. 177-198). New York: Raven.

Malatesta, C. Z., & Haviland, J. M. (1982). Learning display rules: The socialization of emotion expression in infancy. *Child Development, 53,* 991-1003.

Matarazzo, J. D., Weitman, M., Saslow, G., & Wiens, A. N. (1963). Interviewer influence on durations of interviewee speech. *Journal of Verbal Learning and Verbal Behavior, 1,* 451-458.

Matarazzo, J. D., & Wiens, A. N. (1972). *The interview: Research on its anatomy and structure.* Chicago: Aldine-Atherton.

Matsumoto, D. (1987). The role of facial response in the experience of emotion: More methodological problems and a meta-analysis. *Journal of Personality and Social Psychology, 52,* 769-774.

McCaul, K. D., Holmes, D. S., & Solomon, S. (1982). Voluntary expressive changes and emotion. *Journal of Personality and Social Psychology, 42,* 145-152.

Meltzoff, A. N. (1988). Infant imitation after a 1-week delay: Long-term memory for novel acts and multiple stimuli. *Developmental Psychology, 24,* 470-476.

Murphy, G. (1947). *Personality: A biosocial approach to origins and structure.* New York: Harper.

Ohman, A. (1988). Nonconscious control of autonomic responses: A role for Pavlovian conditioning? *Biological Psychology, 27,* 113-135.

Orimoto, L., & Hatfield, E. (1992). *An individual difference measure of emotional contagion.* Unpublished manuscript, University of Hawaii, Honolulu.

Ortony, A., & Turner, T. J. (1990). What's basic about basic emotions? *Psychological Review, 97,* 315-331.

O'Toole, R., & Dubin, R. (1968). Baby feeding and body sway: An experiment in George Herbert Meads' "Taking the Role of the Other." *Journal of Personality and Social Psychology, 10,* 59-65.

Panksepp, J. (1986). The anatomy of emotions. In R. Plutchik & H. Kellerman (Eds.), *Emotion: Theory, research and experience: Vol. 3. Biological foundations of emotion* (pp. 91-124). New York: Academic Press.

Panksepp, J. (in press). A critical role for "affective neuroscience" in resolving what is basic about basic emotions: Response to Ortony and Turner. *Psychological Review.*

Papez, J. W. (1937). A proposed mechanism of emotion. *Archives of Neurology and Psychiatry, 38,* 725-743.

Posner, M. I., & Snyder, C. R. R. (1975). Attention and cognitive control. In R. L. Solso (Ed.), *Information processing and cognition: The Loyola Symposium.* Hillsdale, NJ: Lawrence Erlbaum.

Reay, M. (1960). "Mushroom madness" in the New Guinea Highlands. *Oceania, 31,* 135-139.

Reik, T. (1948). *Listening with the third ear: The inner experience of a psychoanalyst.* New York: Farrar, Straus & Giroux.

Reissland, N. (1988). Neonatal imitation in the first hour of life: Observations in rural Nepal. *Developmental Psychology, 24,* 464-469.

Rutledge, L. L., & Hupka, R. B. (1985). The facial feedback hypothesis: Methodological concerns and new supporting evidence. *Motivation and Emotion, 9,* 219-240.

Schachter, S., & Singer, J. (1962). Cognitive, social, and physiological determinants of emotional state. *Psychological Review, 69,* 379-399.

Scheflen, A. E. (1964). The significance of posture in communication systems. *Psychiatry, 27,* 316-331.

Schmeck, H. M. (1983, September 9). Study says smile may indeed be an umbrella. *The New York Times, 132,* pp. 1, 16.

Shiffrin, R. M., & Schneider, W. (1977). Controlled and automatic human information processing: II: Perceptual learning, automatic attending and a general theory. *Psychological Review, 84,* 127-190.

Simner, M. L. (1971). Newborn's response to the cry of another infant. *Developmental Psychology, 5,* 136-150.

Smith, A. (1966). *The theory of moral sentiments.* New York: Augustus M. Kelley. (Original work published 1759)

Strack, F., Martin, L. L., & Stepper, S. (1988). Inhibiting and facilitating conditions of facial expressions: A non-obtrusive test of the facial feedback hypothesis. *Journal of Personality and Social Psychology, 54,* 768-776.

Sullins, E. S. (1991). Emotional contagion revisited: Effects of social comparison and expressive style on mood convergence. *Personality and Social Psychology Bulletin, 17,* 166-174.

Tansey, M. J., & Burke, W. F. (1989). *Understanding counter-transference: From projective identification to empathy.* Hillsdale, NJ: Analytic Press.

Teoh, J. I., Soewondo, S., & Sidhartha, M. (1975). Epidemic hysteria in Malaysian schools: An illustrative episode. *Psychiatry, 38,* 258-269.

Thompson, R. A. (1987). Empathy and emotional understanding: The early development of empathy. In N. Eisenberg & J. Strayer (Eds.), *Empathy and its development* (pp. 119-145). New York: Cambridge University Press.

Tickle-Degnen, L., & Rosenthal, R. (1987). Group rapport and nonverbal behavior. *Review of Personality and Social Psychology, 9,* 113-136.

Titchener, E. (1909). *Experimental psychology of the thought processes.* New York: Macmillan.

Tomkins, S. S. (1963). *Affect, imagery, consciousness* (Vol. 2). New York: Springer.

Tomkins, S. S. (1982). Affect theory. In P. Ekman (Ed.), *Emotion in the human face* (2nd ed., pp. 353-395). Cambridge: Cambridge University Press.

Tourangeau, R., & Ellsworth, P. C. (1979). The role of facial response in the experience of emotion. *Journal of Personality and Social Psychology, 37,* 1519-1531.

Tronick, E. D., Als, H., & Brazelton, T. B. (1977). Mutuality in mother-infant interaction. *Journal of Communication, 27,* 74-79.

Tseng, W., & Hsu, J. (1980). Minor psychological disturbances of everyday life. In H. C. Triandis & J. D. Draguns (Eds.), *Handbook of cross-cultural psychology: Vol. 6. Psychopathology* (pp. 61-97). Boston: Allyn & Bacon.

Uchino, B. C., Hatfield, E., Carlson, J. G., & Chemtob, C. (1991). *The effect of cognitive expectations on susceptibility to emotional contagion.* Unpublished manuscript, University of Hawaii, Honolulu.

Vaughan, K. B., & Lanzetta, J. T. (1980). Vicarious instigation and conditioning of facial expressive and autonomic responses to a model's expressive display of pain. *Journal of Personality and Social Psychology, 38,* 909-923.

Voglmaier, M. M., & Hakeren, G. (1989, August). *Facial electromyography (EMG) in response to facial expressions: Relation to subjective emotional experience and trait affect.* Paper presented at the Society for Psychophysiological Research, New Orleans, LA.

Warner, R. (1988). Rhythm in social interaction. In J. E. McGrath (Ed.), *The social psychology of time: New perspectives* (pp. 63-88). Newbury Park, CA: Sage.

Warner, R. (1990). *Interaction tempo and evaluation of affect in social interaction: Rhythmic systems versus causal modeling approaches.* Unpublished manuscript.

Warner, R. M., Waggener, T. B., & Kronauer, R. E. (1983). Synchronized cycles in ventilation and vocal activity during spontaneous conversational speech. *Journal of Physiology: Respiratory, Environmental and Exercise Physiology, 54,* 1324-1334.

Webb, J. T. (1972). Interview synchrony: An investigation of two speech rate measures. In A. W. Siegman & B. Pope (Eds.), *Studies in dyadic communication* (pp. 115-133). New York; Pergamon.

Wheeler, L. (1966). Toward a theory of behavioral contagion. *Psychological Review, 73,* 179-192.

Wilson, T. D. (1985). Strangers to ourselves: The origins and accuracy of beliefs about one's own mental status. In J. N. Harvey & G. Weary (Eds.), *Attribution: Basic issues and applications* (pp. 9-36). New York: Academic Press.

Zajonc, R. B., Murphy, S. T., & Inglehart, M. (1989). Feeling and facial efference: Implications of the vascular theory of emotion. *Psychological Review, 96,* 395-416.

Zuckerman, M., Klorman, R., Larrance, D. T., & Speigel, N. H. (1981). Facial, autonomic, and subjective components of emotion: The facial feedback hypothesis versus the externalizer-internalizer distinction. *Journal of Personality and Social Psychology, 41,* 929-944.

7

Toward a Reconsideration of the Gender-Emotion Relationship

MARIANNE LaFRANCE
MAHZARIN BANAJI

Marianne LaFrance is Professor of Psychology at Boston College. She has been a visiting faculty fellow at Yale University, the University of California at San Francisco, and Radcliffe College. Her research is concerned with gender, nonverbal communication, tacit knowledge, and the relationship between language and social cognition.

Mahzarin Banaji is Assistant Professor of Psychology at Yale University. Her research interests concern affect, self, attitudes, stereotyping, and research methodology.

Declarations about how women and men differ emotionally abound in the psychological literature. They can be found in the Parsonian normative construction of family roles, with women described as the "expressive" experts and men as the "instrumental" experts (Parsons & Bales, 1955). They are manifest in measures of gender role identification, where emotion items constitute the key components of identification with the feminine and not masculine sex role (Constantinople, 1973). Emotionality also features prominently in the content of gender stereotypes with at least 75% agreement among subjects (both female and male) that the labels "very emotional" and "very aware of feelings of others" were seen to be more characteristic of females than males (Broverman, Vogel, Broverman, Clarkson, & Rosenkrantz, 1972). A converging result emerges strikingly in Shields's (1987) finding that more than 80% of males and females mention a female target when asked to name the most emotional person they know. Additionally, social pressures tend to facilitate emotionality in mothers as compared with fathers (Shields & Koster, 1989), and clinical thinking about gender underscores females' apparent greater access to their emotions (Chodorow, 1980).

Perhaps because the belief in gender differences in emotionality is so pervasive and perennial, it has tended to mask the complexity of defining what it means to be emotional. That is, how should investigators reach the conclusion that women are more emotional than men or, alternatively, that men are less emotional than women? Research has called upon several modalities of expression to provide information about variability in emotionality, including verbal self-report, nonverbal expressivity, and physiological reactivity. Further, within each modality of expression, there are arrays of measures including emotional intensity, frequency, duration, range, latency, accuracy, and congruence across modalities and measures.

The absence of a single measure of emotion makes the gender-emotion relationship a complicated one. For example, if males report less emotion than females on a self-report measure, should that constitute sufficient evidence of lower emotionality? Further, if gender differences found on self-report measures are absent or reversed on nonverbal or physiological measures, which should be considered the more legitimate measure of emotionality? If gender differences emerge in some contexts and not in others (e.g., public versus private), is an explanation based on basic group differences sufficient or is it necessary to invoke the role of situational influences in explaining gender differences in the expression of emotion?

The purpose of this chapter is twofold: first, to reexamine the gender-emotion relationship with a particular focus on the bench marks used to assess emotionality and, second, to identify the circumstances under which differences in emotionality are likely to be manifest or absent. This review focuses attention on research primarily published in the 1980s (although a few pertinent earlier studies are included). See excellent articles by Brody (1985) and Shields (1987) that review earlier research. Moreover, this review concentrates on adult populations. For a development perspective, see Brody (1985).

The reexamination is organized into three sections, each representing a prominent modality through which emotionality is believed to be manifest. These three modalities are not merely alternative ways of measuring the same underlying construct. Indeed, investigators of emotion are agreed that emotionality is a multidimensional construct and the three modalities are necessary for an adequate understanding of individual variability. We begin by reviewing research on gender and emotionality that focuses on the phenomenal experience of emotion, the data being obtained primarily through verbal self-report measures. Next, we turn to research that assesses the role of gender in nonverbal expressivity, with facial expressivity providing the primary data. Finally, we review research that compares how females and males react physiologically to emotional situations. As will become apparent, there are proportionately more studies that use self-report measures to assess emotionality. Thus the greater amount of the chapter devoted to self-report measures is a reflection of the state of the investigations undertaken.

SELF-REPORT OF EMOTIONALITY

As indicated, verbal self-report indicators of emotionality constitute much of the literature addressing the gender-emotionality relationship. But self-report measures themselves vary in a number of significant ways, and the dimensions along which they differ are critical to understanding how to interpret the results issuing from these indicators. We propose a four-dimensional scheme for characterizing self-reports of emotionality. Specifically, self-reports of emotionality vary in directness (e.g., is the measure a direct probe, such as "how emotional are you?" or is the measure derived from subjects' verbal data, such as the number of emotion words produced?). Second, self-reports vary in whether the experience being reported can be perceived by observers (e.g., does the self-report focus on private, subjective states or on public display?). Third, self-report measures vary in terms of whether the context surrounding the emotional event is included (e.g., does the measure differentiate between interpersonal and impersonal elicitors and/or outcomes of emotion?). Finally, self-reports vary in the specificity of the emotion being probed (e.g., does the measure ask about general emotionality or discrete emotional states?).

The four dimensions of self-report measures are conceptually distinguishable even though in research practice they are not often separated. In this chapter, they serve two objectives. First, these dimensions constitute a useful way to organize and interpret a complex set of findings. Second, a consideration of these dimensions suggests hypotheses to test in future examinations of gender and emotion. In particular, we encourage examination of the following questions: Are gender differences more likely to occur when the measurement is direct rather than indirect, when the domain is public rather than private, when the context is interpersonal rather than impersonal, and when the assessment is of global emotionality rather than of discrete emotional states?

Direct Versus Indirect Self-Reports

The direct-indirect dimension refers to the degree to which the data provided by the subject are used directly, that is, without transformation by the investigator. For example, on a direct measure, subjects may be asked to indicate how emotional, how angry, or how happy they feel. Subjects' rated judgments of their subjective emotional states serve as the data. In addition to obtaining such measures in laboratory research, several personality measures of emotion also use direct self-report such as the Affect Intensity Measure (AIM; Larsen & Diener, 1987), the Affective Communication Test (ACT; Friedman, Prince, Riggio, & DiMatteo, 1980), and the Emotional Expressiveness Questionnaire (EEQ; King & Emmons, 1990). For each scale, a score is derived by summing across multiple items that ask subjects to report how much emotion they feel or express to others.

In contrast, indirect self-report measures also require subjects to generate a verbal self-report but the final emotion score is derived or extracted from subjects' responses. For example, an open-ended verbalization could be coded for incidence of emotion words to derive an indirect index of emotionality. Or an investigator could compute the degree to which the subject spoke about an emotional incident in the past or present tense with theory dictating that the former represents greater emotional "distance" than the latter (Lutz, 1990). Other examples of indirect measures include those that extract information about emotionality from self-descriptions (Mackie, 1980) or from a test of memory for emotional information (Banaji, Greenwald, & Bellezza, 1985). Such indirect measures assume that greater use of emotion terms or better memory for emotional words reveals greater emotionality.

The vast majority of studies of gender and emotion use direct self-report measures. Recent studies in this genre find gender differences, with females reporting greater emotionality than males (see Balswick, 1988), confirming early declarations by Terman and Miles (1936). In addition, assessments of stable individual differences in emotionality are almost without exception direct measures. These include efforts to measure the frequency with which one experiences a range of mood states (McNair, Lorr, & Droppleman, 1981), the stability of emotional dispositions (Spielberger et al., 1979), or the intensity of affect (Larsen & Diener, 1987). These direct measures find that females report greater emotion than males. For example, on the Affective Intensity Measure (AIM), respondents indicate their agreement with such items as this one: "My emotions tend to be more intense than those of most people." On this 40-item questionnaire, females have been found to score higher than males (Diener, Sandvik, & Larsen, 1985).

When indirect self-report measures of emotion are used, the results are much less likely to yield clear and reliable gender differences. For example, in content analyses of subjects' memories about valued possessions, Banaji and LaFrance (1989) found that male and female subjects did not differ in the use of emotion terms (e.g., love, anger), even though females did use more evaluative words (e.g., like, dislike) than males (see Shimanoff, 1983). Other studies using indirect measures have also failed to find gender differences. For example, no gender differences were found when males and females were asked to rate the intensity of 102 positive and negative adjectives drawn from the Depression Adjective Checklist (Lubin, Rinck, & Collins, 1986), when dream diaries were analyzed for emotion content (Stairs & Blick, 1979), when emotional reactions to film segments were coded (McHugo, Smith, & Lanzetta, 1982), or when interpersonal verbs were rated for their degree of similarity (Wier, Phillips, & Stanners, 1987).

Likewise, no gender differences were found when subjects' verbalizations about specific emotional experiences were content analyzed (Lutz, 1990). In this study, descriptions by females and males of recent emotional experiences were coded for the degree to which they "personalized" the emotional experience. One indicator involved the degree to which the respondent distanced the experience from self, such as by using the past or conditional tense or by identifying another as experiencing the emotion. Results showed no differences between male and female speakers in the use of verb tense or in the tendency to focus on the self or another as the experiencer of the emotion. Also, males and females were not distinguishable in terms of the degree to which they negated or denied experiencing emotional states. Shimanoff (1983) also found few gender differences in the incidence of emotion language in natural conversations of both college students and married couples, and Campbell and Muncer (1987) noted few gender differences in talk about anger incidents. It appears that gender differences in emotionality are more likely to emerge depending on whether the self-report is direct rather than indirect.

Public Versus Private Self-Reports

Self-report measures also differ in the degree to which the self-report refers to a private, subjective state or to a public display. At one end of this dimension, for example, are self-reports about privately experienced feelings (e.g., "I feel things more deeply than most people"). At the other end of the dimension are self-reports concerning an overt expression of emotion (e.g., "Most people can tell what I am feeling"). Although both responses represent subjects' beliefs about their emotionality, they differ in the degree to which the report emphasized the private, subjective experience of emotion or the public, communicative aspect of emotion.

Several measures include the public-private dimension of self-reported expression of emotion. They include the Affective Intensity Measure (AIM; Diener et al., 1985) and the Emotional Expressiveness Questionnaire (EEQ; King & Emmons, 1990), and females have been found to score higher than males on both. Although EEQ was designed to measure self-reported expressivity (e.g., "People can tell from my facial expressions how I am feeling"), whereas AIM was designed to tap differences in felt affective intensity, King and Emmons (1990) found EEQ to be significantly and positively correlated with AIM. Thus the possibility exists that AIM assesses not only intensity of felt affect but also intensity of expressed affect. The distinction is important for there is the possibility that overt expression may be somewhat independent of subjective experience, in the sense that there can be both subjective experience without overt expression and overt expression without subjective experience. To the degree to which there is some independence, then self-report measures of emotionality that draw on assessments of expressivity may be amiss in concluding that presence of one aspect, namely, expressivity, is evidence for a presumed difference in another key aspect, namely, subjective experience.

Indeed, the strongest evidence of gender differences in emotionality occurs on self-report measures of expressivity rather than self-reports of subjective experience (Dosser, Balswick, & Halverson, 1983; King & Emmons, 1990; Schenk & Heinisch, 1986; Zuckerman, 1989). An investigation of student populations from several Western European countries and Israel found that females more than males self-reported greater nonverbal expressivity, especially facial reactions, on four emotions (joy, sadness, fear, anger; Wallbott, Ricci-Bitti, & Banninger-Huber,

1986). There were no comparable gender differences on self-reported physiological symptoms, although males reported more unspecified sensations. The authors propose that the greater self-report of expressivity by females than males may be a product of gender-specific display rules that encourage females to be more nonverbally expressive than males. Further evidence for this assertion comes from a recent study in which male and female subjects completed the Differential Emotions Scale under conditions varying in anonymity. Females who were publicly identified scored higher than anonymous females on positive emotions and lower on negative emotions. Males in anonymous conditions scored lower on all emotions than males in identified conditions (O'Grady & Janda, 1989).

Few self-report studies have incorporated an explicit test of the conditions that may or may not generate gender differences. A notable exception is an investigation that combined self-report of private, emotional experience and of public, expressive display (Allen & Haccoun, 1976). Both aspects of emotion were investigated with respect to anger, fear, joy, and sadness. Male and female subjects were surveyed for the degree of self-reported emotional *responsiveness* (e.g., how frequently and intensely each emotion was felt), *expressiveness* (the degree to which the emotion expressed feelings to same- or opposite-sex others), *orientation* (attitudes toward feeling each emotion and about others' emotional expressions), and *social situations* (interpersonal or impersonal situations that lead to each emotion).

On self-reports of public display, females reported being more expressive than males on all four emotions. But, on self-reports of private experience, females scored higher than males only on fear and sadness. Moreover, no gender differences emerged on self-reported orientation toward feeling and perceiving each emotion in others, except for females' somewhat greater positive orientation toward feeling joy. Thus the most unqualified results concerned the greater tendency of females to report being more publicly expressive than males. On measures of private experience, no consistent gender differences emerged.

Other studies have addressed self-reported gender differences in this public aspect of emotionality. For example, when males and females were asked to report on their willingness to reveal their emotional state to others, females reported greater emotional disclosure to others than males (Paprini, Farmer, Clark, & Micka, 1990). In a comparable fashion, results from a study in which college students were asked to indicate their willingness to discuss their emotions with others showed that females, compared with males, indicated more willingness to communicate feelings of depression, happiness, anger, calmness, and fear (Snell, Miller, Belk, Garcia-Falconi, & Hernandez-Sanchez, 1989). Thomas (1989) also found that females say they are more likely than males to discuss feelings of anger with others.

Interpersonal Versus Impersonal Self-Reports

A third dimension along which self-report measures may be differentiated involves the interpersonal versus impersonal context of the emotional response. This includes both the nature of the eliciting conditions as well as the aftermath of the emotional event. With respect to eliciting conditions, respondents might be asked to recall whether specific others evoked an emotional state (interpersonal) or whether the emotion arose from events not necessarily involving others (impersonal).

As there has been relatively little investigation of differences in self-reports regarding elicitors of emotion, a study by Stapley and Haviland (1989) is particularly informative. Adolescent subjects responded to the Elicitors of Emotion Questionnaire (Stapley & Haviland, 1986) about the frequency, intensity, and duration of their experiences of 12 emotions. The study found that females reported more social elicitors to their emotional experiences than males. Moreover, subjects who invoked more interpersonal antecedents also reported a longer duration of the emotional experience and higher average intensity of emotion and produced longer verbal accounts. These findings match those of Allen and Haccoun (1976), who found that although females reported proportionally more interpersonal elicitors than males, there were no gender differences with respect to impersonal elicitors. Note, however, that Phillips and Whissell (1986) failed to find gender differences on emotional elicitors with younger children (6-13 years of age), suggesting that attending to interpersonal elicitors may be a learned behavior, expected more of females than males.

Paralleling the paucity of research on gender effects on the elicitors of emotions is the equally sparse research on self-reported aftermath to emotional states. Nolen-Hoeksema (1987) argued that, in response to depression, men are more likely to engage in distracting behaviors whereas women are more likely to amplify the feeling by ruminating on it. Other research supports the finding that depressed female college students are more likely to respond with more obvious emotional manifestations (e.g., guilt, sadness), while depressed male college students are more likely to report social withdrawal (Hammen & Peters, 1977; Oliver & Toner, 1990). To the extent that social withdrawal is not considered an emotional reaction, it appears that females respond with greater emotion than males. If the definition is broadened to encompass changes in activity or conduct, then males may have demonstrated an emotional response as well.

Recently, this gender difference in self-reported rumination or distraction has been qualified by results that implicate gender role identification rather than gender per se. Conway, Giannopoulos, and Stiefenhofer (1990) show that high femininity scorers compared with low femininity scorers reported more rumination on items such as "I get together with one very close person or friend." In contrast, people who score higher on masculinity reported more distraction behaviors (e.g., "I get away and do something I enjoy"). This finding is consistent with other data linking gender role identification to emotional expressiveness (Ganong & Coleman, 1985).

Global Versus Discrete Emotion Self-Reports

Finally, self-report measures can differ on a global versus discrete dimension. A measure of global emotion elicits self-report about general emotionality that relies on the everyday understanding of what it means to be emotional. A global self-report measure also can be one that sums across self-reports of several emotions. In contrast, measures of discrete emotion elicit self-reports of specific types of emotion (e.g., anger, sadness, joy). Individual difference measures of emotion, such as Izard's Differential Emotions Scale, are often used to assess differences among reported frequency of several emotions (Izard, 1977; Izard, Dougherty, Bloxom, & Kotsch, 1974). Most investigators examining the gender-emotion relationship have tended to favor measures of discrete states rather than global emotion (but see Diener et al., 1985). As a result, the findings reviewed here should be considered suggestive rather than definitive. It remains for future research to provide direct comparisons of self-reports of global and discrete emotion.

We hypothesize that gender differences are more likely to occur when people are asked about global emotionality rather than about particular emotional states. Global assessments (e.g., "How emotional are you?"), drawing as they do on commonplace understanding of the term *emotional* ("showing emotion, especially strong emotion," "easily aroused to emotion"; *Webster's New World Dictionary,* second college edition), will tend to elicit judgments based on stereotypes of emotion. Self-report measures of discrete emotions may show a less clear gender-emotion link both because stereotypes of gender differences in discrete emotions may be more variable and because specific emotions may be more tied to particular circumstances, resulting in gender being only one of several factors effecting differences in reported frequency or intensity of emotion.

The most obvious finding from existing studies investigating gender and self-report of discrete emotions is the lack of any consistent relationship. Shields (1984) found no differences in the degree to which anger, sadness, and anxiety were reported to be felt by males and females. She did find that females self-reported more physiological symptoms associated with each state. Although Thomas (1989) found females to report more physical aspects of anger, Wallbott et al. (1986) found no evidence for gender differences in self-reports of physiological symptoms associated with any emotion.

Among adolescent subjects, studies have investigated gender differences in self-reports of subjective experience and found that results vary as a function of the particular emotion that is judged. Using the Differential Emotions Scale (Izard, 1977), females were found to score higher than males on reports of shame, guilt, and sadness, among others, whereas there were no gender differences on joy, fear, disgust, and anger (Stapley & Haviland, 1989). Other studies show that girls report more intense sadness, whereas boys report more intense anger (Harris & Howard, 1987), while still others report no differences on guilt but greater depression by females and greater arousal by males (Boyle, 1989).

Some investigators have claimed that certain discrete emotions (e.g., anger) are more typical of males, whereas others (e.g., sadness, fear) are more typical of females. In fact, Birnbaum and Croll (1984) showed that, as early as preschool age, children "know" that anger is a male characteristic while fear, sadness, and happiness are female characteristics. When subjects are asked about their ability to express a range of different emotions, few gender differences materialized. For example, Blier and Blier-Wilson (1989) asked male and female college students to rate the confidence they had in their ability to express several emotions, including anger, liking/love and affection, fear, sadness, vulnerability, and loneliness to a male or female other. Although there was no main effect of gender in self-rated expressivity, some discrete emotion effects were obtained. For fear and sadness, females expressed higher confidence in their expressive ability than males but, with respect to anger and liking, the effects varied as a combined function of subject and target gender. That is, males expressed more confidence in their ability to express anger with male than with female targets and females expressed greater confidence than males in their ability to convey liking toward male targets.

Even when the discrete emotion is stereotypically linked to gender (e.g., males show more anger than females), results are far from conclusive. A recurrent theme in the gender and emotion literature is the greater social pressure on women than on men to control and manage both the experience and the display of anger (Smith, Ulch, Cameron, & Cumberland, 1989; Stearns & Stearns, 1986). For example, Gueldner and Clayton (1987) reported low anger-hostility scores on the Profile of Mood States (POMS; McNair, Lorr, & Droppleman, 1981) in a sample of elderly women. Nevertheless, several investigators have noted no statistically reliable gender difference on state or trait anger (Averill, 1982; Kopper & Epperson, 1991; Spielberger, Jacobs, Russell, & Crane, 1983; Stoner & Spencer, 1987; Tavris, 1984). Burrowes and Halberstadt (1987) explored gender differences on a self-report measure designed to tap experienced and expressed anger in social situations. In addition, they obtained a rating of expressivity by a friend or family member for some respondents. Again, no reliable gender differences were found on any measure. In a recent study, Thomas (1989) investigated self-reported anger in a diverse sample of middle-aged males and females using the Framingham Anger Scales (Haynes, Levine, Scotch, Feinleib, & Kannel, 1978). Results showed that gender did not predict the likelihood of either suppressing or expressing anger.

Conclusions Regarding Self-Report of Emotionality

Self-reports of emotionality consist of a heterogeneous set of measures, and the aforementioned dimensions provide insight into the conditions associated with greater or lesser gender variability. Organized this way, the existing literature leads us to suggest the following: Females will report being more emotional than males when the measure is direct rather than indirect, when the self-reported emotion is potentially perceptible by others rather than privately experienced, when the context is interpersonal rather than impersonal, and when global rather than discrete emotion is examined.

We offer these hypotheses with two clear caveats. First, most of the studies under review do not measure both ends of the respective dimensions within the same study, and, second, many of the findings that show lack of strong and consistent gender differences are based on null results. Nevertheless, when direct comparisons are available, there is supportive evidence. When respondents are asked to report on how emotionally demonstrative they are, self-reports bear out the stereotype of greater female emotionality if the focus is on self-rated expressivity rather than self-reported experience. That finding, coupled with results showing no consistent gender effects in the ability to be expressive, suggests strongly that the differences may be due to self-presentational conformity with prescribed sex roles.

It seems to be the case that women and men reporting on their tendency to be generally emotional or visibly expressive may be reporting their beliefs about appropriate or expected gender-linked behavior. If, on the other hand, they are asked about particular feelings in particular situations, self-reports may be more influenced by the circumstances that give rise to the feelings rather than by a gender stereotype. Therefore individual variability rather than sex role adherence becomes apparent.

GENDER AND NONVERBAL EXPRESSIVITY

In this section, we deal with a quite different measure of emotionality. Its most salient characteristic is that the response is behavioral rather than verbal, in most cases involving a measure of facial activity. There is considerable evidence that females are more nonverbally expressive than males. First, observers can more accurately identify emotional states from female than from male faces (Buck, Miller, & Caul, 1974; Fujita, Harper, & Wiens, 1980; Gallagher & Shuntich, 1981; Hall, 1984; Wagner, MacDonald, & Manstead, 1986); second, females show a greater amount of facial activity than males (Buck, Baron, & Barette, 1982; Buck, Baron, Goodman, & Shapiro, 1980); third, female faces show more facial electromyographic activity than male faces (Dimburg, 1988; Schwartz, Brown, & Ahern, 1980).

Nevertheless, the pattern of greater female expressivity is not entirely consistent. For example, some studies find that the superiority in expressivity is not always obtained (Cupchik & Poulos, 1984) or obtained across all emotions (Gitter, Black, & Mostofsky, 1972). Particularly with respect to the emotion of anger, there is some evidence that women are actually more likely than men to suppress its expression presumably because anger is thought to be incompatible with being feminine (Haynes et al., 1978; Lerner, 1985).

In addition, there is some data to show that greater expressivity may not necessarily reflect greater emotionality. For example, one study found females to show more facial activity in response to emotionally loaded questions than males but noted no gender differences in more subtle indications, such as gaze aversion (Cherulnik, 1979). These results mirror those obtained earlier by Buck and his colleagues, who found that females displayed more facial movement than males in response to affect-evoking pictures but corresponding sex differences in the intensity of physiological responsivity were not found (Buck et al., 1974). The issue here is whether gender differences in facial display are indicative of underlying state or whether they are better regarded as social signals. These perceptible signals are important both when they are designed to be *seen* by others, as in the case of females, and when they are designed not to be *seen* by others, as in the case of males. Recent studies show that smiling is more likely to occur in the real or imagined presence of others than as a direct manifestation of positive affect (Fridlund, 1991; Kraut & Johnston, 1979).

Other evidence implicates the nature of the social context in which the display occurs. 'For example, although a number of studies have found that women report crying more often than men (Choti, Marston, Holston, & Hart, 1987; Lombardo, Cretser, Lombardo, & Mathis, 1983; Wallbott, 1988), it is also the case that reports of crying vary by the gender of the partner with females indicating that they cry more with males while males report crying less in the company of females (Choti et al., 1987).

Among preteens, girls with high levels of social competence were better at expressing facial affect than those with less competence but there was no such relationship for boys (Custrini & Feldman, 1989). Among adults, there is evidence that males place a high value on female expressivity. For example, males report greater satisfaction with their dating relationship when the exchange is perceived to have followed sex-typed norms, that is, with the male disclosing less about himself relative to his female partner (Millar & Millar, 1988). Males also report being more attracted to a high expressive opposite-gender person than a low expressive opposite-gender person especially if that person was described as physically attractive (Sprecher, 1989). In a related study among married couples, husbands' marital complaints were found to increase as their wives expressive abilities decreased (Sabatelli, Buck, & Dreyer, 1982).

There are also indications that high expressivity by males is often suspect. Hammen and Peters (1977) studied the reactions of students to descriptions of men and women experiencing depressive emotions and found that perceptibly depressed men were evaluated more negatively than the perceptibly depressed women. This pattern of differential negative evaluation did not occur when the descriptions involved apparently unemotional, that is, detached responses. Depression expressed less obviously (e.g., social withdrawal) appears more acceptable for men. Nevertheless, there are indications that the restricted display of emotions by males is undergoing some change, in particular, that it may occasionally be acceptable for males to express "tender emotions" (Balswick, 1988). Also, concern has been voiced by some about the curtailed expressivity and restricted emotionality of males (Goldberg, 1976; O'Neil, 1982). Narus and Fisher (1982) found, for example, that androgynous males were more emotionally expressive than males scoring high on masculine traits, and Cherulnik and Evans (1984) found that men who score high on self-monitoring were judged to be more expressive than men who score low on this measure.

Accordingly, findings on nonverbal expressivity suggest that expressive behavior is actively managed and that the management requires different displays for females and males. Actually, observers tend to believe that the sexes differ more in the overt display of affect than in the intensity of the feelings themselves (Fabes & Martin, 1991; Johnson & Shulman, 1988). Females find inexpressivity in a situation calling for some overt reaction to be censurable (e.g., a funeral; Graham, Gentry, & Green, 1981), whereas the opposite is true for males, with even young boys anticipating negative reactions for being emotionally expressive (Fuchs & Thelen, 1988).

The usual assumption about the differential management of expressivity is that men suppress overt displays of feeling. The other side of that notion, namely, that women may actively enhance their display, has received less attention. Hochschild (1983) starts from the observation that women are more expressive than men but argues that it stems from the social requirement that women do "emotional labor." Emotional labor requires one to induce or suppress feeling to sustain the outward display that produces the preferred state of mind in others. And because the well-managed display resembles spontaneous display, it is possible to confuse the two. In fact, Bugental, Love, and Gianetto (1971) found that mothers' smiles, unlike fathers' smiles, were unrelated to the pleasantness of the message to their children.

A recent study has shown that observers are sensitive to the possibility that emotional displays by females may be deliberately managed. Males and females were presented with written vignettes in which either a male or a female target got angry or sad in response to a frustrating circumstance. In both conditions, the behavior of the female target was rated as more deliberate and attributed less to the provoking circumstance than was the case for the male target (Egerton, 1988). This is compatible with earlier work on personal influence strategies, which found that more women than men report deliberately showing emotion to "get their way" (Johnson & Goodchilds, 1976).

In sum, there are rather consistent expressivity differences between men and women, particularly with respect to facial display. Nevertheless, these differences may or may not reflect differences in internal affective states. One possibility is that the underlying feelings are essentially comparable but the variation in expressivity results from different gender-based display rules specifying what feelings should be shown and with what intensity (Ekman & Friesen, 1975). Another possibility is that overt display is relatively independent of emotionality and that variation in expressivity is the result of societal requirements that there be observable gender differences. In other words, manifest differences can serve to create and sustain the belief that the sexes are different.

GENDER AND PHYSIOLOGICAL
INDICATORS OF EMOTIONALITY

Studies of the physiological concomitants of emotion reveal a complex and incomplete picture. The complexity has several sources. First, until recently, most research exploring the physiological concomitants of emotionality used single sex research designs, and those more often used male subjects. Second, some of the complexity stems from the reality that physiological reactivity is itself not unidimensional. Third, part of the complexity derives from the fact that there exists no agreed-upon single measure or set of measures that are unequivocally tied to emotionality.

Finally, some of the complexity derives from a pattern of mixed results when gender is considered. For example, early studies reported that females showed higher galvanic skin response (GSR) in response to affectively loaded stimuli (Aronfreed, Messick, & Diggory, 1953; Berry & Martin, 1957) and a recent study found that females were higher on heart rate and diastolic blood pressure on two different types of stressors while males were higher on systolic blood pressure but only on one of the stressors (Stone, Dembroski, Costa, & MacDougall, 1990). Other research, however, shows males to be more reactive, showing greater amine output under stress (Frankenhaeuser et al., 1978) as well as exhibiting larger blood pressure and epinephrine increases under stress than do women (Stoney, Davis, & Matthews, 1987).

When studies employ multiple physiological measures, the results yield no simple gender main effects. As an illustration that multiple physiological measures do not always lead to the same conclusion, Cornelius and Averill (1983) found, in response to a live tarantula, that females showed higher heart rate than men but did not differ from them on skin conductance. A recent study measured levels of low density and high density lipoprotein-cholesterol, triglycerides, free fatty acids, nor-epinephrine, heart rate, and blood pressure of males and females in response to several tasks and found that males had larger low density lipoprotein-cholesterol and blood pressure increases to all the tasks while females had only larger heart rate responses to a videotaped speech task (Stoney, Matthews, McDonald, & Johnson, 1988). More-over, Matthews and her colleagues found that gender-relevant tasks did not influence the extent of sex differences in physiological responses. In fact, males tended to exhibit greater responsivity regardless of the gender orientation of the task (Matthews, Davis, Stoney, Owens, & Caggiula, 1991).

Other studies report finding no gender differences in response to emotion on physiological measures. For example, Kleck and Strenta (1985) found there to be no significant gender differences in subjects upon seeing images of themselves disfigured. In a number of studies conducted by Levenson and his colleagues, subjects' physiological activity is measured in response to the requirement that they voluntarily produce a number of different emotional facial configurations (Levenson, Carstensen, Friesen, & Ekman, 1991; Levenson, Ekman, & Friesen, 1990). In one study that used both professional actors and college students as subjects, there was no evidence that women and men differed significantly in the extent of resulting autonomic activity even though both groups did show that voluntary facial activity produced significant levels of subjective experience of the associated emotion as well as significant levels of autonomic activity (Levenson et al., 1990). The same procedure was also employed in a sample of elderly people and, again, there were no significant differences, with both elderly men and elderly women showing comparable emotional physiology (Levenson et al., 1991).

Some studies have addressed the gender question by using stimuli differing in gender relevance. For example, heart rate responses of male students have been found to increase in response to erotic stimuli while female students' heart rate increased in response to crying baby video segments (Furedy, Fleming, Ruble, Scher, et al., 1989). Similarly, when EMG recordings were taken of males and females exposed to slides of angry and happy faces, results show stronger facial effects for females than males particularly with respect to happy affect (Dimberg & Lundquist, 1990). But other research finds no interaction between subject sex and gender-relevant stimuli. Frodi (1978) took some pains to create sex-appropriate emotional elicitors for anger and found no gender differences on a number of physiological measures including systolic blood pressure, heart rate, and skin conductance.

One of the more intriguing findings regarding the relationship linking gender, emotion, and physiological activity was a study by Buck and his colleagues that found, in response to affect-laden material, that adult females were more facially expressive but showed significantly less autonomic arousal whereas adult males expressed little facially but conveyed more physiologically (Buck et al., 1974). The intuitive reading of this study is that suppression of external display "causes" enhanced internal reactivity. A related interpretation is the speculation from Gottman and Levenson (1986) derived from their studies of interactions of dissatisfied marital couples that men engage in more distracting behaviors (e.g., withdrawal) not because they are less emotional than women but because they are more physiologically reactive than women and strive to avoid arousal. They therefore actively divert or suppress negative affect so as to render it less salient. The explanation, however, remains controversial as other data show positive associations among physiological and expressive measures (Leventhal & Mosbach, 1983). In sum, although the data are not all in as to how gender interacts with physiological aspects of emotionality, the weight of the evidence tends to support the idea that men show more physiological concomitants of emotion than do women.

GENERAL CONCLUSIONS

We began this chapter with the suggestion that the finding of gender differences in emotionality may very well depend on the modality through which it is assessed and the particular emotional dimension that is being tapped. A review of the literature provides support for these propositions. As others have noted, emotions are multidimensional constructs including expressive and behavioral, experiential, and physiological components. Were one to concentrate on expressive aspects, the evidence seems to be there to support the notion that women are more emotionally demonstrative than men, at least with respect to the most visible channel, namely, facial expressivity. Were one to focus instead on the experiential component and hence rely on self-report indicators, the evidence for gender differences is occasionally there, contingent upon a particular set of measurement strategies. Specifically, women appear more emotional than men if they are asked directly, if the emotional domain is observable, if the context is interpersonal, and if the question concerns global emotionality. In the opposite set of conditions, gender effects are either nonexistent or inconsistent. Finally, were one to appeal to physiological indices of emotionality, the appropriate conclusion is that men and women do not show invariable differences.

The correspondence between observed expressivity and self-reported expressivity, on the one hand, and the fact that women show and report more of both raises a number of intriguing questions concerning the role overt display plays in actual or ascribed emotionality. It appears that public display plays a large role in affecting judgments of emotionality both by self and by observers, but whether differences in overt expressivity should be taken as reflecting fundamental emotionality differences is quite another matter. There is also a need to inquire further as to the social functions of observable emotive display and why one group appears to work harder at being demonstrative while the other appears to expend more energy on dampening such expression. More generally, the literature on the gender aspects of emotionality reaffirms its social character.

REFERENCES

Allen, J. G., & Haccoun, D. M. (1976). Sex differences in emotionality: A multidimensional approach. *Human Relations, 29,* 711-722.

Aronfreed, J. M., Messick, S. A., & Diggory, J. C. (1953). Re-examining emotionality and perceptual defense. *Journal of Personality, 21,* 517-528.

Averill, J. R. (1982). *Anger and aggression: An essay on emotion.* New York: Springer-Verlag.

Averill, J. R. (1986). The acquisition of emotions during adulthood. In R. Harré (Ed.), *The social construction of the emotions.* Oxford: Basil Blackwood.

Balswick, J. O. (1988). *The inexpressive male.* Lexington, MA: Lexington.

Banaji, M. R., Greenwald, A. G., & Bellezza, F. S. (1985). *Are women more emotional? Gender differences in reported emotional response do not translate to recall.* Unpublished manuscript.

Banaji, M., & LaFrance, M. (1989, May). *Gender and emotionality: Differences in verbal expression and similarities in rated intensity.* Paper presented to the Eastern Psychological Association, Boston.

Berry, J. L., & Martin, B. (1957). GSR reactivity as a function of anxiety, instructions, and sex. *Journal of Abnormal and Social Psychology, 54,* 9-12.

Birnbaum, D. W., & Croll, W. L. (1984). The etiology of children's stereotypes about sex differences in emotionality. *Sex Roles, 10,* 677-691.

Blier, M. J., & Blier-Wilson, L. A. (1989). Gender differences in self-rated emotional expressiveness. *Sex Roles, 21,* 287-295.

Boyle, G. J. (1989). Sex differences in reported mood states. *Personality and Individual Differences, 10,* 1179-1183.

Brody, L. R. (1985). Gender differences in emotional development: A review of theories and research. *Journal of Personality, 53,* 102-149.

Broverman, D. M., Clarkson, F., & Rosenkrantz, P. S. (1972). Sex role stereotypes: A current appraisal. *Journal of Sex Roles, 28,* 59-78.

Buck, R., Baron, R., & Barette, D. (1982). Temporal organization of spontaneous emotional expression. *Journal of Personality and Social Psychology, 42,* 506-517.

Buck, R., Baron, R., Goodman, N., & Shapiro, B. (1980). Unitization of spontaneous nonverbal behavior in the study of emotion communication. *Journal of Personality and Social Psychology, 39,* 522-529.

Buck, R., Miller, R. E., & Caul, W. F. (1974). Sex, personality and physiological variables in the communication of affect via facial expression. *Journal of Personality and Social Psychology, 30,* 587-596.

Bugental, D. E., Love, L. R., & Gianetto, R. M. (1971). Perfidious feminine faces. *Journal of Personality and Social Psychology, 17,* 314-318.

Burrowes, B. D., & Halberstadt, A. G. (1987). Self- and family-expressiveness styles in the experience and expression of anger. *Journal of Nonverbal Behavior, 11,* 254-268.

Campbell, A., & Muncer, S. (1987). Models of anger and aggression in the social talk of women and men. *Journal for the Theory of Social Behavior, 17,* 489-511.

Cherulnik, P. D. (1979). Sex differences in the expression of emotion in a structured social encounter. *Sex Roles, 5,* 355-361.

Cherulnik, P. D., & Evans, R. M. (1984). Facial expressive behaviors of high self monitors are less sex typed. *Sex Roles, 11,* 435-449.

Chodorow, N. (1980). *The reproduction of mothering.* Berkeley: University of California Press.

Choti, S. E., Marston, A. R., Holston, S. G., & Hart, J. T. (1987). Gender and personality variables in film induced sadness and crying. *Journal of Social and Clinical Psychology, 5,* 535-544.

Constantinople, A. (1973). Masculinity-femininity: An exception to the famous dictum? *Psychological Bulletin, 80,* 389-407.

Conway, M., Giannopoulos, C., & Stiefenhofer, K. (1990). Response styles to sadness are related to sex and sex-role orientation. *Sex Roles, 22,* 579-587.

Cornelius, R. R., & Averill, J. R. (1983). Sex differences in fear of spiders. *Journal of Personality and Social Psychology, 45,* 377-383.

Cupchik, G. C., & Poulos, C. X. (1984). Judgments of emotional intensity in self and others: The effects of stimulus context, sex, and expressivity. *Journal of Personality and Social Psychology, 46,* 431-439.

Custrini, R. J., & Feldman, R. S. (1989). Children's social competence and nonverbal encoding and decoding of emotions. *Journal of Clinical Child Psychology, 18,* 336-342.

Diener, E., Sandvik, E., & Larsen, R. J. (1985). Age and sex effects for emotional intensity. *Developmental Psychology, 21,* 542-546.

Dimburg, U. (1988). Facial electromyography and the experience of emotion. *Journal of Psychophysiology, 3,* 277-282.

Dimburg, U., & Lundquist, L. (1990). Gender differences in reactions to facial expressions. *Biological Psychology, 30,* 151-159.

Dosser, D. A., Balswick, J. O., & Halverson, C. F., Jr. (1983). Situational context of emotional expressiveness. *Journal of Counseling Psychology, 30,* 375-387.

Egerton, M. (1988). Passionate women and passionate men: Sex differences in accounting for angry and weeping episodes. *British Journal of Social Psychology, 27,* 51-66.

Ekman, P., & Friesen, W. V. (1975). *Unmasking the face.* Englewood Cliffs, NJ: Prentice-Hall.

Fabes, R. A., & Martin, C. L. (1991). Gender and age stereotypes of emotionality. *Personality and Social Psychology Bulletin, 17,* 532-540.

Frankenhaeuser, M., von Wright, M. R., Collins, A., von Wright, J., Sedvall, G., & Swahn, C. G. (1978). Sex differences in psychoneuroendocrine stress reactions to examination stress. *Psychosomatic Medicine, 40,* 334-343.

Fridlund, A. J. (1991). Sociality of solitary smiling: Potentiation by an implicit audience. *Journal of Personality and Social Psychology, 60,* 229-240.

Friedman, H. S., Prince, L. M., Riggio, R. E., & DiMatteo, M. R. (1980). Understanding and assessing nonverbal communication of emotion: The Affective Communication Test. *Journal of Personality and Social Psychology, 39,* 333-351.

Frodi, A. (1978). Experiential and physiological responses associated with anger and aggression in women and men. *Journal of Research in Personality, 12,* 335-349.

Fuchs, D., & Thelen, M. H. (1988). Children's expected interpersonal consequences of communicating their affective state and reported likelihood of expression. *Child Development, 59,* 1314-1322.

Fujita, B. N., Harper, R. G., & Wiens, A. N. (1980). Encoding-decoding of nonverbal emotional messages: Sex differences in spontaneous and enacted expressions. *Journal of Nonverbal Behavior, 4,* 131-145.

Furedy, J. J., Fleming, A. S., Ruble, D. N., Scher, H., et al. (1989). Sex differences in small magnitude heart rate responses to sexual and infant-related stimuli: A psychophysiological approach. *Physiology and Behavior, 46,* 903-905.

Gallagher, D., & Shuntich, R. J. (1981). Encoding and decoding of nonverbal behavior through facial expressions. *Journal of Research in Personality, 15,* 241-252.

Ganong, L., & Coleman, M. (1985). Sex, sex roles, and emotional expressiveness. *Journal of Genetic Psychology, 146,* 405-411.

Gitter, A. G., Black, H., & Mostofsky, B. (1972). Race and sex in the perception of emotion. *Journal of Social Issues, 28,* 63-78.

Goldberg, H. (1976). *The hazards of being male: Surviving the myth of masculine privilege.* Plainview, NY: Nash.

Gottman, J. M., & Levenson, R. W. (1986). The social psychophysiology of marriage. In P. Noller & M. A. Fitzpatrick (Eds.), *Perspectives in marital interaction* (pp. 182-200). Philadelphia: Multilingual Matters.

Graham, J. W., Gentry, K. W., & Green, J. (1981). The self-presentational nature of emotional expression: Some evidence. *Personality and Social Psychology Bulletin, 7,* 467-474.

Gueldner, S., & Clayton, G. (1987). *The expression of anger and other mood states in nursing home residents.* Paper presented at the American Nurses' Association International Nursing Research Conference, Arlington, VA.

Hall, J. A. (1984). *Nonverbal sex differences.* Baltimore, MD: Johns Hopkins University Press.

Hammen, C. L., & Peters, S. D. (1977). Differential responses to male and female depressive reactions. *Journal of Consulting and Clinical Psychology, 45,* 994-1001.

Harris, I. D., & Howard, K. I. (1987). Correlates of depression and anger in adolescence. *Journal of Child and Adolescent Psychotherapy, 4,* 199-203.

Haynes, S., Levine, S., Scotch, N., Feinleib, M., & Kannel, W. B. (1978). The relationship of psychosocial factors to coronary heart disease in the Framingham Study. I. Methods and risk factors. *American Journal of Epidemiology, 107,* 362-383.

Hochschild, A. R. (1983). *The managed heart: Commercialization of human feeling.* Berkeley: University of California Press.

Izard, C. E. (1977). *Human emotions.* New York: Plenum.

Izard, C. E., Dougherty, F. E., Bloxom, B. M., & Kotsch, N. E. (1974). *The Differential Emotions Scale: A method of measuring the subjective experience of discrete emotions.* Unpublished manuscript, Vanderbilt University, Department of Psychology.

Johnson, J. T., & Shulman, G. A. (1988). More alike than meets the eye: Perceived gender differences in subjective experience and its display. *Sex Roles, 19,* 67-79.

Johnson, P. B., & Goodchilds, J. D. (1976). How women get their way. *Psychology Today, 10,* 69-70.

King, L. A., & Emmons, R. A. (1990). Conflict over emotional expression: Psychological and physical correlates. *Journal of Personality and Social Psychology, 58,* 864-877.

Kleck, R. E., & Strenta, A. C. (1985). Gender and responses to disfigurement in self and others. *Journal of Social and Clinical Psychology, 3,* 257-267.

Kopper, B. A., & Epperson, D. L. (1991). Women and anger: Sex and sex-role comparisons in the expression of anger. *Psychology of Women Quarterly, 15,* 7-14.

Kraut, R. E., & Johnston, R. E. (1979). Social and emotional messages of smiling: An ethological approach. *Journal of Personality and Social Psychology, 37,* 1539-1553.

Larsen, R. J., & Diener, E. (1987). Affect intensity as an individual difference characteristic: A review. *Journal of Research in Personality, 21,* 1-39.

Lemer, H. (1985). *The dance of anger.* New York: Harper & Row.

Levenson, R. W., Carstensen, L. L., Friesen, W. V., & Ekman, P. (1991). Emotion, physiology and expression in old age. *Psychology and Aging, 6,* 28-35.

Levenson, R. W., Ekman, P., & Friesen, W. V. (1990). Voluntary facial action generates emotion-specific autonomic nervous system activity. *Psychophysiology, 27,* 363-384.

Leventhal, H., & Mosbach, P. A. (1983). The perceptual-motor theory of emotion. In J. T. Cacioppo & R. E. Petty (Eds.), *Social psychophysiology: A sourcebook* (pp. 353-388). New York: Guilford.

Lombardo, W. K., Cretser, G. A., Lombardo, R., & Mathis, S. L. (1983). Fer cryin' out loud: There is a sex difference. *Sex Roles, 9,* 987-995.

Lubin, B., Rinck, C. M., & Collins, J. F. (1986). Intensity ratings of mood adjectives as a function of gender and age group. *Journal of Social and Clinical Psychology, 4,* 244-247.

Lutz, C. A. (1990). Engendered emotion: Gender, power, and the rhetoric of emotional control in American discourse. In C. A. Lutz & L. Abu-Lughod (Eds.), *Language and the politics of emotion.* Cambridge: Cambridge University Press.

Mackie, M. (1980). The impact of sex stereotypes upon adult self imagery. *Social Psychology Quarterly, 43,* 121-125.

Matthews, K. A., Davis, M. C., Stoney, C. M., Owens, J. F., & Caggiula, A. R. (1991). Does the gender relevance of the stressor influence sex differences in psychophysiological responses? *Health Psychology, 10,* 112-120.

McHugo, G. J., Smith, C. A., & Lanzetta, J. T. (1982). The structure of self reports of emotional responses to film segments. *Motivation and Emotion, 6,* 365-385.

McNair, D. M., Lorr, M., & Droppleman, L. F. (1981). *Manual for the Profile of Mood States (POMS).* San Diego: Educational and Industrial Testing Service.

Millar, K. U., & Millar, M. G. (1988). Sex differences in perceived self- and other-disclosure: A case where inequity increases satisfaction. *Social Behavior and Personality, 16,* 59-64.

Narus, L., & Fisher, J. (1982). Strong but not silent: A re-examination of expressivity in the relationship of men. *Sex Roles, 8,* 159-168.

Nolen-Hoeksema, S. (1987). Sex differences in unipolar depression: Evidence and theory. *Psychological Bulletin, 101,* 259-282.

O'Grady, K. E., & Janda, L. H. (1989). The effects of anonymity and dissimulation on the Differential Emotions Scale. *Personality and Individual Differences, 10,* 1033-1040.

Oliver, S. J., & Toner, B. B. (1990). The influence of gender role typing on the expression of depressive symptoms. *Sex Roles, 22,* 775-790.

O'Neil, J. M. (1982). Gender and sex role conflict in men's lives: Implications for psychiatrists, psychologists, and other human service providers. In K. Solomon & M. Levy (Eds.), *Men in transition: Theory and therapy.* New York: Plenum.

Paprini, D. R., Farmer, F. F., Clark, S. M., & Micka, J. C. (1990). Early adolescent age and gender differences in patterns of emotional self disclosure to parents and friends. *Adolescence, 25,* 959-976.

Parsons, T., & Bales, R. (1955). *Family, socialization, and interaction process.* Glencoe, IL: Free Press.

Phillips, E., & Whissell, C. (1986). "What makes you feel?" Children's perceptions of the antecedents of emotion. *Journal of Social Behavior and Personality, 1,* 587-592.

Sabatelli, R., Buck, R., & Dreyer, A. (1982). Nonverbal communication accuracy in married couples: Relationship with marital complaints. *Journal of Personality and Social Psychology, 43,* 1088-1097.

Schenk, J., & Heinisch, R. (1986). Self-descriptions by means of sex-role scales and personality scales: A critical evaluation of recent masculinity and femininity scales. *Personality and Individual Differences, 7,* 161-168.

Schwartz, G. E., Brown, S., & Ahern, G. L. (1980). Facial muscle patterning and subjective experience during affective imagery: Sex differences. *Psychophysiology, 17,* 75-82.

Shields, S. A. (1984). Reports of bodily change in anxiety, sadness, and anger. *Motivation and Emotion, 8,* 1-21.

Shields, S. A. (1987). Women, men and the dilemma of emotion. In P. Shaver & C. Hendrick (Eds.), *Sex and gender.* Newbury Park, CA: Sage.

Shields, S. A., & Koster, B. A. (1989). Emotional stereotyping of parents in child rearing manuals, 1915-1980. *Social Psychology Quarterly, 52,* 44-55.

Shimanoff, S. (1983). The role of gender in linguistic reference to emotive states. *Communication Quarterly, 30,* 174-179.

Smith, K. C., Ulch, S. E., Cameron, J. E., & Cumberland, J. A. (1989). Gender-related effects in the perception of anger expression. *Sex Roles, 20,* 487-499.

Snell, W. E., Miller, R. S., Belk, S. S., Garcia-Falconi, R., & Hernandez-Sanchez, J. E. (1989). Men's and women's emotional disclosures: The impact of disclosure recipient, culture, and the masculine role. *Sex Roles, 21,* 467-485.

Spielberger, C. D., Barker, L., Russell, S., Silva de Crane, R., Westberry, L., Knight, J., & Marks, E. (1979). *Preliminary manual for the State-Trait Personality Inventory (STPI).* Tampa: University of South Florida.

Spielberger, C. D., Jacobs, G., Russell, S., & Crane, R. S. (1983). Assessment of anger: The State-Trait Anger Scale. In J. N. Butcher & C. D. Spielberger (Eds.), *Advances in personality assessment* (Vol. 2). Hillsdale, NJ: Lawrence Erlbaum.

Sprecher, S. (1989). The importance to males and females of physical attractiveness, earning potential, and expressiveness. *Sex Roles, 21,* 591-607.

Stairs, P. W., & Blick, K. A. (1979). A survey of emotional content of dreams recalled by college students. *Psychological Reports, 45,* 839-842.

Stapley, J. C., & Haviland, J. M. (1986). *The elicitors of emotion questionnaire.* Unpublished manuscript, Rutgers, State University of New Jersey, New Brunswick, NJ.

Stapley, J. C., & Haviland, J. M. (1989). Beyond depression: Gender differences in normal adolescents' emotional experiences. *Sex Roles, 20,* 295-308.

Stearns, C. Z., & Stearns, P. N. (1986). *Anger: The struggle for emotional control in America's history.* Chicago: University of Chicago Press.

Stone, S. V., Dembroski, T. M., Costa, P. T., & MacDougall, J. M. (1990). Gender differences in cardiovascular activity. *Journal of Behavioral Medicine, 13,* 137-156.

Stoner, S. B., & Spencer, W. B. (1987). Age and gender differences with the Anger Expression Scale. *Educational and Psychological Measurement, 47,* 487-492.

Stoney, C. M., Davis, M. C., & Matthews, K. A. (1987). Sex differences in physiological response to stress and in coronary heart disease: A causal link? *Psychophysiology, 24,* 127-131.

Stoney, C. M., Matthews, K. A., McDonald, R. H., & Johnson, C. A. (1988). Sex differences in lipid, lipoprotein, cardiovascular, and neuroendocrine responses to acute stress. *Psychophysiology, 25,* 645-656.

Tavris, C. (1984). *Anger: The misunderstood emotion.* New York: Simon & Schuster.

Terman, L. M., & Miles, C. C. (1936). *Sex and personality.* New York: McGraw-Hill.

Thomas, S. P. (1989). Gender differences in anger expression: Health implications. *Research in Nursing and Health, 12,* 389-398.

Wagner, H. L., MacDonald, C. J., & Manstead, A. S. R. (1986). Communication of individual emotions by spontaneous facial expressions. *Journal of Personality and Social Psychology, 50,* 737-743.

Wallbott, H. G. (1988). Big girls don't frown, big boys don't cry: Gender differences of professional actors in communicating emotion via facial expression. *Journal of Nonverbal Behavior, 12,* 98-106.

Wallbott, H. G., Ricci-Bitti, P., & Banninger-Huber, E. (1986). Non-verbal reactions to emotional experiences. In K. R. Scherer, H. G. Wallbott, & A. B. Summerfield (Eds.), *Experiencing emotion: A cross cultural study.* Cambridge: Cambridge University Press.

Wier, M., Phillips, J. L., & Stanners, R. F. (1987). A reexamination of sex differences in interpersonal verbs. *Psychology of Women Quarterly, 11,* 209-218.

Zuckerman, D. M. (1989). Stress, self esteem, and mental health: How does gender make a difference? *Sex Roles, 20,* 429-444.

8

Social Sources and Interactive Functions of Emotion

THE CASE OF EMBARRASSMENT

ROWLAND S. MILLER
MARK R. LEARY

Rowland S. Miller received his Ph.D. from the University of Florida in 1978, moved to Texas, and is now Professor of Psychology at Sam Houston State University. He studies relationship maintenance processes and the causes and consequences of embarrassment. He is coauthor (with Mark Leary) of *Social Psychology and Dysfunctional Behavior: Origins, Diagnosis, and Treatment*.

Mark R. Leary is Professor of Psychology at Wake Forest University. His research interests revolve around how behavior and emotion are affected by people's concerns with what others think of them and include self-presentation, social anxiety, and health implications of impression management. He is the author of *Understanding Social Anxiety: Social, Personality, and Clinical Perspectives; Social Psychology and Dysfunctional Behavior* (coauthored with Rowland Miller); and *Introduction to Behavioral Research Methods*. He is currently Associate Editor of the *Journal of Social and Clinical Psychology*.

Readers who may be wondering why *social* psychologists should study emotion have come to the right place. We assert that our discipline's traditional conceptualization of the origins and effects of emotions has too often been single-mindedly person centered. Emotions are often regarded as response potentials that reside within individuals and that, once elicited by a variety of impersonal or social events, influence the individual's cognitions and behavior. This view has been profitable (as chapters in this volume attest), but it emphasizes the internal, personal effects of emotions at the expense of a richer understanding of their social, interpersonal effects.

Not only do emotions typically emerge from interactions with other people (Clark, 1990; Kemper, 1990), but the manner in which emotions are expressed can substantially determine the outcomes of interactions. Frijda (1986) suggested that many emotional displays are "interactive expressions" that are meant to affect others; they are "shown for the sake of influencing others, appear to have developed for, or because of, such effect, and occur under eliciting conditions in which influencing others in that particular way appears to be of distinct instrumental value" (p. 25; see also Fridlund, 1991; Jones, Collins, & Hong, 1991).

Recent years have seen a growing recognition that our understanding of many emotions would be enhanced by expanding the traditional person-centered view, and this chapter is one attempt to redress our collective neglect of the social side of emotional experience. We will discuss the fact that some emotions spring from social sources, have important effects on interaction, and may even exist because of their social impact. We will try to accomplish this by using embarrassment as an exemplar of an emotion that emerges wholly from our social milieu and whose behavioral displays appear to be primarily communicative, rather than expressive, in nature.

THE SOCIAL ORIGINS OF EMBARRASSMENT

Embarrassment is an aversive state of abashment and chagrin that arises in real or imagined social encounters when people believe that others have formed undesired impressions of them that threaten the public identities they wish to claim (Goffman, 1967; Schlenker, 1980). Embarrassment has sometimes been regarded as a special instance of social anxiety (Buss, 1980; Schlenker & Leary, 1982), but both conceptual arguments and physiological data suggest that embarrassment is not purely an anxiety state (Leary, Britt, Cutlip, & Templeton, in press; Leary, Rejeski, & Britt, 1990). For example, whereas social anxiety is accompanied by increased cardiovascular activity and facial blanching (due to increased activity of the sympathetic nervous system), embarrassed individuals often show decreased heart rate and blood pressure as well as facial blushing due to increased blood volume to the face. Thus, although both social anxiety and embarrassment arise from people's concerns with others' impressions and evaluations of them (Leary, 1983), the experiences are qualitatively distinct (Leary, Rejeski, Britt, & Smith, 1991).

Embarrassment can also be distinguished from shame, a cousin with which it is often confused. Several observers posit shame as one of a handful of fundamental, genetically based emotions (e.g., Izard, 1977) that forcefully direct human conduct (e.g., Frijda, 1986; Scheff, 1990) but recognize no distinction between shame and embarrassment. Indeed, the two emotions have historically been considered synonymous

(Freud, 1900/1953). Nevertheless, shame may be a darker emotion that follows somewhat more weighty events. Some theorists suggest that embarrassment follows relatively trivial social accidents, whereas shame arises from more serious moral transgressions (Buss, 1980; Klass, 1990; Shott, 1979). Whereas embarrassed people feel mortified and foolish, shameful people often feel fearful, disgusted, and regretful (Mosher & White, 1981; Tangney, 1992). Indeed, when people recall past experiences with the two emotions, they often see some humor in their embarrassments but rarely find anything amusing in shame (Miller, Tangney, & Wallstein, 1992). Shame also lasts longer and seems more intense (Tangney, Miller, & Flicker, 1992). Still, both states result from similar social contexts that involve one's concerns with others' evaluations of oneself. Thus much of what we will say about embarrassment applies equally to shame.

By all accounts, embarrassment always arises in real or imagined interpersonal encounters (Goffman, 1967; Leary, 1983; Miller, 1986; Schlenker, 1980). Other people need not be physically present, but others' reactions must be imagined for feelings of embarrassment to occur. Thus, unlike many other emotions that can occur in response to impersonal events (such as anger, joy, or depression), embarrassment is a purely social emotion that can be understood only in terms of its interpersonal antecedents and consequences.

Explanations of Embarrassment

Two major explanations of embarrassment have been offered: the social evaluation (or self-presentational) model and the awkward interaction model. Most theorists have regarded embarrassment as a response to threats to one's public identity or social image that create concerns for how one is being evaluated by others (Edelmann, 1987; Goffman, 1967; Leary, 1983; Miller, 1986, 1992a; Schlenker, 1980; Schlenker & Leary, 1982). People typically feel embarrassed when events have undermined the impressions or images they would like others to hold of them.

An alternative perspective—the awkward interaction model—argues that embarrassment results from the flustered uncertainty that follows the loss of a coherent script in interaction (Parrott, Sabini, & Silver, 1988; Silver, Sabini, & Parrott, 1987). Broadly, this model holds that, regardless of concerns for others' impressions, whenever one's social expectations are disconfirmed, awkward indecisiveness about how to proceed causes the aversive arousal underlying embarrassment.

Both the social evaluation and the awkward interaction models are plausible explanations of embarrassment, and both portray it as a uniquely *social* emotion that depends on the real or imagined presence of others, either as evaluative observers or as interactive partners. In our view, however, the social evaluation perspective fits the available data more parsimoniously than the awkward interaction model. We offer three reasons for this conclusion.

First, the social evaluation model more easily explains the wide variety of disparate events people find embarrassing. Miller (1992b) recently catalogued embarrassing predicaments by obtaining descriptions of "my latest embarrassment" from 350 high school and college student respondents. Most embarrassments resulted when individuals publicly displayed normatively deficient behavior by, for example, inept pratfalls, forgotten zippers, uncontrolled flatulence, and invasion of others' bathrooms. As Table 8.1 shows, however, other predicaments arose from interaction and association with others. These "interactive" embarrassments could occur either when an ongoing interaction suddenly went awry, leaving participants painfully disconcerted (just as the awkward interaction model predicts), or when others with whom one was associated misbehaved in public. Moreover, nearly a fifth of the respondents' recent embarrassments would not have occurred had others not singled them out for teasing, hounding, and needling (see Cupach & Metts, 1990). Most such instances of "audience provocation" occurred when the unfortunate targets had not done anything wrong but were nonetheless made the butt of a joke. Finally, people occasionally became embarrassed by witnessing others' predicaments, even from afar and when they were not associated with the embarrassed other. Such empathic or vicarious embarrassment has been demonstrated in laboratory investigations (Miller, 1987), and it poses, along with several other types of embarrassing circumstances, difficulty for an awkward interaction explanation.

Although many kinds of embarrassments fit the awkward interaction perspective very nicely, the model has trouble with predicaments that involve no scripted interaction whatsoever. Some inept performances and "team" transgressions occur before distant observers with whom one never interacts; for instance, one respondent described becoming embarrassed when one of his companions made loud racist remarks in

TABLE 8.1 Types of Embarrassing Predicaments

Types of Predicament	*Frequency of Mention*
I. Individual behavior	
A. *Normative public deficiencies:* physical pratfalls, cognitive shortcomings, loss of control over possessions or body, and failures of privacy regulation	57%
B. *Abashed harm doing:* embarrassment from inconveniencing others	2%
C. *Conspicuousness:* suffering the attention of others when one is not deficient	7%
II. Interactive behavior	
A. *Awkward interaction:* unsettling uncertainty from unexpected interactive events	8%
B. *"Team" embarrassment:* others in one's group transgress	7%
III. Audience provocation	
A. *Real transgressions:* intentionally or not, others publicize one's past predicaments	5%
B. *No real transgressions:* teasing or hounding from others in absence of any normative deficiency	13%
IV. Bystander behavior	
A. *Empathic embarrassment:* felt for others whose actions do not reflect upon oneself	2%

a shopping mall. Another respondent was embarrassed by tripping on some steps when some other students were in sight down the hall. Rather than resulting from awkward uncertainty about how to proceed, such embarrassments appear to depend more on people's concerns about what any observers are thinking of them. The social evaluation model can account for all the embarrassments an interaction model explains, and others as well.

Second, experimental comparison of the two models demonstrates that, although awkward interactions are indeed embarrassing, concern for one's social image may be the fundamental concern on such occasions. Miller (1992a) tried to disentangle the overlapping effects of awkwardness and social evaluation by having subjects envision being refused a date for either innocuous reasons (the partner had a class to attend) or threatening reasons (the partner said there was a class but was lying). The news of the refusal, however, was conveyed by a messenger who independently believed the rejection to be threatening or innocuous. Subjects thus imagined either an awkward interaction with a messenger who knew they had been snubbed or an innocent interchange with one who thought nothing unusual. They also knew that they had or had not been spurned. The results indicated that the awkwardness of a current interaction clearly affected subjects' embarrassment but that they were also embarrassed by a threatening rejection whether or not that rejection was apparent to the person with whom they were currently interacting. Put differently, concerns for social image influenced embarrassment independently of awkwardness itself. Moreover, despite symmetrical, similar manipulations, the image variable accounted for twice as much variance in the subjects' reports of embarrassment as awkwardness did.

Finally, the best dispositional predictors of susceptibility to embarrassment (and one's propensity to blush) involve concerns with others' evaluations, such as fear of negative evaluation and the motive to avoid social exclusion (Kerschenbaum & Miller, 1991; Leary & Meadows, 1991). In general, people who dread disapproval from others and who especially desire to be liked and accepted tend to be uncommonly embarrassable as well as frequent blushers. In contrast, even though skilled interactants should deftly repair most awkward interactions, global social skill does not predict embarrassability at all. A person's ability to adroitly control his or her self-presentations is moderately, negatively, related to embarrassability, but (a lack of) social skill appears to predict other social anxieties such as shyness much better than embarrassability (Kerschenbaum & Miller, 1991).

In brief, despite the fact that awkward interactions are often embarrassing, evidence links embarrassment more closely to damaged social image or loss of face than to awkwardness per se. Both awkward interactions and the specter of negative social evaluation may induce embarrassment, but evaluation seems the stronger concern (Miller, 1992a). Of course, in many embarrassing situations, both processes may contribute to one feeling flustered and chagrined, and each can exacerbate the other; awkward uncertainty can raise the specter of negative evaluation, and social evaluative concern can rob one of poise and control. Nevertheless, social evaluation appears to be the more common and more central source of embarrassment.

Gender Differences in Embarrassment

Women are more embarrassable than men. Although they experience similar kinds of embarrassing predicaments as men (Miller, 1992b) and are no more likely to blush (Leary & Meadows, 1991), women report stronger fear of negative evaluation and higher dispositional embarrassability on personality measures (Kerschenbaum & Miller, 1991). They also report stronger reactions to both laboratory manipulations of embarrassment (Miller, 1987, 1988) and to naturally occurring embarrassing situations (Miller, in press). Furthermore, these effects are more than just dissimilar self-report; behavioral gender differences in self-conscious emotions can be observed in very young children (Lewis, Sullivan, Stanger, & Weiss, 1989), and, as adults, women work harder than men to remediate embarrassments (Gonzales, Pederson, Manning, & Wetter, 1990). Women also say they are more prone to feelings of shame (Tangney, 1990).

To the extent this gender difference is reliable, it is intriguing but not inconsistent with a social evaluation model. First, women may be socialized to be more astutely aware of and/or sensitive to disapproval from others than men (see Noller, 1984). In addition, because they often hold less social power than men, their outcomes may more often be controlled by others (see Secord, 1983), giving them more reason to be concerned about what others are thinking of them. These explanations are speculative, however, and there may be other influences; clearly, further data are needed.

FUNCTIONS OF SUBJECTIVE EMBARRASSMENT

Altogether, the converging evidence strongly supports the notion that embarrassment and shame substantially depend on people's concerns for others' opinions of them. Embarrassment is thus a uniquely social emotion that emerges only from situations that involve the real or imagined presence of others. Far from being merely an emotional response to self-presentational predicaments, however, embarrassment appears to play an important role in social control, self-regulation, and interpersonal interaction.

Socialization

In many cultures, embarrassment may be an essential component of socialization and social control (Buss, 1980; Goffman, 1967). In the context of socialization, others often induce embarrassment in youngsters to punish them for misdeeds. During the early, uncertain years of toilet training, for instance, children may be teased and taunted for breaches of bladder control. Thereafter, as broader social norms are encountered, children learn that violations of privacy, modesty, and manners will also be met with laughter, ridicule, and disdain. Buss (1980) asserted that socialization, especially in Western societies, exploits the aversiveness of embarrassment by inculcating an internal fear of embarrassment that gradually replaces external teasing or laughter as guides to behavior. Indeed, Semin and Papadopoulou (1990) noted that "child-rearing without the acquisition of such emotions would be a very difficult business" (p. 110), requiring constant supervision, vigilance, and punishment of the child.

Such training takes time, and embarrassment does take years to develop. Buss, Iscoe, and Buss (1979) asked parents whether their children had been recently embarrassed and found that, in preschool children, embarrassment was rare. More than half of the 5-year-olds were judged to have been embarrassed, however, marking a discrete change in the children's emotions. Even then, they may not have been experiencing "adult" embarrassment. Bennett (1989) argued that a feeling of embarrassment in 5- to 8-year-old children is usually based on others' overt reactions toward them and necessitates the presence of an active, derisive audience. He found that 8-year-olds typically reported little embarrassment if their audiences merely watched and silently judged their conduct; only when audiences clearly communicated their disregard did the youngsters become abashed. By the time youngsters are 11- to 13-years-old, however, they finally develop "mature" embarrassment; they are able to imagine others' *assumed* evaluations of them and are embarrassed by any public transgression, whether or not an audience actively reproves them (Bennett, 1989).

Embarrassment's formative period is so prolonged because it requires that people be aware of and care about what others are thinking of them; these require complex role-taking abilities that take years to develop (see Edelmann, 1987; Lewis, 1990). In general, as people's concern for social evaluation gradually changes over time, so, too, does their susceptibility to embarrassment. Thus it's not surprising that adolescents, who are notoriously self-conscious and more concerned with others' impressions of them than either adults or young children (Crozier & Burnham, 1990), suffer both more frequent and more intense embarrassments than anyone else (Horowitz, 1962; Miller, 1992b).

Social Control

In addition to stressing its role in socialization, several scholars have noted the importance of embarrassment as a lifelong agent of social control (Edelmann, 1987; Goffman, 1967; Kemper, 1990; Shott, 1979). Gibbons (1990) stressed that "fear of embarrassment helps bring behavior in line with certain accepted social rules. . . . Without its impact, there would be social anarchy, and social discourse, as it exists, would be virtually impossible" (p. 138). The same can be said for shame (e.g., Scheff, 1990). Crozier (1990) encouraged us to imagine a person who never experiences embarrassment or shame: We would likely assume that such a person "is lacking some important human quality, is insensitive, thoughtless, or uncaring, a 'brazen hussy' or an 'arrogant son of a bitch' " (p. 7). Put differently, the possibility of being embarrassed seems to dictate and constrain a great deal of social behavior; much of what we do and, perhaps more important, what we don't do is based on our desire to avoid embarrassment.

Self-Regulation

By assuring adherence to basic important norms, embarrassment serves an indispensable function for the individual. Because people who are viewed unfavorably are not only derogated but often shunned, punished, or ostracized, it is in the individual's best interests to maintain a minimally acceptable public image in others' eyes (Goffman, 1959; Leary & Kowalski, 1990; Schlenker, 1980).

Subjective embarrassment may serve three functions in deterring actions that might have untoward consequences for the individual. First, embarrassment, like certain other aversive states, may serve as a cue or warning that prompts the individual to evaluate more carefully his or her behavior and others' reactions to it (Baumeister & Tice, 1990). Second, once experienced, the aversiveness and immediacy of embarrassment lead people to take action, when possible, to remedy the situation and thereby reduce their discomfort. Put differently, embarrassment seems to have drive properties that promote attempts to repair threats to one's social image. Third, as we have noted, the mere possibility of embarrassment deters actions that place the individual's social identity in jeopardy. People typically try not to do things that will make them appear unfavorably to others.

Although embarrassment serves these invaluable functions and unquestionably enhances the individual's general well-being, there is a downside: Embarrassment can interfere with the execution of behaviors that, by all accounts, are appropriate but that may engender concerns about social evaluation. For example, a fear of being embarrassed may cause people to fail to intervene in emergencies when other witnesses are present (Latané & Darley, 1970) or to obtain and use birth control (Leary & Dobbins, 1983).

EMBARRASSMENT DISPLAYS

Thus far, we have focused on the subjective experience of embarrassment. In addition to its subjective, affective qualities, however, embarrassment is typically accompanied by behaviors that serve clear social functions for the individual. For instance, Goffman (1967) noted that, by becoming embarrassed, a person "demonstrates that, while he cannot present a sustainable and coherent self on this occasion, he is at least disturbed by the fact and may prove worthy at another time" (p. 111). The characteristic nonverbal and verbal responses that accompany embarrassment may be obvious public communications that influence the subsequent course of an interaction.

Nonverbal Behavior

Embarrassment is typically manifested through a readily recognizable nonverbal display that makes it a reliable emotional communication. When embarrassed, people often decrease their eye contact with others and display a mirthless, silly smile. In addition, they often move about more and their speech becomes less fluent (Asendorpf, 1990; Edelmann, 1990).

Perhaps the most clear-cut index of embarrassment is facial blushing, the visible reddening of the face, ears, and neck caused by the cutaneous vasodilation that often, but not always, accompanies embarrassment (Darwin, 1873/1965; Leary et al., in press). Embarrassment is the most common cause of blushing but, as we will discuss below, people may become embarrassed without blushing and sometimes blush without being embarrassed.

Evidence strongly suggests that such nonverbal indications of embarrassment are more than mere overt expressions of the embarrassed person's inner state. Rather, such behaviors appear to serve a clearly social function. Specifically, by appearing embarrassed, the individual acknowledges that he or she has appeared in a negative light and expresses regret over whatever transgression has occurred (Castelfranchi & Poggi, 1990).

In one test of this idea, Semin and Manstead (1982) found that, when subjects watched a shopper accidentally knock over a grocery store display, they liked the shopper more when he reacted with obvious embarrassment than when he remained poised and calm. Similarly, Levin and Arluke (1982) demonstrated that someone who seemed embarrassed while asking for help from a large class received more volunteer help than someone who was completely composed. Edelmann (1982) and Miller (1988) also showed that appropriate displays of embarrassment elicit favorable reactions from observers, suggesting that embarrassment successfully influences others' impressions by blunting and reducing potential threats of negative social evaluation. In Edelmann's (1982) study, subjects liked an experimenter who informed them of their failures much better when he seemed embarrassed than when he seemed unruffled by the task. Further, Semin and Papadopoulou (1990) showed that mothers levy less punishment and scolding when their children seem embarrassed after a social transgression than when the children seem heedless of their sins.

To the extent that blushing is a particularly salient sign of embarrassment, blushing may likewise serve to lower others' negative reactions to socially inappropriate behavior. Castelfranchi and Poggi (1990) recently argued that, by blushing, embarrassed people demonstrate that "they know, care about, and fear the others' evaluation, and that they share their values deeply; and they also communicate their sorrow over any possible faults and inadequacies" (p. 240). When Landel and Leary (1992) examined the possibility that blushing is an involuntary remedial display, they reasoned that, for blushing to elicit supportive judgments from others, it obviously must be noticed by others. When one's blushing is obvious, it may mollify otherwise critical observers, particularly if the threat to one's identity is minor. If one's blushing is not noticed, however, the threat to one's public identity remains unresolved; in such cases, the individual should be motivated to engage in alternative face-saving strategies designed to enhance the individual's public image.

To test this notion, Landel and Leary (1992) embarrassed subjects by publicly playing (privately recorded) tapes of the subjects singing the song "Feelings." The researcher then either did or did not acknowledge that she saw the subject blush as each tape was played. Consistent with the remedial hypothesis, subjects who believed that the researcher had not seen them blushing subsequently presented a significantly more positive impression of themselves to the researcher than subjects who thought their blush had been noticed (whose self-presentations did not differ from subjects who were not embarrassed at all). When their blushes were public knowledge, subjects did not engage in self-enhancement to repair their social images; however, when blushing could not serve as a remedial gesture, subjects turned to other means of conveying a positive image to the researcher.

Although it is tempting to view blushing solely as a remedial or appeasement gesture that signals embarrassment (Leary & Meadows, 1991), people sometimes blush in situations that pose little or no threat to their social images. For example, people often blush when complimented, when simply stared at by others, or when being serenaded with "Happy Birthday." Leary et al. (in press) proposed that, rather than just being a specific response to embarrassment, blushing results more generally from undesired social attention. Because embarrassment always involves undesired attention from others (i.e., people who fear negative social evaluation do not want to be the focus of others' attention), embarrassment and blushing often coincide. In fact, however, people may be embarrassed without blushing and blush without being embarrassed (Leary et al., 1991).

Verbal Remediation

Cupach and Metts (1990) surveyed college students about the strategies they had used the last time they were embarrassed and found that several distinct remedial tactics were possible. Most often (nearly three fourths of the time), embarrassed people attempted to explain or repair the event by offering a verbal apology or excuse, trying to redress any harm or damage they had caused or using humor to minimize the incident.

About a fourth of the time, people simply avoided mention of their predicaments by quickly changing topics, saying nothing, or actually leaving the interaction altogether. On rare occasions, people challenged or attacked other people presumed to have caused the predicament. Moreover, people often used more than one specific response, stringing together several different strategies into a remedial sequence. Thus embarrassment was hardly ever just ignored; its presence typically changed, however briefly, the patterns of the interactions in which it occurred.

Cupach and Metts (1990) presented an interesting finding that some remedial strategies were used more often for some types of predicaments than for others. Humor and damage repair efforts were more likely after accidental normative public deficiencies (e.g., pratfalls) than after interactive or audience predicaments (see Table 8.1), whereas aggression occurred only after embarrassment that was caused by others' provocation. Moreover, Cupach and Metts clearly demonstrated that witnesses of another person's embarrassment often participated in efforts to cope with the incident. Observers were frequently supportive, quickly reassuring an abashed target of their continued positive regard. (This was the single most common observer strategy, just as a social evaluation perspective would predict.) As Goffman (1967) suggested, embarrassment can pose problems for all the participants in an interaction, so that "much of the activity occurring during an encounter can be understood as an effort on everyone's part to get through the occasion" (p. 41) without embarrassing disruption. When embarrassment does occur, everyone may share the burden of overcoming it.

When embarrassed people receive no reassurance of their social inclusion, their efforts to regain lost social approval may persist for some time (see Landel & Leary, 1992), even carrying over into wholly new interactions. For example, Apsler (1975) had subjects perform either embarrassing or unembarrassing tasks in front of an observer; thereafter, either the observer or another confederate who ostensibly knew nothing about the subjects' performances asked the subjects for help with a class project. Those who were embarrassed were more generous than those who were not abashed and were equally helpful whether or not the requestor knew of their embarrassment. The embarrassing tasks apparently induced a general motive to seek social approval, even from others who were unaware of a person's predicament. Consistent with its social control function, embarrassment evidently temporarily increases people's tendencies to behave in prosocial ways.[1]

Thus embarrassment is not only an emotional reaction to, but often an effective interpersonal defense against, unwanted pitfalls in interaction. This is welcome news but is no doubt hard to remember when we are trapped in the throes of embarrassed abashment and chagrin. Because it *is* aversive, people probably underestimate how adaptive and beneficial embarrassment can be. Miller (1988) found that embarrassed actors (who had performed a variety of embarrassing tasks as an observer watched from an adjacent room) felt they had made poorer personal impressions on their audiences than nonembarrassed actors did, whereas, in truth, the audiences actually liked them better than the nonembarrassed actors. Fear of embarrassment is substantially misplaced; embarrassment is best avoided, of course, but, when predicaments do occur, embarrassment and its accompanying remedial displays are often useful, if not desirable.

THE EVOLUTIONARY SIGNIFICANCE OF EMBARRASSMENT

Several scholars have suggested that universal human emotions must be adaptive or they would not have evolved (e.g., Izard, 1977; Plutchik, 1980). Thus "the reason the primary, prototypic emotions developed in the first place, were shaped and reshaped over the millennia, and continued to survive, was because they were adaptive" (Hatfield & Rapson, 1990, p. 129).

Such emotions could confer reproductive advantage via two routes. On the one hand, adaptive emotions could alert one and/or prepare one to face a variety of impersonal and physical dangers. On the other hand, emotions might facilitate one's dealings with others, minimizing the possibility of rejection (or attack) from potential mates or peers.

Many theorists acknowledge the evolutionary desirability of emotions that diminish social threats. Plutchik (1980) even suggested that all emotional expressions have an important social function: "They communicate information from one animal to another about what is likely to happen and thereby affect the chances of survival" (p. 5). Over millennia, then, the capacity for such useful emotions would gradually be genetically encoded in "a specific innately determined neural substrate" (Izard, 1977, p. 83) that would result in these emotions becoming universal transcultural phenomena. Indeed, Baumeister and Tice (1990) recently argued that the threat of social exclusion would have been so worrisome to early tribal humans that concern over one's acceptance by others might have been the ancient prototype for most human anxiety.

Although not without its weaknesses, this argument may be useful in the case of socially based concerns. Social discomfort—social anxiety, embarrassment, shame, and the like—may have evolved because persons who experienced distress over concerns with others' impressions of them were more likely to survive as reproductive members of the group than persons who acted with disregard for others' opinions of them (who were likely to be ostracized or banished, if not killed; Baumeister & Tice, 1990; Leary, 1990). By sensitizing an individual to the opinions of the social group, such emotions ensured that one would be responsive to the criticism that forewarned abandonment. Moreover, the desire to avoid such painful social emotions probably motivated individuals to develop social skills that assured their acceptance and made for a stronger group (Izard, 1977). Effective behavior also attracted more desirable mates, so that a capacity for appropriate embarrassment probably enhanced an individual's breeding potential (Gilbert & Trower, 1990). Thus an evolutionary perspective implies that, over time, embarrassment became the social counterpart to physical pain; just as it would be hard to survive if we had no pain to warn us of threats to our physical well-being, we would not last long if we had no social anxiety or embarrassment to warn us of possible rebuke and rejection.

Similar evolutionary arguments can be applied to certain behavioral concomitants of embarrassment. As we have seen, when embarrassed, people tend to display a nervous, silly grin, lower their gaze, and blush. Such grinning and gaze behaviors are part of the appeasement displays of other primates (Altmann, 1967; Morris, 1967; van Hooff, 1972), so there are reasons to suspect that such nonverbal behaviors may serve a similar function in humans. Among humans, nervous smiling, gaze aversion, and blushing help to "appease" those who have witnessed the actor's social infraction as well as divert onlookers' attention from him or her (because people find it uncomfortable to attend to those who are obviously embarrassed; Leary et al., in press; Miller, 1987).

Altogether, an evolutionary perspective suggests that some emotions are adaptive and may gradually have become innate because of their social effects. Embarrassment and blushing appear to be responses to social threat that may have helped forestall social rejection, perhaps in two different ways. Individually, they were intrinsically aversive, promoting (socially desirable) behavior designed either to ameliorate them or to avoid them entirely. Interactively, they were readily recognizable, signaling one's chagrin to any attentive observer (Castelfranchi & Poggi, 1990). In our dim past, group members who appeared embarrassed after some misdeed may have been more likely to survive the transgression than were those who remained poised and calm. Of course, nothing in an evolutionary analysis is inconsistent with the assertion that social influences shape displays of embarrassment and teach people when and where such displays are appropriate (Buck, 1989).

EMOTIONS AS SOCIAL PHENOMENA

We have suggested that embarrassment is a common human emotion because it has conferred evolutionary advantages that are social in nature, that we are taught through social seasoning when to experience embarrassment, and that our capacities for embarrassment and shame are agents of social control throughout our lives. Further, we have stressed that embarrassment and its concomitants have important effects on interaction by communicating one's chagrin to observers, motivating attempts at remediation, and decreasing the likelihood of social rejection. Finally, we have argued, as have others, that embarrassment is a social emotion that depends on the implied presence and attention of others; it is based on our concerns for what others are thinking of us and would not occur if we were unaware of others' presence or did not care what they thought. Embarrassment is thus an exemplar that makes a point too often overlooked in the social psychology of emotion: At least some "emotions are not mere cognitive responses to physiological, cultural, or structural factors. They are interactive processes best studied as social acts involving interactions with self and interactions with others" (Denzin, 1984, p. 61).

NOTE

1. This is another important way in which shame and embarrassment differ. Whereas embarrassment typically motivates ingratiatory, helpful behavior, shame seems to make people angry at both themselves and others (Tangney, 1992). Shameful people lack empathy and evidence hostility toward others (Tangney, 1990), another indication that, despite their similar evolutionary and social control functions, shame and embarrassment are not one and the same.

REFERENCES

Altmann, S. A. (1967). The structure of primate communication. In S. A. Altmann (Ed.), *Social communication among primates.* Chicago: University of Chicago Press.

Apsler, R. (1975). Effects of embarrassment on behavior toward others. *Journal of Personality and Social Psychology, 32,* 145-153.

Asendorpf, J. (1990). The expression of shyness and embarrassment. In W. R. Crozier (Ed.), *Shyness and embarrassment: Perspectives from social psychology* (pp. 87-118). Cambridge: Cambridge University Press.

Baumeister, R. F., & Tice, D. M. (1990). Anxiety and social exclusion. *Journal of Social and Clinical Psychology, 9,* 165-195.

Bennett, M. (1989). Children's self-attribution of embarrassment. *British Journal of Developmental Psychology, 7,* 207-217.

Buck, R. (1989). Emotional communication in personal relationships: A developmental-interactionist view. In C. Hendrick (Ed.), *Close relationships* (pp. 144-163). Newbury Park, CA: Sage.

Buss, A. H. (1980). *Self-consciousness and social anxiety.* San Francisco: Freeman.

Buss, A. H., Iscoe, I., & Buss, E. H. (1979). The development of embarrassment. *Journal of Psychology, 103,* 227-230.

Castelfranchi, C., & Poggi, I. (1990). Blushing as a discourse: Was Darwin wrong? In W. R. Crozier (Ed.), *Shyness and embarrassment: Perspectives from social psychology* (pp. 230-251). Cambridge: Cambridge University Press.

Clark, C. (1990). Emotions and micropolitics in everyday life: Some patterns and paradoxes of "place." In T. Kemper (Ed.), *Research agendas in the sociology of emotion* (pp. 207-237). Albany: SUNY Press.

Crozier W. R. (1990). Introduction. In W. R. Crozier (Ed.), *Shyness and embarrassment: Perspectives from social psychology* (pp. 1-15). Cambridge: Cambridge University Press.

Crozier, W. R., & Burnham, M. (1990). Age-related differences in children's understanding of shyness. *British Journal of Developmental Psychology, 8,* 179-185.

Cupach, W. R., & Metts, S. (1990). Remedial processes in embarrassing predicaments. In J. Anderson (Ed.), *Communication yearbook 13* (pp. 323-352). Newbury Park, CA: Sage.

Darwin, C. R. (1965). *The expression of the emotions in man and animals.* Chicago: University of Chicago Press. (Original work published 1872)

Denzin, N. K. (1984). *On understanding emotion.* San Francisco: Jossey-Bass.

Edelmann, R. J. (1982). The effect of embarrassed reactions upon others. *Australian Journal of Psychology, 34,* 359-367.

Edelmann, R. J. (1987). *The psychology of embarrassment.* Chichester, UK: John Wiley.

Edelmann, R. J. (1990). Embarrassment and blushing: A component-process model, some initial descriptive data and cross-cultural data. In W. R. Crozier (Ed.), *Shyness and embarrassment: Perspectives from social psychology* (pp. 205-229). Cambridge: Cambridge University Press.

Freud, S. (1953). *The interpretation of dreams.* London: Hogarth. (Original work published 1900)

Fridlund, A. J. (1991). Sociality of solitary smiling: Potentiation by an implicit audience. *Journal of Personality and Social Psychology, 60,* 229-240.

Frijda, N. H. (1986). *The emotions.* Cambridge: Cambridge University Press.

Gibbons, F. X. (1990). The impact of focus of attention and affect on social behavior. In W. R. Crozier (Ed.), *Shyness and embarrassment: Perspectives from social psychology* (pp. 119-143). Cambridge: Cambridge University Press.

Gilbert, P., & Trower, P. (1990). The evolution and manifestation of social anxiety. In W. R. Crozier (Ed.), *Shyness and embarrassment: Perspectives from social psychology* (pp. 144-177). Cambridge: Cambridge University Press.

Goffman, E. (1959). *The presentation of self in everyday life.* New York: Anchor.

Goffman, E. (1967). *Interaction ritual: Essays on face-to-face behavior.* Garden City, NY: Anchor.

Gonzales, M. H., Pederson, J. H., Manning, D. J., & Wetter, D. W. (1990). Pardon my gaffe: Effects of sex, status, and consequence severity on accounts. *Journal of Personality and Social Psychology, 58,* 610-621.

Hatfield, E., & Rapson, R. L. (1990). Passionate love in intimate relationships. In B. Moore & A. Isen (Eds.), *Affect and social behavior* (pp. 126-151). Cambridge: Cambridge University Press.

Horowitz, E. (1962). Reported embarrassment memories of elementary school, high school, and college students. *Journal of Social Psychology, 56,* 317-325.

Izard, C. E. (1977). *Human emotions.* New York: Plenum.

Jones, S. S., Collins, K., & Hong, H. (1991). An audience effect on smile production in 10-month-old infants. *Psychological Science, 2,* 45-49.

Kemper, T. D. (1990). Social relations and emotions: A structural approach. In T. Kemper (Ed.), *Research agendas in the sociology of emotion* (pp. 207-237). Albany: SUNY Press.

Kerschenbaum, N. J., & Miller, R. S. (1991, August). *Predicting susceptibility to embarrassment: Social skill versus social esteem.* Paper presented at the meeting of the American Psychological Association, San Francisco.

Klass, E. T. (1990). Guilt, shame, and embarrassment: Cognitive-behavioral approaches. In H. Leitenberg (Ed.), *Handbook of social and evaluative anxiety* (pp. 385-414). New York: Plenum.

Landel, J., & Leary, M. R. (1992, March). *Social blushing as a face-saving display.* Paper presented at the meeting of the Southeastern Psychological Association. Knoxville, TN.

Latané, B., & Darley, J. (1970). *The unresponsive bystander: Why doesn't he help?* New York: Appleton-Century-Crofts.

Leary, M. R. (1983). *Understanding social anxiety: Social, personality, and clinical perspectives*. Beverly Hills, CA: Sage.

Leary, M. R. (1990). Responses to social exclusion: Social anxiety, jealousy, loneliness, depression, and low self-esteem. *Journal of Social and Clinical Psychology, 9,* 221-229.

Leary, M. R., Britt, T. W., Cutlip, W. D., II, & Templeton, J. L. (in press). Social blushing. *Psychological Bulletin.*

Leary, M. R., & Dobbins, S. E. (1983). Social anxiety, sexual behavior, and contraceptive use. *Journal of Personality and Social Psychology, 45,* 1347-1354.

Leary, M. R., & Kowalski, R. M. (1990). Impression management: A literature review and two-component model. *Psychological Bulletin, 107,* 34-47.

Leary, M. R., & Meadows, S. (1991). Predictors, elicitors, and concomitants of social blushing. *Journal of Personality and Social Psychology, 60,* 254-262.

Leary, M. R., Rejeski, W. J., & Britt, T. (1990, June). Emotional blushing. In W. H. Jones (Chair), *Embarrassment and blushing.* Symposium presented at the meeting of the American Psychological Society, Dallas, TX.

Leary, M. R., Rejeski, W. J., Britt, T., & Smith, G. E. (1991). *Physiological differences between embarrassment and social anxiety.* Manuscript submitted for publication.

Levin, J., & Arluke, A. (1982). Embarrassment and helping behavior. *Psychological Reports, 51,* 999-1002.

Lewis, M. (1990). Social knowledge and social development. *Merrill-Palmer Quarterly, 36,* 93-116.

Lewis, M., Sullivan, M. W., Stanger, C., & Weiss, M. (1989). Self development and self-conscious emotions. *Child Development, 60,* 146-156.

Miller, R. S. (1986). Embarrassment: Causes and consequences. In W. Jones, J. Cheek, & S. Briggs (Eds.), *Shyness: Perspectives on research and treatment* (pp. 295-311). New York: Plenum.

Miller, R. S. (1987). Empathic embarrassment: Situational and personal determinants of reactions to the embarrassment of another. *Journal of Personality and Social Psychology, 53,* 1061-1069.

Miller, R. S. (1988, August). *Embarrassability and reactions to the threat of embarrassment.* Paper presented at the meeting of the American Psychological Association, Atlanta.

Miller, R. S. (1992a). *Delineating the causes of embarrassment: Awkward interaction versus social-evaluation.* Manuscript submitted for publication.

Miller, R. S. (1992b). The nature and severity of self-reported embarrassing circumstances. *Personality and Social Psychology Bulletin, 18,* 190-198.

Miller, R. S., Tangney, J. P., & Wallstein, C. C. (1992, August). *Differentiating embarrassment and shame.* Paper presented at the meeting of the American Psychological Association, Washington, DC.

Morris, D. (1967). *Primate ethology.* Chicago: Aldine.

Mosher, D. L., & White, B. R. (1981). On differentiating shame and shyness. *Motivation and Emotion, 5,* 61-74.

Noller, P. (1984). *Nonverbal communication and marital interaction.* Oxford: Pergamon.

Parrott, W. G., Sabini, J., & Silver, M. (1988). The roles of self-esteem and social interaction in embarrassment. *Personality and Social Psychology Bulletin, 14,* 191-202.

Plutchik, R. (1980). *Emotion: A psychoevolutionary synthesis.* New York: Harper & Row.

Scheff, T. J. (1990). Socialization of emotions: Pride and shame as causal agents. In T. Kemper (Ed.), *Research agendas in the sociology of emotion* (pp. 281-304). Albany: SUNY Press.

Schlenker, B. R. (1980). *Impression management: The self-concept, social identity, and interpersonal relations.* Monterey, CA: Brooks/Cole.

Schlenker, B. R., & Leary, M. R. (1982). Social anxiety and self-presentation: A conceptualization and model. *Psychological Bulletin, 92,* 641-669.

Secord, P. F. (1983). Imbalanced sex ratios: The social consequences. *Personality and Social Psychology Bulletin, 9,* 525-543.

Semin, G. R., & Manstead, A. S. R. (1982). The social implications of embarrassment displays and restitution behavior. *European Journal of Social Psychology, 12,* 367-377.

Semin, G. R., & Papadopoulou, K. (1990). The acquisition of reflexive social emotions: The transmission and reproduction of social control through joint action. In G. Duveen & B. Lloyd (Eds.), *Social representations and the development of knowledge* (pp. 107-125). Cambridge: Cambridge University Press.

Shott, S. (1979). Emotion and social life: A symbolic interactionist analysis. *American Journal of Sociology, 84,* 1317-1334.

Silver, M., Sabini, J., & Parrott, W. G. (1987). Embarrassment: A dramaturgic account. *Journal for the Theory of Social Behavior, 17,* 47-61.

Tangney, J. P. (1990). Assessing individual differences in proneness to shame and guilt: Development of the Self-Conscious Affect and Attribution Inventory. *Journal of Personality and Social Psychology, 59,* 102-111.

Tangney, J. P. (1992). Situational determinants of shame and guilt in young adulthood. *Personality and Social Psychology Bulletin, 18,* 199-206.

Tangney, J. P., Miller, R. S., & Flicker, L. (1992, August). *A quanitative analysis of shame and embarrassment.* Paper presented at the meeting of the American Psychological Association, Washington, DC.

van Hooff, J. (1972). A comparative approach to the phylogeny of laughter and smiling. In R. A. Hinde (Ed.), *Non-verbal communication* (pp. 209-241). Cambridge: Cambridge University Press.

9

The Cybernetics of Happiness

THE RELATION OF GOAL ATTAINMENT, RUMINATION, AND AFFECT

WILLIAM D. McINTOSH
LEONARD L. MARTIN

William D. McIntosh received his Ph.D. from the University of Georgia in 1990. He is now a temporary Assistant Professor at Georgia Southern University. His primary research interest is happiness.

Leonard L. Martin received his Ph.D. in 1983 from the University of North Carolina at Greensboro. He then spent a year and a half at the University of Illinois, first as a visiting Assistant Professor and then as an NIMH postdoctoral researcher. He is currently Associate Professor at the University of Georgia. His research interests include the use of information in judgments, cognition-emotion interactions, and the role of goals in thoughts and feelings.

> Our desires always increase with our possessions. The knowledge that something remains yet unenjoyed impairs our enjoyment of the good before us.
>
> Samuel Johnson

There are situations in which people's feelings fluctuate from moment to moment. For example, when we learn that our winning lottery ticket is not in fact a winner, our extreme elation may turn quickly to disappointment. If we learn that people are laughing *at* us rather than *with* us, our joy may turn quickly to embarrassment. Alongside of these momentary fluctuations in emotion, however, people also have more long-term affective experiences.

In this chapter, we explore the determinants of such experiences. Put another way, we explore the determinants of happiness and unhappiness. We begin by defining happiness and its relation to affect. Then, we discuss research indicating that people's objective life situations are not very good predictors of their happiness. Finally, we propose a model of happiness and describe some preliminary research derived from this model. In brief, the model proposes that happiness is a function of three interacting factors: peoples' beliefs about goal attainment, the affect they experience when they achieve or fail to achieve those goals, and the extent to which they sustain that affect through ruminative thought.

We believe that this model explains much of the (sometimes paradoxical) data that have come out of research on happiness. For example, it provides an explanation for why objective life situations are not good predictors of happiness, and it describes the relationship between short-term affect and long-term happiness. We begin, however, by examining the nature of happiness.

WHAT IS HAPPINESS?

First and foremost, happiness is a judgment. The statements "I am happy" and "I am unhappy" may be based on experiences a person is currently having or has had, but the statements themselves constitute inferences. As Schwarz and Strack (1991) described it: "Reports about happiness and satisfaction with one's life are not necessarily valid readouts of an internal state of personal well-being. Rather, they are judgments which, like other social judgments, are subject to a variety of transient influences" (p. 28). Similarly, Veenhoven (1984) has suggested that "happiness is not a simple sum of pleasures, but rather a cognitive construction which the individual puts together from his various experiences" (p. 22).

Other investigators have characterized happiness in a similar way. For example, Fordyce (1972) has defined happiness as "an overall evaluation made by the individual in accounting all his pleasant and unpleasant affective experiences in the recent past" (p. 227). Wessman and Ricks (1966) have suggested that happiness

> appears as an overall evaluation of the quality of the individual's own experience in the conduct of his vital affairs. As such happiness represents a conception abstracted from the flux of affective life indicating a decided balance of positive affectivity over long periods of time. (pp. 240-241)

And Veenhoven (1984) has suggested that happiness is "the degree to which an individual judges the overall quality of his life-as-a-whole favorably" (p. 22).

Given that people are *judging* their happiness, what information do they use to make this judgment? According to Ross, Eyman, and

Kishchuk (1986), people use their current mood, their assessment of the past and the future, and their standing relative to other people. More specifically, Ross et al. (1986) asked people how they decided whether or not they were happy and found that between 41% and 53% of the reasons people gave pertained to their current mood, 22% to 40% of the reasons pertained to their future expectations, 5% to 20% pertained to their assessment of the past, and 5% to 13% pertained to social comparisons. According to Diener, Sandvik, and Pavot (1991), the *single best* predictor of happiness is the *frequency* with which people experience positive affect.

So, happiness might safely be described as a judgment about one's overall life quality based largely upon the way people feel but also including people's assessments of their past and future and how they think they are doing relative to other people.

THE PARADOX OF GOAL ATTAINMENT

The definition just outlined might lead one to believe that it would be relatively easy to determine the causes of happiness. People who have consistently attained their goals should experience more positive affect, should assess their future more optimistically, should assess their past as more productive, and should feel that they are better off than people who have not attained their goals. In short, one might expect that, the better a person's objective life situation, the more likely it is that the person would report being happy.

The problem, of course, is that this is not always the case. Objective life situations are not good predictors of happiness. We know, for example, that poor people are sometimes happier than rich people (Easterlin, 1974) and that recent lottery winners are sometimes no happier than control subjects and only slightly happier than recently paralyzed accident victims (Brickman, Coates, & Janoff-Bulman, 1978). In fact, in a nationwide survey, Andrews and Withey (1976) found that the optimum combination of people's age, sex, race, education, income, religion, occupation, employment status, and size of city accounted for only 11% of the total variance in judgments of subjective well-being. According to Kammann (1982), most objective life circumstances account for less than 5% of the variance in judgments of subjective well-being, and combinations of circumstances in as many as a dozen domains rarely account for more than 10% of the variance.

Of course, objective life situations are not completely unrelated to happiness. Some situations are predictors (see Diener, 1984). For example, married people tend to be happier than single people, and people who live in extreme deprivation tend to be unhappy (Veenhoven, 1984). In general though, objective life situations exert much less influence on one's happiness than might commonly be believed.

The fact that objective life situations do not explain much of the variance in people's happiness judgments forces us to confront two logical problems:

1. If affect is an integral part of people's happiness judgments (Diener et al., 1991; Ross et al., 1986), and if attaining goals leads to positive affect (Hsee & Abelson, 1991), how is it that goal attainment is not related to long-term happiness?

2. If improvements in one's objective life situations do not lead to happiness, then why do people (at least some of them) attempt to improve their objective life situation to make themselves happy?

We address the former question first.

ADAPTATION LEVEL AND ASSESSMENTS OF LIFE SATISFACTION

One reason that improved life situations may not lead to greater levels of happiness is that people's assessments of their outcomes shift with their experiences. For example, winning $100 may seem great to a relatively poor person but may seem paltry to a millionaire. By the same reasoning, winning a million dollars may seem great to a millionaire but seem relatively paltry to a billionaire.

These examples can be understood in terms of adaptation-level theory (Brickman et al., 1978; Helson, 1964). According to that theory, judgments are made relative to a subjective neutral point. Outcomes above the neutral point of a positive-negative dimension are seen as positive, whereas outcomes below that point are seen as negative. Outcomes that match the neutral point are experienced as neutral. The theory also assumes that people's neutral points slide up or down to match their experiences. So, events that at one time had seemed very positive may be perceived as less positive when people get used to experiencing those kinds of events. Events that at one time had seemed very negative may be perceived as less negative when people get used to experiencing those kinds of events.

Positive and negative events can also influence happiness by serving as standards against which current events can be compared (Strack, Schwarz, & Gschneidinger, 1985; Tversky & Griffin, 1991). People who grew up during the Great Depression, for example, tend to report higher levels of subjective well-being in their current lives compared with similar people who did not experience the Depression (Elder, 1974). In addition, the more these people suffered during the Depression, the greater their current satisfaction. Similarly, survivors of cancer treatments report greater happiness three years after their treatments than do a healthy control group (Irwin, Allen, Kramer, & Danoff, 1982). Presumably, the survivors used their brush with death as a negative baseline against which their current life appears quite good.

Similarly, Brickman et al. (1978) asked recent lottery winners and recently paralyzed accident victims to judge how much they enjoyed a number of day-to-day activities, such as eating breakfast and reading the newspaper. The recent lottery winners reported less enjoyment of these simple pleasures than did either control subjects or the recently paralyzed accident victims.

Apparently, eating breakfast and reading the newspaper are not especially enjoyable when one could be sailing a yacht. On the other hand, what the person gains in joy by sailing the yacht may be offset by the fact that he or she experiences less enjoyment in everyday activities.

But, if a continual adaptation and balancing out were all that there was to happiness, then we might expect everyone to be equally happy in the long run, and this is not the case. People differ in their reported levels of happiness, and these reports are reasonably stable across time (Bradburn & Carpovitz, 1965). Why then are some people better able than others to maintain their happiness?

As we have seen (Brickman et al., 1978), the objective events in people's lives appear to be less important in determining happiness than are people's *perceptions* of those events. This point has been made in the coping literature as well (e.g., Lazarus & Folkman, 1984). That work has made it clear that people's mental and physical health is more dependent on the ways in which people interpret and cope with an event than on the event itself. We suggest that the key to maintaining long-term happiness is similar. In other words, happiness may be as much, if not more, a function of what people *think* is happening than of what actually is happening. Of course, this is a rather glib statement without further elaboration. We attempt that elaboration in the following sections.

GOAL NONATTAINMENT AND RUMINATION

One thought process that may be important in determining happiness is rumination. Rumination is a class of thinking in which thoughts about a given object or event come to people's minds frequently and unbidden (Martin & Tesser, 1989). Ruminative thoughts are experienced by the person as repetitive, intrusive, and aversive. These thoughts may stay in people's consciousness for some time despite people's best efforts to eliminate the thoughts. According to Martin and Tesser (1989), ruminative thoughts are generated by the failure to attain an important goal (see Zeigarnik, 1938). Of course, people may spend extended periods of time thinking about something other than a goal they cannot reach, but only blocked goals seem to result in the aversive, repetitive, intrusive thinking unique to rumination.

It is important to point out that rumination is instigated by the failure to attain *higher-order* goals (Martin & Tesser, 1989). For example, an executive may be more likely to ruminate about the size of his or her office if he or she considers office size to be an indicator of success. Having a small office may be an inconvenience, but by itself this may not elicit rumination. On the other hand, if important people have large offices, and if I do not have a large office, then I must not be important. Threats to one's self may instigate rumination. How might ruminative thoughts influence feelings and happiness? First, ruminative thoughts are unpleasant (Millar, Tesser, & Millar, 1988). They focus on what people want but do not have (Martin & Tesser, 1989), and when people focus on such discrepancies, they experience negative affect (e.g., Higgins, 1989). And this negative affect will continue for as long as the people ruminate—which is until they attain the goal or abandon the desire for it (Martin & Tesser, 1989).

Rumination may also influence people's happiness through its polarization effect. It has been shown (Tesser, 1978) that the more people think about something toward which they initially had a slightly favorable or slightly negative attitude, the more extreme their attitudes become. So, if feelings about an object are initially negative, these feelings can become even more negative as the person continues to think about the object. As we just noted, experiencing a discrepancy between what one has and what one wants is aversive (Hsee & Abelson, 1991; Millar et al., 1988). So, if people ruminate about this discrepancy, then the more they ruminate, the more aversive their situation will appear.

In sum, rumination can lead to negative affect because (a) it is aversive in and of itself and (b) it may cause people to polarize the negative feelings they associate with their failure to attain their goals. Moreover, rumination may persist until the individual either attains the goal or abandons the desire for it. Thus rumination can provide a mechanism for the persistent, long-term experience of negative affect (i.e., unhappiness).

LINKERS AND NONLINKERS

Suppose two people strongly desire a new car. One wants it simply because he thinks it would be fun to drive, and one wants it because he thinks it will improve his social life. During the time when neither has the car, which person would be ruminating? According to our previous discussion, it would be the person who links the attainment of the car to an improved social life (assuming that an improved social life is a goal of a higher order than simply having fun). So, we have two people in objectively similar positions. Both want a car and neither has a car. Yet, one person will be ruminating, and the other will not be. And, for the reasons we described earlier, the ruminating person should experience more negative affect and unhappiness than the nonruminating person.

More generally, if people believe that attaining a given outcome will make them happy, then a failure to attain that outcome will in fact make them unhappy. And this is true regardless of whether lack of the outcome is aversive in and of itself. There is evidence, for example, that single people are less happy than are married people (Diener, 1984). So, two single people might both be less happy in general than two married people. The single person who ruminates about the mate he or she wants but does not have, however, will experience more unhappiness than the single person who does not ruminate.

In sum, when attainment of a given outcome does not lead to happiness, believing that it does can cause a person to ruminate about not having it, and this will make him or her unhappy. On the other hand, when attainment of an outcome *does* lead to happiness, ruminating about not having it can add to the objective unhappiness associated with not attaining the outcome.

We use the term *linking* to refer to the belief that the attainment of specific goals will lead to happiness. Linking means believing that goals are *necessary* for happiness. It means believing that happiness can be achieved *only if* certain things fall into place. In effect, linking entails placing situational contingencies on one's happiness. By comparison, *nonlinking* means seeing specific outcomes as important and desirable but not believing that the attainment of these goals determines happiness.

In this chapter, we may refer to *linking* and *nonlinking* as if these were dichotomous. We do this because it is easier to talk in these terms. Linking, however, is probably best conceptualized as a continuum. A person's beliefs about the relation between goal attainment and happiness may fall anywhere from completely linked to completely nonlinked. In addition, people can be more or less linked to any given goal, and different people may link varying numbers of goals to their happiness.

Notice also that there is a distinction between linking the attainment of goals to happiness and holding goal attainment as important. People can believe that a goal is worth pursuing without believing that attainment of that goal will make them happy. For example, maintaining good oral hygiene is important, but few people would say that flossing their teeth would make them *happy*. They would be more likely to say that they would be happy playing tennis, winning a million dollars, or taking a trip.

The distinction between importance and linking is a critical one to make as the two may have very different implications for people's well-being. As research on learned helplessness suggests, if people do not strive to attain their goals, then they will have difficulty functioning normally day to day (Dweck, 1978; Miller & Seligman, 1975). After all, humans are goal-oriented organisms. Most of our actions are performed with the attainment of some goal in mind (e.g., Carver & Scheier, 1981; Miller, Galanter, & Pribram, 1960). It is healthy to actively seek goals.

On the other hand, the evidence suggests that, in most cases, attaining specific outcomes does not lead to greater long-term happiness. So, believing that they do means operating from a false premise. This may lead to disappointment when the goal is attained and happiness does not result. It may also lead to long-term negative affect as people ruminate during the (possibly lengthy) time during which they have not attained the desired outcome. So, although attainment may not lead to happiness, nonattainment may very well lead to unhappiness.

Of course, linking the attainment of lower-order goals to happiness does not mean frustration and rumination all of the time. Even linkers can experience positive affect when the goal to which they have linked their happiness is obtained or when progress toward the goal is made (Carver & Scheier, 1990; Hsee & Abelson, 1991). But, because attaining goals does not lead to long-term happiness, the positive affect is likely to be short-lived (Brickman et al., 1978). It may quickly dissipate as people adjust to the new adaptation level and consider other unattained goals. Therefore the positive affect people experience when they reach a goal or make progress toward it may be better described as pleasure than as happiness. Nonlinkers will also experience positive affect when they achieve desired goals, but they do not pay the price of negative affect and unhappiness when the goal is not reached.

This might best be illustrated with an example. Imagine that a person is attached to the goal of owning a new BMW. This person believes that she would be happy if she could just get behind the wheel of this car. By believing that the car will make her happy, she implicitly believes that not having the car means that she cannot be happy. She often thinks about how much she wants the car. This rumination is unpleasant and distracting, and it continues until she finally gets the car.

The BMW gives her a great deal of pleasure at first. Indeed, it may actually give her more intense pleasure than it would have if she did not link its attainment to her happiness, because she has built this goal up to be very significant. But, as Diener et al. (1991) point out, it is not the intensity of affect that leads to long-term happiness, but the frequency. And, after a while, the BMW owner will get used to seeing the car in the driveway, and the positive affect will dissipate.

If this same person does not link the attainment of the car with happiness, then she still gets to experience the brief pleasure from attaining the car. She is, however, less upset and distracted if she has trouble getting the BMW, and she does not experience the negative affect during the time when she wants but does not have the car. Therefore she is better able to enjoy what positive features her life holds while the car is not in her possession.

So, it may well be that linking the attainment of specific goals with happiness will result in as much positive affect upon attainment of the goal as does nonlinking. It is the rumination and focus on the discrepancy between what one wants but does not have that is the difference. Unpleasant rumination about desired outcomes that people currently want but do not have will add a *chronic negative* to the balance of positive and negative affect people experience in their day-to-day lives (see Figure 9.1). And this will make them more unhappy than if they did not link attainment of those goals with their happiness. In short, it is the *ruminating* about not having rather than the not having that causes people to be unhappy.

One question that arises from the preceding argument concerns why people attempt to attain goals to make themselves happy when, as the evidence suggests, attaining goals will probably not make them happy. Why do people not realize this and stop doing it?

PEOPLE DO NOT ALWAYS KNOW
WHAT MAKES THEM HAPPY

One reason people may pursue goals in order to be happy is that they are following culturally shared theories rather than their own feelings (Csikszentmihalyi & LeFevre, 1989; Wilson, Laser, & Stone, 1982). Such theories can cause people to perceive covariations where none exist and to miss covariations where they do exist (Chapman & Chapman, 1967; Nisbett & Wilson, 1977). In other words, theories can make people think they would be happy engaging in a given behavior when in fact they would not be. At the same time, the theories could make people fail to realize that some behaviors in which they are engaging are in fact making them happy.

Evidence to this effect was obtained by Csikszentmihalyi and LeFevre (1989). They found that people were three times more likely to experience "flow" (a good correlate of happiness) when they were working than when they were engaging in leisure activities. This suggests that people were happier at work than at play. Yet, these same people were more likely to say they "would rather be somewhere else" when they

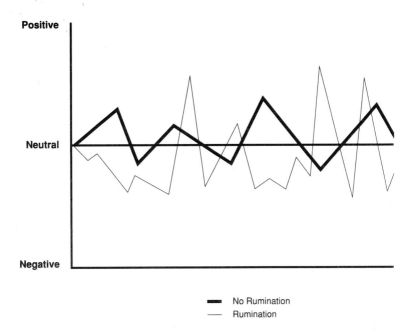

Figure 9.1. Positive and Negative Experiences of Ruminating and Nonruminating Persons

were at work than when they were engaging in leisure activities. Apparently, they missed the correlation between work and enjoyment, because enjoying work more than leisure is inconsistent with our cultural theories. As Csikszentmihalyi and LeFevre (1989) describe it: "In deciding whether they wish to work or not, people judge their desires by social conventions rather than by the reality of their feelings" (p. 821).

Wilson, Laser, and Stone (1982) provided related evidence for people's understanding of the determinants of their moods. They asked subjects to rate their moods once a day for five weeks. In addition, they asked the subjects to indicate the context of their rating (i.e., weather, day of week, hours of sleep). At the end of the five weeks, subjects were given a list of the contextual variables that had surrounded their mood ratings and were asked to estimate how much each of these variables correlated with their mood.

Wilson et al. (1982) then computed a correlation between the weights assigned to the contextual variables by the subjects with the weights assigned to them by a regression analysis. The correlation between these two sets of weights was .42. Thus there was a decent correlation between what subjects think affected their moods and what actually did. There was an interesting correlation of .45, however, between the weights the subjects assigned to the contextual variables and the weights assigned by people who responded only to a list of the contextual variables. In other words, these people who had not explicitly noted their moods and the surrounding contexts for five weeks were just as accurate in estimating the correlation between mood and contextual factors as were subjects who had kept track of their moods for five weeks.

Even more interesting was the degree to which the estimates of the actual subjects matched those of the people not in the experiment. This correlation was .94. This finding suggests that both groups based their estimates on the same information: culturally shared theories of what factors lead people to feel good or bad.

More generally, we might suggest that peoples' theories about happiness can make them miss the true relation between the activities they perform and their resultant happiness. The role of goal beliefs and rumination in producing unhappiness is depicted graphically in Figure 9.2. As noted previously, we are not construing linking as a personality trait or an individual difference per se. Rather, it is a set of beliefs about goals. As people switch from goal to goal, they return to the question: "Believe attainment of outcome leads to happiness?" From here, they could answer either yes or no. Of course, some people are likely to link more goals to happiness than are others, and in that sense we can talk about people as linkers and nonlinkers. In fact, this is what we do in our research.

From the model, we can derive the following predictions:

(1) For linkers, the nonattainment of a lower-order goal (get a car) is associated with the nonattainment of a higher-order goal (be happy). For nonlinkers, however, nonattainment of a lower-order goal is simply nonattainment of a lower-order goal. Because rumination is instigated

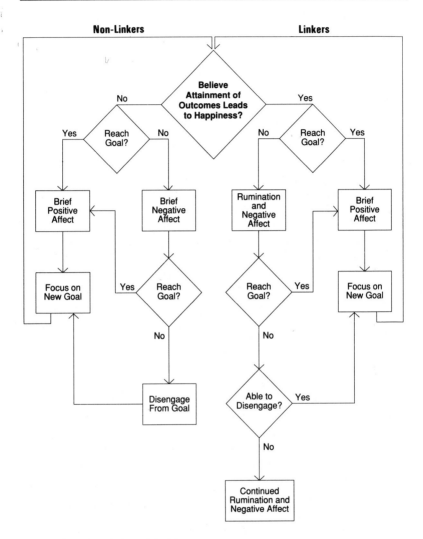

Figure 9.2. The Linkage Model

by the failure to attain higher-order goals, then, upon failure to attain a goal, linkers should be more likely to ruminate than should nonlinkers.

(2) Rumination should be positively related to people's experiences of negative affect and unhappiness. As noted earlier, rumination is unpleasant in and of itself, and it may polarize the unpleasantness associated with goal nonattainment. So, the more people ruminate, the more unhappy they should be.

(3) Linking results in more negative affect and unhappiness than does nonlinking but it does not lead to less positive affect and happiness. This is because rumination adds a chronic negative to the mixture of positive and negative affect people experience on a day-to-day basis. But linkers and nonlinkers may not differ in the frequency with which they attain their goals. Hence they should experience the same frequency of positive affect.

(4) Rumination mediates *the relationship between linking and unhappiness.* That is, the relationship is causal. Linking the attainment of an outcome with happiness leads to rumination when that outcome is not attained, and this, in turn, leads to long-term experiences of negative affect.

(5) All of these effects will be restricted to outcomes people want but do not have. This is because people do not ruminate about outcomes they have attained or do not desire.

EMPIRICAL EVIDENCE

We have obtained some preliminary evidence to support each of the previously described derivations of the model (McIntosh & Martin, 1989). We first had to develop a means of assessing people's beliefs about the links between the attainment of specific goals and happiness. The measure we developed looks at people's *global* linking tendencies. More specifically, we asked subjects four separate questions about a variety of goals (e.g., a romantic relationship, financial security, ideal weight). First, subjects were asked to make two concurrent judgments about each goal: (a) How happy would they be if they never achieved this goal? (b) How happy would they be if they had this goal now? Next, subjects were asked to indicate on the list the goals that they wanted but did not have. A subject's *initial* linking score was then determined by taking the average differences between questions 1 and 2 for the goals that they wanted but did not have. The larger this discrepancy, the happier subjects believe they would be if they attained this goal. In the case of goals the subjects want but do not have, the discrepancy tells us that subjects believe they would be happy if only they had those goals.

Finally, subjects were asked to rate how important each goal was to them. We measured importance for two reasons. First, we wanted to demonstrate that, although importance and linking are conceptually similar, they should predict a person's affective and ruminative experiences very differently. As noted previously, holding goals as important is adaptive. Linking happiness to the attainment of those goals, however, may lead to rumination and negative affect. Second, we reasoned that anyone would react more strongly to not attaining an important as opposed to an unimportant goal. At any given level of importance, however, linkers should respond more strongly than should nonlinkers. Thus importance might cloud the relationship between linking and unhappiness. That is, importance might act as a suppressor variable. By statistically removing the effect of importance, we may derive a purer measure of the effects of linking on rumination and unhappiness.

We also measured subjects' tendencies to ruminate. This was done using a 10-item questionnaire that contained items such as "When I have a problem, I tend to think about it a lot of the time," "I often think about the future," and "I often become lost in thought." Subjects responded to these items on 7-point Likert scales with the poles labeled "does not describe me well" and "describes me well."

To measure happiness, we asked subjects to estimate the percentage of time they felt happy, unhappy, and neutral (Fordyce, 1977). This measure is good for two reasons. It allows us to obtain independent assessments of the amount of time subjects spend happy and the amount of time they spend unhappy. These have been shown to vary independently (Bradburn, 1969; Diener & Emmons, 1984), and our model makes separate predictions for the two. The measure also reflects the *frequency* with which people experience happiness and unhappiness. According to Diener et al. (1991), frequency of affective experience is the single best predictor of happiness. Along with happiness and unhappiness, we also measured positive and negative affect, using the Positive and Negative Affect Scale (Watson, 1988).

The results of this study provided strong support for our hypotheses. We started with simple correlations involving the subjects' *initial* linking scores (i.e., importance is *not* partialed out). These correlations revealed, as predicted, that the more people linked goals to happiness, the more they ruminated ($r = .30, p < .001$). The more people ruminated, the more unhappiness ($r = .37, p < .001$) and negative affect ($r = .29, p < .01$) they reported. And the more people believed that attaining goals that they did not have would make them happy, the more negative affect they experienced ($r = .18, p < .05$). Linking, however, was not related to the amount of unhappiness people reported ($r = .12$, n.s.).

This last finding, the lack of a relationship between linking and unhappiness, may appear inconsistent with our model. Recall our assumption, however, that goal importance would act as a suppressor variable in the relation between linking and unhappiness. Everyone would be more likely to ruminate about important as opposed to unimportant goals. At any given level of importance, however, linkers should ruminate more than nonlinkers. So, we conducted additional analyses using importance as a covariate. More specifically, when we regressed unhappiness simultaneously on linking and importance, the relation between linking and unhappiness increased to significance ($ß = .19, p = .056$). Thus linking the attainment of goals to happiness is something other than holding goals as important, and removing the effect of importance increases the relation between subjects' goal beliefs and their unhappiness.

As expected, there was little relation between linking and the degree of *positive* affect and *happiness* subjects reported. Linking (with importance partialed out) was unrelated to either experiences of positive affect ($ß = .04$, n.s.) or happiness ($ß = −.01$, n.s.).

We also obtained evidence that rumination is a *mediator* of the relation between linking and unhappiness. That is, linking influences unhappiness through its effect on rumination. Baron and Kenny (1986) describe four criteria for determining whether a variable is a mediator. In terms of this experiment, the criteria are that (a) linking must be related to unhappiness, (b) rumination must also be related to unhappiness, (c) linking must be related to rumination, and (d) when rumination and linking are regressed simultaneously onto unhappiness, the relationship between linking and unhappiness should disappear, while the relation between rumination and unhappiness should remain. This is what was found (see Figure 9.3).

Evidence for the first three criteria was reported earlier. In terms of the fourth criteria, when rumination was included in the regression with linking and importance, the relation between linking and unhappiness was removed (from $\beta = .19$, $p = .056$ to $\beta = .09$, n.s.), as was the relationship between linking and negative affect (from $\beta = .20$, $p < .05$ to $\beta = .13$, n.s.). Both the relation between rumination and unhappiness ($\beta = .37$, $p < .001$) and the relation between rumination and negative affect ($\beta = .26$, $p < .05$), however, remained significant. These results suggest that rumination can be considered a true mediator of the relationship between linking and happiness. When people have not attained goals that they link to their happiness, they ruminate about those goals, and this rumination, in turn, leads them to experience negative affect and ultimately unhappiness.

The results are also consistent with our assumption that, for a goal to elicit rumination, it must be "charged." That is, it must currently be desired yet remain unattained (Martin & Tesser, 1989). When the linkage score was based on subjects' ratings of the goals that they reported *already having,* there were no significant effects. Linkers did not ruminate more than did nonlinkers ($r = .06$), they were not more unhappy ($r = -.08$), and they did not report greater negative affect ($r = .02$).

As noted earlier, the linking score is determined by taking the difference between subjects' ratings of (a) how happy they would be if they never reached a given goal and (b) how happy they would be if they had the goal now. Linkers and nonlinkers differ on their answers to both questions. Using a median split, we found that linkers judged that they would be less happy than nonlinkers if they never reached a given goal (linkers: M = 2.54; nonlinkers: M = 3.88), and they judged that they would be happier attaining the goal (linkers: M = 8.94; nonlinkers: M = 7.93).

Rumination, however, was significantly related to people's judgments of how happy they would be if they had the goal now ($r = .22$, $p < .05$) but not with their judgments of how happy they would be if they never reached the goal ($r = -.10$, n.s.). Evidently, it is the promise of being happier if they reach their goals rather than the affective consequences of never reaching their goals that is more pressing for linkers.

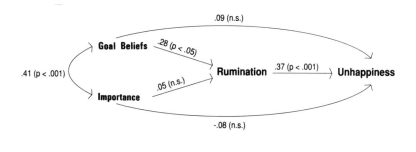

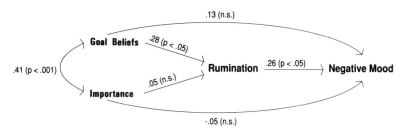

Figure 9.3. Path Analyses Assessing the Mediational Function of Rumination

To summarize, the results provided strong support for our model. Linking was related to rumination and to negative affect and unhappiness, but only when the linking score was based on subjects' ratings of the goals they wanted but had not yet attained. And, when rumination was included in the equation, the relation between linking and unhappiness disappeared, indicating that rumination mediates the relation between linking and unhappiness. We also obtained evidence that goal importance and linking are not identical concepts. And, finally, we found no differences in the happiness or positive affect linkers and nonlinkers experienced.

In the study just described, we used a *global* measure of rumination. Because of this, we cannot be sure that we were measuring only goal-directed rumination. We may have also tapped into a more general individual difference related to negative affect, such as neuroticism.

Also, a global measure does not allow us to determine the *content* of the subjects' ruminations. We assumed that our subjects were ruminating about their unattained goals; however, we have no direct evidence of this. So, in a second experiment, we measured rumination in a way that allowed us to assess goal-specific thoughts.

We began, as before, by blocking subjects as linkers and nonlinkers. Then, we identified a goal that some subjects wanted but did not have and that others wanted and already had. The goal we chose was "a romantic relationship." We thought this would be a goal of high importance to our subjects, and our previous research had indicated that about half of our subjects wanted a romantic relationship but did not have one, and about half wanted and already had a romantic relationship.

We made this goal salient by asking all of our subjects to complete a short questionnaire about their recent love life. They answered questions such as these: "When was the last time you were on a date?" "Do you currently have a steady boyfriend/girlfriend?" Once subjects were reminded (through the questionnaires) that they had either attained or not attained the desired outcome of being in a romantic relationship, they proceeded to the task in which we measured rumination.

In this task, subjects were presented with a sequence of 12 words. Each word first appeared on the computer screen as a string of asterisks. Then, the word was revealed one letter at a time. The subjects' task was to identify the words before all of the letters had been revealed. Four of the words dealt with romantic relationships (e.g., *romance*), four dealt with self-worth (e.g., *likable*), and the remaining four were irrelevant control words (e.g., *adjective*).

The assumption behind this task is that, the more subjects are ruminating about a given goal, the more accessible information related to that goal should be. Therefore subjects ruminating about a goal should recognize words related to it faster than should subjects not ruminating about that goal (Fuhrman & Shavitt, 1990; Martin & Tesser, 1989; Meyer & Schvaneveldt, 1971; Warren, 1972).

From the model, we can derive the following predictions:

(1) For subjects who want but do not *have a romantic relationship, linkers should ruminate more than nonlinkers (i.e., they should be faster at recognizing words related to a romantic relationship).*

(2) Among people who have *a romantic partner, linkers should ruminate about romantic relationships* less *than nonlinkers.* Because the goal has already been met, linkers may quickly lose interest in it.

Once a goal has been reached, the urgency surrounding it is removed, and other salient unmet goals that promise happiness may quickly become the focus. Nonlinkers, on the other hand, are not preoccupied with intrusive thoughts of unmet goals. Therefore thoughts of romantic relationships should remain somewhat salient, because they have recently completed a questionnaire on the subject.

(3) Looked at another way, linkers who want but do not have a romantic relationship should ruminate more about romantic relationships than linkers who want and have a relationship. Nonlinkers, however, should not vary significantly in their rumination regardless of whether they are in a relationship or not.

Figure 9.4 summarizes the average reaction time (in seconds) to recognize words related to romantic relationships. The results showed the predicted crossover interaction. Linkers who wanted a romantic relationship ruminated more than did linkers who currently had a romantic relationship. Nonlinkers did not vary in how much they ruminated about romantic relationships, however, regardless of whether they currently had one or not. Looked at another way, among people who want but do not have a romantic relationship, linkers ruminated more than nonlinkers. And, among people who currently had a romantic relationship, linkers ruminated about romantic relationships *less* than did nonlinkers.

It is important to point out that the recognition time differences we described were observed only for words related to romantic relationships. There were no differences between linkers and nonlinkers in the time it took them to recognize any of the other words. Thus we know that subjects were ruminating about the unattained goal and that our measure does not reflect a general tendency to ruminate.

SUMMARY

We started with the assumption that people do not directly detect their happiness the way they would detect a bright light, for example. Rather, they infer or judge their happiness. This judgment appears to be based largely upon one's affective state. According to Diener et al. (1991), the single best predictor of happiness is the frequency with which one experiences positive affect. Therefore, to understand happiness, one must understand the determinants of the frequency of affective experiences.

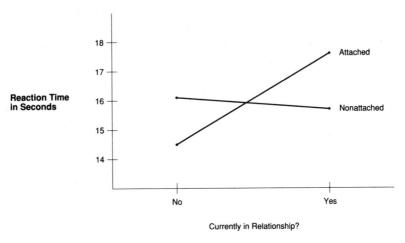

Figure 9.4. Time to Recognize Goal-Related Words as a Function of Status of Relationship and Linkage Score

Because people's life situations do not correlate well with their levels of happiness (Diener, 1984; Veenhoven, 1984), we assume that the determinants must be subjective. We have focused on people's beliefs that attainment of objective outcomes will make them happy. The more beliefs people hold that link the attainment of goals to their long-term happiness, the more likely it is that they will ruminate about goals they want but do not have. This rumination is aversive and lasts until the goal is either attained or abandoned. Thus it adds a long-term negative pall to people's overall affective states. The end result is that linkers spend significantly more of their time *unhappy* than do nonlinkers.

Future Directions

The model of happiness we have proposed makes some novel predictions with regard to the determinants of happiness. In addition, the model allows us to make sense of some of the diverse, and often contradictory, findings in research on happiness. And, finally, we have obtained preliminary evidence to support the basic assumptions of our model. On the other hand, our work in this area has only just begun, and there is still a great deal that needs to be done. The following are a few of the possibilities suggested by our model:

(1) To this point, the data supporting the relationship between linking and unhappiness are correlational. If we are correct in maintaining that linking is a belief system rather than a stable personality trait, then it should be possible to *manipulate* these beliefs. For example, we might simply tell subjects that the attainment of outcome X leads to happiness but that the attainment of outcome Y does not. If our model is correct, then, regardless of whether subjects are globally linkers or nonlinkers, they should ruminate more and experience more negative affect when they fail to attain a goal that they believe will lead to happiness than when they fail to attain a goal that they believe does not lead to happiness.

(2) Also, it should be possible, under the right conditions, to change people more generally from linkers to nonlinkers, and vice versa. We speculate that this change would involve much the same factors as are involved in attitude change more generally (for a review, see Petty & Cacioppo, 1981). People might be more likely, for example, to hold false beliefs about outcomes they have not directly experienced than about outcomes they have experienced directly. Similarly, people with low self-confidence may be more likely to accept someone else's (i.e., culturally shared) theories of happiness than would people with confidence in their abilities.

(3) Linkers should have a more difficult time than nonlinkers in disengaging from a goal. If a goal is being pursued for its own sake (i.e., nonlinkers), and proves to be more trouble than it's worth, it can be abandoned or replaced without much difficulty. But people will be very reluctant to give up a goal that promises long-term happiness. They may cling to such goals even in the face of much negative affect.

This hypothesis carries the additional implication that linkers may be more likely than nonlinkers to attain a given goal. After all, linkers may cling to the goal longer than nonlinkers, and this extra effort may improve their chances of eventual attainment. Remember, however, that, even if linking does lead to a greater likelihood of goal attainment, this means little in terms of people's happiness. Attaining goals does not lead to happiness.

(4) Nonlinkers should be better able than linkers to detect covariations between external events and their internal states. Linkers are

pursuing happiness in a manner that generally does not lead to happiness. They rely on culturally derived, a priori theories of how to achieve happiness rather than on paying attention to what circumstances actually do and do not influence their happiness. This may reflect a general inability on their part to detect covariations between external events and their internal states. One way to test this proposition would be to replicate the previously mentioned study by Wilson et al. (1982). Nonlinkers should be more accurate than linkers at estimating how much the external variables correlate with their mood.

GENERAL CONCLUSIONS

It seems intuitively plausible that attaining desired outcomes should lead to happiness. Based on the plausibility of this culturally derived theory, some people pursue specific outcomes in the hopes of becoming happy. But research has found that getting one's objective life situation to fit one's desires does not lead to long-term happiness. We have found, however, that if people believe they cannot be happy until certain things take place in their lives, then they ruminate about those things and make themselves unhappy. Thus it is the ruminating rather than the nonattaining that makes people unhappy. Our research suggests that little needs to be added to people's lives to make them happy. Rather, something needs to be subtracted. What needs to be subtracted is their belief that they will be happy only if they reach their goals. In most cases, this is a false belief. Yet, holding this belief can lead to rumination and unhappiness.

REFERENCES

Andrews, F. M., & Withey, S. B. (1976). *Social indicators of well-being*. New York: Plenum.

Baron, R. M., & Kenny, D. A. (1986). The moderator-mediator variable distinction in social psychological research: Conceptual, strategic, and statistical considerations. *Journal of Personality and Social Psychology, 51,* 1173-1182.

Bradburn, N. M. (1969). *The structure of psychological well-being*. Chicago: Aldine.

Bradburn, N. M., & Carpovitz, D. B. (1965). *Reports on happiness: A pilot study of behavior related to mental health*. Chicago: Aldine.

Brickman, P., Coates, D., & Janoff-Bulman, R. (1978). Lottery winners and accident victims: Is happiness relative? *Journal of Personality and Social Psychology, 36,* 917-927.

Carver, C. S., & Scheier, M. F. (1981). *Attention and self-regulation: A control-theory approach to human behavior.* New York: Springer-Verlag.

Carver, C. S., & Scheier, M. F. (1990). Origins and functions of positive and negative affect: A control-process review. *Psychological Review, 97,* 19-35.

Chapman, L. J., & Chapman, J. P. (1967). Genesis of popular but erroneous diagnostic observations. *Journal of Abnormal Psychology, 72,* 193-204.

Csikszentmihalyi, M., & LeFevre, J. (1989). Optimal experience in work and leisure. *Journal of Personality and Social Psychology, 56,* 815-822.

Diener, E. (1984). Subjective well-being. *Psychological Bulletin, 235,* 542-822.

Diener, E., & Emmons, R. A. (1984). The independence of positive and negative affect. *Journal of Personality and Social Psychology, 47,* 1105-1117.

Diener, E., Sandvik, E., & Pavot, W. (1991). Happiness is the frequency, not the intensity, of positive versus negative affect. In F. Strack, M. Argyle, & N. Schwarz (Eds.), *Subjective well-being.* New York: Pergamon.

Dweck, C. S. (1978). Achievement. In M. E. Lamb (Ed.), *Social and personality development.* New York: Holt, Rinehart & Winston.

Easterlin, R. A. (1974). Does economic growth improve the human lot? Some empirical evidence. In P. A. David & M. W. Reder (Eds.), *Nations and households in economic growth.* New York: Academic Press.

Elder, G. H. (1974). *Children of the Great Depression.* Chicago: Chicago University Press.

Fordyce, M. W. (1972). *Happiness, its daily variation and its relation to values.* San Diego, CA: United States International University.

Fordyce, M. W. (1977). Development of a program to increase personal happiness. *Journal of Counseling Psychology, 24,* 511-521.

Fuhrman, R. W., & Shavitt, S. (1990). *The effects of goal priming on the speed and favorableness of attitude judgments.* Paper presented at the Midwestern Psychological Association, Chicago.

Helson, H. (1964). *Adaptation Level Theory.* New York: Harper & Row.

Higgins, E. T. (1989). Knowledge accessibility and activation: Subjectivity and suffering from unconscious sources. In J. S. Uleman & J. A. Bargh (Eds.), *Unintended thought: The limits of awareness, intention, and control* (pp. 75-123). New York: Guilford.

Hsee, C. K., & Abelson, R. P. (1991). Velocity relation: Satisfaction as a function of the first derivative of outcome over time. *Journal of Personality and Social Psychology, 60,* 341-347.

Irwin, P. H., Allen, G., Kramer, S., & Danoff, B. (1982). Quality of life after radiation therapy: A study of 309 cancer survivors. *Social Indicators Research, 10,* 187-210.

Kammann, R. (1982). *Personal circumstances and life events as poor predictors of happiness.* Paper presented at the annual convention of the American Psychological Association, Washington, DC.

Lazarus, R. S., & Folkman, S. (1984). *Stress, appraisal, and coping.* New York: Springer.

Martin, L. L., & Tesser, A. (1989). Toward a motivational and structural theory of ruminative thought. In J. S. Uleman & J. A. Bargh (Eds.), *Unintended thought: The limits of awareness, intention, and control.* New York: Guilford.

McIntosh, W. D., & Martin, L. L. (1989). *Happiness, rumination, and situational contingencies.* Paper presented at the annual convention of the Midwestern Psychological Association, Chicago.

Meyer, D. E., & Schvaneveldt, R. W. (1971). Facilitation in recognizing pairs of words: Evidence of a dependence between retrieval operations. *Journal of Experimental Psychology, 90,* 227-234.

Millar, K. U., Tesser, A., & Millar, M. (1988). The effects of a threatening life event on behavior sequences and intrusive thought: A self-disruption explanation. *Cognitive Therapy and Research, 12,* 441-457.

Miller, G. A., Galanter, E., & Pribram, K. N. (1960). *Plans and the structure of behavior.* New York: Holt, Rinehart & Winston.

Miller, W. R., & Seligman, M. E. P. (1975). Depression and learned helplessness in man. *Journal of Abnormal Psychology, 84,* 228-238.

Nisbett, R. E., & Wilson, T. D. (1977). Telling more than we know: Verbal reports on mental processes. *Psychological Review, 84,* 231-259.

Petty, R. E., & Cacioppo, J. T. (1981). *Attitudes and persuasion: Classic and contemporary approaches.* Dubuque, IA: William C. Brown.

Ross, M., Eyman, A., & Kishchuk, N. (1986). Determinants of subjective well-being. In J. M. Olson, C. P. Herman, & M. Zanna (Eds.), *Relative deprivation and social comparison.* Hillsdale, NJ: Lawrence Erlbaum.

Schwarz, N., & Strack, F. (1991). Evaluating one's life: A judgment model of subjective well-being. In F. Strack, M. Argyle, & N. Schwarz (Eds.), *Subjective well-being.* London: Pergamon.

Strack, F., Schwarz, N., & Gschneidinger, E. (1985). Happiness and reminiscing: The role of time perspective, mood, and mode of thinking. *Journal of Personality and Social Psychology, 49,* 1460-1469.

Tesser, A. (1978). Self-generated attitude change. In L. Berkowitz (Ed.), *Advances in experimental social psychology* (Vol. 2, pp. 289-338). New York: Academic Press.

Tversky, A., & Griffin, D. (1991). Endowment and contrast in judgments of well-being. In F. Strack, M. Argyle, & N. Schwarz (Eds.), *Subjective well-being.* London: Pergamon.

Veenhoven, R. (1984). *Conditions of happiness.* Dordrecht: Reidel.

Warren, R. (1972). Stimulus encoding and memory. *Journal of Experimental Psychology, 94,* 90-100.

Watson, D. (1988). The vicissitudes of mood measurement: Effects of varying descriptors, time frames, and response formats on measures of positive and negative affect. *Journal of Personality and Social Psychology, 55,* 128-141.

Wessman, A. E., & Ricks, D. F. (1966). *Mood and personality.* New York: Holt, Rinehart & Winston.

Wilson, T. D., Laser, P. S., & Stone, J. I. (1982). Judging the predictors of one's own mood: Accuracy and the use of shared theories. *Journal of Experimental Social Psychology, 18,* 537-556.

Zeigarnik, B. (1938). On finished and unfinished tasks. In W. D. Ellis (Ed. and Trans.), *A source book of Gestalt psychology.* New York: Harcourt, Brace, & World. (Original work published 1927)

10

The Impact of Positive Affect on Persuasion Processes

DIANE M. MACKIE
ARLENE G. ASUNCION
FRANCINE ROSSELLI

Diane M. Mackie is Associate Professor of Psychology at the University of California, Santa Barbara. Her research focuses on the role of cognitive, motivational, and affective processes in persuasion and intergroup perception. She is currently Associate Editor of the *Personality and Social Psychology Bulletin.*

Arlene G. Asuncion is an Assistant Professor in social psychology at The University of Texas, Arlington. Her current research investigates the effects of positive mood on persuasion and the impact of elaboration of on-line versus memory-based attitude judgments. Other interests include the effects of affectively and cognitively inconsistent information on stereotype change.

Francine Rosselli is a graduate student in social psychology at the University of California, Santa Barbara. Currently, her research examines the mediating factors of positive mood effects in persuasion and the allocation of attention during information processing.

Research concerned with the ways affective processes interact with cognitive processes to produce social judgments has developed apace in recent years (for reviews, see Bower, 1981; Fiedler, 1990; Forgas, 1990; Isen, 1984, 1987; Schwarz & Clore, 1988). Despite this flurry of activity, tracing the impact of affect on many domain-specific judgments has proven difficult because little is known about the cognitive processes involved in making such judgments. In the attitude domain, however, much is now known about the various processes that underlie attitude formation and change (Eagly & Chaiken, 1984; Petty & Cacioppo, 1986; Sherman, 1987). This knowledge provides a basis for predicting the

AUTHORS' NOTE: Preparation of this chapter was supported by NIMH grant MH43041 to the first author and a University of California President's Dissertation Fellowship to the second author. We take this opportunity to thank Margaret S. Clark, Richard E. Petty, and several anonymous reviewers who provided comments on an earlier version of this chapter. Correspondence concerning this chapter should be addressed to Diane M. Mackie, Department of Psychology, University of California, Santa Barbara, Santa Barbara, CA 93106.

impact of affective states on persuasive processes and outcomes as well as a baseline for interpreting research findings when affect is introduced into the persuasive context.

In this chapter, we first provide a processing model of persuasion as a foundation for discussing ways in which affect could be expected to influence the various substages of persuasive processing. Focusing on the implications of affect-induced category activation, we review what is known about the impact affect has on persuasion-relevant processes. Our review focuses on the impact of *positive affect* on persuasion both because positive mood has been successfully considered within an information processing perspective (see Isen, 1987; Schwarz, Bless, & Bohner, 1991; Srull, 1983) and because there is now a small but growing body of research on positive affect and persuasion conducted from such a perspective.[1] In reviewing the literature, we are primarily concerned not with attitudinal *outcomes* but with the impact of positive mood on the *subprocesses* underlying persuasion. In focusing on processes, we attempt to draw out the implications of an information processing view of mood effects on persuasion and to indicate potentially fruitful directions for future research.

A PROCESSING MODEL OF PERSUASION

Persuasion can be modeled as an information processing sequence that culminates in a privately accepted attitudinal judgment. Such judgments reflect evaluation of the attitude object and represent either formation of a new attitude or modification of a prior attitude (for more detailed reviews, see Eagly & Chaiken, 1984; Petty & Cacioppo, 1986). To provide a framework for the multiple ways in which positive affect could affect persuasion, we focus on three "subprocesses" that contribute to persuasion: reception, elaboration, and integration. To make the description of these subprocesses more concrete, consider a persuasive message depicting a dentist recommending a new toothpaste.

Reception Processes

Reception comprises encoding and comprehension of some subset of information in the persuasive context. Such information may include the attitude object (the toothpaste), the advocated position (the consumer should purchase the toothpaste), presented arguments or object attributes (flavor, effectiveness, cost), any influence source (the dentist) or audience present, and so on. Encoding and comprehension entail forming a mental representation and general understanding of the attended information. Encoding of the attitude object may be accompanied by either automatic or deliberate activation of any relevant preexisting attitudes (e.g., "I like this brand") from long-term memory. Related semantic and persuasion knowledge structures will also be activated during encoding of information. Such structures may include persuasion-relevant rules, such as persuasion heuristics. Thus, for example, in addition to activating information about the features of experts, encoding the presence of an expert source—like a dentist—may also activate the inference that expert sources hold valid attitude positions (Chaiken, 1987). Encoding of any particular piece of information does not necessarily require extensive allocation of attentional capacity. In many cases, activation of relevant semantic or persuasion knowledge is spontaneous and routinized. Attempts to encode extremely difficult or extensive information, however, will be subject to motivational and capacity constraints.

Elaboration Processes

The encoded items of information become candidates for allocation of further processing capacity that allows attribution, inference drawing, and evaluation to occur. Particularly crucial in this stage is the formation of evaluative inferences and evaluative elaborations of encoded information (Greenwald, 1968; Petty & Cacioppo, 1986). For example, information that a particular toothpaste contains baking soda may produce the positive inference of healthier gums or the negative inference of reduced flavor. Particular arguments may be extended or amplified from prior knowledge. For example, knowing that a friend had improved dental exams following use of the toothpaste may amplify arguments of cavity fighting effectiveness. Responses and reactions of endorsement or disparagement may also be added to or associated with encoded arguments. For example, one may decide that the presented arguments are very compelling or rather inane. Elaborative processes are resource intensive and can be limited by both capacity or motivational deficits. The outputs of elaboration may serve to draw attention to other information in the persuasion context, may act as retrieval cues for other semantic or persuasion-relevant information, or may be forwarded directly to the integration stage.

Integration Processes

Attitude judgments are made by assembling, weighting (by strength, importance, and the like), and integrating some combination of currently presented encoded material, relevant retrieved material, and output of elaboration of either currently encoded or retrieved material. The reception and elaboration processes will continue to provide inputs to this integration process until the recipient attains a desired point of subjective certainty or validity (the "sufficiency" threshold; Chaiken, Liberman, & Eagly, 1989), at which time a judgment is made. That is, the recipient will continue to encode, retrieve, and elaborate information until such information can be combined to yield a judgment that satisfies the recipients' desired level of judgmental confidence. These integration processes may be relatively resource-free, consisting only of retrieval of a prior evaluation of the object, reliance on an activated heuristic, or use of one dimension of information. Other integration processes may be resource-intensive strategies, such as weighting and combining multiple input items.

During encoding, elaboration, and integration, selected information is processed and the output of any one process may provide input for another process. That is, some subset of the information available in the persuasion context will receive attention and be encoded. Some subset of this information may then be evaluatively elaborated. Finally, some subset of the raw products of reception and/or the output of elaboration will provide the basis for a judgment. This view is compatible with on-line models of attitude formation wherein the attitude judgment is continually updated as information is encoded, elaborated, and combined until subjective validity is achieved. It is also compatible with memory-based models of attitude formation wherein information is retrieved from memory or held in working memory until input has ceased and then is evaluated and interpreted.

POSITIVE AFFECT WITHIN A
PROCESSING FRAMEWORK

In this chapter, we consider the experience of positive affect as a state characterized or accompanied by *activation of particular kinds of content* from long-term memory (Isen, 1984, 1987; Srull, 1983, 1987). Both network models (Bower, 1981; Clark & Isen, 1982; Singer & Salovey,

1988) and constructionist theories (Bransford, 1979) of memory imply that positive mood results in continued activation and reactivation of positive material (Isen, 1984, 1987; Isen, Shalker, Clark, & Karp, 1978). Either because activation spreads through associated nodes of similar valence, or because similar material is retrieved in response to a positively valenced cue or probe, these models suggest that positive mood will be accompanied by a flux of predominantly positive material in active memory. Because of its everyday prevalence, positive mood may be associated with both substantial amounts of and a substantial diversity of largely positive material. The activation of this amount and kind of material may create a *complex cognitive context* (Isen, 1987) as a backdrop for other simultaneous processing tasks occur.[2]

How might the activation of substantial amounts of diverse but predominantly positive content affect reception, elaboration, and integration processes? In general, the activation of such material is likely to have effects on both the *extent* and the *nature* of other ongoing processes.

Extent of processing on simultaneous tasks might be affected because of the distracting quality of the continually activated and reactivated material. First, affectively valenced material is inherently attention grabbing (e.g., Erdelyi & Blumenthal, 1973). Second, its positive valence might make it a preferable attentional target (Isen, 1987). Third, even attempting to suppress such thoughts to continue a processing task may impair attentional allocation to other tasks (Wegner, Schneider, Carter, & White, 1987). As a consequence of any of these three effects, the presence of such material in working memory is likely to interfere with attentional allocation to other tasks (Mackie & Worth, 1989, 1990). With simple tasks, resource competition or even resource sharing may not impede performance. In fact, performance on tasks that require creativity or diversity of solutions may be enhanced by the complex cognitive context provided by affect-induced activation (Isen, 1987; Isen, Johnson, Mertz, & Robinson, 1985). As processing tasks increase in their requirements for concentrated, sequential, and capacity-intensive attentional allocation, however, they might be increasingly disrupted by positive mood. The extent of elaboration and complex integration are thus more likely to be vulnerable to positive mood effects than the extent of encoding and simple integration.

The presence of a diversity of positive material will also influence the *nature of persuasion processes.* At encoding, the presence of this material facilitates selective attention to and encoding of valence-congruent information (Bower, 1981; Forgas & Bower, 1987; Mischel, Ebbesen, & Zeiss, 1973; Ritchie, 1986). Similarly, elaboration is likely to be biased toward positive inferences, interpretations, and extensions (Forest, Clark, Mills, & Isen, 1979; Forgas, Bower, & Krantz, 1984; Isen et al., 1985). The presence of multiple—and perhaps changing—category activations may also allow presented information to be interpreted in multiple diverse and creative ways (Isen & Daubman, 1984; Isen et al., 1985; Murray, Sujan, Hirt, & Sujan, 1990). Finally, selection and integration might be biased toward mood-congruent content (Blaney, 1986; Natale & Hantas, 1982; Singer & Salovey, 1988), especially in retrieval-based judgments (Teasdale & Fogarty, 1979).

In sum, the conceptualization of positive mood as activating a diversity of largely positive material implies that the extent and nature of encoding, elaboration, and integration will be influenced in predictable ways by a positive mood state. We now review the relevant literature to assess empirical support for these ideas.

THE IMPACT OF POSITIVE AFFECT ON PERSUASION PROCESSES

What is now known about the impact of positive mood on the encoding, elaboration, and integration of persuasive communications? Despite the fact that theories of positive mood provide predictions about its impact on encoding and integration, most persuasion studies of positive affect have focused on its consequences for elaboration. We first review the results of these studies before turning to a consideration of the possible ways positive mood might influence encoding and integration.

Positive Mood and Elaboration of Persuasive Messages

Because of its centrality to current theories of attitude change, message elaboration is among the most studied processes in contemporary persuasion research. The extent and nature of elaboration are usually assessed in two ways. First, reactions to manipulations of argument quality are used to assess the extent to which message content is elaborated. Strong arguments are by definition more compelling than weak arguments and should thus result in more persuasion. Therefore greater attitude change to strong as compared with weak versions of a message is taken as evidence that message content has been evaluated. Second, "thought listing" instructions are used to elicit subjects' "cognitive responses" to the persuasive message, which are coded as favorable and unfavorable message and content evaluations. Strong arguments typically engender more favorable thoughts whereas weak arguments engender more unfavorable thoughts. Therefore cognitive response patterns of more favorable thoughts to strong arguments and more unfavorable thoughts to weak arguments can provide further evidence for message elaboration. These two measures together have been used to evaluate the impact of positive mood on the extent and nature of elaboration.

Extent of elaboration. The results of multiple experiments converge on the conclusion that positive mood undermines systematic elaboration of persuasive messages. The attitude change and cognitive responses shown by elated subjects are not determined by the quality of presented arguments. In an initial demonstration of these effects, we presented subjects in either a positive or a neutral affective state with strong or weak arguments about controlling acid rain (Worth & Mackie, 1987). Subjects in a neutral mood responded more favorably to and were significantly more persuaded by strong arguments than weak ones. In contrast, subjects in a positive mood showed no differences in attitude change or cognitive responses to the strong and weak messages.

These findings have been replicated with a variety of mood manipulations, attitudinal issues, and subject populations. Positive moods have been induced by having subjects watch humorous video clips, consider positive life events, listen to a series of positive self-statements, or read warm and happy stories. Attitude issues and objects have ranged from gun control, tuition hikes, banking services, comprehensive examinations, and concentration of the media in the hands of a powerful few. And the effect has been replicated with American, German, and Australian students (Batra & Stayman, 1990; Bless, Bohner, Schwarz, & Strack, 1990; Innes & Ahrens, 1990; Mackie & Worth, 1989). In the relevant conditions of all these studies, elated subjects failed to show different attitude change to strong and weak arguments. Typically, elated subjects fail to respond with positive elaborations of strong messages or unfavorable elaborations of weak ones (Batra & Stayman, 1990; Bless et al., 1990; Mackie & Worth, 1989; Worth & Mackie,

1987). In addition, elated subjects' cognitive responses are not typically predictive of the attitude change they show (compared with those in a neutral mood: Batra & Stayman, 1990; Mackie & Worth, 1989; Sinclair, 1988). The crucial role of reduced elaboration at encoding in producing these effects has been further documented by studies showing that (a) they are obtained even if mood is present only at encoding and not when the attitude judgment is made (Bless, Mackie, & Schwarz, in press), (b) distraction at encoding produces the same results in processors in a neutral mood (Bless et al., 1990, Experiment 2), and (c) when people in a positive mood do elaborate at encoding, they are consequently persuaded by strong arguments and not persuaded by weak ones (Mackie & Worth, 1989). This reduced differentiation might be due to an overall reduction in elated subjects' elaboration (Batra & Stayman, 1990).

The nature of elaboration. Undifferentiated elaboration could also result, however, from biases in elaboration, such as the production of predominantly positive elaborations. In fact, three experiments have documented an increase in the proportion of positive thoughts generated by happy subjects. In one study, elated subjects presented with strong or weak attributes about a banking service produced a smaller proportion of counterarguments than did neutral subjects, particularly in response to weak arguments (Batra & Stayman, 1990).[3] In the other studies, Petty and his colleagues (Petty, Schumann, Richman, & Strathman, cited in Petty, Gleicher, & Baker, 1990) report that elated subjects experiencing high motivation to elaborate produced a greater proportion of positive elaborations than did neutral subjects in the same conditions. This bias to elaborate both strong and weak arguments positively reduces the negative thoughts and counterarguments usually generated in response to weak arguments, thereby producing undifferentiated elaboration.

Whereas Batra and Stayman (1990) found that increased motivation *decreased* thought positivity in positive mood subjects, Petty et al. (1990) showed that heightened motivation *increased* the positivity of elated subjects' thoughts. We can only speculate as to how these findings can be reconciled. One possibility is that the degree of bias possible in elaboration will be constrained by the extent to which arguments are ambiguous in their implications. Elaboration of ambiguous arguments—which may not provide strong evidence for the advocated position—may be biased toward mood congruency. Thus the more elaboration that occurs, the more bias there will be. This may explain

Petty and his colleagues' results: The realistic messages used may have resulted in a weaker manipulation of argument quality (no argument quality effects are reported on attitude change), enabling mood-biased elaboration to occur more easily. When elaboration is biased, the more elaboration occurs, the more bias there will be. When arguments are clearly strong and clearly weak, however, it may be more difficult to bias elaboration (Chaiken et al., 1989). In these cases, elaboration is unbiased, and therefore increased elaboration produces greater differentiation, as Batra and Stayman (1990) found.

Diversity of elaboration. The impact of the complex cognitive context activated by positive mood might also make itself felt in the diversity and creativity of elaborations produced. Elaborations might appear undifferentiated because message recipients are responding creatively to arguments rather than focusing on their strength or quality. Unfortunately, of course, cognitive responses are not usually coded on the basis of creativity. Innes and Ahrens (1990) did, however, attempt to assess the impact of creativity goals on elaboration by asking happy and neutral subjects to "react creatively" or "be critical" as they read strong and weak message content. Compared with their reactions when "being critical," neutral mood subjects were more persuaded by a weak message and somewhat less persuaded by a strong message when trying to react creatively to the arguments. Thus use of the creativity goal produced attitudinal outcomes similar to those produced by the induction of positive mood. The possibility that elated recipients take a more creative approach to argument elaboration, and that so doing reduces the impact of argument quality on attitude change, warrants more research attention.

Conditions of reduced differential elaboration. Much recent research focuses on whether the reduced systematic processing of message content shown by subjects in a positive mood occurs only under conditions of low motivation. Such findings would support the idea that positive mood has its effects primarily through motivational mechanisms. Finding processing interference even under conditions of high motivation, however, suggests that at least some of the attentional allocation effects of positive mood may be relatively inescapable. In fact, mood-related decrements in systematic processing have been produced in situations that typically invoke motivation to process. In our early studies, for example, subjects were asked to evaluate the speaker and his speech; these instructions provoked systematic processing of message content in the neutral, but not in the happy, subjects (Mackie & Worth, 1989; Worth & Mackie, 1987). Similarly, Batra and Stayman (1990) found decreased elaboration by elated message processors even when all subjects were explicitly instructed to "evaluate the bank and its marketing efforts," an instruction known to invoke careful product evaluation (Hastak & Olson, 1989).

Other studies have gone to greater lengths to increase processing motivation. Innes and Ahrens (1990) induced what can only be described as a highly motivating processing set. Subjects in happy or neutral mood were presented with strong or weak messages and were told adopt "a critical set, to read the message as if they had to present an appraisal of the contents to another group for class discussion and criticism, and possible assessment" (1990, p. 228). Neutral mood subjects given this instruction showed considerable acceptance of the strong arguments and rejected the position supported by the weak arguments. In contrast, subjects in a positive affective state failed to differentiate the messages. And, in another study, we told subjects that they would be paid according to how well they completed the task of evaluating the content of a presented message (Worth, Mackie, & Asuncion, cited in Mackie & Worth, 1990). Although subjects in this condition reported being motivated and trying hard, elated subjects failed to differentiate the strong and weak arguments.[4]

Despite these motivating processing sets, most studies have presented subjects with counterattitudinal—and thus disagreeable—persuasive messages. From a motivational perspective, elated subjects may avoid processing such disagreeable messages but may systematically process more agreeable ones. In one of our early studies, proattitudinal as well as counterattitudinal communications were presented (Worth & Mackie, 1987). Proattitudinal messages were no more differentiated by elated subjects than counterattitudinal ones. And Innes and Ahrens (1990) presented proattitudinal messages specifically to ensure that elaboration likelihood would be "moderate to high," yet failed to produce differentiation. As a more direct test of these ideas, we exposed subjects to a message that stressed either the healthful benefits associated with performing breast self-examinations or the unpleasant costs of not doing so. Subjects in a positive mood spent more time processing *both* the costs and the benefits message than did subjects in a neutral mood—although they were more persuaded by the benefits than the costs message (Asuncion, Rosselli, & Mackie, 1990). Elated subjects' failure to differentiate between strong and weak message content seems quite robust, even in conditions of relatively high motivation. This is not to say that mood effects are not influenced by motivational concerns, an issue we return to below.

Conclusions. Most studies of positive affect and persuasion have focused on the effects of elaboration, and the evidence bears out the crucial nature of this processing stage. Positive mood reduces the differentiated nature of elaboration that usually marks systematic processing of strong and weak arguments. There is some evidence for both a general reduction in differentiated elaboration and for an increase in positive elaboration (or reduction in negative elaboration). This is consistent with the idea that mood influences both the extent and the nature of elaboration. Although more empirical evidence is clearly necessary, a reduction in differentiated processing by those in a good mood has been documented in a range of situations usually thought of—at least in laboratory settings—as involving considerable motivation.

Although evaluative elaborations have received much research attention, the effects of mood on other potentially important aspects of elaboration have been ignored. As noted above, more exploration of the role of multiple and diverse elaborations on attitude change resulting from weak and strong arguments seems warranted. For example, the possibility of multiple interpretations might result in an overestimation of the number of items of information presented, which may increase persuasion via heuristic or peripheral mechanisms (the length equals strength heuristic; Chaiken, 1987; Petty & Cacioppo, 1986). Asking happy subjects about the number of arguments they think a message contains could help assess this possibility. No published study appears to have investigated the impact of inference and conclusion drawing or attributional processing in positive mood. Experimental paradigms currently used to investigate spontaneous inferences to persuasive communications (Kardes, 1988; Pittman & D'Agostino, 1989) could be adapted to include positive mood. Similarly, paradigms designed to demonstrate the impact of attributional processing on persuasion (Eagly, Chaiken, & Wood, 1981) could also be modified to examine the impact of positive affect on such processing.

Positive Mood and the Reception of Persuasive Messages

Despite the benefits of focusing on elaboration, the impact of affect on reception processes deserves increased research attention (Chaiken & Stangor, 1987; Mackie & Asuncion, 1990). Reception differences may explain affect-induced increases in persuasion that are not due to elaboration or integration effects. For instance, positive mood may increase the use of persuasion heuristics to increase non-elaboration-mediated attitude change. In addition, even when differences in elaboration occur, these differences may be due, in part, to the elaborated item's initial encoding. For example, a piece of information encoded positively is more likely to give rise to further positive elaboration than an item given a negative twist at encoding.

With the assumption that recognition is the least contaminated measure of reception (Jacoby, Craik, & Begg, 1979), studies that have included such measures have provided little evidence of mood-induced limits, selectivity, or bias in interpretation at encoding (Bless et al., 1990; Lawson, 1986). Srull (1987) has also provided evidence that mood has minimal effects on encoding. In this study, different affective states were induced in subjects by asking them to recall a positive, neutral, or negative life event. Following this, subjects were shown 10 separate attributes about a Mazda RX7. Subjects read the items at their own pace either simply to understand what was said (an encoding without elaboration goal) or with the goal of evaluating the car in relation to others (an elaborative attitude formation goal). Then, 48 hours later, the subjects—now in a neutral mood—reported their evaluations of the product. Our interest is particularly in the memory-based conditions; the conditions in which subjects read the arguments but did not form an evaluation. In these conditions, subjects in a positive mood at encoding rated the car no differently than those in a neutral mood at encoding. This suggests that mood had no impact on how the arguments were encoded, as evaluations based on later retrieval of the arguments were identical in positive and neutral mood encoding conditions.[5]

Potential problems with investigating mood effects at encoding. Even the conclusions of these few studies, however, need to be qualified by several considerations. First, experimental studies of persuasion hardly ever offer the possibility of finding limits on encoding, given that they present relatively few arguments of a relatively coherent nature to a relatively verbal population (Eagly & Chaiken, 1984). Second, most studies fail to use recognition measures as an index of encoding. Thus the use of recognition measures would be a first step in investigating the effects of positive mood on reception processes.[6] Third, regarding selective encoding, it is not clear what kind of persuasive arguments are in fact congruent with a positive mood. Neither proattitudinal arguments nor information about the benefits of an advocated position are *affect congruent* in the sense in which this term is generally used. Listing positive product attributes might provide affectively congruent information, but persuasive arguments are typically much more complicated in form and content and may not be clearly enough differentiated to provide a good test of selective encoding. Fourth, mood effects on interpretation are likely to have maximal impact with ambiguous material; manipulations of message position and argument quality, on the other hand, call for the use of unambiguously clear and strong arguments. Fifth, it would be useful to know how subjects in a positive mood rate arguments and attributes as individual items of information *before* elaboration or integration occurs. Thus more direct ratings of arguments, before further processing has taken place, are needed to determine whether happy recipients consider more or more varied interpretations of individual arguments. Finally, it is also possible that mood influences how the situation as a whole is interpreted (Forgas et al., 1984). If elated subjects are more likely to view the presentation of persuasive arguments as "sharing helpful tips" or "giving friendly advice" rather than "trying to coerce" or "making a hard sell," persuasion-relevant mechanisms might not come into play. Thus further study on how positive mood influences interpretation of the persuasion situation in general is needed.

Attention to heuristic cues. What impact does positive mood have on encoding of heuristic cues? In two studies, subjects read weak or strong arguments presented by expert or nonexpert sources (Mackie & Worth, 1989, Experiment 2; Worth & Mackie, 1987). Elated, but not neutral, recipients' attitude change reflected the presence of a heuristic cue rather than argument quality. These studies are often cited as evidence that happy people are more heavily influenced by heuristic cues than their neutral mood counterparts. In neither of our studies, however, was the expertise of the source rated differently by happy and neutral subjects: Differences appeared only in the impact of the source on postmessage attitudes. Our interpretation therefore is somewhat different. We believe that positive and neutral mood subjects are likely to encode and interpret heuristic cues in a similar fashion. Differences in output attitude measures are more likely to reflect attenuation of the heuristic cues' impact by the additional systematic processing engaged in by neutral, but not positive, mood subjects (in fact, attitude change found in high elaboration conditions reflects *both* heuristic cue use and argument elaboration; Maheshwaran & Chaiken, 1991). Resolution of this issue requires experimental designs that compare subjects in positive and neutral moods receiving messages in the presence of one of the following: an expert, a nonexpert, or no source.

One heuristic that does seem worthy of further study, however, is the liking-agreement heuristic (Chaiken, 1987). This heuristic appears to be based on an affective reaction of liking or attractiveness. Because a pleasant source may be congruent with a positive affective state, such affect congruence might give this type of source certain encoding advantages. Therefore happy influence targets may be more likely to encode a pleasant source more positively than other message recipients.

Positive Mood and Integration Processes in Persuasion

Like reception, integration processes have been relatively neglected in the experimental study of persuasion. Only one or two studies have independently manipulated affect at encoding and at integration to isolate the impact of mood on these processes (Bless et al., in press; Srull, 1987). Even fewer have attempted to have subjects make memory-based (versus on-line) judgments to show the impact of mood on retrieval and integration processes alone. We now turn to some aspects of the integration process that deserve further research attention.

Nature of integrated material. Mood at retrieval has been found to enhance the recall of mood-congruent information. For example, subjects who had received a gift to boost their mood were better able to recall positive features of the consumer products they already owned (Isen et al., 1978). In another study, Srull (1987) attempted to isolate the effects of mood on recall of items encoded in a neutral state. Prior to a mood manipulation, subjects read a description of an automobile with the goal of simply reading the information for comprehension or of forming an evaluation of the car. Then, 48 hours later, mood states were induced by asking subjects to think about a positive, a neutral, or a negative life event. Following this, subjects were asked to evaluate the automobile. Results indicated that subjects who had formed the judgment at *encoding* showed no effects of the mood manipulation. In contrast, when subjects retrieved and integrated attributes to make the judgment, evaluations were influenced by their affective state. That is, happy subjects expressed more favorable ratings than subjects in other mood conditions.

Further research is necessary to pinpoint the exact integration mechanism influenced by mood in this case. It could be that only positive information about the car was retrieved. Alternatively, positive attributes could be more heavily weighted in integration. It could also be that positive elaboration of the material took place after retrieval. Each of these possible mechanisms that may operate during integration deserves further research attention.

Extent of retrieval and use of integration strategies. Although retrieving a prior attitude is probably the most cognitively simple attitudinal response, there is little evidence that subjects in a positive mood use this strategy predominantly. In fact, research into mood and persuasion was prompted largely by the finding that happy influence targets show *more* attitude change than others (Dribben & Brabender, 1979; Galizio & Hendrick, 1972; Janis, Kaye, & Kirschner, 1965).

There is some evidence that, when making a judgment, subjects in a positive mood might use simpler integration rules than those in a neutral mood. Isen and Means (1983), for example, reported that happy subjects tended to use an "elimination-by-aspects" rule, in which alternatives that did not surpass some set point on one particular dimension were eliminated from consideration. On the basis of studies in which positive affect was independently manipulated at reception and at judgment, Bless et al. (1989) provided evidence that subjects in a positive mood simplify integration by relying on accessible summary judgments. Finally, as noted, happy subjects may also be more likely to rely on heuristic cues to make judgments without gathering further information. Thus it may be fruitful to investigate the kinds of integration strategies in which positive mood subjects engage to determine whether they are simpler or not.

Mood state as a heuristic. If individuals in a good mood wish to simplify judgments, they might use their own experience of positive affect as a piece of information to make the judgment. Use of this strategy would make happy subjects' judgments more positive than those of neutral subjects. In two studies, happy subjects showed attitude change directly related to their subjective experience of mood that was not mediated by message elaboration (Batra & Stayman, 1990; Petty et al., 1990). Whether this direct effect of mood on integration is due to simple association between the positive state and the advocated position (such as in classical conditioning) or whether it is due to the operation of the "how-do-I-feel-about-it?" heuristic (Schwarz & Clore, 1988) and a misattribution of mood state to the object remains unclear. Several authors have noted the need to clarify the nature of the integration processes underlying these effects (Eagly & Chaiken, in press; Petty et al., 1990; Schwarz et al., 1991).

Positive affect, confidence, and subjective certainty. Although both motivational and capacity decrements resulting from positive mood may produce a tendency to rely on fewer and simpler pieces of information at integration, similar effects would also occur if positive affect increased subjects' subjective certainty. Elated subjects may cross the "sufficiency threshold" sooner if positive mood increases general feelings of optimism, efficiency, and willingness to take risks (Fiedler, 1990; Johnson & Tversky, 1983; Kavenaugh & Bower, 1985). Although these ideas seem plausible—and although happy subjects have been found to use less information in making decisions (Isen & Means, 1983; Sinclair, 1988)—we are aware of no published data that bear directly on elated message recipients' feelings of attitudinal or judgmental confidence. Given that subjective confidence may determine the extent to which reception, elaboration, and integration occur, the impact of affect on the sufficiency threshold seems an area particularly worthy of future investigation.

CONCEPTUAL ISSUES AND
THEORETICAL IMPLICATIONS

In this chapter, we considered positive affect to be a state characterized by activation of diverse but predominantly positive material in working memory. The activation of this complex cognitive context was assumed to have an impact on the extent and nature of the encoding, elaboration, and integration that contribute to persuasion. We then reviewed empirical evidence that positive affect operated in predictable ways on these subprocesses.

Underlying our concern with the impact of mood on persuasion processes is the assumption that persuasive outcomes are related to those processes in predictable ways. This assumption has several implications regarding the impact of positive mood. First, rather than assuming that mood plays a different role in producing persuasion at, for example, different levels of motivation (Petty et al., 1990), we assume that mood always has the same effects on a particular subprocess but that that subprocess may play a more or less dominant role in persuasion at any given time. For example, it is not so much that mood increases reliance on heuristics to produce persuasion under conditions of low motivation. Rather, under any conditions that cause encoding to dominate the persuasion process (that is, little more than encoding and simple judgment occur), the particular impact that mood has on encoding (and thus heuristic activation) will be reflected in any attitude change produced. Positive affect has certain effects on particular processes, and those effects will be magnified or attenuated as the role that those processes play in producing persuasion waxes and wanes.

Second, to the extent that mood operates on a particular subprocess, the more that process occurs, the greater the opportunity for mood to influence it. Similarly, the more subprocesses that operate on any input, the more opportunities contextual effects, including the impact of activated affect, have to influence the resultant output (Fiedler, 1990). Thus mood effects might be minimal at encoding but might increase as elaboration and extensive integration occur.

A third implication of the processing approach is that, to the extent that mood affects the nature and extent of persuasion processes, some remnant of these operations will remain even if other factors override them. Our view has never been that capacity restrictions completely debilitate positive mood subjects from processing persuasive messages. We fully expect that motivational manipulations will have some influence on persuasive processing regardless of affective state. Instead, we have argued that, *if* positive affect influences the extent and nature of persuasive *processing,* and *if* these effects are relatively automatic and inescapable, they should be observable on some index, even when motivational considerations lead elated subjects to produce attitude outcomes identical to those produced by subjects in a neutral mood (Chaiken et al., 1989; Mackie & Worth, 1989). Thus our goal has been to try to assess the impact of activation of positively valenced material on attention and elaboration processes even under conditions of increased motivation.

As a parallel for our reasoning, consider the operation of cognitive and motivational variables on the Stroop effect (Stroop, 1935). When subjects are asked to report the color of the ink (say, blue) in which a color word (say, red) is written, the highly overlearned meaning of the color word (red) is more available. By the motivated application of attention to the task, however, respondents can overcome the tendency to report "red" and correctly report "blue." This finding does not, of course, suggest that the Stroop effect itself is motivational: People aren't prone to answer "red" because they aren't trying. Instead, the consequences of one process can often be overridden by the output of a different process under the appropriate circumstances (Bargh, 1989; Logan, 1989; Spielman, Pratto, & Bargh, 1988). But some consequences of that overriding should be observable. When subjects do respond correctly on the Stroop test, they respond more slowly, reflecting the competition between the two responses and the "correction" of the initial response. When the outcome of one process overrides the outcome of another process, the overriding itself should have measurable consequences.

In the same way, any attentional processing deficits or difficulties caused by positive mood could presumably be overridden by motivational goals. We should still be able to find some evidence of their occurrence, however. Our reasoning here is speculative, but two kinds of evidence appear consistent with this suggestion.

First, we reported two cases in which subjects in a positive mood showed systematic differentiation of strong and weak messages when told they could look at the persuasive message as long as they wanted (Mackie & Worth, 1989). Although the attitude change shown by happy and neutral mood subjects was the same, happy subjects took longer to complete the processing task. This increased processing time provides some evidence of compensation for attentional deficits under conditions of high motivation.

In another study recently completed in our lab, we presented happy subjects with a counterattitudinal message about either a highly relevant or a not very relevant issue (Asuncion, Mackie, Rosselli, & Aguirre, 1991). Subjects reported much higher motivation in the high relevance conditions than found in our earlier studies. Under these conditions, happy subjects' attitude change reflected argument quality. In addition, message elaborations predicted the persuasion produced in the high, but not the low, motivation conditions. Clearly, then, our motivational manipulation produced attitude change and argument elaborations reflective of extensive content-based processing of the messages. Even under these conditions, however, we did find some evidence for compensatory strategies. Although there was no difference in the overall amount of time elated subjects spent processing the message in the high or low motivation conditions, some intriguing findings did emerge. In the high involvement conditions, the more positive subjects felt at the beginning of the processing task, the longer they took to process the message. In contrast, the more positive subjects felt as they began processing in the low motivation conditions, the less time they tended to spend on the message. In addition, subjects in the high motivation conditions produced as many content-free comments (such as "he made good points") as content-based elaborations. Thus it appeared that these subjects were relying somewhat on surface features of the messages to provide cues as to the likely strength of the arguments as well as or perhaps instead of carefully considering message content.

If so, use of such cues might help explain the results of a prior study in which elated subjects told to focus on argument evaluation showed increased differentiation of strong and weak arguments (Bless et al., 1990). In that study, elated subjects' differentiated attitude change was not mediated by systematic message elaboration. Again, subjects may have been using some surface cue concerning argument quality to guide judgments without carefully processing message content (see Maheshwaran & Chaiken, 1991, for other examples of heuristic use under high motivation and processing difficulty). Thus some evidence of compensation may be found even when conditions of high motivation produce attitude change that shows no obvious sign of the influence of mood.

Finally, motivational and cognitive consequences of positive mood may be inextricably intertwined because people understand (if only implicitly) the relation between affective states and processing consequences. Although increasing effort might be one means of overcoming any perceived limitations of positive mood, decreasing effort—abandoning processing as a hopeless task—is clearly another. Yet another reaction might be to control the mood state itself rather than its consequences. Careful processing of a message might be of such importance that elated recipients consciously "get out of a good mood" so that they can concentrate better. Moods may signal when and how to regulate the processing environment, but moods may also be regulated to deal with that same environment.

A processing analysis demonstrates the predictive value of integrating affective states into information processing perspectives. Although it has long been accepted that positive mood increases persuasion, the means by which it might do so, and the limits on this effect, are now becoming better understood. This progress has come as researchers turn from examining persuasive outcomes to investigating the impact of positive affect on persuasive processes. We have attempted to highlight process issues—particularly ones related to encoding and integration—that still demand research attention and that might further increase our ability to predict just how and when positive affect will influence persuasion.

NOTES

1. Although *positive affect* (which we define as mild feelings of subjective well-being and pleasantness) is more abstract than the term *positive mood,* we use the terms interchangeably here. We do wish to distinguish these from the experience of positive emotion and arousal (see Schwarz, 1990, for a discussion of the differences between mood and emotion and Isen, 1984, and Isen, Daubmen, & Nowicki, 1987, for a discussion of why mood effects cannot be explained by arousal).

2. Positive affect might also activate specific motivational goals. The mood maintenance hypothesis (Isen, 1970, 1987), for example, suggests that happy subjects avoid any extensive processing that might eliminate their mood. Elaboration would thus be reduced. Informational theories of affect and emotion (Schwarz, 1990) argue that positive affect informs the individual that the environment is nonthreatening and does not require any specific action. Therefore individuals experiencing a positive mood may be less likely to expend the cognitive effort to engage in capacity-exhaustive processes such as elaboration (unless required by other goals). Such theories imply increased motivation will eliminate the reduced elaboration generally associated with positive mood, an issue we discuss later.

3. These authors argue that reduced elaboration and reduced negative elaboration give a special advantage to weak arguments: Their results do not replicate the more moderated responses to strong arguments found in other work (Bless et al., 1990; Innes & Ahrens, 1990, Experiment 2; Mackie & Worth, 1989; Worth & Mackie, 1987). No increase in positivity of cognitive responding was reported in these latter studies.

4. Bless et al. (1990) explicitly directed subjects to focus on evaluating arguments in the presented message. Although the authors interpret this manipulation as increasing motivation, it could also be seen as focusing attention and thus manipulating ability to perform the processing task efficiently.

5. When subjects evaluated the automobile at encoding, subjects in a positive mood reported more favorable ratings than did subjects in a neutral mood.

6. Although recall has been interpreted as reflecting encoding differences, it is also prone to storage, elaboration, and retrieval biases (Chaiken & Stangor, 1987). Elated subjects have exhibited reduced recall of message arguments in some studies (Mackie & Worth, 1989, Experiment 1; Worth & Mackie, 1987) but not in others (Bless et al., 1990, Experiment 1; Mackie & Worth, 1989, Experiment 2). It would be tempting to suggest that the lack of recall differences in the latter studies reflects the minimal impact of mood at encoding but that the reduction in recall by elated subjects in the former studies reflects biased elaboration rather than encoding of arguments.

REFERENCES

Asuncion, A. G., Mackie, D. M., Rosselli, F., & Aguirre, Z. (1991). *Tracing the impact of mood-induced motivational deficits in persuasion.* Unpublished manuscript, University of California, Santa Barbara.

Asuncion, A. G., Rosselli, F., & Mackie, D. M. (1990). *Positive mood and persuasion: The impact of positive and negative content in persuasive messages.* Unpublished manuscript, University of California, Santa Barbara.

Bargh, J. A. (1989). Conditional automaticity: Varieties of automatic influence in social perception and cognition. In J. S. Uleman & J. A. Bargh (Eds.), *Unintended thought: Limits of awareness, intention, and control* (pp. 3-51). New York: Guilford.

Batra, R., & Stayman, D. M. (1990). The role of mood in advertising effectiveness. *Journal of Consumer Research, 17,* 203-214.

Blaney, P. H. (1986). Affect and memory: A review. *Psychological Bulletin, 99,* 229-246.

Bless, H., Bohner, G., Schwarz, F., & Strack, F. (1990). Mood and persuasion: A cognitive response analysis. *Personality and Social Psychology Bulletin, 16,* 331-345.

Bless, H., Mackie, D. M., & Schwarz, N. (in press). Mood effects on attitude judgments: The independent effects of mood before and after message elaboration. *Journal of Personality and Social Psychology.*

Bower, G. H. (1981). Mood and memory. *American Psychologist, 36,* 129-148.

Bransford, J. D. (1979). *Human cognition.* Belmont, CA: Wadsworth.

Chaiken, S. (1987). The heuristic model of persuasion. In M. Zanna, J. Olson, & C. Herman (Eds.), *Social influence: The Ontario Symposium* (Vol. 5, pp. 3-39). Hillsdale, NJ: Lawrence Erlbaum.

Chaiken, S., Liberman, A., & Eagly, A. H. (1989). Heuristic and systematic information processing within and beyond the persuasion context. In J. S. Uleman & J. A. Bargh (Eds.), *Unintended thought: Limits of awareness, intention, and control* (pp. 212-252). New York: Guilford.

Chaiken, S., & Stangor, C. (1987). Attitudes and attitude change. *Annual Review of Psychology, 38,* 575-630.

Clark, M. S., & Isen, A. M. (1982). Toward understanding the relationship between feeling states and social behavior. In A. H. Hastorf & A. M. Isen (Eds.), *Cognitive social psychology.* New York: Elsevier.

Dribben, E., & Brabender, V. (1979). The effect of mood inducement upon audience receptiveness. *Journal of Social Psychology, 107,* 135-136.

Eagly, A. H., & Chaiken, S. (1984). Cognitive theories of persuasion. In L. Berkowitz (Ed.), *Advances in experimental social psychology* (Vol. 17, pp. 267-359). New York: Academic Press.

Eagly, A. H., & Chaiken, S. (in press). *The psychology of attitudes.* New York: Harcourt Brace Jovanovich.

Eagly, A. H., Chaiken, S., & Wood, W. (1981). An attribution analysis of persuasion. In J. H. Harvey, W. J. Ickes, & R. F. Kidd (Eds.), *New directions in attribution research* (Vol. 3). Hillsdale, NJ: Lawrence Erlbaum.

Erdelyi, M. H., & Blumenthal, D. G. (1973). Cognitive masking in rapid sequential processing: The effect of an emotional picture on preceding and succeeding pictures. *Memory and Cognition, 1,* 201-204.

Fiedler, K. (1990). On the task, the measures and the mood in research on affect and social cognition. In J. P. Forgas (Ed.), *Emotion and social judgments* (pp. 83-104). Oxford: Pergamon.

Forest, D., Clark, M. S., Mills, J., & Isen, A. M. (1979). Helping as a function of feeling state and nature of the helping behavior. *Motivation and Emotion, 3,* 161-169.

Forgas, J. P. (1990). Affect and social judgments: An introductory review. In J. P. Forgas (Ed.), *Emotion and social judgments* (pp. 3-29). Oxford: Pergamon.

Forgas, J. P., & Bower, G. H. (1987). Mood effects on person perception judgments. *Journal of Personality and Social Psychology, 53,* 53-60.

Forgas, J. P., Bower, G. H., & Krantz, S. E. (1984). The influence of mood on the perception of social interaction. *Journal of Experimental Social Psychology, 20,* 497-513.

Galizio, M., & Hendrick, C. (1972). Effect of musical accompaniment on attitude: The guitar as a prop for persuasion. *Journal of Applied Social Psychology, 2,* 350-359.

Greenwald, A. G. (1968). Cognitive learning, cognitive response to persuasion, and attitude change. In A. G. Greenwald, T. C. Brock, & T. M. Ostrom (Eds.), *Psychological foundations of attitudes.* New York: Academic Press.

Hastak, M., & Olson, J. C. (1989). Assessing the role of brand-related cognitive responses as mediators of communication effects on cognitive structure. *Journal of Consumer Research, 15,* 444-456.

Innes, J. M., & Ahrens, C. R. (1990). Positive mood, processing goals and the effects of information on evaluative judgment. In J. P. Forgas (Ed.), *Emotion and social judgments* (pp. 221-239). Oxford: Pergamon.

Isen, A. M. (1970). Success, failure, attention and reactions to others: The warm glow of success. *Journal of Personality and Social Psychology, 15,* 294-301.

Isen, A. M. (1984). Toward understanding the role of affect in cognition. In R. Wyer & T. Srull (Eds.), *Handbook of social cognition* (Vol. 3, pp. 179-236). Hillsdale, NJ: Lawrence Erlbaum.

Isen, A. M. (1987). Positive affect, cognitive processes, and social behavior. In L. Berkowitz (Ed.), *Advances in experimental social psychology* (Vol. 20, pp. 203-253). New York: Academic Press.

Isen, A. M., & Daubman, K. A. (1984). The influence of affect on categorization. *Journal of Personality and Social Psychology, 47,* 1206-1217.

Isen, A. M., Daubman, K. A., & Nowicki, G. P. (1987). Positive affect facilitates creative problem solving. *Journal of Personality and Social Psychology, 52,* 1122-1131.

Isen, A. M., Johnson, M. M. S., Mertz, E., & Robinson, G. F. (1985). The effects of positive affect on the unusualness of word associations. *Journal of Personality and Social Psychology, 48,* 1413-1414.

Isen, A. M., & Means, B. (1983). The influence of positive affect on decision making strategy. *Social Cognition, 2,* 18-31.

Isen, A. M., Shalker, T. E., Clark, M. S., & Karp, L. (1978). Affect, accessibility of material in memory and behavior: A cognitive loop? *Journal of Personality and Social Psychology, 36,* 1-12.

Jacoby, L. L., Craik, F. I. M., & Begg, I. (1979). Effects of decisional differences on recognition and recall. *Journal of Verbal Learning and Verbal Behavior, 18,* 585-600.

Janis, I. L., Kaye, D., & Kirschner, P. (1965). Facilitating effects of "eating while reading" on responsiveness to persuasive communications. *Journal of Personality and Social Psychology, 1,* 181-186.

Johnson, E. J., & Tversky, A. (1983). Affect, generalization, and the perception of risk. *Journal of Personality and Social Psychology, 45,* 20-31.

Kardes, F. R. (1988). Spontaneous inference processes in advertising: The effects of conclusion omission and involvement on persuasion. *Journal of Consumer Research, 15,* 225-233.

Kavenaugh, D. J., & Bower, G. H. (1985). Mood and self-efficacy: Impact of joy and sadness on perceived capabilities. *Cognitive Therapy and Research, 9,* 507-525.

Lawson, R. (1986). The effects of mood on retrieving consumer product information. *Advances in Consumer Research, 12,* 399-403.

Logan, G. D. (1989). Automaticity and cognitive control. In J. S. Uleman & J. A. Bargh (Eds.), *Unintended thought: Limits of awareness, intention, and control* (pp. 52-74). New York: Guilford.

Mackie, D. M., & Asuncion, A. G. (1990). On-line and memory-based modifications of attitudes: Determinants of message recall-attitude change correspondence. *Journal of Personality and Social Psychology, 59,* 5-16.

Mackie, D. M., & Worth, L. T. (1989). Processing deficits and the mediation of positive affect in persuasion. *Journal of Personality and Social Psychology, 57,* 27-40.

Mackie, D. M., & Worth, L. T. (1990). "Feeling good but not thinking straight": Positive mood and persuasion. In J. P. Forgas (Ed.), *Emotion and social judgments* (pp. 201-220). Oxford: Pergamon.

Maheshwaran, D., & Chaiken, S. (1991). Promoting systematic processing in low motivation settings: The effect of incongruent information on processing and judgment. *Journal of Personality and Social Psychology, 61,* 13-25.

Mischel, W., Ebbesen, E., & Zeiss, A. (1973). Selective attention to the self: Situational and dispositional determinants. *Journal of Personality and Social Psychology, 27,* 129-142.

Murray, N., Sujan, H., Hirt, E. R., & Sujan, M. (1990). The influence of mood on categorization: A cognitive flexibility interpretation. *Journal of Personality and Social Psychology, 59,* 411-425.

Natale, M., & Hantas, M. (1982). Effect of temporary mood states on selective memory about the self. *Journal of Personality and Social Psychology, 42,* 927-934.

Petty, R. E., & Cacioppo, J. T. (1986). *Communication and persuasion: Central and peripheral routes to attitude change.* New York: Springer.

Petty, R. E., Gleicher, F., & Baker, S. M. (1990). Multiple roles for affect in persuasion. In J. P. Forgas (Ed.), *Emotion and social judgments* (pp. 181-200). Oxford: Pergamon.

Pittman, T. S., & D'Agostino, P. R. (1989). Motivation and cognition: Control deprivation and the nature of subsequent information processing. *Journal of Experimental Social Psychology, 25,* 465-480.

Ritchie, R. G. (1986). Momentary affect and attention allocation. *Motivation and Emotion, 10,* 387-395.

Schwarz, N. (1990). Feeling as information: Informational and motivational functions of affective states. In R. Sorrentino & E. T. Higgins (Eds.), *Handbook of motivation and cognition* (Vol. 2, pp. 527-561). New York: Guilford.

Schwarz, N., Bless, H., & Bohner, G. (1991). Mood and persuasion: Affective states influence the processing of persuasive communications. *Advances in Experimental Social Psychology, 24,* 161-199.

Schwarz, N., & Clore, G. L. (1988). How do I feel about it? Informative functions of affective states. In K. Fiedler & J. Forgas (Eds.), *Affect, cognition, and social behavior* (pp. 44-62). Toronto: Hogrefe.

Sherman, S. J. (1987). Cognitive processes in the formation, change, and expression of attitudes. In M. Zanna, J. Olson, & C. Herman (Eds.), *Social influence: The Ontario Symposium* (Vol. 5, pp. 75-106). Hillsdale, NJ: Lawrence Erlbaum.

Sinclair, R. C. (1988). Mood, categorization breadth, and performance appraisal: The effect of order of information acquisition and affective state on halo, accuracy, information retrieval, and evaluations. *Organizational Behavior and Human Decision Processes, 42,* 22-46.

Singer, J. A., & Salovey, P. (1988). Mood and memory: Evaluating the network theory of affect. *Clinical Psychology Review, 8,* 211-251.

Spielman, L. A., Pratto, F., & Bargh, J. A. (1988). Automatic affect: Are one's moods, attitudes, evaluations, and emotions out of control? *American Behavioral Scientist, 31,* 296-311.

Srull, T. K. (1983). Affect and memory: The impact of affective reactions in advertising on the representation of product information in memory. In R. Bagozzi & A. Tybout (Eds.), *Advances in consumer research* (Vol. 10, pp. 520-525). Ann Arbor, MI: Association for Consumer Research.

Srull, T. K. (1987). Memory, mood, and consumer judgment. In M. Wallendorf & P. Anderson (Eds.), *Advances in consumer research* (Vol. 14, pp. 404-407). Provo, UT: Association for Consumer Research.

Stroop, J. R. (1935). Studies of interference in serial verbal reactions. *Journal of Experimental Psychology, 18,* 643-662.

Teasdale, J. D., & Fogarty, J. (1979). Differential effects of induced mood on retrieval of pleasant and unpleasant events from episodic memory. *Journal of Abnormal Psychology, 88,* 248-257.

Wegner, D. M., Schneider, D. J., Carter, S., III, & White, L. (1987). Paradoxical consequences of thought suppression. *Journal of Personality and Social Psychology, 53,* 1-9.

Worth, L. T., & Mackie, D. M. (1987). Cognitive mediation of positive affect in persuasion. *Social Cognition, 5,* 76-94.

11

Changes in the Valence of the Self as a Function of Mood

CONSTANTINE SEDIKIDES

Constantine Sedikides is Assistant Professor of Psychology at the University of Wisconsin—Madison, where he has been since receiving his Ph.D. in social psychology from The Ohio State University in 1988. His research interests are in the area of the self. He studies the relation between mood and the self, the process of self-evaluation, the impact of close relationships on the self, and the way in-group and out-group members are perceived when the self joins a group.

The topic of the self has produced some of the most prolific investigations in social cognition. Representative empirical foci are the structural properties of the self (Higgins, Van Hook, & Dorfman, 1988; see Higgins & Bargh, 1987, for a review), the memorial, processing, and judgmental consequences of the self (for reviews, see Kihlstrom et al., 1987; Markus & Wurf, 1987), and the cognitive bases of trait self-descriptiveness judgments (Klein & Loftus, in press).

An additional empirical trend has sought to place the self in context, whether social, cognitive, or affective. The social context is composed of the physical or imagined presence of others. The cognitive context is broadly defined in terms of constructs stored in memory. Affective context refers to affective states. The affective context is of particular relevance to this chapter.

Research placing the self in affective context has taken two general directions. One direction explores the effects of the self on affective states. This line of research has generated several interesting findings. For example, discrepancies between the actual and the ideal self generate dejection-related emotions, whereas discrepancies between the actual and ought self engender agitation-related emotions (Higgins, 1987); self-complexity is associated with reduced negative affect (Linville,

AUTHOR'S NOTE: I thank Margaret Clark for her extensive editorial feedback. I also thank Peter Salovey and several anonymous reviewers for helpful comments on earlier drafts. Address correspondence to Constantine Sedikides, Department of Psychology, University of Wisconsin—Madison, 1202 West Johnson Street, Madison, WI 53706.

1987); and both upward and downward social comparison of the self to others can elicit either negative or positive affect (Buunk, Collins, Taylor, VanYperen, & Dakof, 1990).

The second research direction has explored the consequences of affective states and, more specifically, the consequences of mood for the self. The objectives of this chapter are to (a) review published experiments pertaining to mood effects on the self, (b) integrate these empirical findings in a theoretically parsimonious manner, and (c) point to new research directions. The overarching goal of the chapter is to clearly demarcate the focus of inquiry, methods, findings, and prospects of the emerging area of consequences of mood states for the self.

The review has implications for several issues of interest to self researchers. One implication concerns the issue of stability versus malleability of the self. Research has demonstrated the malleability of the self as a function of social context (Markus & Kunda, 1986; McGuire, McGuire, & Cheever, 1986; Schlenker & Trudeau, 1990) and cognitive context (Chaiken & Baldwin, 1981; Salancik & Conway, 1975). This review seeks to establish the malleability of the self as a function of affective (i.e., mood) context.

Demonstration that mood can lead to temporary changes in the self is of paramount importance. As Jones (1990) put it, "Temporary and trivial are not the same thing" (p. 71). Temporary changes in the self (i.e., the phenomenal self or working self, according to Jones & Gerard, 1967, and Markus & Wurf, 1987, respectively) can lead to fluctuations in self-esteem (Jones, Rhodewalt, Berglas, & Skelton, 1981; Rhodewalt & Agustdottir, 1986) and, most important, evoke alterations in expectations and behavior (Fazio, Effrein, & Falender, 1981; Harris & Snyder, 1986; Snyder & Swann, 1978).

The review also has practical implications. Understanding which aspects of the self are most amenable to change as a function of mood has intervention consequences. For example, aspects of the self (e.g., perceptions of self-efficacy, judgments of physical health, future planning) that are vulnerable to the effects of negative mood can be inoculated and further consolidated by therapists, relatives, or friends.

DEFINITIONAL CONCERNS

Next, I consider definitional issues regarding the two major terms used in this review: *mood* and the *self.*

Defining Mood

The review is concerned with normal, everyday mood states. Wood, Saltzberg, and Goldsamt (1990, p. 900) defined *mood* as "a general and pervasive feeling state that is not directed toward a specific target." Schwarz and Clore (1988, p. 58) concurred that "a central characteristic of mood states is their diffuse and unfocused quality." Mayer and Salovey (1988, p. 88) thought of mood as "a feeling state (e.g., angry, happy, sad) that involves multiple psychological subsystems, including the hormonal, facial expressive, postural, and cognitive systems." Simon (1982, p. 335) stated that "mood provides a more general, non-interruptive context for cognition." Finally, Isen (1984, pp. 186-187) maintained that mood states "occur quite frequently, often in response to seemingly small everyday occurrences," and, in most cases, mood states

> are not terribly attention-getting—even when they are having a pronounced effect on thought and behavior. Unlike strong emotion, these states do not interrupt our thought and behavior; rather, they gently color and redirect ongoing thoughts and actions, influencing what will happen next but almost without notice and certainly without ostensibly changing the context or basic activity.

In summary, mood states are frequent, relatively long and pervasive, but typically milder in intensity than emotions. As a result, they do not usually interrupt the regular thinking process; instead, they are unfocused and general (in contrast to emotions, which are object specific) and provide the context for subsequent cognitive activity. (For a noteworthy attempt to streamline mood as a distinctive and independent construct, see Morris, 1989.)

Defining the Self

Broadly defined, a person's self is the person's mental representation of information pertaining to him or her. More specifically, the self is defined in terms of its content and structure.

The content of the self is uniquely rich and diverse (Fiedler, 1990). It includes information about one's personality and behavioral characteristics, activities and important life events, physical qualities, demographic attributes, feelings, thoughts, goals, values, standards, rules for behavioral regulation, significant relationships with individuals, group memberships, and possessions (Kihlstrom & Cantor, 1984; Markus, 1983). The content of the self is dynamic. It varies across cultures (Markus & Kitayama, 1991; Marsella, De Vos, & Hsu, 1985), and it is altered as a function of different social environments (e.g., home versus school; McGuire et al., 1986) and life transitions (Deutsch, Ruble, Fleming, Brooks-Gunn, & Stangor, 1988).

The content of the self has been described in terms of psychological dimensions such as well-being, sociability, competence, and unconventionality (Mortimer, Finch, & Kumka, 1982) and also achievement-leadership, congeniality-sociability, masculinity-femininity, and adjustment (Monge, 1975). Self-conceptions can additionally vary in terms of their valence (i.e., negativity-positivity). The valence dimension is of particular relevance to this review.

Self-conceptions are interrelated. The structure of the self has been conceptualized as a schema (Markus, 1977), a hierarchy (Rogers, 1981), a prototype (Kuiper, 1981; Rogers, Rogers, & Kuiper, 1979), a location in multidimensional trait space (Breckler, Pratkanis, & McCann, 1991; Hoelter, 1985), and in terms of propositional memory networks (Bower & Gilligan, 1979; Kihlstrom & Cantor, 1984). Further, the self has been structurally subdivided into the private, public, and collective self (Greenwald & Pratkanis, 1984), the actual, ought, and ideal self (Higgins, 1987), and the desired versus undesired self (Ogilvie, 1987). Although the structure of the self is not directly pertinent to this review, the subject will be given additional consideration in a later section of the chapter.

CURVING THE SCOPE OF THE REVIEW

Having defined *mood* and *self,* I will now proceed to spell out clearly the scope and range of this review.

Concern for Causality

This chapter will review experiments that examine mood effects on the self. The review focuses exclusively on the effects of manipulated rather than natural mood, so that causal inferences regarding the relation between mood and the self can be drawn. All experiments included in this review randomly assigned subjects to mood conditions.

Restriction to Sad and Happy Moods

The review limits itself to experiments that manipulated sad versus happy moods only. There is a pragmatic reason for doing so, namely, availability of sources. Almost all experiments examining mood effects on the self have used sadness versus happiness as their mood manipulation.

There are additional reasons for constraining the review to sad and happy moods. Such moods are presumed to be omnipresent in everyday human functioning and to have powerful and profound consequences. Furthermore, this mood dimension has particular relevance to clinical phenomena. Sadness, for instance, is a primary correlate of depression.

Assessment of the Valence of the Self

The review will be exclusively concerned with the effects of mood on the valence of the self and specifically on the valence of (a) memories and judgments of one's own past or current personality, behavioral, and demographic characteristics; (b) goals or expectations involving the self; and (c) behaviors that are originated by the self and are directed toward the self (i.e., self-directed behaviors).

Why be preoccupied with the valence of the self? One reason is pragmatic. The vast majority of the research linking mood to the self has focused on the effects of sadness versus happiness on the valence of self-conceptions.

A second reason has to do with the omnipresence of the valence dimension in research on the self. Valence of the self determines, in part, the nature of interpersonal feedback that is accepted, the pattern of attributions about the self, choices and persistence in achievement-related tasks, and goal setting—to mention only a few domains of influence (for reviews, see Markus & Nurius, 1986; Strube, 1990; Swann, 1990; Taylor & Brown, 1988; for parallel findings demonstrating the prominence of the valence dimension in the perception and classification of environmental objects, see Abelson & Sermat, 1962; Eysenck, 1960; Hastorf, Osgood, & Ono, 1966; Osgood & Suci, 1955; Scherer, Koivumaki, & Rosenthal, 1972).

Certainly, the sad-happy and negative-positive dimensions deserve distinct conceptual statuses: one dimension is affective, the other is evaluative (Peeters & Czapinski, 1990). At the same time though, the two dimensions share semantic and process similarities. They can arguably be subsumed under a general unpleasant-pleasant dimension. Further, they bear analogously pivotal consequences for human functioning. If sadness and happiness are likely to exert any effects on the self, such effects should be most prevalent in the case of self valence. At least, self valence would be a good place to begin studying the impact of sadness and happiness on the self.

Exclusion of Success Versus Failure Manipulations

The review does not include experiments that manipulated success versus failure feedback. Such manipulations have been shown to affect self-esteem (Cunningham, 1988b), self-competence (Kazdin & Bryan, 1971), expectations for future success or failure (Feather, 1966), and expectations for rewards that match previous success or failure (the "deservingness" norm; see Long & Lerner, 1974). Consequently, it is unclear whether the effects of success or feedback manipulations are due to (a) changes in self-esteem, competence, or expectations; (b) changes in mood states; or (c) some combination of these variables. (For a successful attempt to establish the independence of the mood and self-esteem constructs, see Heatherton & Polivy, 1991.)

THEORETICAL PERSPECTIVES ON MOOD

Two theoretical frameworks will be used to parsimoniously accommodate results of the literature pertaining to mood effects on self valence. These frameworks are the *mood congruency* and *mood incongruency* hypotheses.

Why restrict the review to these two formulations? Because much of the research in the extant literature has been conducted as a test of at least one of these two formulations. Pragmatic reasons notwithstanding, the two hypotheses are general and at the same time precise enough to accommodate most of the existing literature.

The two hypotheses will be pitted against one another. Granted, there have been reservations raised by several investigators concerning the value of between-theory testing as well as preferences expressed in favor of within-theory testing (Greenwald, 1975; Ostrom, 1977; Tetlock

& Levi, 1982). Between-theory testing, however, does serve the purposes of this review quite well. Framing the issues from a between-theory perspective has heuristic value, because it contributes to an elegant and all-encompassing summary of the extant literature. Additionally, between-theory testing has the potential of elucidating the effects of *sad* mood on self valence. (For an example of a between-theory attempt pitting mood congruency against mood incongruency, see Parrott & Sabini, 1990.)

Mood Congruency Hypothesis

General form of the hypothesis. The mood congruency hypothesis states that mood will affect the self in a congruent manner. That is, sadness will elicit negatively valenced, whereas happiness will evoke positively valenced, self-relevant cognitions (e.g., memories, judgments, expectations) and/or self-directed behaviors.

On mediation. What are the processes through which mood alters self valence? According to one line of reasoning, mood acts as a priming cue affecting retrieval of self-relevant information (Bower, 1981; Clark & Isen, 1982; Forgas, Bower, & Moylan, 1990; Isen, Shalker, Clark, & Karp, 1978). Upon induction, happy mood activates (Collins & Loftus, 1975) favorable self-relevant information in memory, and sad mood activates unfavorable self-relevant information. Thus mood-congruent material becomes more cognitively accessible. Subsequent judgments of the self will be based on the overly represented mood-congruent memories; as a result, self-judgments will also be mood congruent. Self-directed behaviors, to the extent that they are influenced by memory and judgments, will similarly be mood congruent.

Mood can also have its effects at the encoding stage of information processing. Mood renders evaluatively congruent interpretive concepts accessible in memory. New ambiguous information is encoded according to the most accessible and applicable concepts (Sedikides & Skowronski, 1991). Consequently, mood-activated concepts are most likely to be used for encoding of self-relevant information, resulting in mood-congruent selective encoding. Judgments about the self and self-directed behaviors are also likely to be mood congruent.

Another view on mediation, the cognitive priming view (see Riskind, 1983; as well as Mayer, Gayle, Meehan, & Haarman, 1990), asserts that it is not the affective quality of mood manipulations that produces the recorded results but their cognitive quality. That is, mood manipulations are effective because of the information embedded in them. This information acts as a cognitive prime, activating semantically similar information in memory.

Additional attempts to explicate the processes through which mood exerts congruent effects on the valence of the self converge on the view that humans are motivated to maintain their current mood state, whether sad or happy. More specifically, one variant proposes that mood affects the self by inducing a general sense of sadness or happiness without necessarily the mediation of accessible and evaluatively similar information (Mischel, Coates, & Raskoff, 1968; Mischel, Ebbesen, & Zeiss, 1973, 1976). Ensuing judgments or behaviors will be geared toward maintaining this global sense of sadness or happiness. Another variant posits that, although people in a happy mood find their affective state pleasant and worth maintaining, people in a sad mood find their affective state unpleasant; however, sad mood people are energy depleted and thus incapable (at least for a relatively short time span) of engaging in any tedious cognitive or behavioral efforts to overcome it.

A hybrid variant can also offer some insight into the mechanisms through which mood affects self valence. Such a variant would accept that humans are motivated to sustain their current affective state but also suggest that the mechanisms humans employ to preserve affective consistency are cognitive in nature. Humans, when encountering information whose valence is mood incongruent, tend to activate mechanisms (at the attention, encoding, or retrieval stages) that are likely to suppress such information. Hence mood-incongruent information is undersampled and underrepresented in working memory.

A clarification. The purpose of the current review is *not* to distinguish among alternative mediating mechanisms. Indeed, the review does not have the potential to achieve this goal, because the relevant experiments were not conducted as crucial tests of alternative mediating mechanisms. Rather, the purpose of the review is to test the general form of the mood congruency hypothesis.

Mood Incongruency Hypothesis

General form of the hypothesis. The mood incongruency hypothesis posits that whether mood will affect the self in a congruent or incongruent manner depends on the nature of mood. A happy mood will exert congruent effects on self valence, eliciting positively valenced memories, judgments, expectations, or behaviors. A sad mood, however, will exert incongruent effects on self valence, evoking positively valenced (instead of negatively valenced) memories, judgments, expectations, or behaviors. In fact, a sad mood could even surpass the positivity of self valence elicited by a happy mood.

On mediation. What are the mechanisms through which mood might produce incongruent effects on self valence? Humans are assumed to be motivated to achieve and maintain a happy mood state, because it is pleasant and rewarding per se. People in sad moods will find their state aversive and will attempt to alleviate it in any of several ways. Thus they may block out mood-sustaining information at a preattentive stage (see Bargh, 1989, for an informative discussion). Alternatively, they may initiate (either consciously or nonconsciously) self-regulatory strategies (Frijda, 1986; Scheier & Carver, 1982) aiming at changing the undesirable affective states. Such self-regulatory strategies can be positive thinking, rationalization, or external distraction. Finally, people may act toward *themselves* in a way that directly counters the effects of sad mood. For example, they may engage in behavior that is directly self-rewarding. (For relevant treatises, see Clark & Isen, 1982; Fiske & Taylor, 1984; Isen, 1984.)

A clarification. It should again be clarified that the purpose of this review is *not* to test the mediating mechanisms of the mood incongruency hypothesis, given that primary-level experiments did not intend to accomplish this goal. Instead, the purpose is to test the general form of the hypothesis.

Pitting Mood Congruency Against Mood Incongruency

To recap, mood congruency and mood incongruency make indistinguishable predictions as far as happy mood is concerned. Both formulations predict that happy moods will increase self valence. The two hypotheses make opposing predictions, however, in the case of sad mood. The mood congruency hypothesis predicts decreases in self valence, whereas the mood incongruency hypothesis predicts increases in self valence. A finding where self valence becomes more positive in the case of sad than neutral and/or happy mood would be in line with the mood incongruency hypothesis.

EMPIRICAL EVIDENCE

This section of the chapter will detail the circumstances under which a result should be interpreted as supportive of mood congruency versus mood incongruency. Next, the section will examine empirical evidence directly relevant to the viability of the two hypotheses.

What Constitutes Support for Each Hypothesis?

A critical issue concerns the exact circumstances under which an empirical finding is taken as backing the mood congruency versus the mood incongruency hypothesis. In an attempt to specify these circumstances, several hypothetical designs will be described below, accompanied by interpretations of possible results.

The Case of Recall

2 × 2 designs. Imagine a 2 (mood: happy, sad) × 2 (self-relevant information: favorable, unfavorable) mixed-factors design, with the second factor being within subjects. After mood has been induced and *its presence verified* through manipulation checks, subjects are asked to recall information concerning the self. The mood congruency hypothesis would be supported if happy mood produced higher recall of favorable information than sad mood, and sad mood produced higher recall of unfavorable information than happy mood. On the other hand, the mood incongruency hypothesis would be supported if sad mood elicited higher recall of favorable and lower recall of unfavorable information than happy mood. The results would be nondiagnostic if no difference was observed between happy and sad mood in the amount of either favorable or unfavorable information recalled (see Table 11.1, Design I).

The above predictions would hold, with minor modifications, for designs manipulating either happy and neutral moods only or sad and neutral moods only. In the case of happy/neutral moods, happy mood leading to higher recall of favorable information and lower recall of unfavorable information than neutral mood would indicate support for the mood congruency hypothesis, whereas the absence of difference between happy and neutral mood in the amount of either favorable or unfavorable information recalled would be nondiagnostic (see Table 11.1, Design II). In the case of sad/neutral moods, the mood congruency hypothesis would be supported if a significant difference between sad

TABLE 11.1 Mood Congruency Versus Mood Incongruency: Hypothetical
Designs, Possible Results, and Interpretations

Possible Result	*Interpretation*
Design I: 2 (mood: happy, sad) × 2(self-relevant information: favorable, unfavorable) Mixed Factors	
HM leads to higher recall of FSI than SM, and SM leads to higher recall of USI than HM	Support for mood congruency
SM leads to higher recall of FSI and lower recall of USI than HM	Support for mood incongruency
No difference between HM and SM in the recall of FSI and/or USI	Results are nondiagnostic
Design II: 2 (mood: happy, neutral) × 2 (self-relevant information: favorable, unfavorable) Mixed Factors	
HM leads to higher recall of FSI and lower recall of USI than NM	Support for mood congruency
No difference between HM and NM in the recall of FSI and/or USI	Results are nondiagnostic
Design III: 2 (mood: sad, neutral) × 2 (self-relevant information: favorable, unfavorable) Mixed Factors	
SM leads to higher recall of USI and lower recall of FSI than NM	Support for mood congruency
SM leads to higher recall of FSI and lower recall of USI than NM	Support for mood incongruency
No difference between SM and NM in the recall of FSI and/or USI	Results are nondiagnostic
Design IV: 3 (mood: happy, neutral, sad) × 2 (self-relevant information: favorable, unfavorable) Mixed Factors	
HM leads to higher recall of FSI than NM, and NM leads to higher recall of FSI than SM; further, SM leads to higher recall of USI than NM, and NM leads to higher recall of USI than HM	Support for mood congruency
SM leads to higher recall of FSI than NM and (possibly but not necessarily) HM; further, SM leads to lower recall of USI than NM and (possibly but not necessarily) HM	Support for mood incongruency
HM leads to higher recall of FSI than SM and NM (with the difference between SM and NM being nonsignificant), and SM leads to higher recall of USI than HM and NM (with the difference between HM and NM being nonsignificant)	Support for mood congruency
HM and SM lead to higher recall of FSI and lower recall of USI than NM (with the difference between HM and SM being nonsignificant)	Support for mood incongruency
No differences among HM, NM, and SM in the recall of FSI and/or USI	Results are nondiagnostic

NOTE: HM = happy mood; SM = sad mood; NM = neutral mood; FSI = favorable self-relevant information; and USI = unfavorable self-relevant information.

and neutral mood was obtained such that sad mood subjects recalled more unfavorable and less favorable information than neutral mood subjects. The mood incongruency hypothesis would be supported if sad mood elicited higher recall of favorable and lower recall of unfavorable information than neutral mood. Null results (i.e., no difference between sad and neutral mood in the amount of either favorable or unfavorable information recalled) would be nondiagnostic (see Table 11.1, Design III).

3 × 2 designs. Now imagine a 3 (mood: happy, neutral, sad) × 2 (self-relevant information: favorable, unfavorable) mixed-factors design, with the second variable treated as a repeated measures factor. For the mood congruency hypothesis to be supported, (a) happy mood should elicit higher recall of favorable information than neutral mood, with neutral mood evoking higher recall of favorable information than sad mood, and (b) sad mood should elicit higher recall of unfavorable information than neutral mood, with neutral mood eliciting higher recall of unfavorable information than happy mood. Conversely, for the mood incongruency hypothesis to be supported, (a) sad mood should lead to higher recall of favorable information than neutral mood and (possibly but not necessarily) happy mood, and (b) sad mood should elicit lower recall of unfavorable information than neutral mood and (possibly but not necessarily) happy mood. The results would be non-diagnostic if happy, neutral, and sad moods did not produce differential amounts of favorable or unfavorable information recalled (see Table 11.1, Design IV).

Several additional potential results of the 3 × 2 experiment are of theoretical interest. Consistent with the logic underlying interpretation of the outcomes of previous hypothetical designs (Table 11.1, Designs I, II, and III), results will be taken as supportive of the mood congruency hypothesis if happy mood elicits higher recall of favorable information than sad and neutral mood (with the difference between the latter two being nonsignificant) and sad mood elicits higher recall of unfavorable information than happy and neutral mood (assuming that the difference between the latter two is not significant). On the other hand, the results will be in line with the mood incongruency hypothesis if happy and sad moods lead to higher recall of favorable information and lower recall of unfavorable information than neutral mood (provided that the difference between happy and sad mood is not significant; see Table 11.1, Design IV).

Recall and Beyond

2 × 2 and 3 × 2 designs. The above noted interpretations would be generally applicable to the effects of mood induced at retrieval and to the effects of mood on additional dependent measures assessing the valence of self-relevant information that is attended to, the valence of judgments and expectations regarding the self, and the valence of self-directed behaviors.

A Caveat

As a reminder to the reader, the effects of happy mood alone are nondiagnostic with regard to mood congruency and mood incongruency. It is the effects of sad mood that are capable of discriminating between the two formulations. This discrepancy in the theory testing potential of sadness versus happiness has led to an important assumption underlying the entire review. According to this assumption, if there is evidence for mood congruency (or incongruency) operating in the case of sad moods, then that essentially constitutes evidence for mood congruency (or incongruency) for happy moods as well.

This assumption certainly lends parsimony to the review. Nevertheless, it should be acknowledged that the same process or mechanism does not necessarily have to operate under both sadness and happiness. Consequently, the effects of happiness are surrounded by some uncertainty regarding the underlying process or mechanism. This, of course, does not mean that the part of the review focusing on the effects of happiness on self valence is not useful. In fact, this part has the potential to yield important and interesting findings.

REVIEW AND DISCUSSION OF EMPIRICAL FINDINGS

I searched *Psychological Abstracts* (1970-1991) for experiments examining mood effects on the self. I used the following selection criteria. First, mood should be experimentally manipulated. Second, mood should not be induced through success and failure feedback. Third, the presence of mood should be verified through postinduction mood assessments. Fourth, the dependent measures should tap aspects of the self in terms of attention, memory, judgment, goals/expectations, and/or behaviors.

I located 43 published reports. These reports contained 84 tests of the hypotheses. The tests correspond to dependent measures assessed. The reports and the tests can be found in Table 11.2.

There are several bits of information for each of the 84 tests provided in Table 11.2. The parent article is referenced, the mood induction procedure (e.g., Velten [1968], hypnosis, self-generated imagery) is listed, the timing of mood induction (e.g., encoding versus retrieval) is recorded, and the design of each experiment is noted only with regard to mood (e.g., sad, neutral, or happy mood) and self-relevant information (favorable, unfavorable), when applicable. Finally, the hypothesis supported by each test is indicated.

The results were overwhelmingly in favor of the mood congruency hypothesis. Specifically, of the 84 tests reported, 52 (62%) lent support to the mood congruency hypothesis, 10 (12%) favored the mood incongruency hypothesis, and 22 (26%) were nondiagnostic. The mood congruency hypothesis was supported irrespective of the particular mood induction procedure involved (e.g., Velten [1968], hypnosis, music, self-generated imagery) and regardless of whether mood was induced at the encoding (25 tests) or retrieval (27 tests) stage.

Strongest support for the mood congruency hypothesis was obtained for cognitive measures: attention, recall, judgments, and expectancies. Of the total number of relevant tests (i.e., 72), 49 (68%) tests yielded results supportive of the mood congruency hypothesis, only 1 (1%) test favored the mood incongruency hypothesis, and 22 (31%) tests were nondiagnostic. Thus subjects in a sad mood (compared with subjects in a happy and/or neutral mood) attend more to unfavorable self-relevant information, recall higher amounts of unfavorable self-relevant information, judge the self less favorably, and have more negative performance expectancies. The effects of mood on self-judgments and recall of self-relevant information are pervasive.

In contrast, it was the mood incongruency hypothesis that received weaker support with regard to behavioral measures (i.e., self-disclosure, self-reward, self-gratification). Of the total number of relevant tests (i.e., 12), 3 (25%) were in line with the mood congruency hypothesis, and the remaining 9 (75%) backed the mood incongruency hypothesis. Specifically, subjects in the experiments that supported the mood congruency hypothesis (a) had more intimate self-disclosures when in a happy than sad mood (Cunningham, 1988a), (b) praised themselves more and criticized themselves less when in a happy mood compared with either a neutral or a sad mood (Jones & Thelen, 1978), and (c) rewarded themselves with more money when in a happy mood as opposed to either a neutral or sad mood (Underwood, Moore, & Rosenhan, 1973). Subjects (mostly children) in the experiments that favored the mood incongruency hypothesis (a) rewarded themselves with more tokens when happy and sad compared with being in a neutral mood state (Baumann, Cialdini, & Kenrick, 1981); (b) were more likely to resist temptation, such as playing with a mobile, when in a happy rather than neutral or sad mood state (Fry, 1975); (c) chose immediate rewards when in a sad mood but chose delayed rewards when in a happy mood (Knapp & Clark, 1991; Schwarz & Pollack, 1977); and (d) indulged themselves with candies when in a happy and/or sad mood more so than when in a neutral mood (Rosenhan, Underwood, & Moore, 1974).

There may be several reasons for the outcome discrepancy between the cognitive and behavioral measures. First, it should be noted that relatively few experiments that included behavioral measures were available for the review. Thus conclusions regarding such measures must be made cautiously. Nonetheless, one explanation for the relative support for the mood incongruency hypothesis in the case of behavioral measures is that the impact of sad mood on self-directed behaviors became attenuated due to the mediation of a relatively large number of intervening (e.g., cognitive, situational, norm-related) variables. Another possibility is that sad mood initially produced mood-congruent effects, that is, negatively valenced self-conceptions; however, these effects were countered by the organism via mobilization (Taylor, 1991) and self-rewarding behavior. Mood affects self-relevant cognitions in a congruent manner but may affect self-directed behaviors in an incongruent manner.

A sizable minority of the tests produced nondiagnostic results. Of the 22 nondiagnostic tests, 16 (or 73%) were due to mood failing to affect self-related measures despite its presence as detected by manipulation checks. This attests to the relatively weak effects of mood on self valence. The remaining tests (6 or 27%) produced results that were hard to interpret under the rules specified in Table 11.1. For example, subjects in a happy mood recalled less information that was unfavorable

Text continued on page 300

TABLE 11.2 Research Testing the Hypotheses

Area	Experiment	Mood Induction Procedure; Timing of Mood Induction; Design[a]	Results	Hypothesis Supported
I. Attention	Mischel, Ebbesen, & Zeiss (1973, p. 139)	Imagery of tape-recorded scenes; encoding mood; 3 × 2	HM[b] Ss[c] spent more time attending to FSI[d] and less time attending to USI than NM Ss; NM Ss spent more time attending to FSI and less time attending to USI than SM Ss.	Mood congruency
II. Recall				
A. Free Recall	Berkowitz (1987, Expt. 2)	Self-generated imagery; encoding mood; 2 × 2	HM Ss produced more FSI and less USI than SM Ss.	Mood congruency
	Bower (1981, Expt. 1)	Hypnosis; retrieval mood; 2 × 2	HM Ss recalled more FSI and less USI than SM Ss.	Mood congruency
	Bower (1981, Expt. 2)	Hypnosis; retrieval mood; 2 × 2	HM Ss recalled more FSI and less USI than SM Ss.	Mood congruency
	Brown & Taylor (1986)	Velten (1968), self-generated imagery; encoding mood; 2 × 2	HM and SM Ss recalled an equal amount of FSI. HMS recalled less USI than SM Ss.	Nondiagnostic results
	Bullington (1990)	Velten, music; retrieval mood; 2 × 2	HM Ss recalled more FSI and less USI than SM Ss.	Mood congruency

Study	Method; design	Results	Conclusion
Forgas, Bower, & Krantz (1984)	Hypnosis, self-generated imagery; encoding mood; 2 × 2	Mood produced no significant results.	Nondiagnostic results
Laird, Cuniff, Sheehan, Shulman, & Strum (1989)	Facial expressions; retrieval mood; HM, SM, and ANGRY mood	HM Ss recalled more FSI than Sm Ss. SM Ss recalled more USI than HM Ss but not significantly so.	Mood congruency
Madigan & Bollenbach (1982, Expt. 2)	Velten; retrieval mood; HM, SM	HM Ss produced more pleasant associations to stimulus words than SM Ss.	Mood congruency
Mathews & Bradley (1983)	Velten, music; retrieval mood; NM, SM	SM Ss recalled more USI than NM Ss.	Mood congruency
Natale & Hantas (1982)	Hypnosis, Velten; retrieval mood; 3 × 2	HM Ss recalled more FSI than NM S; Nm Ss recalled more FSI than SM Ss. HM Ss recalled less USI than either NM or SM Ss.	Mood congruency
Parrott & Sabini (1990, Expt. 3)	Music; retrieval mood; 2 × 2	HM Ss recalled more FSI and less USI than SM Ss.	Mood congruency
Parrott & Sabini (1990, Expt. 4)	Music; retrieval mood; 2 × 2	Mood did not reliably affect the valence of the self-relevant information recalled. (The Mood main effect was not significant)	Nondiagnostic results
Parrott & Sabini (1990, Expt. 5)	Music; retrieval mood; 2 × 2	HM Ss recalled less FSI and more USI than SM Ss.	Mood incongruency
Salovey & Singer (1989, Expt. 1)	Self-generated imagery and guided imagery; retrieval mood; 3 × 2	Mood did not reliably affect the valence of self-relevant information recalled.	Nondiagnostic results

continued

TABLE 11.2 Continued

Area	Experiment	Mood Induction Procedure; Timing of Mood Induction; Design[a]	Results	Hypothesis Supported
	Salovey & Singer (1989, Expt. 2)	Self-generated imagery; retrieval mood; 3 × 2	HM elicited higher recall of FSI than either NM or SM; SM tended to elict higher recall of USI than NM or HM.	Mood congruency
	Salovey & Singer (1989, Expt. 3)	Self-generated imagery; retrieval mood; 3 × 2	HM elicited higher recall of FSI than either NM or SM; SM tended to elict higher recall of USI than NM or HM.	Mood congruency
	Snyder & White (1982, Expt. 1)	Velten; retrieval mood; 2 × 2	HM Ss recalled more FSI and less USI than SM Ss.	Mood congruency
	Teasdale & Taylor (1981)	Velten; retrieval mood; 2 × 2	HM Ss recalled more FSI and less USI than SM Ss.	Mood congruency
	Teasdale, Taylor, & Fogarty (1981)	Velten; retrieval mood; 2 × 2	HM Ss recalled more FSI and less USI than SM Ss.	Mood congruency
	Wright & Mischel (1982)	Self-generated imagery; encoding mood; 3 × 2	HM Ss recalled more FSI than NM Ss; NM Ss recalled more FSI than SM Ss. HM Ss recalled less USI than NM Ss; NM Ss recalled less USI than SM Ss.	Mood congruency
B. Recognition Memory				
	Forgas et al. (1984)	Hypnosis, self-generated imagery; encoding mood; 2 × 2	Mood produced no significant results.	Nondiagnostic results

Study	Method	Results	Conclusion
Natale & Hantas (1982)	Hypnosis, Velten; retrieval mood; 3 × 2	SM Ss discriminated less between FSI items than either Hm or NM Ss; however, mood did not affect the ability to discriminate between old and new USI and NSI.	Nondiagnostic results
Siegel, Johnson, & Sarason (1979)	Velten; retrieval mood; 3 × 2	Mood had no effect on recognition.	Nondiagnostic results
C. Retrieval Latencies			
Riskind (1983, Expt. 1)	Facial and body posturing; retrieval mood; 2 × 2	HM Ss took less time to retrieve FSI and more time to retrieve USI than SM Ss.	Mood congruency
Riskind (1983, Expt. 2)	Facial and body posturing; retrieval mood 2 × 2	HM Ss took less time to retrieve FSI and more time to retrieve USI than SM Ss.	Mood congruency
Riskind, Rholes, & Eggers (1982)	Velten; retrieval mood; 2 × 2	HM Ss took less time to retrieve FSI and more time to retrieve USI than SM Ss.	Mood congruency
Teasdale & Fogarty (1979)	Velten; retrieval mood; 2 × 2	HM Ss took less time to retrieve FSI than SM Ss. HM and SM Ss took approximately equal time to retrieve USI.	Nondiagnostic results
Teasdale & Taylor (1981)	Velten; retrieval mood; 2 × 2	HM Ss took less time to retrieve FSI and more time to retrieve USI than SM Ss.	Mood congruency

continued

TABLE 11.2 Continued

Area	Experiment	Mood Induction Procedure; Timing of Mood Induction; Design[a]	Results	Hypothesis Supported
	Teasdale et al. (1981)	Velten; retrieval mood; 2 × 2	HM Ss took less time to retrieve FSI and slightly more time (not significantly so) to retrieve USI than SM Ss.	Mood congruency
III. Judgments				
A. Overall Self-Evaluations	Wright & Mischel (1982)	Self-generated imagery; encoding mood; HM, SM, NM	HM Ss rated the self more favorably than NM Ss; NM Ss rated the self more favorably than SM Ss.	Mood congruency
B. Self-Efficacy	Cunningham (1988b, Expt. 2)	Velten; encoding mood; HM, SM, NM	Mood did not affect self-perception of ability in social-passive tasks.	Nondiagnostic results
			Mood did not affect self-perception of ability in social-active tasks.	Nondiagnostic results
			Mood did not affect self-perception of ability in nonsocial-passive tasks.	Nondiagnostic results
			Mood did not affect self-perception of ability in nonsocial-active tasks.	Nondiagnostic results

Kavanagh & Bower (1985)	Hypnosis; encoding mood; HM, SM, NM	HM Ss made more positive and less negative self-efficacy judgments than NM and SM Ss.	Mood congruency
Natale (1978)	Velten; encoding mood; HM, SM, NM	HM Ss scored higher on internality, whereas SM Ss scored higher on externality (compared with NM Ss) on the Rotter Locus of Control Scale.	Mood congruency
Salovey & Birnbaum (1989, Expt. 2)	Self-generated imagery; retrieval mood; HM, SM, NM	HM Ss and NM Ss felt more capable of successfully implementing health promoting behavior than SM S.	Mood congruency
C. Global Self-Behavior Assessment			
Forgas et al. (1984)	Hypnosis, self-generated imagery; encoding mood; HM, SM	Mood produced no significant results.	Nondiagnostic results
D. Continuous Self-Behavior Interpretation			
Forgas et al. (1984)	Hypnosis, self-generated imagery; encoding mood, HM, NM	HM Ss interpreted their behavior more favorably than SM Ss.	Mood congruency
E. Performance Based Self-Evaluation			
Esses (1989, Expt. 1)	Velten, and Izard (1972), procedures; encoding mood; HM, SM	HM Ss were more likely to evaluate themselves in accordance with positive feedback than SM Ss. SM Ss were more likely to evaluate themselves in accordance with negative feedback than HM Ss.	Mood congruency
Esses (1989, Expt. 2)	Velten; encoding mood; HM, NM	HM Ss were as likely to change self-ratings in the direction of positive feedback as NM Ss were.	Nondiagnostic results

continued

TABLE 11.2 Continued

Area	Experiment	Mood Induction Procedure; Timing of Mood Induction; Design[a]	Results	Hypothesis Supported
	Wright & Mischel (1982)	Self-generated imagery; encoding mood; HM, SM, NM	HM Ss reported higher evaluations of their performance than NM Ss; NM Ss reported higher evaluations of their performance than SM Ss.	Mood congruency
F. Self-Perception on Task-Relevant Attributions				
	Cunningham (1988b, Expt. 2)	Velten; encoding mood; HM, SM, NM	HM Ss reported more positive self-perception of energy in social-passive tasks than NM and SM Ss.	Mood congruency
			HM Ss reported more positive self-perception of energy in social-active tasks than NM and SM Ss.	Mood congruency
			Mood did not affect self-perception of energy in nonsocial-passive tasks.	Nondiagnostic results
			Mood did not affect self-perception of energy in nonsocial-active tasks.	Nondiagnostic results
G. Appraisal of Physical Symptoms				
	Croyle & Uretsky (1987, Expt. 1)	Velten; retrieval mood; HM, SM	HM Ss judged their health more favorably than SM Ss.	Mood congruency

Study	Method	Results	Conclusion
Croyle & Uretsky (1987, Expt. 2)	Videotapes; retrieval mood; HM, SM	HM Ss judged their health more favorably than SM Ss.	Mood congruency
Salovey & Birnbaum (1989)	Self-generated imagery; retrieval mood; HM, SM, NM	Mood affected reporting of ambiguous symptoms: SM Ss reported more aches, pains, and discomfort than HM Ss, with NM Ss falling in between.	Mood congruency
		Mood did not affect reporting of unambiguous symptoms (nasal congestion, stomach discomfort, sleeping irregularities).	Nondiagnostic results

H. Probability Estimates of Future Health Events

Study	Method	Results	Conclusion
Salovey & Birnbaum (1989, Expt. 2)	Self-generated imagery; retrieval mood; HM, SM, NM	Mood produced no significant effects.	Nondiagnostic results
Salovey & Birnbaum (1989, Expt. 3)	Self-generated imagery; retrieval mood; HM, SM, NM	HM Ss gave lower estimates of negative outcomes occurring to them than NM Ss, who in turn gave lower estimates than SM Ss. Mood had no effects on positive outcomes.	Mood congruency

I. Ratings of Past Recalled Experiences

Study	Method	Results	Conclusion
Madigan & Bollenbach (1989, Expt. 1a)	Velten; retrieval mood; HM, SM, NM	HM Ss rated personal memories they generated as more pleasant than SM Ss. Neither HM nor SM Ss differed in their ratings from NM Ss.	Mood congruency

continued

TABLE 11.2 Continued

Area	Experiment	Mood Induction Procedure; Timing of Mood Induction; Design[a]	Results	Hypothesis Supported
	Madigan & Bollenbach (1982, Expt. 1b)	Velten; retrieval mood; HM, SM, NM	HM Ss rated personal memories they generated as more pleasant than SM Ss. Neither HM nor SM Ss differed in their ratings from NM Ss.	Mood congruency
J. Time Spent Engaging in Positive or Negative Events				
	Snyder & White (1982, Expt. 2)	Velten; retrieval mood; HM, SM	HM Ss reported spending more time during the past week in pleasant activities and less time in negative activities than SM Ss.	Mood congruency
K. Stability Attributions for the Causes of Success				
	Brown (1984)	Velten; encoding mood; HM, SM	HM Ss perceived the causes of their successful performance as more stable than SM Ss; however, HM Ss did not perceive the causes of their failure as less stable than SM Ss.	Nondiagnostic results
	Forgas, Bower, & Moylan (1990, Expt. 2)	Videotapes; encoding mood; HM, SM, NM	HM and NM Ss made more stable attributions for their successes than their failures compared with SM Ss.	Mood congruency

L. Causal Attributions for Success and Failure Outcomes		
Baumgardner & Arkin (1988)	Videotapes; encoding mood; HM, SM, NM	HM Ss made internal attributions for their successes to a higher degree than NM Ss, who in turn made internal attributions for their successes to a higher degree than SM Ss; however, no differences were generally found among HM, SM, and NM Ss with regard to attributions for their failures.	Nondiagnostic results
Forgas et al. (1990, Expt. 2)	Videotapes; encoding mood; HM, SM, NM	HM and NM Ss tended to make more internal attributions for successes and external attributions for failure compared with SM Ss.	Mood congruency
M. Estimates of Past Successes		
Teasdale & Spencer (1984)	Music; retrieval mood; HM, SM	HM Ss provided higher estimates of their past successes than SM Ss.	Mood congruency
N. Judgments of Personal Satisfaction		
Dermer, Cohen, Jacobsen, & Anderson (1979, Expt. 2)	Guided imagery; encoding mood; PHM, SM	PM Ss expressed significantly lower satisfaction with life and health than NM Ss. PM Ss expressed significantly higher satisfaction with their financial situation than NM Ss. PM and NM Ss did not significantly differ in their judged satisfaction of physical appearance, relationships, and sex life.	Nondiagnostic results

continued

TABLE 11.2 Continued

Area	Experiment	Mood Induction Procedure; Timing of Mood Induction; Design[a]	Results	Hypothesis Supported
	Schwarz & Clore (1983, Expt. 1)	Self-generated imagery; encoding mood; HM, SM	PM Ss expressed more personal satisfaction and happiness with their life than NM Ss.	Mood congruency
	Strack, Schwarz, & Gschneidinger (1985)	Self-generated imagery; encoding mood; HM, SM	PM Ss expressed more personal satisfaction and happiness with their life than NM Ss (this finding held only when mood was induced by having Ss imagine current rather than past life events).	Mood congruency
	Strack et al. (1985, Expt. 2)	Self-generated imagery; encoding mood; HM, SM	PM Ss expressed more personal satisfaction and happiness with their life than NM Ss (this finding was observed only when mood was induced by having Ss imagine life events vividly rather than pallidly).	Mood congruency
	Strack et al. (1985, Expt. 3)	Self-generated imagery; encoding mood; HM, SM	PM Ss indicated more personal satisfaction and happiness with their life than NM Ss (this finding was only observed when mood was induced by having Ss describe how rather than why the event occurred).	Mood congruency

IV. Expectancies

A. Goal Setting			
Wright & Mischel (1982)	Self-generated imagery; encoding mood; HM, SM, NM	Mood produced no significant effects.	Nondiagnostic results
B. Outcome Expectancies			
Forgas et al. (1990, Expt. 2)	Videotapes; encoding mood; HM, SM, NM	HM Ss expected to receive a better grade in the next exam than NM Ss, who in turn expected to receive a better grade than SM Ss.	Mood congruency
Masters & Furman (1976)	Self-generated imagery; encoding mood; HM, SM, NM	HM Ss had higher performance expectancies for a future task than either SM or NM Ss; however, NM Ss did not have higher expectancies than SM Ss.	Mood congruency
Wright & Mischel (1982)	Self-generated imagery; encoding mood; HM, SM, NM	HM Ss had higher performance expectancies than NM Ss, who in turn had higher performance expectancies than SM Ss.	Mood congruency
C. Retrospective Expectancies			
Forgas et al. (1990, Expt. 2)	Videotapes; encoding mood; HM, SM	HM Ss reported higher retrospective expectancies than SM Ss; however, the estimates of both HM and SM Ss were not higher than the estimates of NM Ss.	Mood congruency
D. Confidence of Success			
Brown (1984)	Velten; encoding mood; HM, SM	HM Ss were more confident of their successes than SM Ss	Mood congruency

continued

TABLE 11.2 Continued

Area	Experiment	Mood Induction Procedure; Timing of Mood Induction; Design[a]	Results	Hypothesis Supported
V. Behaviors				
A. Self-Disclosure				
	Cunningham (1988a)	Videotapes; encoding mood; HM, SM	HM Ss self-disclosed more and longer to a partner than SM Ss.	Mood congruency
B. Self-Gratification				
	Baumann, Cialdini, & Kenrick (1981)	Self-generated imagery; encoding mood, HM, SM, NM	HM and SM Ss self-gratified more than SM Ss.	Mood incongruency
	Fry (1975)	Self-generated imagery; encoding mood; HM, SM, NM	HM Ss resisted temptation longer than NM Ss, who in turn resisted temptation longer than SM Ss.	Mood incongruency
	Jones & Thelen (1978)	Velten; encoding mood; HM, SM, NM	HM Ss rewarded themselves more than either NM or SM Ss. The latter two groups did not differ from one another. HM Ss punished themselves less than either NM or SM Ss, and NM Ss punished themselves less than SM Ss.	Mood congruency
	Knapp & Clark (1991, Expt. 1)	Guided imagery; encoding mood; HM, SM, NM	SM Ss were less able to delay gratification than NM and HM Ss.	Mood incongruency
	Knapp & Clark (1991, Expt. 2)	Guided imagery; encoding mood; SM, NM	SM Ss delayed gratification less than NM Ss.	Mood incongruency

Study	Design/factors	Results	Mood (in)congruency
Moore, Clyburn, & Underwood (1976)	Self-generated imagery; encoding mood; HM, SM, NM	HM Ss made more delayed-reward choices than did NM Ss, and SM Ss made more immediate-reward choices than did NM Ss.	Mood incongruency
Rosenhan, Underwood, & Moore (1974)	Self-generated imagery; encoding mood; HM, SM, NM	HM and SM Ss did not differ in terms of self-gratification; however, both HM and SM Ss self-gratified more than HM Ss.	Mood incongruency
Schwarz & Pollack (1977, Expt. 1, first assessment)	Guided and self-generated imagery; encoding mood; HM, SM	HM Ss made more delayed-reward choices than SM Ss.	Mood incongruency
Schwarz & Pollack (1977, Expt. 2, first assessment)	Guided and self-generated imagery; encoding mood, HM, SM, NM	HM Ss made more delayed-reward choices than NM Ss, who tended to make more delayed-reward choices than SM Ss.	Mood incongruency
Schwarz & Pollack (1977, Expt. 3, first assessment)	Guided and self-generated imagery; encoding mood, HM, SM, NM	HM Ss made more delayed-reward choices than NM Ss, who tended to make more delayed-reward choices than SM Ss.	Mood incongruency
Underwood, Moore, & Rosehan (1973)	Self-generated imagery; encoding mood; HM, SM, NM	HM Ss self-gratified more than either NM or SM Ss. The later two groups did not differ from one another.	Mood congruency

NOTES: a. Whenever the experimental design is factorially notated, the first factor refers to mood, and the second factor refers to self-relevant information (favorable, unfavorable). A three-level mood factor indicates happy, sad, and neutral mood. A two-level mood factor denotes happy and sad mood.

b. HM = happy mood; SM = sad mood; NM = neutral mood.

c. Ss = subjects.

d. FSI = favorable self-relevant information; USI = unfavorable self-relevant information; NSI = neutral self-relevant information. (FSI refers to either information that compliments the self or information that is generally pleasant to the self; USI refers to information that either threatens the self or is generally unpleasant to the self; NSI refers to information that is neutral to the self.)

to the self compared with subjects in a sad mood, but subjects in both mood conditions recalled an equal amount of favorable self-information (Brown & Taylor, 1986). Or happy mood subjects made internal rather than external attribution for their successes (in comparison with neutral and happy mood subjects), but they also made internal attributions (as subjects in a sad and neutral mood state did) for their failures.

The current review uncovered symmetrical mood effects; that is, the effects of happy mood on self valence were the opposite of the effects of sad mood. Such a pattern has not always been obtained. Several experiments examining the impact of mood on non-self-related dependent measures (e.g., Fiedler, Pampe, & Scherf, 1986; Gotlib & McCann, 1984, Experiment 2; Hasher, Rose, Zacks, Sanft, & Doren, 1985; Isen, 1985; Mecklenbrauker & Hager, 1984) have yielded mood-asymmetrical results (see Taylor, 1991, for a review). Why does mood tend to elicit symmetrical effects on self-related measures but oftentimes asymmetrical effects on non-self-related measures?

Based on a review of the work by Mecklenbrauker and Hager (1984), Hasher et al. (1985), and Fiedler et al. (1986), Schwarz and Clore (1988) concluded that mood congruency effects "may be limited to relatively unstructured material and tend to be difficult to find when material is presented in narrative form, such that positive and negative elements are interconnected or otherwise well organized" (p. 46). Self-knowledge fulfills the requirements for obtaining mood congruency effects. It is unlikely to be tightly structured due to its richness, multidimensionality, and plasticity (Markus & Wurf, 1987); further, it is not, of course, presented to subjects, let alone presented in narrative form with positive and negative self-conceptions being structurally interconnected. It follows that whether one obtains mood-symmetrical versus mood-asymmetrical effects depends on the nature of the cognitive material associated with moods, with self-relevant material likely to yield mood-symmetrical effects (Blaney, 1986; Bullington, 1990; Forgas et al., 1990).

The review establishes that people in both a happy and a sad mood tend to maintain their affective states. This finding is not surprising as far as happy mood is concerned. As Isen (1984) observed, "positive affect is very common . . . [whereas] negative affect is more rare" (p. 187). Thus one can reasonably assume that most people are usually in a slightly happy mood state. Given the necessity of positive affect for effective everyday functioning (Lazarus, Kanner, & Folkman, 1980), people tend to maintain their mildly happy moods by engaging in mood-congruent thinking (e.g., activating positively valenced self-conceptions) or behavior (e.g., engaging in positive self-directed behaviors, such as self-reward).

It is only because of disruptive and/or stressful life events that people delve into a temporary sad state (Isen, 1984). But how are sad mood states sustained? In part, by such activities as ruminating (Martin & Tesser, 1989), adopting a problem-focus strategy (i.e., consulting others about the unpleasant life occurrence), socializing with people in a similar affective state (Rosenblatt & Greenberg, 1991), or choosing likewise valenced activities (e.g., reading a sad book, listening to sad music, watching a sad movie).

Still, how do individuals ever manage to break their sad mood state? One possibility is that people take no particular action to snap out of their sad mood—it simply fades away, especially as a result of processing new information or engaging in new tasks. Another possibility is that people in a sad mood state unintentionally divert attention externally; sad thoughts and accompanying unfavorable thoughts about the self become diffuse, because of the impact of incoming information. Alternatively, people may focus attention on objects of personal significance, either social (e.g., friends, relatives) or nonsocial (e.g., valued possessions) and, as a result, neutral or favorable self-relevant thoughts become more accessible in memory than unfavorable thoughts (see Wyer & Srull, 1989). It is also possible that people make conscious decisions that maximize the chances of exiting the sad mood state, such as socializing, thinking thoughts that are generous to the self (Beck, Rush, Shaw, & Emery, 1979), making self-serving attributions (Kuiper, 1978), seeking explanations (Abele, 1985), or engaging in activities that are likely to breed a sense of self-worth and accomplishment (Diener, 1984). The time is ripe for future research to focus on the exact strategies people use to regulate their sad mood states.

CONCLUDING REMARKS

The main objective of this review was to define and establish the area of consequences of mood states for the self as an independent domain of investigation. As a first step toward this objective, the review examined empirical work on the changes occurring in the valence of the self as a function of mood. The review showed that self valence is affected by mood in a congruent manner. In so doing, the review affirmed the viability of the mood congruency hypothesis.

The relevancy of another theoretical view, the *mood as information* view, should also be entertained. This view (Schwarz & Clore, 1983, 1988) credits mood (and affect in general) with informative value. The experience of mood provides people with cues relevant to the evaluation of the situation in which they currently find themselves. For example, feeling happy cues people favorably, whereas feeling sad cues people unfavorably, toward a target. In either case, people use their perceived mood states as information to infer that they like or dislike the target.

On the face of it, the mood as information view would seem to account reasonably well for the obtained results—at least as well as the mood congruency hypothesis. Upon closer inspection, however, the mood as information view appears to be constrained in several regards. First, this view was offered as an alternative explanation for the effects of mood states on *evaluative judgments,* whereas the mood congruency hypothesis has a broader scope: It encompasses mood effects on attention, recall, recognition, retrieval latencies, expectancies, judgments, and behaviors. Second, to demonstrate experimentally the validity of the mood as information view, one will have to include a condition in which subjects are oblivious to the source of their mood (in which case the predictions of the mood as information view would be identical to the predictions of the mood congruency hypothesis) *and* also a condition in which subjects are led to attribute their mood to an environmental source (e.g., the weather, an unpleasant room). In the latter case, the mood as information view predicts that mood will be attributionally discounted, that is, it will not have any effects on judgments. Only 4 of the 78 tests reported in this review satisfied this latter crucial requirement. These four tests were by Schwarz and Clore (1983, Experiment 1) and Strack, Schwarz, and Gschneidinger (1985, Experiments 1, 2, and 3). Given the more extensive applicability of the mood congruency hypothesis and the limited experimental tests of the mood as information hypothesis, it is concluded that, currently, the mood congruency hypothesis provides a more comprehensive and adequate theoretical umbrella for the interpretation of mood effects on self valence.

This chapter demonstrated that mood has reliable effects on attention, memory, judgments, expectations, and behaviors regarding the self. This is testimony to the malleability of the self as a function of affective context. The findings of the review qualify mood as a powerful determinant of temporary changes in the self.

Furthermore, the findings of the review have intervention implications. Given the potency of the effects of sad mood on the self, momentary fluctuations in the favorableness of self-evaluations as a function of mood would appear hard to prevent. One step toward prevention is to help individuals become conscious of the effects moods have on them. In corroboration of this suggestion, recent research has showed that the effects of mood are diminished when subjects' attention is directed toward their mood state (Berkowitz & Troccoli, 1990; Strack et al., 1985). Another form intervention might take is to cultivate effective coping strategies that individuals could activate and use after the occurrence of unfavorable self-evaluations. Such strategies could range from challenging the negativity of inferences about the self via selective recall of favorable self-relevant information to diffusing the lingering effects of mood on the self through engagement in externally oriented activities.

Having established mood congruency effects on the self, the final section of this chapter will explore fruitful avenues that research on the consequences of mood on the self can follow.

DIRECTIONS FOR FUTURE RESEARCH

Mood Congruency Hypotheses: Searching for Process Specificity

An important task for future research is to identify the mechanism(s) that best accounts for the influence of mood on the self. Several mechanisms were discussed under the heading "Mood Congruency Hypothesis." An additional mechanism might also be worth examining, namely, the possibility of differential mood effects on central (i.e., self-descriptive and important) versus peripheral (i.e., non-self-descriptive and unimportant) self-conceptions. Mood, for example, may be more likely to affect the self through peripheral rather than central self-conceptions, because peripheral self-conceptions are less likely to be resistant to change than central self-conceptions.

Mood Effects on the Structure of the Self

Future research needs to focus on whether mood produces structural changes in the self. Does mood change the structural interconnections of favorable and unfavorable self-relevant information? Does mood predominantly affect the public versus private self, the actual versus ideal self, and the desired versus undesired self?

Effects of Additional Mood Dimensions on the Self

The influence of additional mood states (e.g., anger, fear, disgust) on the self is worth exploring in the laboratory. Mood congruency effects may be obtainable with other mood states. As an illustration, a recent experiment that induced an angry mood (along with a happy and a sad mood) obtained mood-congruent effects, with angry subjects tending to retrieve anger-related personal life events from memory (Laird, Cuniff, Sheehan, Shulman, & Strum, 1989).

Final Recommendations

Future researchers will do well to adopt a more systematic approach in attempting to enhance our understanding of mood effects on self-perception. Whenever possible, a 3 (mood: happy, sad, neutral) × 3 (self-relevant information: favorable, neutral, unfavorable) design should be employed. The difficulties in defining neutral self-relevant information notwithstanding, such a design would provide a most rigorous evaluation of the mood congruency and mood incongruency hypotheses.

The effects of mood along different information processing stages would also need to be explored. How does mood affect initial self-categorization, the organization of new self-information in memory and its recall, and the retrieval of such information for self-evaluation purposes? To explore this, one could begin to investigate the effects of mood on such self-related measures as free-style self-descriptions, amount of recall and cognitive organization of self-relevant information, response times for feedback concerning the self, self-complexity, self-evaluative judgments with regard to personal and social standards, and social comparison attempts.

REFERENCES

(Experiments preceded by an asterisk were included in Table 11.2.)

Abele, A. (1985). Thinking about thinking: Causal, evaluative and finalistic cognitions about social situations. *European Journal of Social Psychology, 15,* 315-332.

Abelson, R. P., & Sermat, V. (1962). Multidimensional scaling of facial expressions. *Journal of Experimental Psychology, 63,* 546-554.

Bargh, J. A. (1989). Conditional automaticity: Varieties of automatic influence in social perception and cognition. In J. S. Uleman & J. A. Bargh (Eds.), *Unintended thought* (pp. 3-51). New York: Guilford.

*Baumann, D. J., Cialdini, R., & Kenrick, D. (1981). Altruism as hedonism: Helping and self-gratification as equivalent processes. *Journal of Personality and Social Psychology, 40,* 1039-1046.

*Baumgardner, A. H., & Arkin, R. M. (1988). Affective state mediates causal attributions for success and failure. *Motivation and Emotion, 12,* 99-111.

Beck, A. T., Rush, A. J., Shaw, B. F., & Emery, G. (1979). *Cognitive therapy of depression.* New York: Harper & Row.

*Berkowitz, L. (1987). Mood, self-awareness, and willingness to help. *Journal of Personality and Social Psychology, 52,* 1-9.

Berkowitz, L., & Troccoli, B. T. (1990). Feelings, direction of attention, and expressed evaluations of others. *Cognition and Emotion, 4,* 305-325.

Blaney, P. H. (1986). Affect and memory: A review. *Psychological Bulletin, 99,* 229-246.

*Bower, G. H. (1981). Mood and memory. *American Psychologist, 36,* 129-148.

Bower, G. H., & Gilligan, S. G. (1979). Remembering information related to one's self. *Journal of Research in Personality, 13,* 420-461.

Breckler, S. J., Pratkanis, A. R., & McCann, C. D. (1991). The representation of self in multidimensional cognitive space. *British Journal of Social Psychology, 30,* 97-112.

*Brown, J. (1984). Effects of induced mood on causal attributions for success and failure. *Motivation and Emotion, 8,* 343-353.

*Brown, J. D., & Taylor, S. E. (1986). Affect and the processing of personal information: Evidence for mood activated self-schemata. *Journal of Experimental Social Psychology, 22,* 436-452.

*Bullington, J. C. (1990). Mood congruent memory: A replication of symmetrical effects for both positive and negative moods. In J. W. Neuliep (Ed.), *Handbook of replication research in the behavioral and social sciences* [Special issue]. *Journal of Social Behavior and Personality, 5,* 123-134.

Buunk, B. P., Collins, R. L., Taylor, S. E., VanYperen, N. W., & Dakof, G. A. (1990). The affective consequences of social comparison: Either direction has its ups and downs. *Journal of Personality and Social Psychology, 59,* 1238-1249.

Chaiken, S., & Baldwin, M. W. (1981). Affective-cognitive consistency and the effect of salient behavioral information on the self-perception of attitudes. *Journal of Personality and Social Psychology, 41,* 1-12.

Clark, M. S., & Isen, A. M. (1982). Toward understanding the relationship between feeling states and social behavior. In A. Hastorf & A. M. Isen (Eds.), *Cognitive social psychology* (pp. 73-108). New York: Elsevier.

Collins, A. M., & Loftus, E. F. (1975). A spreading-activation theory of semantic processing. *Psychological Review, 82*, 407-428.

*Croyle, R. T., & Uretsky, M. B. (1987). Effects of mood on self-appraisal of health status. *Health Psychology, 6*, 239-253.

*Cunningham, M. R. (1988a). Does happiness mean friendliness? Induced mood and heterosexual self-disclosure. *Personality and Social Psychology Bulletin, 14*, 283-297.

*Cunningham, M. R. (1988b). What do you do when you're happy or blue? Mood, expectancies, and behavioral interest. *Motivation and Emotion, 12*, 309-331.

*Dermer, M., Cohen, S. J., Jacobsen, E., & Anderson, E. A. (1979). Evaluative judgments of aspects of life as a function of vicarious exposure to hedonic extremes. *Journal of Personality and Social Psychology, 37*, 247-260.

Deutsch, F. M., Ruble, D. N., Fleming, A., Brooks-Gunn, J., & Stangor, C. (1988). Information-seeking and maternal self-definition during the transition to motherhood. *Journal of Personality and Social Psychology, 55*, 420-431.

Diener, E. (1984). Subjective well-being. *Psychological Bulletin, 95*, 542-575.

*Esses, V. M. (1989). Mood as a moderator of acceptance of interpersonal feedback. *Journal of Personality and Social Psychology, 57*, 769-781.

Eysenck, H. J. (1960). *The structure of human personality.* New York: Macmillan.

Fazio, R. H., Effrein, E. A., & Falender, V. J. (1981). Self-perceptions following social interaction. *Journal of Personality and Social Psychology, 41*, 232-242.

Feather, N. T. (1966). Effects of prior success and failure on expectations of success and subsequent performance. *Journal of Personality and Social Psychology, 3*, 287-298.

Fiedler, K. (1990). Mood-dependent selectivity in social cognition. In W. Stroebe & M. Hewstone (Eds.), *European review of social psychology* (Vol. 1, pp. 1-32). Chichester, UK: John Wiley.

Fiedler, K., Pampe, H., & Scherf, U. (1986). Mood and memory for tightly organized social information. *European Journal of Social Psychology, 17*, 243-246.

Fiske, S. T., & Taylor, S. E. (1984). *Social cognition.* Reading, MA: Addison-Wesley.

*Forgas, J. P., Bower, G. H., & Krantz, S. E. (1984). The influence of mood on perceptions of social interactions. *Journal of Experimental Social Psychology, 20*, 497-513.

*Forgas, J. P., Bower, G. H., & Moylan, S. J. (1990). Praise or blame? Affective influences on attributions for achievement. *Journal of Personality and Social Psychology, 59*, 809-819.

Frijda, N. H. (1986). *The emotions.* Cambridge: Cambridge University Press.

*Fry, P. S. (1975). Affect and resistance to temptation. *Developmental Psychology, 11*, 466-472.

Gotlib, I. H., & McCann, C. D. (1984). Construct accessibility and depression: An examination of cognitive and affective factors. *Journal of Personality and Social Psychology, 47*, 427-439.

Greenwald, A. G. (1975). On the inconclusiveness of "crucial" cognitive tests of dissonance versus self perception theory. *Journal of Experimental Social Psychology, 11*, 490-499.

Greenwald, A. G., & Pratkanis, A. R. (1984). The self. In R. S. Wyer, Jr., & T. K. Srull (Eds.), *Handbook of social cognition* (Vol. 3, pp. 129-178). Hillsdale, NJ: Lawrence Erlbaum.

Harris, R. N., & Snyder, C. R. (1986). The role of uncertain self-esteem in self-handicapping. *Journal of Personality and Social Psychology, 51*, 451-458.

Hasher, L., Rose, K. C., Zacks, R. T., Sanft, H., & Doren, B. (1985). Mood, recall, and selectivity effects in normal college students. *Journal of Experimental Psychology: General, 114,* 104-118.

Hastorf, A. H., Osgood, C. E., & Ono, H. (1966). The semantics of facial expressions and the prediction of meanings of stereoscopically fused facial expressions. *Scandinavian Journal of Psychology, 7,* 179-188.

Heatherton, T. F., & Polivy, J. (1991). Development and validation of a scale for measuring state self-esteem. *Journal of Personality and Social Psychology, 60,* 895-910.

Higgins, E. T. (1987). Self-discrepancy: A theory relating self to affect. *Psychological Review, 94,* 319-340.

Higgins, E. T., & Bargh, J. A. (1987). Social cognition and social perception. *Annual Review of Psychology, 38,* 369-425.

Higgins, E. T., Van Hook, E., & Dorfman, D. (1988). Do self-attributes form a cognitive structure? *Social Cognition, 6,* 177-207.

Hoelter, J. W. (1985). The structure of self-conceptions: Conceptualization and measurement. *Journal of Personality and Social Psychology, 49,* 1392-1407.

Isen, A. M. (1984). Toward understanding the role of affect in cognition. In R. S. Wyer, Jr., & T. K. Srull (Eds.), *Handbook of social cognition* (Vol. 3, pp. 179-236). Hillsdale, NJ: Lawrence Erlbaum.

Isen, A. M. (1985). Asymmetry of happiness and sadness in effects on memory in normal college students. *Journal of Experimental Psychology: General, 114,* 104-118.

Isen, A. M., Shalker, T., Clark, M., & Karp, L. (1978). Affect, accessibility of material in memory and behavior: A cognitive loop? *Journal of Personality and Social Psychology, 36,* 1-12.

Izard, C. E. (1972). *Patterns of emotions: A new analysis of anxiety and depression.* New York: Academic Press.

Jones, E. E. (1990). Constrained behavior and self-concept change. In J. M. Olson & M. P. Zanna (Eds.), *Self-inference processes: The Ontario Symposium* (Vol. 6, pp. 69-86). Hillsdale, NJ: Lawrence Erlbaum.

Jones, E. E., & Gerard, H. B. (1967). *Foundations of social psychology.* New York: John Wiley.

Jones, E. E., Rhodewalt, F., Berglas, S., & Skelton, J. S. (1981). Effects of strategic self-presentation on subsequent self-esteem. *Journal of Personality and Social Psychology, 41,* 407-421.

*Jones, G. F., & Thelen, M. H. (1978). The effects of induced mood states on self-reinforcement behavior. *Journal of Psychology, 98,* 249-252.

*Kavanagh, D. J., & Bower, G. H. (1985). Mood and self-efficacy: Impact of joy and sadness on perceived capabilities. *Cognitive Therapy and Research, 9,* 507-525.

Kazdin, A. E., & Bryan, J. H. (1971). Competence and volunteering. *Journal of Experimental Social Psychology, 7,* 87-97.

Kihlstrom, J. F., & Cantor, N. (1984). Mental representations of the self. In L. Berkowitz (Ed.), *Advances in experimental social psychology* (Vol. 17, pp. 1-47). New York: Academic Press.

Kihlstrom, J. F., Cantor, N., Albright, J. S., Chew, B. R., Klein, S. B., & Neidenthal, P. M. (1987). Information processing and the study of the self. In L. Berkowitz (Ed.), *Advances in experimental social psychology* (Vol. 21, pp. 145-177). New York: Academic Press.

Klein, S., & Loftus, J. (in press). The mental representation of trait and autobiographical knowledge about the self. In T. K. Srull & R. S. Wyer, Jr. (Eds.), *Advances in social cognition* (Vol. 5).

*Knapp, A., & Clark, M. S. (1991). Some detrimental effects of negative mood on individuals' ability to solve resource dilemmas. *Personality and Social Psychology Bulletin, 17,* 678-689.

Kuiper, N. A. (1978). Depression and causal attributions for success and failure. *Journal of Personality and Social Psychology, 36,* 236-246.

Kuiper, N. A. (1981). Convergent evidence for the self as prototype: The "inverted-URT effect" for self and other judgments. *Personality and Social Psychology Bulletin, 7,* 438-443.

*Laird, J. D., Cuniff, M., Sheehan, K., Shulman, D., & Strum, G. (1989). Emotion specific effects of facial expressions on memory for life events. In D. Kuiken (Ed.), *Mood and memory: Theory, research, and applications* [Special issue]. *Journal of Social Behavior and Personality, 4,* 87-98.

Lazarus, R. S., Kanner, A. D., & Folkman, S. (1980). Emotions: A cognitive-phenomenological analysis. In R. Plutchik & H. Kellerman (Eds.), *Theories in emotion: Vol. 1. Emotion: Theory, research, and experience* (pp. 189-217). San Diego, CA: Academic Press.

Linville, P. W. (1987). Self-complexity as a cognitive buffer against stress-related illness and depression. *Journal of Personality and Social Psychology, 52,* 663-676.

Long, G. T., & Lerner, M. J. (1974). Deserving, the "personal contact" and altruistic behavior by children. *Journal of Personality and Social Psychology, 29,* 551-556.

*Madigan, R. J., & Bollenbach, A. K. (1982). Effects of induced mood in retrieval of personal episodic and semantic memories. *Psychological Reports, 50,* 147-157.

Markus, H. R. (1977). Self-schemata and processing information about the self. *Journal of Personality and Social Psychology, 35,* 63-78.

Markus, H. R. (1983). Self-knowledge: An expanded view. *Journal of Personality, 51,* 543-565.

Markus, H. R., & Kitayama, S. (1991). Culture and the self: Implications for cognition, emotion, and motivation. *Psychological Review, 98,* 224-253.

Markus, H., & Kunda, Z. (1986). Stability and malleability of the self-concept. *Journal of Personality and Social Psychology, 51,* 858-866.

Markus, H., & Nurius, P. (1986). Possible selves. *American Psychologist, 41,* 954-969.

Markus, H., & Wurf, E. (1987). The dynamic self-concept: A social psychological perspective. *Annual Review of Psychology, 38,* 299-337.

Marsella, A. J., De Vos, G., & Hsu, F. L. K. (1985). *Culture and self.* New York: Tavistock.

Martin, L. L., & Tesser, A. (1989). Toward a motivational and structural theory of ruminative thought. In J. S. Uleman & J. A. Bargh (Eds.), *Unintended thought* (pp. 306-326). New York: Guilford.

*Masters, J. C., & Furman, W. (1976). Effects of affect inductions on expectancies for serendipitous positive events, success on task performance and beliefs in internal or external control of reinforcement. *Developmental Psychology, 12,* 176-179.

*Mathews, A., & Bradley, B. (1983). Mood and the self-reference bias in recall. *Behavior, Research and Therapy, 21,* 233-239.

Mayer, J. D., Gayle, M., Meehan, M. E., & Haarman, A. K. (1990). Toward better specification of the mood-congruency effect in recall. *Journal of Experimental Social Psychology, 26*, 465-480.

Mayer, J. D., & Salovey, P. (1988). Personality moderates the interaction of mood and cognition. In K. Fiedler & J. Forgas (Eds.), *Affect, cognition, and social behavior* (pp. 87-99). Toronto: Hogrefe.

McGuire, W. J., McGuire, C. V., & Cheever, J. (1986). The self in society: Effects of social contexts on the sense of self. *British Journal of Social Psychology, 25*, 259-270.

Mecklenbrauker, S., & Hager, W. (1984). Effects of mood on memory: Experimental tests of a mood state-dependent retrieval hypothesis and of a mood-congruity hypothesis. *Psychological Research, 46*, 355-376.

Mischel, W., Coates, B., & Raskoff, A. (1968). Effects of success and failure on self-gratification. *Journal of Personality and Social Psychology, 10*, 381-390.

*Mischel, W., Ebbesen, E. B., & Zeiss, A. R. (1973). Selective attention to the self: Situational and dispositional determinants. *Journal of Personality and Social Psychology, 27*, 129-142.

Mischel, W., Ebbesen, E. B., & Zeiss, A. R. (1976). Determinants of selective memory about the self. *Journal of Consulting and Clinical Psychology, 44*, 92-103.

Monge, R. H. (1975). Structure of the self-concept from adolescence through old age. *Experimental Aging Research, 1*, 281-291.

*Moore, B. S., Clyburn, A., & Underwood, B. (1976). The role of affect in the delay of gratification. *Child Development, 47*, 237-276.

Morris, W. N. (1989). *Mood: The frame of mind.* London: Springer-Verlag.

Mortimer, J. T., Finch, M. D., & Kumka, D. (1982). Persistence and change in development: The multidimensional self-concept. In *Life span development and behavior* (Vol. 4, pp. 263-313). New York: Academic Press.

*Natale, M. (1978). Effect of induced elation and depression on internal external locus of control. *Journal of Psychology, 100*, 315-321.

*Natale, M., & Hantas, M. (1982). Effect of temporary mood states on selective memory about the self. *Journal of Personality and Social Psychology, 42*, 927-934.

Ogilvie, D. M. (1987). The undesired self: A neglected variable in personality research. *Journal of Personality and Social Psychology, 52*, 379-385.

Osgood, C. E., & Suci, G. J. (1955). Factor analysis of meaning. *Journal of Experimental Psychology, 50*, 325-338.

Ostrom, T. M. (1977). Between-theory and within-theory confrontation in explaining context effects in impression formation. *Journal of Experimental Social Psychology, 13*, 492-503.

*Parrott, W. G., & Sabini, J. (1990). Mood and memory under natural conditions: Evidence for mood incongruent recall. *Journal of Personality and Social Psychology, 59*, 321-336.

Peeters, G., & Czapinski, J. (1990). Positive-negative asymmetry in evaluations: The distinction between affective and informational negativity effects. In W. Stroebe & M. Hewstone (Eds.), *European review of social psychology* (Vol. 1, pp. 33-60). Chichester, UK: John Wiley.

Rhodewalt, F., & Agustdottir, S. (1986). Effects of self-presentation on the phenomenal self. *Journal of Personality and Social Psychology, 50*, 47-55.

*Riskind, J. H. (1983). Nonverbal expressions and the accessibility of life experience memories: A congruency hypothesis. *Social Cognition, 2*, 62-86.

*Riskind, J. H., Rholes, W. S., & Eggers, J. (1982). The Velten mood induction procedure: Effects on mood and memory. *Journal of Consulting and Clinical Psychology, 50*, 146-147.

Rogers, T. B. (1981). A model of the self as an aspect of the human information processing system. In N. Cantor & J. Kihlstrom (Eds.), *Personality, cognition, and social interaction* (pp. 193-214). Hillsdale, NJ: Lawrence Erlbaum.

Rogers, T. B., Rogers, P. J., & Kuiper, N. A. (1979). Evidence for the self as cognitive prototype. The "false alarm effect." *Personality and Social Psychology Bulletin, 5*, 53-56.

Rosenblatt, A., & Greenberg, J. (1991). Examining the world of the depressed: Do depressed people prefer others who are depressed? *Journal of Personality and Social Psychology, 60*, 620-629.

*Rosenhan, D. L., Underwood, B., & Moore, B. (1974). Affect moderates self-gratification and altruism. *Journal of Personality and Social Psychology, 30*, 546-552.

Salancik, G. R., & Conway, M. (1975). Attitude inferences from salient and relevant cognitive content about behavior. *Journal of Personality and Social Psychology, 32*, 829-840.

*Salovey, P., & Birnbaum, D. (1989). Influence of mood on health-relevant cognitions. *Journal of Personality and Social Psychology, 57*, 539-551.

*Salovey, P., & Singer, J. A. (1989). Mood congruency effects in recall of childhood versus recent memories. In D. Kuiken (Ed.), *Mood and memory: Theory, research, and applications* [Special issue]. *Journal of Social Behavior and Personality, 4*, 99-120.

Scheier, M. F., & Carver, C. S. (1982). Cognition, affect, and self-regulation. In M. S. Clark & S. T. Fiske (Eds.), *Affect and cognition* (pp. 157-183). Hillsdale, NJ: Lawrence Erlbaum.

Scherer, K. R., Koivumaki, J., & Rosenthal, R. (1972). Minimal cues in the vocal communication of affect: Judging emotions from content-masked speech. *Journal of Psycholinguistic Research, 1*, 269-285.

Schlenker, B. R., & Trudeau, J. V. (1990). Impact of self-presentations on private self-beliefs: Effects of prior self-beliefs and misattribution. *Journal of Personality and Social Psychology, 58*, 22-32.

*Schwarz, J. C., & Pollack, P. R. (1977). Affect and delay of gratification. *Journal of Research in Personality, 11*, 147-164.

*Schwarz, N., & Clore, G. (1983). Mood, misattribution and judgments of well-being: Informative and directive functions of affective states. *Journal of Personality and Social Psychology, 45*, 513-523.

Schwarz, N., & Clore, G. L. (1988). How do I feel about it? The informative function of affective states. In K. Fiedler & J. Forgas (Eds.), *Affect, cognition, and social behavior* (pp. 44-62). Toronto: Hogrefe.

Sedikides, C., & Skowronski, J. J. (1991). The law of cognitive structure activation. *Psychological Inquiry, 2*, 169-184.

*Siegel, J. M., Johnson, J. H., & Sarason, I. G. (1979). Mood states and the reporting of life changes. *Journal of Psychosomatic Research, 23*, 103-108.

Simon, H. (1982). Affect and cognition: Comments. In M. S. Clark & S. T. Fiske (Eds.), *Affect and cognition: The Seventeenth Annual Carnegie Symposium on Cognition* (pp. 333-342). Hillsdale, NJ: Lawrence Erlbaum.

Snyder, M., & Swann, W. B. (1978). Behavioral confirmation in social interaction: From social perception to social reality. *Journal of Experimental Social Psychology, 14,* 148-162.

*Snyder, M., & White, P. (1982). Moods and memories: Elation, depression, and the remembering of the events of one's life. *Journal of Personality, 50,* 149-167.

*Strack, F., Schwarz, N., & Gschneidinger, E. (1985). Happiness and reminiscing: The role of time perspective, mood, and mode of thinking. *Journal of Personality and Social Psychology, 49,* 1460-1469.

Strube, M. J. (1990). In search of self: Balancing the good and the true. *Personality and Social Psychology Bulletin, 16,* 699-704.

Swann, W. B., Jr. (1990). To be adored or to be known? The interplay of self-enhancement and self-verification. In E. T. Higgins & R. M. Sorrentino (Eds.), *Handbook of motivation and cognition: Foundations of social behavior* (Vol. 2, pp. 408-448). New York: Guilford.

Taylor, S. E. (1991). Asymmetrical effects of positive and negative events: The mobilization-minimization hypothesis. *Psychological Bulletin, 110,* 67-85.

Taylor, S. E., & Brown, J. D. (1988). Illusion and well-being: A social psychological perspective on mental health. *Psychological Bulletin, 103,* 193-210.

*Teasdale, J. D., & Fogarty, S. J. (1979). Differential effects of induced mood on retrieval of pleasant and unpleasant events from episodic memory. *Journal of Abnormal Psychology, 88,* 248-257.

*Teasdale, J. D., & Spencer, P. (1984). Induced mood and estimates of past success. *British Journal of Clinical Psychology, 23,* 149-150.

*Teasdale, J. D., & Taylor, R. (1981). Induced mood and accessibility of memories: An effect of mood state or of mood induction procedure? *British Journal of Clinical Psychology, 20,* 39-48.

*Teasdale, J. D., Taylor, R., & Fogarty, S. J. (1981). Effects of induced elation-depression on the accessibility of memories of happy and unhappy experiences. *Behaviour, Research, and Therapy, 18,* 339-346.

Tetlock, P. E., & Levi, A. (1982). Attribution bias: On the inconclusiveness of the cognition-motivation debate. *Journal of Experimental Social Psychology, 18,* 68-88.

*Underwood, B., Moore, B. S., & Rosenhan, D. L. (1973). Affect and self-gratification. *Developmental Psychology, 8,* 209-214.

Velten, E. (1968). A laboratory task for induction of mood states. *Behaviour Research and Therapy, 6,* 473-482.

Wood, J. V., Saltzberg, J. A., & Goldsamt, L. A. (1990). Does affect induce self-focused attention? *Journal of Personality and Social Psychology, 58,* 899-908.

*Wright, J., & Mischel, W. (1982). Influence of affect on cognitive social learning person variables. *Journal of Personality and Social Psychology, 43,* 901-914.

Wyer, R. S., Jr., & Srull, T. K. (1989). *Memory and cognition in its social context.* Hillsdale, NJ: Lawrence Erlbaum.